Bank Accounts

Bank Accounts

A World Guide to Confidentiality

EDOUARD CHAMBOST

Avocat au Barreau de Paris

Translated by

Peter Walton and Margaret Thompson

JOHN WILEY & SONS

Chichester · New York · Brisbane · Toronto · Singapore

Copyright © 1983 by John Wiley & Sons Ltd.

All rights reserved.

No part of this book may be reproduced by any means, nor transmitted, nor translated into a machine language without the written permission of the publisher.

Library of Congress Cataloging in Publication Data

Chambost, Édouard.
  Bank accounts.
  Translation of: Guide mondial des secrets bancaires.
  Bibliography: p.
  Includes index.
  1. Confidential communications—Banking. I. Title.
HG1720.C413   1983   332.1'2   82-17532
ISBN 0-471-90076-1

British Library Cataloguing in Publication Data

Chambost, Edouard
  Bank accounts.
  1. Bank accounts.   2. Confidential communications
  —Banks.
  I. Title.
  332.1'752   HG1660
  ISBN 0-471-90076-1

Phototypeset by Dobbie Typesetting Service, Plymouth, Devon.
Printed by Page Bros., (Norwich) Ltd.

Contents

Foreword   x

I   Concept and uses of banking secrecy   1

1. THE GENERAL HISTORY OF BANKING SECRECY   3

   Hammourabi and the banker-god   Trapezites—not circus performers   The gnomes of Rome   Banking secrecy and the Knights Templar   The Gestapo plays at being Father Christmas   The American eagle takes over from the German eagle and gets a gold carrot   Another carrot for the Jewish martyrs

2. THE DESIRE FOR BANKING SECRECY   9

   Parasites on society and taxpayers   Bank deposit certificates—with no name

3. THE RECENT HISTORY OF BANKING SECRECY   27

   The competence of the banker is the principal instrument of banking secrecy   A treaty above all suspicion   A judge who was also a cowboy?   Political society and commercial society   The monkeys imitate the gnome

4. THE SWISS ASPECT OF THE QUESTION   33

   Motives behind the Swiss banking convention   Legal standing of the convention   The originality of the convention

5. THE DIRECT INSTRUMENTS OF BANKING SECRECY   39

   The envelope with a number or a false name?   Muller with one 'l' or two   There is no subscriber at that number   Someone with a big family   Gonzales the phantom becomes Mr Muller's representative   An instrument which will not have any effect until the moment it should be revoked   Postmortem instrument and safe deposit box   A safe with no key or almost the last stage in confidence   A particularly vicious circle

6. THE INDIRECT INSTRUMENTS OF BANKING SECRECY   58

Structures with local exchange control and private agreements   Structures with no local exchange control but private agreements   Structures which really are anonymous

7. THE ROLLS-ROYCES OF BANKING SECRECY   68

Free captives   Interest at wholesale prices   'Offshore' financial platforms   Heavy reserves   Paper banks   The rules of the game   The rules of the club

8. BANKING SECRECY AT THE TIME OF DEATH   76

Moral or physical person   A postmortem instrument equates to a will

9. BANKING SECRECY AND POLITICS   81

The anatomy (autopsy?) of a political affair

II   The common law banking infernos   91

10. GREAT BRITAIN: A WORLD CELEBRITY FOR LESS THAN TEN POUNDS   93

Jurisprudence is not necessarily justice   Unusual transactions   The investigators will not pay the bills   A woman beaten by the horses

11. UNITED STATES: JUSTICE WORTHY OF THE NAME   98

From banking to bigamy   Public relations, yes—but on whose behalf?   April Fool's Day joke   The summonsing of an American Mr Dupont   A castle and a bank   United States *v.* Nixon

12. CANADA: FORESTS WITHOUT SECRETS   103

Canadian snow versus Swiss snow   Legal decisions and the law of gravity   The golden rule   Fishing for taxpayers   Wall Street is not a wall between the snow and the palm trees

13. SOUTH AFRICA: A BLACK FUTURE FOR BANK SECRECY   107

Bank secrecy going back to Abrahams   South African and Canadian interpretation

14. AUSTRALIA: A COUNTRY WHICH GOES BEYOND REASONABLE BOUNDS   110

Beyond reasonable bounds   An oath on the bible but lies on paper   The kangaroo pouches of Australian banks hold no secrets when there are duplicate keys

III The Roman law infernos 113

15. THE FEDERAL REPUBLIC OF GERMANY: THE RIGHT OF MIGHT 115

Truth on this side of the Rhine Powers and limitations The judicial and fiscal 'Anschluss' of 1977

16. FRANCE: FROM CASH UNDER THE MATTRESS 118

Obliged by the law to be informers Is there a price for free justice? If you do not work for me free of charge you will be convicted Authorities with an interest Safe-deposits but not so safe Wholesale fishing The Supreme Court decides the size of the nets The authorities obliged to protect a 'legal evasion'

17. ITALY: A *'GUARDIA DI FINANZIA'* — SOMETHING LESS THAN CIVIL 126

An Italian salad Departures made use of by opponents

18. DENMARK: THE KING WORE NO CLOTHES 129

The little mermaid, an alarm signal as much as a siren Something rotten in the State of Denmark

19. JAPAN: KAMIKAZE DEPOSITORS 132

Regulated *shinto-shokai* An Eastern inferno

20. PORTUGAL: SECRECY BORN OF EXCESS 134

A climate of confidence An unknown banking haven A legal provision does not make a haven

21. SWEDEN: SOCIALISM WITHOUT PENALTIES 137

Scandinavian commonsense The Swedish reality Fishing for the happy salmon

22. SOME OTHER ROMAN LAW INFERNOS 140

Belgium: a Walloon or Flemish transfer Spain: the banking bullfight has begun Finland: the end of the earth but perhaps in the springtime of banking secrecy Mexico: banking secrecy which is well bronzed but not well muscled Norway: fjords with no secrets The Netherlands: accounts which the authorities enter like windmills

IV The traditional banking havens — 145

23. ANDORRA: THE MIDDLE AGES OF BANK SECRECY — 148

24. BAHREIN: THE OFFSHORE BANKING UNITS (OBUs) OF INTERNATIONAL FINANCE — 153

25. HONG KONG: THE BAND OF THREE — 158

26. BRITISH VIRGIN ISLANDS: BANKING VIRGINITY STILL PRESERVED — 163

27. JERSEY AND GUERNSEY: A NEW CARD UP ONE'S SLEEVE — 168

28. LUXEMBOURG: THE BLUE BLOOD OF BANKING SECRECY — 175

29. ISLE OF MAN: AN ISLE OF MAN FOR THE BUSINESSMAN — 181

30. USSR: SEE NO EVIL, SPEAK NO EVIL, HEAR NO EVIL — 185

V Banking havens which have chosen their vocation — 191

31. THE BAHAMAS: NOTHING BUT THE SEA IS TRANSPARENT — 193

32. CAYMAN ISLANDS: A STRONG BANKING CASTLE — 202

33. HUNGARY: LIBERTY—FOR FLOATING CAPITAL — 209

34. LIECHTENSTEIN: A SWISS TRANSFER — 215

35. VANUATU: SECRECY SPRINGS FROM EXEMPTION — 220

36. PANAMA: A CANAL FOR FLOATING CAPITAL — 226

37. SINGAPORE: A BAD NUMBER FOR NUMBERED ACCOUNTS — 233

38. SWITZERLAND: A CURRENCY—EVEN FOR THE BLIND — 239

VI Other havens and banking loopholes   251

39. THE OTHER BANKING HAVENS   253

Lebanon: in the absence of a chef, it is no longer a good kitchen   Malaysia: a malaise in Malaysia   Nauru: banking secrecy, but only one main course   Austria: will the eagle of banking secrecy fly away?   Costa Rica: a passport for banking secrecy   Kleinwalsertal: bearer bank deposit books   Jungholz: a baby bank haven   St Vincent: secrets in the shadow of a volcano   Turks and Caicos Islands: banking effects for denuded islands

40. BANKING LOOPHOLES   260

Bearer certificates and net losses   Funds with floating morality   *Mu-kimei* accounts with *natsu-in toku-betsu* receipts   Seals have their uses   Recreation of bearer instruments   Third-party accounts in Switzerland and subjective or objective theory in Japan   Good sense does not harm the law   The Japanese State and *mu-kimei* accounts

41. CONCLUSION   269

APPENDIX I: GLOSSARY   284

APPENDIX II: BIBLIOGRAPHY   290

APPENDIX III: CONVENTION ON THE NEED FOR CAUTION WHEN ACCEPTING DEPOSITS AND ON THE USE OF BANKING SECRECY   304

Index   315

Foreword

Banking havens are to secrecy what tax havens are to taxation. They are places of refuge in a world which is economically oppressive and instable. Their existence and indeed their *raison d'être* often spring more from the faults of their neighbours than from their own qualities.

The difference which marks them from international financial centres, which they sometimes also may be (as is the case with Switzerland), is the fact that their principal attribute is above all the maximum of banking secrecy and therefore discretion.

A 'banking haven' can be defined as a country which gives—as far as its law can reach—any individual or legal entity a degree of banking secrecy which is much more extensive than that to be found in other countries. It is therefore only by comparison with 'banking infernos' that banking havens may be defined, since no country in the world allows *absolute* banking secrecy.

It was from the idea of a comparison that the conception of a world guide was born, although the achievement of this has not been made any easier by the fact that discretion is a principal characteristic of a banking haven, and that no other general work of comparison exists.

Banking secrecy has numerous forms which owe their origin to different legal frameworks, practices and systems and which have given birth to the most unlikely mythology in which modern dreamers recreate the bulging treasure ships of their childhood imaginings.

This natural tendency to join banking secrecy to adolescent fantasy has the result that many 'roving depositors', bewitched by secrecy which in practice they often do not need, behave in an almost infantile way. An analogy with dogs which bury bones springs to mind.

The consequence of this irrational attitude is that these same roving depositors forget for the most part to examine thoroughly the relevant documentation of the banking haven which they are studying. They content themselves with such vague information as corresponds to their imaginings and omit even the most elementary precautions just as soon as some professional adviser, usually foreign, waves the lure of banking secrecy under their noses. The experience of the professionals is that most of the people attracted by banking havens are neither dropouts nor international adventurers, but rather respectable heads of families who wish to have something put aside for their families secure from political hazards—which often have bad side-effects in terms of taxation and exchange control.

Is it reasonable to criticize these 'respectable family men' for not complying with laws which are as unfortunate as they are temporary, when they know that in many countries the politicians who created the law are doing, or have done, the same thing only on a larger scale? That is not the object of this work —even if the author did disapprove of their attitude in the face of systematic, organized plundering which should be prevented—not by violating laws but by organized political action devoted to changing laws which are unjust and counterproductive.

The object of this guide, conceived purely as a technical work, is to explain the advantages, risks and disadvantages of the principal banking havens and the forms of secrecy available to combat official constraints. The book is a guide and does not set out to be encyclopedic in a field where no encyclopedia exists. The author is more concerned with the realities rather than the letter of the law, which, like bank secrecy, is only as effective as the people operating it.

Leaving aside the underlying principle of the work (which is in itself a matter open to debate), the author is aware that some readers may be critical of omissions. These spring from the fact that the work is the first of its type and is therefore necessarily open to improvement.

Before examining the individual havens, it seemed appropriate to consider the origins of banking secrecy and those who make use of it and describe its current situation in the world. To allow further comparison it is also necessary to study the techniques used and the direct and indirect means of control: these topics are dealt with in the first section under the heading 'Concept and use of banking secrecy'.

Professional readers may remark with curiosity that the question of secrecy within the family has not been dealt with. This deliberate omission springs from the fact that the question does not really arise in bank havens, and in most countries considered to be banking infernos it is quite commonly the case that while any tax or customs official whatsoever has the right to examine freely a resident's bank account, the holder's spouse is refused access in the name of a highly debatable morality . . . .

In order to provide the essential basis for comparison required in this method of presenting the subject, sections II and III deal with the economically more important countries which are banking infernos, while sections IV to VI then examine the banking havens.

A substantial amount of space has deliberately been given up to the reproduction of banking documents which have never previously been published. The systematic publication of these documents would alone have justified this book and the author thanks sincerely those banking friends in the world in general, and in Switzerland in particular, who after the publication of *Guide des Paradis Fiscaux* gave him copies of documents whose existence is normally kept extremely confidential. In return the author extends to these banking friends the protective anonymity which they strive so hard to give to their clients.

As this book is a guide the reader will follow, for ease of presentation in his search for discretion, an imaginary traveller called the 'roving depositor'.

This explorer, like the 'tax explorer' in *Guide des Paradis Fiscaux* is looking for legal solutions to his problems.

As with all guides, the good addresses change in time. But unlike tax havens, the good addresses in banking secrecy change slowly; one of the basic essentials of such a 'good address' is *confidence*—and then 'the important thing is moral integrity'.*

---

*M Alfred E. Sarasin, President of the Swiss Bankers' Association, in his opening address at the Bankers' Day, Lucerne, 30 September 1977.

I

Concept and uses of Banking Secrecy

1 The general history of banking secrecy

The principle of confidentiality in financial transactions is bound up with the history of banking and has only recently become a problem to the extent that the state, wishing to take over the rights of the individual, has taken on an inquisitorial role in the modern world in pursuit of restrictive taxation complemented by a ruinous exchange control.

HAMMOURABI AND THE BANKER-GOD

It was in the reign of Hammourabi at Babylon, about 4000 years ago, that the role of bankers began to be defined. Some unkind wits suggest that it was one of the world's first two professions. This is not true—tax collectors existed before bankers, from which fact perhaps springs the dislike of the former for the latter since it may have been the cause of banking secrecy. At the time of the first author of a legal code which carried its creator's name (an idea subsequently taken up by Napoleon), the banker who plied his trade in the temple was highly respected.

If the Hammourabi Code does not contain in the version which has survived the principle of banking secrecy, it provides that the banker—who to an extent performed the functions of a notary as well—might make public his records in the event of a dispute with his client. This provision, allowing for a departure from secrecy, leads one to suppose that there must therefore have been a general understanding on banking secrecy.

Since the gods—even bankers—have the tendency to come down off their pedestals in the face of financial realities, they became more or less officials (already!) and there are numerous examples of 'transfers' between Rome and Alexandria (on scrolls) for the movement of precious metals.

TRAPEZITES—NOT CIRCUS PERFORMERS

The Greeks, who are traders by inclination as much as necessity, left this activity to moneychangers who operated from tables (*trapeza*) in the streets. They became, in fact, bankers little by little, thanks notably to possessing a staff of devoted slaves (we are not trying to rewrite history).

The Romans succeeded the Greeks, although in effect their social structure owed much to the Greeks; through the medium of moneychangers whose main function was to identify counterfeit coins, the Romans took up this profession which was destined to such a brilliant future. Imitating the Greeks and Phoenicians, the Romans struck their coins in a temple—that of Juno the Counsellor, who was also known as 'Moneta', hence the word money. The bankers themselves had the pleasant name of *argentarii* and both took deposits and made loans.

THE GNOMES OF ROME

It may be that the adage *'pecunia non olet'* ('money has no taint') dates from this period. In any event it seems that the bankers played an important role and even plotted against Julius Caesar. With the decline of Rome they pursued their vocation at Alexandria.

If the Romans had already given the principle of banking secrecy official status in their statutes with the *actio injurarium*, the bloodthirsty barbarians who were going to replace them, and from whom for better or worse the majority of Europeans are descended, were as interested in money as they were in blood. The common law of the barbarian tribes therefore already recognized in the *lex visigothorum* the principle of secrecy in financial transactions.

BANKING SECRECY AND THE KNIGHTS TEMPLAR

The Templars were the first to take on banking as an organized group, which they did from their base in Jerusalem. They are credited with having conceived the idea of the current account. Their role as bankers to princes and kings was not without its disadvantages. Happily, even the most powerful chairmen of banking groups no longer have the power to mete out fate like that of Jacques de Molay who maintained in his ashes if not the secrets of their banking clients at least the secrets of the Templars themselves.

With the Italian Renaissance banking became the prerogative of the Medicis at Florence. Louis XI, anticipating modern anti-avoidance legislation but above all to satisfy his father-in-law Louis of Savoy, had already ruined trade in Geneva by forbidding all merchants to take part in the Geneva fairs.

Florence had as many as 80 banking enterprises with branches in the principal cities of Europe. It is likely that they did not observe very strictly the prohibition placed by the Catholic Church on the lending of money for interest. The prohibition was supported by St Thomas Aquinas who said: 'interest is the price of time, and time is the gift of God'.

The more practical Protestants supported economic activity, and in his letter on usury, in 1545, Calvin removed the ban on charging interest, as long as the rate charged was moderate (5 per cent), on the grounds that it was illogical that the owner of capital could not make any profit on it while the owner of land was allowed to charge rent. It is not irrelevant to note that at the time Calvin was taking refuge in Geneva* where he died in 1564, leaving a deep impression on the place after a 25-year stay.

Honesty requires it to be pointed out that banking secrecy, that is secrecy of financial transactions, was not the main preoccupation at that time of inquisitors—their interest was more religious than legal or fiscal. This happy time (for banking) continued throughout the periods dominated by the English, Dutch and Germans.

In reality it was only in the aftermath of the First World War, with the birth of exacerbating national exchange controls and spoliatory states offering valueless pieces of paper including a reproduction of their tyrant in exchange for goods or work, that international banking secrecy in the true sense was born. The first serious conflict, which is at the same time the principal and the most important piece of international financial litigation, is the German-Swiss confrontation which was to be the basis of the modern concept of banking secrecy and the structures which are derived from it.†

In 1933 national socialist Germany published a series of regulations requiring all German citizens to make a declaration of their overseas assets. The penalty for failing to make this declaration was death.‡ One of the brilliant organizations charged with following up this legislation was the *Geheime Stadt Polizei* (city secret police force—abbreviated to 'Gestapo') who used numerous techniques to obtain the names of German citizens with bank accounts abroad.

THE GESTAPO PLAYS AT BEING FATHER CHRISTMAS

One of the techniques used was for a Gestapo agent to go into a bank and give the cashier a sum of money to be credited to the account of Mr X. Too great a hesitation on the cashier's part was sufficient (the Gestapo was not looking for judicial proof but sufficient evidence to support the confession which they would do a great deal to obtain). This would be enough for heavy pressure to be exerted on the lawbreaker and instructions to be extracted from him to arrange for the return of the funds from the Swiss Bank.

The Swiss bankers have long since obviated such a risk and the cashiers and

---

*The name Geneva probably derives from the Ligurian language where '*gen*' means 'coming out' and '*ava*' means 'water'—a curious twist of fate which has made a water source into a repository for liquid capital.

†Since that test many countries have railed against banking secrecy as being contrary to international morality, including East Germany which sells its emigrants to West Germany just as Nazi Germany sold some Jews, and uses the same economic justification that the country has made an investment in the education of these human cattle!

‡The German text (in the version published subsequent to the 1936 order) shows evidence of a profound humanity worthy of the better current declarations made by the rulers of so-called popular democracies on human rights: 'Any German national who, deliberately or otherwise, activated by a base selfishness or any other vile motive, has amassed his wealth abroad or left capital outside the country, shall be punished by death'. Since that time humanity has made extraordinary progress and an identical law published in 1976 in Italy has substituted a heavy prison sentence for the death penalty. You cannot stand in the way of progress!

employees of worthwhile banks are unaware of the identity of the owners of numbered accounts or those in false names—which are used in that way for precisely this reason. The execution of three Germans in 1934 caused the Swiss authorities to incorporate in their legal code the traditional banking secrecy which had for a long time been an unwritten rule. Its codification extended the protection of the Swiss Penal Code to the clients of Swiss banks since any violation of secrecy would constitute an offence. This legislation had the object of bringing bankers and their employees within the reach of criminal penalties and thereby protecting at a stroke the clients, the bankers and the bank employees, since it is not legally possible to oblige anyone to commit a criminal offence.

The most serious attack on Swiss banking secrecy finally arose not from the Gestapo but from the United States where the absence of any concept of bank secrecy would not allow the acceptance of foreign legal systems.

At the beginning of hostilities in the Second World War the Germans, Italians and Japanese repatriated their American deposits. The Swiss bankers, not expecting—and apparently rightly so—any blocking of their assets, did not take the same action. On the contrary, after the fall of France, Switzerland transferred its physical reserves of gold to New York as it feared that the Germans would ultimately invade Switzerland.

Certain American officials had the idea that German groups might be hiding behind the Swiss deposits and in 1941, convinced of the accuracy of their intuition, they wanted to obtain legal evidence to prove it. On the face of it such information would be easy to obtain since the branches and subsidiaries of the Swiss banks are obliged to comply with American law and would not therefore be able to conceal anything from the government.*

The American officials were extremely annoyed to discover that all the investments were held in the names of banks and not of their clients,† and that these investments amounted to US$1 billion. The American authorities then demanded that the identity of these investors should be divulged to them. To which the Swiss, who had already resisted all the efforts of the Gestapo, replied that their law of 1934 prevented them, on pain of criminal penalties, from divulging such information.

---

*One of the basics of the international banking system is that branches or subsidiaries of banks in foreign countries must submit, as far as secrecy is concerned, to the law of the country in which they are operating. Therefore the branch or subsidiary of a Swiss bank abroad does not benefit from Swiss banking secrecy, and on the contrary the branch or subsidiary of a foreign bank in Switzerland benefits from secrecy and must comply with it. The same system applies to American banks and (by way of example) it is therefore highly debatable what legal authority the American government had to block Iranian assets in banks 'under American control' outside the United States.

†Under the system of 'fiduciary' contracts, a sort of mandate where the banks take the place of the account holder: perfectly legal in current Swiss law and also to an extent in Anglo-Saxon law in the form of a trust. The investments made under a fiduciary contract do not form part of the bank's balance sheet, by comparison with guaranteed parallel financing—more commonly known as 'back-to-back loans'.

THE AMERICAN EAGLE TAKES OVER FROM
THE GERMAN EAGLE AND GETS A GOLD CARROT

The American reaction was of a brutality which went beyond blackmail for on 14 June 1941, that is 6 months before the entry of the United States into the war, not only were all the Swiss investments and assets in the United States blocked, but this extended as far as the gold reserves that the Swiss government had had taken to the United States because they were afraid of a German invasion! On top of that 1300 Swiss companies were placed on a boycott list for trading with the Germans (a list which was reduced to 600 companies in 1945).

At the end of the war the Swiss banks had not done marvellous business with Germany; supplies of goods had not been paid for, the value of investments in German industry which by then had been destroyed was next to nothing, and the stories of vast deposits belonging to German leaders were much overstated: they really believed in the 1000 year Reich, which state of mind precludes foreign bank deposits.

In these circumstances the Swiss banks needed the assets frozen in the United States, but the American government would not negotiate except with the Swiss government, whereas within the Swiss federal system the only body really in a position to negotiate was the Swiss Bank Association.

It was not finally until 25 May 1946 after many ups and downs and the exertion of much pressure that an agreement was ratified under whose terms the German assets (as defined by Swiss law) were shared between Switzerland and the Allies and used for the reconstruction of Europe. In order to determine the amount of the German assets it was left to each bank to provide a total figure, which produced the sum of $60 million for the Allies.*

ANOTHER CARROT FOR THE JEWISH MARTYRS

This same principle was going to be attacked again, and this time by the Jewish community and the state of Israel who, while it was making its attacks, was also depositing the major assets of its new banks in Switzerland. It is obvious that after the war (which some of our contemporaries refuse to call the Second World War because they prefer to forget what happened before) a substantial number of bank deposits and deposit boxes were left without apparent inheritors, despite the real efforts made by the Swiss banks in 1946 to find heirs. It is equally obvious that if the whole of these 'forgotten' deposits did not belong to Jews, then at least a very large part of them did.

Their fate was regulated by a decree made on 20 December 1962 which was to remain valid for 10 years and came into force on 1 September 1963.

---

*Certain authors (and notably T. R. Fehrenbach) have reported that the Swiss contribution to the reconstruction of Europe was in fact equal to that of the Marshall Plan, that is $3 billion. It seems that this figure should be checked.

This decree, which was a compromise between banking secrecy and the obvious injustice of maintaining it under the circumstances, applied to Swiss assets whose last known owners were foreigners or stateless persons and from whom there had been no positive contact since 9 May 1945—and who it was presumed or known had been the victims of racial, religious or political persecution.

This decree which applied not only to bankers but also to other guardians of professional secrets (lawyers, accountants etc.) provided that all assets whose last-known owners were covered by the decree should be declared to the 'missing persons' asset bureau'.

Subject to certain restrictions which are very well set out in Maurice Aubert's remarkable book *Le Secret bancaire suisse**, the sum which came to light was relatively modest. To take account of the Jewish origin of most of the original owners two-thirds was passed to the Swiss Federation of Israeli communities in Zurich and one-third to the Central Office for helping refugees, also at Zurich.

That should be seen as a favour done by the Swiss banks in the same way as the one which they did for the United States. All the critics of the Swiss banking system, generally forgetting what happens in their own country, omit to mention that in their country estates which are left without heirs pass to the state. It seems that in these cases the Swiss bankers have shown themselves to be excellent businessmen, knowing when to go beyond their own law. If this skill has made a great deal of money for them, that is due ultimately to their merits and only less able people are likely to criticize them for it.

---

*Aubert, Kernen and Schoenle *Le Secret bancaire suisse*, Berne, Editions Staempfle.

2 The desire for banking secrecy

The modern world in which we live continues to base society on the individual and his immediate surroundings — particularly on his emotional and economic surroundings, or rather the family cell in which he *lives* (for a long time the cell has been relieved by the community hospital of the birth and death of the individuals which make it up).

This society with its democratic nature (like others elsewhere, since there is no dictatorship of the right or left which does not also use the term), while it allows this basic cell to continue to exist gives it ever-reducing rights. One of the most important, and in practice one of the most frequently attacked, rights of a liberal world is the right to secrecy. It is attacked on many levels, even including medical, but the attack is at its most virulent in the area of finance.

In effect the modern states whose new, brilliant citizens have the irritating tendency of looking for a milch-cow themselves have a desperate need for money to finance the allowances which are demanded of them.

PARASITES ON SOCIETY AND TAXPAYERS

In such conditions all techniques of checking on the financial state of the parasites are good, since they can then be made to pay back in a different way what they demand of the state as their due. Obviously the state, the 'collective provider' will not be prepared to see itself opposed in its search for money by any sort of secrecy, and particularly not bank secrecy even if it has an interest in it.

This situation works itself out in one of two ways. Either the state allows a general banking secrecy (accompanied mostly by an absence of exchange controls) in effect gambling that the losses from its own citizens will be largely compensated for by the inflow from abroad. This is the case in Switzerland. Alternatively the state which is less confident in itself denies banking secrecy to its own residents but allows it to non-residents. In other words they allow it to residents of other countries on the basis that it is worth taking in that way what they could not otherwise have reached.

The result of this situation is that the countries with a large population (with the exception of Switzerland) reject banking secrecy or use it as a weapon at the expense of their neighbours while withholding it from their own residents. The withholding of bank secrecy is not always total and only takes place in matters which concern the 'provider state'. The amusing result of this is that in most of the countries where the basic unit of society is still the family, a wife has no means of examining her husband's bank transactions and would even have the greatest difficulty in tracing them in a divorce action to demonstrate that his management of his affairs might be dishonest.

On the other hand, again in most countries, the husband even though designated as the head of the family would not be able to get to know his wife's banking transactions. However, in the same countries any employee of the state in the area of taxation or customs has the power to demand that a banker unveils the activities of any client. The banker cannot protest professional secrecy and indeed may in some countries be required by national legislation to act as an agent of the state or as an informer to the state.

Clearly in such circumstances the few countries where true bank secrecy still exists are bound to enjoy a certain attraction, just as tax havens do. What then supplies the impetus which leads to these havens, so often prohibited by legislation? It seems that there is no one specific motive, but rather a whole series of them which may or may not occur together.

MOTIVES

In search of security

This is undoubtedly the most important motive. It is the only one which would explain, for example, the considerable flow of funds both to and through Switzerland from the Gulf States. Gulf citizens are not afraid of taxation which they consider excessive and are trying to avoid since in general there is no taxation in those countries. Equally there is no exchange control to tie up funds and which someone might seek to escape simply to avoid having his money tied up even if he had no other motive to take the money out.

The motivation of the Gulf citizens is purely and simply common sense— they seek a skilled banking system in which the state has no part and a currency in which they can have confidence. This latter is a quality which excludes countries that have exchange control since those countries themselves have confidence neither in the currency nor in their banking institutions.

The other reasons for seeking banking secrecy have nothing to do with a desire to find a particular quality, but rather to escape something. Of course, a fair number of states allow non-residents a 'supervised freedom' and allow them to keep accounts in convertible currency, but it seems that those regimes which give only a semi-liberty receive in return only a semi-confidence from depositors.

Tax avoidance

Tax avoidance is a modern technique which consists of the taxpayer looking for legal means, often international, whereby he pays the minimum tax possible, while living in, or spending some time in states which try to extract the maximum.

This procedure is practised either through tax havens which raise little or no taxation or through a conduit of legal structures in different countries which have voluntarily created loopholes in their tax systems.*

The steps taken by someone who uses tax havens are very different from tax evasion. The avoider is someone who, seeing the same object for sale in two shops, goes in and buys at the shop where it is cheaper. The behaviour of the tax evader is much more crude and consists of going into either one of the shops and taking the object without paying. He does not differentiate between the shops since he has no intention of paying either one.

At present certain countries and the OECD (in its official documents) are trying to create confusion between avoidance and evasion. This is an unfortunate and intellectually dishonest move.

It is evident that multinational corporations, dynamic businessmen and rich people taking their retirement in a tax haven must plan their banking operations with the same care and sound legal base as the taxation which they are going to avoid. Their preference in banking will be for secrecy and technical skill and, since one of the rules for the use of tax havens is not to use the tax haven of residence (be it physical or legal), they will need to find a banking haven, that is a country which, given an adequate level of technical skill, provides the maximum banking secrecy.

Tax evasion

This is a subject which creates great phantoms in the soul of the state and great fantasies in the mind of the individual.

In reality, as has been pointed out above, tax evasion is a form of dishonesty which consists of making your fellows pay what you should pay yourself. It is evident that certain tax burdens (Algeria, Great Britain) reach a level which implies either simple plundering or mental deficiency and clearly taxation under such conditions becomes totally impossible. Nevertheless in such circumstances a solution must be found either through the ballot box or by leaving the country (which is still possible in those countries which have a democracy not of the 'popular' kind) rather than by tax evasion.

Nevertheless, if one is to avoid following the habits of the ostrich, it must be admitted that tax evasion exists, even if it does not achieve the status of an institution. It is obvious that money deriving from tax evasion cannot be brought back legally and officially into the banking system where this system is not closed to the tax authorities.

BANK DEPOSIT CERTIFICATES — WITH NO NAMES

It is necessary to point out that it is patently obvious at what point certain countries organize officially the 'recycling of dirty money'. This is the

---

*See Edouard Chambost, *Using Tax Havens Successfully*, Institute for International Research, London.

situation in France (and this is far from being the only situation) with bank deposit certificates issued without names.* Any tax inspector who was both reasonably diligent and moderately intelligent could find out about these if he were authorised to do so (see Chapter 16 on France) but discovery is apparently prevented by the existence in the country of large credits which relate to seasonal businesses connected with high fashion.

It is in the area of tax evasion and its consequences that banking secrecy can conceal some unpleasant surprises concerning the fact that not only is banking secrecy never absolute but the definition of evasion differs from one country to another.

For example, a businessman could decide to make use of false invoicing in order to reduce his taxable profits. This procedure which is much to be condemned but which is also much used requires amongst other things some complicity in the fraud and a false use of commercial practices.

The businessman buys from another company a false invoice which he can deduct from his taxable profit by way of operating expenses incurred in the creation of the profit. The businessman writes out a cheque to the supplier company and, to be absolutely safe, goes to the bank with the manager of the supplier company to pay in the cheque and receive cash in exchange by way of a 'commission'.

Clearly this operation creates some 'dirty money' which will in time form the object of a transfer (itself illegal) and for which the owner will look for absolute banking secrecy.

If at some stage or other the operation does not run according to plan, the businessman will pretend that he was obliged to extract the money in this way in order himself to pay hidden commissions. Of course this poor defence would be very unfavourably received by the courts.†

---

*The bank deposits are placed for fixed terms of 1, 3, 6 or 12 months and receive a certain amount of interest. The anonymity of the owners of these deposits is preserved by the deduction of a withholding tax from the interest credits given by the banks—credits which are already very modest in any event.

†At the moment there is no country which forbids such transactions (apart from the United States where the inhabitants suffer from a basic puritanism which drives them, after committing the worst excesses, to a desire to recreate their lost virginity). Generally speaking businesses involved in this sort of area reach agreement in advance wih the appropriate authorities on the amounts involved so that there is no subsequent question about their being allowed as business expenses.

Such practices are carried out without any basis in law. In France the authorities insist that the recipient of the commission is named but the information is given in a sealed envelope and kept in a safe. These formal measures are clearly a waste of time since the opening of one single envelope, if it came to light, would risk ruining a major part of France's foreign trade. They should be seen simply as the desire on the part of the authorities to intimidate the businessmen on the grounds of a possible 'sharing of the loot'.

The Italians, who are much more practical, will allow without any documentation a flat rate of deduction from exports of between 10 and 33⅓ per cent! The authorities of this country are not unaware that the businessmen will find their own accounts by way of a contract (with a Swiss agent) of a type which the Italian Ministry of Finance will recommend if the businessmen are not intelligent enough to think of it for themselves. What do sharing or fraud matter since the Italian economy benefits by having markets for its products which it has acquired in the last 15 years, notably in the Common Market—but so what? In any case Switzerland will certainly find its share, and who should complain at that?

If the operation takes place as intended by the businessman, but ultimately he is put under pressure by the tax authorities, or blackmailed, or the helpful supplier is arrested (such people are normally crooks), he will think he is safely protected by his numbered Swiss account—provided that he has found a bank to accept his money or rather that he has succeeded in concealing from his Swiss banker the true origin of the money.

It is then that he risks getting a very considerable shock. Granted the existence of Swiss banking secrecy which may not be breached by the Swiss tax authorities—and therefore even less so by foreign taxmen—even in the face of tax evasion carried out by people who are residents or citizens of Switzerland, this banking secrecy has its limits, which also delineate Swiss honesty.

In a situation where the evasion includes transactions which are themselves illegal (which would be the case in our example) and illegal in Switzerland (which is also the case in our example), banking secrecy no longer applies: our dishonest businessman will suddenly see his banker from a new angle which is likely to be as expensive as it was unforeseen.*

Bankruptcy and fiscal bankruptcy

There are other forms of disagreement between the taxpayer and the tax gatherers which to a greater or lesser degree have some bearing on bank secrecy and in which the tax authority is only one of the taxpayer's creditors.

If it is accepted in a number of Latin countries, and notably in France, that a taxpayer cannot be make bankrupt for fiscal debts,† that is not the case in Great Britain. Because of this the British tax authority sued in the Jersey courts a man who had been made bankrupt for tax debts in the United Kingdom but had previously taken refuge in Jersey, a 'sovereign' state.

My tailor is still rich in Jersey

The 'poor' British taxpayer, whose name was Taylor and who had reached the venerable age of 84, was sued for principal and interest due to the British tax authority of the not inconsiderable sum of £190 718.82.

Mr Taylor, through his lawyers, advanced the argument that on constitutional grounds a sovereign power cannot sue the resident of another sovereign power for tax debts. He was given much support by Barclays Bank in Jersey who, having been served with a notice blocking Mr Taylor's account entered a counter-plea in the courts.

---

*Some Swiss professionals disagree with this interpretation—they are wrong, although perhaps commercial motives may have something to do with their views.

†For some reason which is apparently clear to French jurists, fiscal debts are civil in nature and do not permit of bankruptcy proceedings, while other debts of virtually the same sort (due to URSSAF for example—the organization which collects social security contributions) are considered to have a different nature and would permit the bankruptcy of the same person. Hurrah for such a subtle distinction and so much the better for the dishonest taxpayer!

The British Inland Revenue were not put off by this and asked the Jersey courts to seize Mr Taylor's assets. The Royal Court went ahead with this general seizure 'for the account of whoever owns them' and named an administrator who would provide Mr Taylor with subsistence from the assets until a decision was reached as to their disposition.

The British Treasury and Mr Taylor's lawyers exchanged opinions and finally the Attorney General of Jersey intervened in the affair (this episode is interesting from several points of view and is studied in detail in Chapter 27 on Jersey and Guernsey).

If at first you don't succeed, don't try again

The whole thing should have ended in an important decision of principle. It was nothing. It is true that the lawyers at the British Treasury had written prior to the court action to the Jersey Treasury to suggest some transaction which was refused. An out-of-court settlement was reached in the affair—details of which have never been revealed—following on the opinion given by the Jersey Attorney General. It is reasonable to bet that the terms were, however, quite favourable for the 'poor' British taxpayer, as the British authorities would have wanted to avoid at any cost a court ruling which would have constituted a precedent.*

This policy towards the law is relatively lacking in courage, but is nonetheless much wiser than the violent American attacks against banking secrecy in the Cayman Islands (see chapters 11 and 32 on the United States and the Cayman Islands) where a consideration of the principles resulted in a reinforcement of the Cayman law.

It is true that on a financial level, if Jersey and Guernsey have sometimes enabled money to be removed from Great Britain, as in the Taylor case, the activities of the two islands as tax havens and financial centres have for a long time brought needed foreign currency into the reduced 'sterling area'. Whereas the Cayman Islands live at the expense of the United States which has no connection with the Cayman dollar—whose most curious feature is to carry a portrait of Queen Elizabeth in the place usually occupied by George Washington. It is no doubt as a result of this difference in interests that there has been the difference in legal approach. It is also true that the Cayman situation was not strictly concerned with a bankruptcy.

It is worth noting here that if in general international collaboration in dealing with bankruptcy does not work on a high level, it can nevertheless provide some surprises. Quite a number of residents of various countries have set up an 'alternative inheritance' under differing circumstances and for different reasons, but one of these can be so that in the event of bankruptcy their 'alternative means' can be kept out of the hands of their creditors!

---

*The Anglo-Saxon system of common law is built on 'precedents'. That is, that in a set of circumstances which have already been considered by a higher or equal court, the decision of that earlier hearing is binding.

In such a situation the country which holds the money has to run with the hare and hunt with the hounds to arrive at a balanced treatment of the interests of the bankrupt, protected by banking secrecy, and those—no less legitimate —of the creditors.

Maurice Aubert, who is one of the most eminent Swiss specialists in this area, takes the view that 'the rights of the creditors over assets deposited must be examined according to Swiss law'.* As if there was any doubt about that!

But what lies behind that comment? If we let him continue:

Information can only be obtained through mutual cooperation agreements on criminal law when there is a case outstanding overseas against the bankrupt for some bankruptcy offence, false titles, fraud etc. Nevertheless, in order that the veil of banking secrecy can be lifted, it is necessary that the request should come from a state which has signed a convention with Switzerland—either the European Convention on reciprocal envorcement of judgements in civil matters, to which the principal European countries are signatories, or by application of the treaty on this subject with the United States.

In reality, as the author of that passage notes very properly, there are numerous obstacles to a foreign bankruptcy being recognized in Switzerland; only an international treaty which harmonized bankruptcies could achieve that.

A French bankruptcy is the same as a Swiss bankruptcy

To be precise, there exists an old international treaty, apparently little known, between France and Switzerland dating from 15 June 1869. This deals with legal jurisdiction and the execution of judgments and affirms the principle of universality of bankruptcy between the two countries.†

The effects of this treaty are, however, limited since article 6, 1 of the treaty states:

The bankruptcy of a French person with a business establishment in Switzerland may be decided by the Swiss tribunal responsible for the place in which his business is established and similarly a Swiss national having a place of business in France may be pronounced bankrupt by a French tribunal.

When these conditions are fulfilled and an order of execution‡ obtained

---

*Special edition of *Banque*, 22 September 1978.
†Convention on legal jurisdiction and the execution of judgments on civil matters, 15 June 1869, published in France by decree of 19 October 1869 (*JO*, 2-3 November 1869). To this treaty has been added an interpretative protocol (which does not concern bankruptcy except as regards the procedures for execution) and an additional section on 4 October 1935 (which similarly does not deal with bankruptcy).
‡Articles 16 and 17 of the convention provide for a summary procedure of execution 'in France by a tribunal after a report requested by the president has been prepared by a magistrate and the Public Ministry has commented; and in Switzerland by the competent authority designated by the law'. Given the peculiarities of the Swiss legal system, the diplomats thought it worth adding in the interpretative protocol: 'the meaning of the words "competent authority" . . . in Switzerland the request for an executive order should be lodged, according to canton, with either the whole tribunal, or the president alone or even the executive authority . . . it may in case of difficulty be lodged with the Federal Council which acts in this case as a higher court.'

it is interesting to note that under the terms of the same article 6(3) the receiver may proceed:

according to the laws of the country in which they are situated, to sell the assets, fixed or other of the bankrupt.

This situation excludes bank secrecy from which the bankrupt was benefiting and whose benefit then passes on to the creditors in the two countries. It is the only treaty signed by Switzerland on this subject which is still current (by way of reassurance to non-French readers whose affairs are in a dubious state).

Etiquette in banking matters normally demands that the contingency of a client becoming bankrupt should be considered, but never that of the bank going into liquidation, but this may happen, and it may pose serious difficulties in verifying creditors and serious questions of secrecy concerning the anonymous depositor/creditor. Depositors can relax, however, since if this should happen to a bank, the liquidators who verify the creditors are subject to the banking secrecy laws and when they draw up a list of creditors give them numbers rather than names—that is a case of getting a numbered account without having to ask for it!

Exchange control

For reasons which are as much historical as political, countries allowing wide banking secrecy adopt a very complaisant attitude towards breaches of the exchange control regulations of other countries—exchange controls are not generally to be found in banking havens.

Exchange controls are in effect legislation through which a country in a particular situation protects, or believes it is protecting, its economy by preventing in particular the free conversion of its currency on the grounds that the currency would not survive market pressures.

About 80 per cent of the world's governments have adopted the 'easy' policy of forbidding their residents to hold overseas bank accounts* and obliging new residents to make a declaration and to 'repatriate' their overseas assets within a time limit.† These same countries forbid, or allow only after special authorization, the holding of any overseas asset.‡ Nevertheless certain of these countries may constitute banking havens specifically for non-residents (which is the case for the Bahamas or Guernsey and Jersey for example§) or even,

---

*Overseas is generally defined as 'countries which are outside the currency zone of the country of residence'.
†For France this time limit is 30 days, for example.
‡The French are allowed only to acquire fixed assets abroad whose value is less than Fr. 150 000.
§It should be noted in relation to these two 'sovereign' states that Great Britain withdrew exchange controls with effect from 24 October 1979 and therefore the distinction between residents and non-residents no longer applies.

since they are within the boundaries of a strict exchange control exercised by a large country, may constitute a tax haven used for this reason by the residents of that large country in preference to other havens which may have more advantages or be closer to hand (this was the case for Guernsey and Jersey in relation to Great Britain and is to a certain extent the case of French Polynesia to France).

As for the 20 per cent of governments which do not operate exchange control in the strict sense of the term, some of them have set up statistical checks on the flows of funds which would allow them, should it prove necessary, to enact almost instantly whatever legislation might seem appropriate (which is the case in the United States and West Germany).

If we abandon the concept of the State as a milch-cow and take up that of the State as a managing director, the procedure of having an exchange control would consist for an employer of refusing to pay his employees (on the grounds that his management was not good) in money which could be used to buy the products of other companies, but rather paying them in tokens which were only valid for the purchase of goods made by the company for which the employee worked.

Incompetence defeating itself

You may imagine what the reaction of the trade unions would be in such a situation. As far as states go, there are no parallels because not only are there no trade unions for citizens neither are there strictly speaking any sanctions against incompetence when the recruitment of top administrators in a country is done (unlike the methods used in a great democratic state like the United States) not on the basis of competence and proven professional ability, but on the basis of having been educated at a national school where the teaching is done by graduates of the same school! This happy system, called a technocracy, scarcely differs from a theocracy—whose terrible effects in the past are well known.

The stability of a country's currency is affected by the confidence which the 'administered'* have in their administrators. This element of confidence is obviously missing in a technocracy, despite the clear abilities of some individuals—abilities which derive from the individual and are often endorsed by an electorate, rather than being generated by the system which carries within it the principle of its own exclusivity and leads to a poor development of the confidence-currency relationship.

An old economic adage has it that 'bad money drives good money out of circulation'† which is to say that if at a given time there are two or more currencies in circulation in a country, the one in which people have the most confidence will be hoarded, set on one side, often outside the country, to the

---

*Not to be confused with shareholders. The shareholder can always sell out.
†This is no novel idea—this economic truth was pointed out more than 400 years ago by Sir Thomas Gresham (1519-79) who was Chancellor to Queen Elizabeth I of England.

detriment of the one inspiring less confidence which will stay in circulation. It is clear that many governments whose skill in governing inspires only a limited degree of confidence have a tendency to institute strict exchange controls in order to prevent, at least theoretically, their residents from depositing their money in another country whose government inspires less mistrust.*

This is particularly true when a government makes too great a use of its printing plates, knowing very well that it will inevitably result in a devaluation of the currency. French banknotes carry the following inscription:

Article 129 of the Penal Code stipulates perpetual imprisonment (you should have the means of carrying out your policies) for those who counterfeit or falsify bank notes authorised by the law, as well as those who have used such counterfeit or false notes. Those who have brought them into France will be punished with the same penalty.

Of course, there is no mention anywhere of those who have violated their right to issue, and you may be reasonably certain that those few people who have such authority would find that thought in very bad taste.

They have nothing to fear in France as the criminal laws are restrictive in their interpretation so no magistrate could convict them, and as for public opinion, in many countries its function is not to judge but to be manipulated.

Genuine imitations, or imitations of the genuine?

Legal counterfeiting can sometimes take a more precise form. In France there is a price differential on the markets between that of a Napoleon on the one hand and that of a gold ingot, or gold bar, on the other.

This differential, that is this difference in price between the Napoleon and the ingot judged in relation to the metal content alone, does not spring from its value to coin collectors, nor from the extra cost of the metal being stamped. It derives from the laws of supply and demand—small savers want to buy the gold coin because its unit weight, and therefore also its unit price, is much lower than that of a gold ingot.

Up to that point all is quite normal. If, for example, the number of coins struck during Napoleon's time is limited and the demand is considerable, the price will be greater than the simple value of the gold. It would, of course, be a great temptation to someone in those circumstances to melt down ingots in

---

*On this subject it is appropriate to congratulate in particular the British government under Mrs Thatcher for having had the courage to abolish the British exchange control after more than 40 years. The lawyers should note that it is the exchange control which has been lifted rather than the 1947 Act which has been abolished, which means that the measure could be reinstated immediately without requiring a debate in Parliament. The only European prime minister who is a woman, and at the same time the only one who behaves like a 'man', did not perhaps completely have the courage of her convictions. It is a pity that the measure, which is incomplete and lacks any amnesty provision, but was designed to permit the repatriation of capital which had previously been in contravention of controls, is quite insufficient and ultimately could be dangerous.

order to make napoleons. He should take care, however, as such an exercise would certainly land him in prison.*

If on the other hand a state had kept the original die and had proceeded to melt down ingots to make more napoleons, it would no longer be a question of imitations, but of genuine imitations (or imitations of the genuine?). In any event the coiner (one could not dare say counterfeiter) would make a very good profit on the price differential. It seems that the original dies for gold coins struck carrying impressions of Caesar and Vercingetorix have disappeared; so much the worse for them since they have therefore fallen into monetary obscurity. Good luck, however, to Napoleon—there are very few heads of state who can pride themselves on continuing to have their effigy struck more than 150 years after their death and with a premium at that, which reached 125 per cent in September 1976.† Such practices‡ are clearly not very encouraging for the worthy family man who, with an eye to safeguarding his family, conducts his business in a way which his country regards as unpleasant cheating.

Duty to the family or to the state?

Law-breaking in the area of temporary financial regulations has a vocabulary whose use is sufficient in itself to make you think, and also consider, perhaps rather sadly, the example of the spider's web—it catches only the smallest insects. If our worthy family man (living in a country which has severe exchange controls which forbid the export of capital) attempts to protect part of his capital by physically removing it to another country, or by using some intermediary, he is called a currency smuggler§ and as such receives a severe sentence (provided that is that amongst other things his intermediary has not disappeared with his fortune). The same man, if he had better connections, would be able to call on the services of a friend in the diplomatic service, whose passport—and above all whose suitcase—which is also considered to be diplomatic and theoretically untouchable, and would be assured of both a much more comfortable amount and a much smaller risk.

---

*When this kind of operation is practised officially and therefore legally by a state like Mexico the premium is quite low. Thus the premium on a modern 50 pesos coin is only 0.58 per cent (June 1979) compared with 35 per cent for the napoleon (Fr.20 coin at the same time). These figures ignore the wild fluctuations of a purely speculative nature which have taken place more recently.
†This striking of new coins was officially admitted during a televised debate a few years ago by the Governor of the central bank of an important country. Those grumblers who say that the English are malicious have really very little idea. In any event certain technicians in the know suggest that when flotation of the pound began to take on the characteristics of a submarine, there was a massive buying of napoleons in Switzerland—a poor glory? In any case some kind of glory since according to Rene Sedillot (*Vie française* 20 August 1979) there exist 10 napoleons per person in France and 27 per household.
‡Those of Phillippe le Bel, known as one of the 'great' kings of France, were even more primitive since he was accustomed to clip the gold coins issued carrying his image—every age has its own customs!
§The popular press amuses itself with stories which are as silly as they are spicy of starlets who try to smuggle money in the linings of their mink coats (so discreet) or other means as farcical as they are original.

It is perhaps worth noting that the diplomatic bag, which came into use at a time when there were 'gentlemen', to allow them to transport diplomatic documents, has come to be used for some very strange purposes since the arrival on the international scene of new countries whose diplomats are not necessarily 'gentlemen'. It was for this reason that one of the few countries which is internationally bankrupt as far as its balance of payments is concerned (let alone its situation as regards liberty, since having been passed through the rollers of the party presses in this 'democracy' the term has only as much substance as the rice paper on which it is printed) saw several of its diplomats arrested for drug trafficking by means of diplomatic bags.

Moreover it was thanks to profits gained from intoxication that this same government was able to take large advertisements in the international press with a view to intoxicating the readers of the 'free' press in a different way by extolling the virtues of their leader.

There at least, by way of revenge, their defeat was total.

If we return to our family man, and the problem of providing himself with a nest egg, there is a good chance that he could find—even in a country with severe exchange controls—a bank which would do him the service of performing a (locally) illicit contra deal—that is, an exchange between the funds which he wishes to take out of the country and those which a foreign company wishes to invest within the country. This quite substantial kind of operation is called 'an unauthorized clearing' technically speaking.

Finally, if our same man were at the peak of power and influence and were head of a multinational enterprise, he would have all sorts of means at his disposal: realization of profits outside the exchange control net (and if possible in a low tax jurisdiction); use of parallel financing ('back-to-back loans'); use of captive banks or insurance companies.

If he is well-organized, in the last example our family man could achieve the whole operation in a way which was perfectly legal in all the countries concerned but which would escape all exchange controls and even perhaps from all taxation.

The market for banking secrecy and its requirements

The countries which offer complete banking secrecy generally also offer, as a necessity of the marketplace, a warm welcome to capital which has escaped from the exchange controls of a neighbouring country:

The limits of banking secrecy only conform to the needs of the marketplace if they resist abuses and remain as diligent as they are expected to be. These expectations would be thrown over if banking secrecy was raised to help the legal authorities in other countries in the event that their exchange controls had been violated; the prohibition on exporting currency goes against those needs. Consequently banking secrecy must guarantee complete protection to currency and assets deposited and must observe the obligation to be diligent,* even if that does not suit the financial rulings of other countries.†

It is true that Switzerland not only does not have exchange controls in the strict sense of the word, but nor is it a signatory to the Bretton Woods agreement, whose 137 signatories might find such a statement not to their taste, even if some of them have become banking havens. There is in that agreement a clause, which is both famous and misunderstood, and which requires in particular:

Foreign exchange contracts which involve the currency of a member state and are in contravention of the exchange regulations of that state set up in accordance with the terms of this agreement, shall not be enforceable in the territories of other member states.‡

This little clause is at the same time both a little-known global check to legislation and the source of the most amazing official dishonesty. Without going into the complex details of the interpretation of this agreement nor the statutes arising from it in the member states,§ you could conclude at the risk of oversimplification, that a contract between residents of two member states could not be enforced by law if that agreement ran counter to the exchange controls of one of the countries, as the legislation of each country must be considered as being an integral part of the other country's.

The idea could have been acceptable and could even have worked in law if the defendant could not cite breaches of his own exchange control or the plaintiff escape a breach of his native laws.‖ But it is quite different as can be seen in this simplified example. X, or company X, a resident of one of the member states borrows $1 million from Y, or company Y, an American. When the repayment falls due X fails to perform his part and Y issues a writ in either his own country or that of X. X replies through his lawyers that he has indeed borrowed $1 million, but the exchange control legislation in his country requires that overseas borrowing should be authorized and he has omitted to obtain this authorization. The repayment cannot therefore be enforced in law. It is a marvellous piece of legal chicanery! ☆

---

*The obligation set in the Convention of 1 June 1977.
†Hugo Sieber speaking at the 64th Conference of the Association of Swiss Bankers, Lucerne, 30 September 1977.
‡Article 8, section 2b (*JO*, 27 December 1945).
§See in particular the very remarkable book by Dominique Carreau: *Souverainité et Cooperation monétaire international*, and in particular Chapter IV: 'Un exemple de cooperation judiciaire et administrative' (*Sovereignty and International Monetary Cooperation:* An example of official legal cooperation).
‖The plaintiff must have 'clean hands' in the sight of the law. Similar rules exist in legal systems based on Roman law in the form of adages such as 'a person may not enforce a benefit arising from his own failure to observe the law'.
☆Several decisions have been given on these lines in situations which were much more complex, but based on the same principle.

Tell me where you live, and I'll tell you who you may legally defraud

In effect therefore, before entering into a contract with a resident of another country you need to know the details of his exchange control statutes (there are currently 137 IMF members and therefore that many different sets of legislation). If this is easy in some countries (United States, West Germany) and possible in others whose statutes are complicated but more or less clear (France, Great Britain) it becomes difficult in certain cases (Australia) and reaches the proportions of a Chinese puzzle—in Japan.*

Quite apart from the basic morality of the question, the first reaction of a jurist would be to note that there is gain without justification, or at least that a clear fault on the part of the debtor should bring about a liability to compensate the lender for the damage he has suffered. This view would not be acceptable in the New York Court of Appeal nor in the jurisdictions of most member countries. One of the few judiciaries to have the courage to find in the opposite way was that of the Paris Court of Appeal in a similar case (where the other country was indeed Japan).†

After criticizing the judgment, one lawyer's review concluded—correctly as far as the law is concerned—that the Paris Court of Appeal was wrong to base its decision in equity‡ and added, with a maladroitness surprising in a professional:

. . . international monetary ethics are translated into legal form in the articles of the International Monetary Fund. National courts are obliged to make them effective. It is to be regretted that the Appeal Court has sacrificed them.

This type of conclusion (incorrect as to its facts given that there exist perfectly respectable countries such as Switzerland which are not signatories) follows the same kind of unacceptable reasoning where the man§ for whom laws are made is replaced by the jurist and not the reverse. This brings us back after a necessary digression to the problem of banking secrecy, since laws only have the value of the men who apply them.

---

*Certain lawyers who specialize in this field give the view, apparently justified, that the Japanese government has deliberately made even more complicated its legislation, which is in any event quite unclear, in order to allow Japanese businessmen, with the authorities' connivance, to use the law as a weapon against international competition when it occurs.
†4th Chamber, 14 May 1970, under the presidency of M. Abgral.
‡For some legal academics justice corresponds to the law, irrespective of situations where the law strays from equity.
§In this type of reasoning the operations of the *Geheime Stadt Polizei* (Gestapo) complied perfectly with the national socialist laws, and readers will be surprised to learn that the incarceration of Soviet dissidents in psychiatric hospitals is perfectly acceptable in terms of formal Soviet *legality* even if it offends Soviet *morality*.

Crossing the iron curtain will help

To avoid the application of the terms of the agreement it would appear to be sufficient for one of the contracting parties to reside in a state which is not a member. This principle was applied by the New York Appeal Court in relation to Cuba* and more recently by the Federal Court in West Germany in dealing with two Germans who were domiciled in East Germany (the Soviet zone) and had gone to the West. A legal relationship had been entered into during the time that these two lived in the East, and one was suing the other subsequently in the West. The defendant, who certainly had not lost his bearings, argued that according to East German law there could be no agreement between them. But the court ruled against him on the basis that the East German exchange control touched human rights and were in effect a political measure of a kind which should not be sustained, even if, according to the general principles of international law followed by West Germany the operation would be controlled by the law of the Soviet zone. 'It can only be treated differently if it concerns contracts between countries which are signatories of the Bretton Woods agreement or other international exchange agreements.'†

The Bretton Woods trap

To escape from the Bretton Woods trap it is apparently necessary, and sufficient, if one of the contracting parties belongs to a country which is not a signatory—which can be arranged in an apparently legal manner.

Taking the earlier example where the loan came from an American, and assuming he wishes to avoid the risks of such an agreement with Japan and its incomprehensible laws, he can make his loan through the intermediary of, for example, a Bahamian bank which would make the loan in its own name. Such an operation, which is performed frequently in the international field and in particular by the so-called multinational companies, is called 'Parallel guarantee financing' ('back-to-back loan')‡

Under these conditions the operation would have financial repercussions in three directions. Firstly, in the absence of a double taxation agreement between Japan and the Bahamas, or whichever banking haven was chosen to be the screen, the borrowing country could charge the maximum withholding tax on the interest. Then the Bahamian bank in whose balance sheet the operation will appear would take its fees in the form of a percentage of the

---

*Cuba, which was one of the founder members, withdrew from the IMF on 2 April 1964.
†See Dominque Carreau's excellent book, cited above.
‡This operation could be carried out perfectly legally as far as the United States is concerned as long as the American declares the loan made to the Bahamian bank to the IRS (International Revenue Service, the US tax authority). It should be remembered that in this hypothetical case the American is not concerned with breaking his own country's exchange control laws but simply with avoiding the trap of the Japanese exchange controls into which the borrower might make him fall.

interest received on the sum lent to Japan and that paid to the American bank for making the loan possible by way of the collateral deposit.

Finally, if the operation is not to become prohibitively expensive, it is necessary that the banking haven should not impose a withholding tax on the interest paid by the bank to the American depositor.

For these reasons the examination of each of the banking havens will include details of any factors militating against the operation of back-to-back loans and of whether the haven is itself a signatory to the Bretton Woods agreement (as is the case with the Bahamas) which would only transfer the problem to a new place. It should be noted that in a case where the banking haven is an IMF signatory, it would give the borrower the possibility of finding a breach of exchange control on the part of the lender, regardless of whether the lender was based in the territory of a signatory or not. No judgment has yet been passed to lift banking secrecy in a haven on this basis. However, it is conceivable that such a decision could be made on the basis of double incrimination, if exchange controls do exist in the banking haven, and even if the latter is not a party to the Bretton Woods agreement.

Crime — organized or not

If by some scarcely possible chance there should be criminals or criminal organizations amongst the readers of this book, looking for 'good' sources of information, their disappointment will be intense. The bankers in countries which have complete banking secrecy have, aside from discretion, one major characteristic in common — their hate of criminals and criminal organizations. The juxtaposition of these qualities is not, of course, without its ambivalence and the general public is shocked from time to time to learn that such and such a criminal organization keeps its funds in such and such a banking haven. This situation does not arise because the owners want banking secrecy as such, but rather they want the maximum protection. Criminals no doubt, but not necessarily weakminded!

It is obvious that the money would not have been accepted as such* and would be received by the banks only after 'laundering'† done by the criminal organization which would prevent the banker from discovering its true origin. In such circumstances the money would be accepted by absolutely any bank in any country.

Given that the Americans are a people endowed with a powerful sense of organization, it was their criminal groups and Mafia 'families' which attempted between the wars not only to enjoy their illgotten gains openly but even, in pursuit of respectability (much more than profitability), to invest this

---

*If a banker were knowingly to receive funds from a criminal source, this could in certain countries (Switzerland for example) constitute the specific crime of receiving stolen property.
†International 'laundering' techniques receive a remarkable analysis in the book by Clarke and Tigue, *Dirty Money* (see bibliography, page 291).

'dirty money' in legitimate businesses; the expression 'laundering' was born at this time.

Contrary to an opinion as popular as it is wrong, the origin of the word does not derive from the activity of making things clean, but from the fact that payment in that business is usually made in cash. The criminal organizations proceeded to buy up laundry chains so that they could then show officially a legitimate, taxable profit—which would conceal the source of the money (a sort of tax planning in reverse—we are a long way from tax havens).

Today the same criminal organizations prefer casinos to laundries: the results are quicker. So rumour has it that the Las Vegas casinos and certain floating casinos (in the Caribbean) are used as laundries by different 'families'. The more malicious would suggest that the New York 'family' is involved with European casinos—'from New York with love!'

Other organizations which have remained at the laundry stage have been modernized by going onto automatic carwashes. This is the reason why the American IRS is interested in profits which are too large as well as tax evasion. Clarke and Tigue quote, in *Dirty Money*, an example where the IRS discovered in the course of a tax audit of a carwash operator that on a particular day the operator had apparently washed an average of 200 cars per operating unit. However, on that particular day there was a blizzard with over a metre of snow falling, and all traffic completely at a standstill! It was obvious in the face of such a situation in the pursuit of organized crime that a serious lack of agreement would arise between Switzerland and the United States. The American government said it wanted to have Swiss banking secrecy lifted on grounds of taxation, but really with the idea that its legal system would allow it to fight criminals via investigations for tax evasions.[*] The Swiss authorities for their part did not see things that way and took the view, apparently with some cause, that if the American legal system had some omissions it was not the duty of the Swiss system to be changed to remedy the situation.

This dialogue between apparently deaf entities led after limited negotiations to the signature of a treaty between Switzerland and the United States[†] which provided that banking secrecy could be lifted in certain circumstances, provided that sufficient evidence existed of a criminal origin of funds which had not been discerned by the banker—despite the obligation on him to be diligent—at the time the funds were deposited. Such situations are part of the history of modern banking secrecy.

Banking secrecy and political secrets

There is no doubt—and it has been known for a long time—that certain political parties are financed from abroad by countries which support them[‡]

---

[*] It was for tax evasion—and only tax evasion—that the American authorities were able to convict their most famous gangster, Al Capone.
[†] See Chapter 3 on the recent history of banking secrecy.
[‡] The fact has been analysed sufficiently by various political journalists not to merit specific references.

and that in order to be discreet the funds are channelled through banking havens. In the same way governments in power use the havens for 'discreet' financing of their various activities and the agents of the services (themselves secret) responsible for carrying them out.

Heads of state currently in power (and on the way to being eliminated) and revolutionary organizations of all persuasions (on their way to replace the heads of state) have deposits in banking havens to safeguard for the former their 'future' and for the latter the 'sinews of war' coming from collections and foreign aid.*

Curiously some sums of money, occasionally enormous, seem to have disappeared in this way, or at least become 'unavailable'. This topic comes up regularly in the newspaper headlines in which the reader can find the most fantastic allegations in the form of a serious analysis.

As is the case with the story of the FLN (Algerian National Liberation Front) war chest which paid the newspapers' expenses for a long time and for which we shall attempt to explain the principal mechanics which led to its 'unavailability'. This business is explained in Chapter 9. It is necessary that the reader, in order to understand this, familiarizes himself with the different instruments of banking secrecy which are explained before that.

---

*The same applies here, particularly as far as the KGB and CIA are concerned.

3 The recent history of banking secrecy

The recent history of banking secrecy is that of a continual fight between the individual and society. This struggle comes within the wider context of professional secrecy whose function is to protect the individual rather than society in the collective sense. Unless you consider (as simple good sense would demand) that society, which is a collection of individuals living together, is made for these individuals, rather than the individual being made for a general, abstract, collective society misappropriated for the benefit of political vested interests, then it is not possible to refute the need for banking secrecy.

But that is exactly how some states occupy their time, even if they describe themselves as both modern and democratic, and in the first rank of these is the United States, which with Switzerland is one of the most democratic countries in the world.

Why should there be such opposition and such confrontation between these two true democracies? It is the legal concepts—which form part of the intellectual superstructure of a collective society which changes with time but also lags behind events—to which no doubt we should look for some sort of answer to this question, even if the answer is an awkward and not wholly satisfactory one.

Switzerland and the United States have numerous points in common, even if their respective inhabitants may for the most part be ignorant of this. Both countries were originally populated by refugees who had been driven from their homes as a result of their religious beliefs, which in their time qualified as the 'reform' view. As a result they created new communities which were extremely liberal—as a response to persecution, but at the same time immovable as to the value of work and its product (that is, money) which in both countries is highly respected.

The result of these qualities possessed by both countries is that they are looked upon as a refuge by the nationals of other less stable countries. The difference between them stems from the fundamental point that Switzerland is quite lacking in natural wealth whereas the United States has almost unlimited natural resources. To avoid extending these observations into a comparative economic history, the serious nature of the inhabitants and the quality of their work, in short, leads to an inevitable result: Switzerland had to offer services to the world, while the United States offers good investments.

The apparently simplistic synthesis of this position is that money earned by work in less serious and less stable countries passes through Switzerland to be invested in the United States, to the mutual satisfaction of both countries. This conclusion, which is borne out by a large number of examples, has nevertheless been distorted by several factors.

THE COMPETENCE OF THE BANKER IS THE PRINCIPAL INSTRUMENT OF BANK SECRECY

In the first place the Swiss, as providers of services, make their living from their steady approach and the quality of their work—which is based on competence and discretion. On their side, the Americans look for investment and work on condition that these are integrated in a society which is as much concerned with reality as novelty and where there should in principle be no secrecy. At one time it was an important, even vital, consideration to know your neighbours well. Doubtless it is that historical detail, specific to the Americans, which makes them at the same time both the most democratic and the most xenophobic community in the world in their basic reactions.

From this difference in attitudes came the most recent and the most important confrontation as regards banking secrecy and one which has shaped its subsequent development.

The second factor which upset Swiss-American relations was the fact that some Americans (although their number has been considerably overestimated by the American authorities) began to use Swiss banks in order to escape from the American tax net and used the banks to invest in the United States (and generally nowhere else) money which had not been assessed to tax. A number of American politicians aroused public opinion for their own political ends against the 'secret' foreign investments made under the cover of Swiss banks, and also their potential abuse by criminal organizations.

A TREATY ABOVE ALL SUSPICION

A series of long and arduous negotiations lead to the Swiss-American Treaty of 25 May 1973 which came into force on 27 January 1977 and caused the shedding of much ink. This treaty was both the result and the resolution of a difference of interpretation.

While it is not our intention to criticize the American legal system which is undoubtedly one of the most democratic in the world, one result of its possibly excessive zeal in protecting the rights of the individual has been that organized crime cannot be attacked except indirectly through tax evasion. A similar situation has not arisen with the Swiss legal system, although that too is very democratic.

It is really at this stage and on the subject of pursuing criminals (of whom the Swiss have never made national heroes) where both the conflict and its solution were found. The United States wanted a complete lifting of banking secrecy where tax evasion was concerned and Switzerland would accept it only for criminal investigations. Switzerland has pointed out repeatedly that tax evasion could only constitute a criminal act in very exceptional cases.

A JUDGE WHO WAS ALSO A COWBOY?

The whole business was not made any easier by the views held by a certain number of American jurists, reflected in the judgment given in 1971 in the 'Vesco affair'. A leading judge pronounced that it was of no importance to know whether or not it was in the public interest of Switzerland to safeguard the secrecy of certain business transactions, given that it was clear that this was not in the public interest of the United States. In effect, where the public interest of the United States finds itself in opposition to the public interest of a foreign state, he said that it is the American interest which should prevail.*
Fortunately not all the American courts displayed such chauvinism which ill accords with true American democracy.

It was in these circumstances, and under strong American pressure that the treaty was signed; its principal motive of allowing bank secrecy to be lifted could only be called on in matters of tax evasion on condition that evidence made it seem likely that the suspect was connected with organized crime, that normal evidence was insufficient to allow prosecution for anything other than tax evasion, and that assistance from the Swiss authorities was essential to obtain a prosecution. 'This treaty is the most concrete thing to have happened to Swiss bank secrecy in the last forty years.'† It is also one of the most significant in terms of its minimal use.

Banking secrecy, which has existed since time immemorial but has become a major factor in the modern world, has proved itself, and because it attracts money will never fail to attract new disciples whose interest is sometimes matched by their ineffectiveness, but some of whom are bound to have some sort of impact.

In this way most countries who have made themselves into tax havens to attract the rich residents of their neighbours, or their financial and commercial activities through the medium of tax-exempt companies using different but always attractive formulae also attempt to become banking havens by producing laws to protect banking secrecy and creating in some cases penalties for violation of secrecy which are even greater than those applicable in Switzerland. Such an attempt leaves aside a number of fundamental factors which should be examined briefly.

In the first place for the roving depositor, assuming he wishes to reside in a place where there are no taxes or only minimal ones, there will not in general be any obligation to deposit all his money in the same place. It is in fact a rule of good sense and a means of spreading risks to do the opposite. The only tax haven which to an extent practices such an obligation is the Principality of

---

*DNJ, 1971, Civil, 585-71.
†*Harry Browne's Complete Guide to Swiss Banks*, McGraw-Hill, 1976.

Monaco whose residents (except those of French origin) are free of any form of taxation from the moment they arrive but are subject to French exchange controls after 2 years. This exchange control does not require the new residents to transfer all their assets but rather to repatriate the earnings from those assets. This situation does not pose any problems from the point of view of tax since the new residents of Monaco would not be taxable. But in return, a measure which is both natural and ill-considered, the subsequent re-export of these earnings is subject to authorization. The result is simple: earnings are not 'repatriated' and nearly all the foreigners resident in Monaco are guilty of breaking French exchange controls. This hybrid situation does, however, work quite successfully since in effect it does not hurt anyone too much: the Monaco residents know that thanks to Swiss banking secrecy they are in fact sheltered from all suspicion and cannot in practice be prosecuted; the Monaco authorities benefit from the partial repatriation which the residents make for their day-to-day living; France gains some benefit since Monaco is within the franc zone and the remittances are made in foreign currency; the Swiss bankers naturally also have their morsel since the money is in their country.

Who is in the right in this hypocritical game? Perhaps everyone—but then what curious chain of historical events gave rise to the situation where French exchange controls do not apply in that other tax haven, the co-principality of Andorra, when the President of France is a co-prince? There can be no doubt that there *is* an answer to such a stupid and improper question. There are even in some countries colleges which exist—at the taxpayers' expense—to train senior administrators whose job is to answer these questions. It is probably thanks to this splendid training that the taxpayers, who are not as delicate as those for whose training they have paid would like them to think, have only a moderate degree of confidence in the skills of their administrators and often prefer to place the fruits of their labours in the hands of people for whom money is something more than a legal concept, the object of exchange controls and the subject of plunder.

Exchange control is the most extraordinary economic nonsense which modern governments use together with their printing presses for banknotes. The darkly oppressive effect of the creation of the continuation of exchange controls is probably the most absurd—and the least well-known—phenomenon of the modern economy. There is no question of criticizing the control of foreign investment in a country, which is a quite different matter. Every country has the right, even the duty, to protect itself against foreign competition provided that it also stands by the international agreements it has signed. Although there is no statistical evidence available to support this point, there is no example of a country or an institution where exchange control has proved profitable.

POLITICAL SOCIETY AND COMMERCIAL SOCIETY

Exchange control measures, brought in by governments in case their economic management should prove bankrupt, immediately provoke the flight of capital through lack of confidence. This capital would very probably not have been exported if the exchange controls, or the fear of them, had not existed. The normal solution to bad management is to remove it, but democratic regimes are much slower to remove their bad managers than are commercial companies. This derives from the fact that the taxpayer regards as lost the investment which he makes in paying his taxes to the collective entity of the society in which he lives, while he regards any investment made in a commercial company as directly productive and he holds the management directly responsible for its performance. The result is that political managers are able to mask their incompetence by bringing in exchange controls, and do not deny themselves this support. Sometimes though these same managers maintain exchange controls which they have inherited from a previous crisis, through a desire not to upset the opposition.

The problem does not have any impact on major capital which is diversified throughout the world in the same way as the multinational companies. It is at the level of the medium-sized fortune or enterprise that the imposition of a legal constraint provokes the desire to escape. Human ingenuity being limitless there is no example of a country which has brought in exchange controls and not caused a haemorrhage of capital. It is of course true that once this haemorrhage goes underground, the official statistics will improve enormously and the brilliant rulers of such badly run countries can present their false figures with impunity.

The continuance of a useless exchange control is just as ill-fated even if less dangerous and prevents the open return of capital which its owners wish to reinvest. This unfortunate situation obtains in Morocco whose king, who could not be more ill-advised, maintains useless exchange controls and *dahirs* (decrees) for the 'maroccanization' of assets.

There is similarly no example in the opposite vein where the abolition of exchange controls has not brought about the repatriation of capital. In particular this is the case when it is intelligently accompanied by an amnesty in respect of the previous breaches by which the capital was originally exported, and also by a tax amnesty.*

It is in fact a lack of confidence in their own economic management which causes the administrators of a country with a relatively stable economy to maintain useless and counter-productive controls. Man's natural tendency is to want to enjoy freely the goods which he has accumulated and the administrators do not realize that it is lack of confidence in them or their laws which brings their 'subjects' to use the mechanisms and secrecy of foreign banks which prevent them from enjoying their money in the country where they live. This situation of general mistrust and the corresponding evasion of capital controls has been the making of Switzerland's fortune and

---

*It is worth noting here that when exchange controls were withdrawn in Great Britain (23 October 1979) this was not accompanied by such measures, which was a great risk in a high-tax country after 40 years of maintaining controls; nevertheless this 'risky' choice has not apparently led to any catastrophes.

countless countries have attempted to emulate Switzerland since the last war.

APING THE GNOMES

Overall, the success of these imitations has been quite limited. Capital is exported through lack of confidence if not through fear, pure and simple! The new bank's havens have clearly enacted laws which are often very well thought-out. But it is not really a question of laws since banking secrecy implies a degree of confidence which exceeds the law, since the capital which seeks it has often had to break laws to reach it. It is therefore not only in the laws themselves but in the stability of the country where they are applied and in the competence of the banks which put it to use that the true banking secrecy of the modern world is to be found. That defines the whole of the difficulties—and also perhaps the interest—in a guide on a question where practice takes precedence over statute.

4 The Swiss aspect of the question

While a fair number of small countries and certain large socialist countries are striving to copy Swiss legislation on banking secrecy and even sometimes enacting even stiffer penalties, Switzerland itself, like a modern sorcerer's apprentice, is trying to limit its effects.

It was in the wake of the Credit Suisse affair, called the 'Chiasso affair' from the name of the town in which its guilty branch was situated, indeed only 50 days after 14 April 1977 when the scandal first became public, that a convention was signed. It has the pompous title: 'Convention on the need for caution when accepting deposits and on the use of banking secrecy'. This agreement has a number of interesting aspects: in the first place the motives behind it are not well understood, then its legal standing is ill-defined and finally its rather odd nature is not recognized.

MOTIVES BEHIND THE SWISS BANKING CONVENTION

The really deep motive behind the signature of this convention does not seem to be made clear in official comments, although these are certainly revelatory:

The convention signed by the Swiss banks and our Association with the Banque Nationale relating to the obligation to use diligence in accepting deposits . . . constitutes an original attempt to define, on the basis of a private contract with the Banque Nationale, some rules of behaviour with an ethical and moral content. The fact that the Swiss banks have accepted this agreement does not imply that they have previously acted improperly . . . . It is unfortunate that isolated fraudulent acts have created the circumstances which make necessary the signature of this agreement.*

Obligation to use diligence, but no result

You may consider banking secrecy to be an objective which determines economic policy in banking matters but also as a means of guaranteeing for the banking client the privacy which most people in the commercial world regard as being just as important as the professional secrecy extended by doctors, lawyers and other professionals . . . . The limitations of banking secrecy comply with this system only if they prevent abuses and remain within the terms defined by the convention requiring the use of diligence. These terms would be broken if secrecy was lifted to provide legal cooperation to foreign

---

*From a speech made by M Alfred E. Sarasin, President of the Association of Swiss Bankers, at a Bankers' Day in Lucerne, 30 September 1977.

countries whose exchange controls had been breached, because prohibitions on the export of capital are completely contrary to the system. It follows that secrecy must guarantee complete protection to deposits and assets which have been accepted within the terms of the convention on diligence, even if that action is not acceptable to foreign financial authorities. Any other approach would make our banks the agents of these authorities and the executors of their measures against the system. This would be too high a price to pay for the approval of the outside world. It would also be quite unacceptable to use this means to influence the exchange rate of the Swiss franc. For in that case the principle of freedom to import currency, which arises from a market economy, would be sacrificed in favour of a low exchange rate which would benefit an exporting economy.*

The text of the convention signed on 1 June 1977 between the banks based in Switzerland, the Swiss National Bank at Zurich and the Swiss Bankers Association at Basle was the subject of a joint explanatory statement by the two last organizations which was published on 9 December 1977.†

This joint statement, which is not startlingly clear, was itself the subject of a commentary by the Geneva Business Law Association at a meeting on 1 March 1978 at the Hotel des Bergues at which it did not occur to any of the speakers‡ to indicate the true origin of the convention which is perhaps of disconcerting simplicity—Switzerland is too rich.

Too much money is dangerous

Too much capital has been attracted for too long by banking secrecy and the skills of the Swiss bankers; too much money has been converted into Swiss francs.§ Switzerland has therefore less need of new deposits and, wanting to renew its virginity, adopted this convention to safeguard its future. That is the only reason which can explain why Switzerland should have undertaken restrictions in its dealing towards other countries which are more onerous than those practised by the other countries. It leads to an apparently theoretical debate on the legal nature of the convention, but the debate does take on a certain interest viewed from this angle.

LEGAL STANDING OF THE CONVENTION

The question of the legal standing of the convention has been raised and extensively debated. Some writers maintain the theory that the agreement is made under administrative law, but most consider that it is an agreement

---

*An address by Pr Hugo Sieber at the 64th Bankers' Day of the Swiss Bankers Association, Lucerne, 30 September 1977.
†The original five year term of the convention expired in 1982 and it was replaced with a slightly amended version which came into force in October 1982. In view of the importance of the convention, the new version is given in full in Appendix III.
‡Including M Lusser, the Director of the Swiss Bankers Association at Basle.
§See the question of negative bank interest in Chapter 38 on Switzerland.

under commercial law,* to be treated more as an ethical code. Both groups, of course, have apparently incontrovertible arguments in their favour. One of these is that if the agreement were purely in the commercial field, then it could have been signed by some or all of the bankers and not between the bankers and the Swiss National Bank.

Legal nature is only apparent

The answer to this question of juridical standing has been given by the following formula:

The matter is a private one for the banks and also a public one; thus it is a matter for the Federal Banking Commission which should concern itself with the conduct of the banks and also one for the Swiss National Bank which should look after the public interest.†

The convention, which came into force on 1 July 1977 for a 5-year period, is then extended automatically at the end of that period, according to article 15, in a series of 1-year periods, except that the signatories may terminate it by giving 3 months' notice prior to the end of a contractual year.

What is the point of this seemingly obscure debate in which the Swiss jurists are ultimately inclined to believe in general that the convention is made under commercial law? Leaving aside some implications internal to Switzerland which are really secondary, the point is political: the convention contains obligations which are in general rather greater than those which a state would enter into unilaterally with one or more other states. It was imperative that the Swiss Government would not find its hands tied in some future negotiations and could even receive unofficial help from the bankers who could threaten not to renew the convention: its existence could then become useful as a negotiating weapon.

THE ORIGINALITY OF THE CONVENTION

Here is a question which is easily answered: what is the only country in the world in which, without being obliged to do so by some international treaty, a professional subgroup has undertaken to observe the laws of other countries? There can be only one answer: Switzerland and its bankers.

The convention of 1 June 1977 includes firstly a rigorous check not only on the person contracting with the bank, that is the person opening the account, but also on the beneficiary. Therefore, if someone opens an account but then issues a power of attorney in favour of someone else, the bank must check the identity of the person in whose name the power of attorney is issued.

---

*For example M Maurice Aubert in an article published in *L'Expert Comptable Suisse* March, 1978.
†An address by M Ersham, director of the Swiss National Bank at a meeting of Geneva Private Law Association, 1 March 1978.

In the same way, where an account is opened in the name of a company which qualifies as a 'domiciliary company' that is, it has no direct economic activity, irrespective of whether it is a Swiss company or a foreign one, the bank must look into the people who 'control' the company economically: according to the commentary 'the person or group of persons who own directly or indirectly more than half the share capital or voting capital or who exercise a controlling influence in a recognisable manner'. The bank must acquire as much information about these people as if they were themselves becoming direct clients of the bank.

It can be seen already, before reaching 'recognition' of the laws of other countries, that the obligations which are laid on the Swiss banker in opening an account are much more severe than those laid on their colleagues practising in the banking infernos—that is the countries where if professional secrecy is practised it cannot hold out against the tax or exchange authorities. But there is much more relating to the transfer of capital, in particular the following paragraph (which is article 8):

The banks agree not to provide any active help in the transfer of capital from countries whose statutes include restrictions on the placement of funds abroad.

This article places a general prohibition on help, and the interpretation (paragraph 55(c) of the commentary) even specifies that it is forbidden to supply any indications of people who organize the transfer of capital or who act as agents in organizing such transfers.

Active help and passive resistance

There are two observations to be made here. On the one hand it is 'active' help which is forbidden and the Swiss banker is not therefore turned into a police informer; on the other hand the rule concerning 'indications' is criticized by certain Swiss lawyers on the grounds that there is no point in forbidding something whose existence cannot materially be proved (Swiss lawyers are practical people). There are even in this convention some clauses which relate to external morality, such as article 9:

The banks must not assist their clients in manoeuvres intended to deceive the Swiss and foreign authorities—in particular tax authorities—by means of incomplete statements or other means which may induce an error.

This is a splendid example of international morality and there can be no other country in the world which has adopted such clauses outside any international treaty. Would Switzerland, contrary to the suggestions of the overzealous federal advisers, really be above all suspicion?

What is the real impact of such an engagement? The reply might almost be considered as casuistry when it comes to 'back-to-back' loan operations.

The operation consists, for reasons of anonymity (which often have nothing to do with taxation or exchange control), of placing a certain amount of money with a bank and arranging a loan from the bank of the same amount in the same currency for the duration of the deposit. The bank will thus appear as the source of the loan, and with the loan appearing in the balance sheet it will give the appearance of a real transaction which would not have been the case if the banker had been replaced by an intermediate 'screening' company. For the transaction to be technically viable there must be only a small withholding tax, or none at all, on the interest paid by the bank* to the depositor as the counterpart of that charged to the loan beneficiary who is usually, either directly or indirectly, the same person. This operation is often carried out at a national level under much more expensive circumstances† and is also quite familiar to Swiss banks. Of course as it is apparently a real loan it is necessary for the bank to be able to certify it should the beneficiary request that. The concern with morality has become such that some Swiss lawyers consider that the certificate should mention the existence of the guarantee! This is a good example of overextended morality, which if practised in Switzerland would have made Luxemburg's fortune.

Knowledgable witnesses!

In reality the true effect of the convention is not on banking secrecy but rather when this is lifted:

The result is that the banks cannot pretend to be unaware of facts which they are obliged to check. In addition when the banker is relieved of his secrecy obligations he must give evidence of this information. The Swiss banks can therefore be obliged to provide, principally to the legal authorities, information which is more complete than banking establishments would be able to provide in other countries which do not require in a statutory way that they know about the accounts opened by their clients and the nature of the transactions which take place through them.‡

Enormous contractual fines

In legal matters a rule without sanctions becomes a moral rule. It was therefore necessary that the convention requiring the exercise of diligence should be accompanied by sanctions to apply for breaches of it to give it legal force. That is where the shoe pinches. If a commission is set up by the convention and empowered in the event of breaches to impose a fine which can go as high as a million francs (Swiss francs!), certain Swiss lawyers query the possibility of enforcing the execution of such a penalty which derives from

---

*In particular this is the case in Luxemburg.
†This happens in France, where in certain industries bearer certificates of deposit are used to guarantee overdrafts which are apparently too high in relation to the assets of the companies to whom the facilities have been granted.
‡Maurice Aubert in *L'Expert Comptable Suisse*, March, 1978.

a private agreement. They should take heart, there are ways other than those depending solely upon legal sanctions!

The power of rhetoric and that of the *gulag*

The sanctions within a professional group are generally unofficial; the pressure exerted by the group on one of its members works better to achieve the desired result than the sanction itself. This is preserved as the ultimate threat because of its official nature and consequent publicity. There are also legal rules which are not capable of being enforced but whose effects are ultimately observed. This happened in the little-known case of the return of the journalist Bloch who was kidnapped by the Gestapo on neutral Swiss territory on Hitler's personal authority. The reason for this was the personal attacks on the German leader made by the journalist.

In certain situations there is a tendency to observe the rule of law even if its observance cannot be enforced. It is for this reason that the Soviet democracy allows dissidents to emigrate when they have had the chance to become famous, often thanks to the party machine, while the *gulags* are full of unknown dissidents—that is, if they have not disappeared altogether.

It is doubtless the unspecified sanctions of the professional body which come into play in this area and which are a form of justice, however indirect.

5 The direct instruments of banking secrecy

The instruments which are used to achieve banking secrecy are either direct, and form part of the technical side of banking, or indirect, and derive from external legal techniques. In this chapter only the 'direct' instruments will be examined.

When examining these, care should be taken not to confuse the techniques with the principles; a technique is merely an instrument of the principle and is of no interest if the principle is absent or limited in application, even simply in the minds of the people applying the technique. For example, the majority of countries with a modern banking system have legislation permitting the use of numbered accounts. But if this technique of secrecy is aimed at keeping the client's identity secret from minor bank employees, it is of almost no interest in a country where banking secrecy is very limited or non-existent in the face of certain official bodies.

Given that the imagination of mankind in general and bankers and lawyers in particular is limitless, there no doubt exist techniques other than those which appear here, but they will be outside the main stream as far as banking is concerned since innovation is not regarded favourably in that quarter. In order to review the direct instruments of secrecy we shall go to Switzerland to open an account—assuming that this would be allowed by the exchange control body in the country of residence of the intended account holder—and to examine the means which are available to protect the holder's privacy.

THE 'ENVELOPE' WITH A NUMBER OR A FALSE NAME?

These are the famous 'numbered accounts' with their appendage the 'lettered accounts' (this type of account does not exist in the Latin countries) which with the more recent innovation of the 'pseudonym accounts' are the basis of the system. It is of course not pure chance which has led to the choice of Switzerland to illustrate this chapter from amongst a good number of other possibilities which in certain circumstances might appear more useful. It is a waste of time to discuss Swiss banking secrecy, however briefly, if stress is not laid on the practical aspects of it. Institutions, like laws, can have only that value which is placed on them by the men who are applying them. The main reason for the quality of Swiss banking secrecy is the honesty and efficiency of the Swiss bankers and their staff.

Regulations in themselves would not have been sufficient. It serves no purpose whatsoever to create laws which provide serious penalties for the breach of conditions which you wish to enforce if people's mental attitudes and professional skills are not suited to the purpose.

This brief thought leads us to the heart of Swiss banking secrecy, its practicality. This has been evolved following two precepts which would not necessarily have occurred to the theoretician:

1. The protection of the minor employees of the banks from third parties and from themselves.
2. The protection of the clients from the same employees.

These two objects (which are in effect the same object since the fewer the secrets there are to know, the less there is to give away) have resulted in different internal practices within the banks which in the constant search for secrecy differ from one bank to another. This has led in particular to different systems for numbering accounts which has in turn become the legend of the numbered bank account and more recently the accounts in false names. As far as the employees are concerned, it is worth noting that their contracts of employment mention the obligation to practise secrecy and when they leave their job this fact is also included in their testimonial. This requirement, both legal and contractual, is reinforced by the system of accounts with numbers or false names which we shall study at a Swiss bank which we will call the Secret Bank of Geneva and in whose system we shall follow the steps of a local Mr Smith or M Dupont, who according to the Swiss custom we shall call M (or Mr) Muller.

MULLER—WITH ONE 'L' OR TWO

It is clear that the technical examples which follow will not be exactly the same at every bank, but this is a difference of the order of Muller being spelt sometimes with one 'l' and sometimes with two. These are the hypotheses:

1. Mr Muller wants a classic account with banking secrecy, but which will allow him to withdraw money over the counter.
2. Mr Muller wants a numbered account.
3. Mr Muller is worried and wants an account in another name.

1. Mr Muller wants to open a traditional account from which he can make withdrawals over the counter

In this case Mr Muller will go to the Secret Bank of Geneva, and before he makes his deposit he will be given the 'Agreement for the opening of an account or deposit' which appears as Figure 1, parts 1–4, p. 41 show the pages to be completed while pp. 42–44 show the general terms of business of the bank. On the first page the name Jean Muller will appear in

Figure 1

SECRET BANK OF GENEVA LTD.
Geneva

AGREEMENT FOR THE OPENING OF AN ACCOUNT AND DEPOSITING SECURITIES

The contracting parties,
of the first part   Jean Muller
                                                                    (the depositor)

    Nationality: Swiss
    Residence: 1, Banking Haven Square
                           Geneva

of the second part
                      Secret bank of Geneva Ltd. at Geneva   (the bank)

agree as follows:
1. Opening of an account
The bank will open an account in the name of
                      Jean Muller
under the normal terms of business except if specified otherwise in writing.
2. Opening a security deposit
If the depositor gives into the banks keeping any securities or other valuables, the bank will hold these under the same name as the account.
3. Joint-account and joint-deposit
If there are several co-holders they are responsible jointly and severally for the obligations towards creditors on the account or deposit, in conformity with article 150 of the Federal Code of Obligations. As a result, each co-holder will have the right to dispose freely of part or all credit in the account on his sole signature; at the same time he will be authorized to increase, reduce or charge the securities deposited or even withdraw all the shares and securities previously deposited. This rule may also apply to a co-holder or co-holders in the event of the death or legal incapacity of one of the co-holders. In the event of the death of one of the co-holders, the other co-holder or co-holders will preserve the sole rights to dispose of the credit on the account and the securities which have been deposited. In carrying out its obligations towards one of the co-holders the bank will have equally satisfied its obligations towards the others. The co-holders may substitute by common agreement one or more representatives to operate the account, but the mandate then can only be withdrawn by common agreement.

    In the absence of instructions to the contrary, the bank will have the right to place in the deposit or account any securities or sums of money which it receives in the name of one of the co-holders.

    If the co-holders are married they give each other unrestricted power to dispose of the assets in the joint-account or joint-deposit; the wives give express permission to their husbands to act, where the situation passes beyond the normal day to day administration of the conjugal property.
4. Accounting
In the absence of specific instructions the bank will credit the depositor's account with dividends and other income arising from the securities deposited with the bank and will enter on that account all items which arise in respect of the depositor. As far as possible, and in the absence of alternative instructions, the bank will credit all receipts in currencies other than that in which the account is held to the account.
5. Correspondence
All correspondence will be
*sent automatically to   Jean Muller
                                          1, Banking Haven Square (Geneva)

*held by the bank and sent   *only when requested   *once a quarter   *once every six months
*once a year to

Correspondence sent to the address indicated or retained in accordance with the instructions given will be considered as having been dispatched to the depositor. The latter retains the

Figure 1 *continued*

responsibility for all the consequences, losses and damages which may result from the application of his instructions concerning the dispatch or retention of correspondence.

6. Applicability of General Conditions and Deposit Regulations

The contractual relations between the depositor and the Secret Bank of Geneva, and in particular the relevant laws and the competent tribunal, are further set out in the General Conditions, which relate to current accounts and other business transactions with clients, and the Deposit Regulations. Copies of these are attached hereto and form part of this contract.

Subject to special agreement, the Bank refuses any obligation to take action without a specific mandate.

7. Special arrangements

Geneva. (date)

           The Bank   The Depositor
Secret Bank of Geneva Ltd.   (usual signature)

*delete as appropriate

GENERAL CONDITIONS

Subject to regulations which apply to certain types of business, normal banking usage and special agreements, the General Conditions are intended to regulate the relations between the Secret Bank of Geneva and its clients.

Article 1   Right of disposal and control of signatures

Notwithstanding the appearance of conflicting signatures in the Commercial Register or any other publication, only the signatures communicated in writing to the bank will be acted on until they are revoked.

The bank is required to make a careful check on the signature of its clients and their proxies but it is not obliged to carry out a more detailed check on identity. Damages arising out of undiscovered forgery or absence of proof will be the client's responsibility, except where the bank has committed a serious error.

Article 2   Legal incapacity

Any damages arising from the legal incapacity of a client or his agent will fall to the client unless information about the legal incapacity has been published in an official gazette in Switzerland in the case of the client, and unless the bank has been informed in writing in the case of his agent.

Article 3   Communications from the bank

All communications from the bank will be considered to have reached the client if they were sent to the last address supplied by the client. The date which appears on the bank's copies of correspondence will be treated as the date of communication. Correspondence retained by the bank on the client's instructions will be considered as having been sent on the date given in the correspondence.

Article 4   Errors in transmission

Any losses arising from any means of transmission or from the use of a carrier, and in particular because of loss, delay, misunderstanding, mutilation or duplicate communications will be at the client's expense, except where the bank has committed a serious error.

Article 5   Defective execution of an instruction

Where damages arise as a result of a failure to execute or a delayed execution of an order (excluding stock exchange orders), the bank will be liable only for the loss of interest except where the bank has been put on notice that the specific case may involve more extensive damages.

Article 6 Clients' complaints
Any inquiry by a client concerning the execution or non-execution of a particular instruction, or any disagreement concerning his statement or his security deposit or any other communication, should be made on receipt of the document concerned and in any event no later than the time limits fixed by the bank in the particular instance. If a client does not receive a particular document, he should institute inquiries at the time when the document would normally have been received.

Article 7 Current accounts
The bank will at its convenience debit to the account any interest, commission or fees (either specially arranged or normal) as well as any tax or duties due from the client at the end of a quarter, six months or a year. The bank reserves the right to alter its interest and commission rates at any time, but in particular if there is any change in the money markets, and to inform the client in whatever way is appropriate.

In the absence of a specific disagreement made within a month of dispatch, statements of account will be assumed to have been accepted, even if the acknowledgement form sent with the statement has not been returned by the client. The acceptance of the statement, be it express or tacit, will be assumed to include acceptance of all the entries on it as well as any deductions made by the bank.

If the client has issued various instructions whose total value exceeds the available credit balance on the account or the credit allowed by the bank, the bank then reserves the right to decide which of these orders shall be fulfilled in part or in whole, regardless of the dates of each instruction or the date on which they were received by the bank.

Foreign currency credits will be placed competitively with correspondent banks in whom the bank has confidence either inside or outside the relevant monetary zone. The placements will be in the bank's name but on the client's behalf and at the client's risk — particularly in respect of possible legal or governmental restrictions, as well as for taxes and duties in the countries concerned.

The client may draw on his foreign currency credits by selling, making transfers or by drawing or buying cheques. Any other methods of disposal would require the prior approval of the bank. Cash paid in or withdrawn from the account may be charged with a commission by the bank.

Article 8 Bills of exchange, cheques and similar instruments
The bank has the right to recharge to the account the proceeds of bills of exchange, cheques or similar instruments which have been discounted or credited against a future receipt. If such obligations are not settled, the bank is free to exercise its right to recover the sums by debiting the client's current account and need not take account of the situation of the current account at that time. Until such a debt has been satisfied, the bank retains its rights of payment against all guarantors of the instrument in question for the full sum as well as incidental expenses, irrespective of whether it is a bill of exchange or other instrument.

Article 9 Lien and compensation
The bank has a lien, and where it is a creditor a right to seek compensation, on all shares and other valuables deposited with it by the client and held either on its own premises or elsewhere, in respect of money owed to it without regard to the timing of its claims nor the currency involved, and disregarding whether credit has been given against specific guarantees or not. In the event that the client defaults, the bank may at its discretion realize the securities by mutual agreement or by seeking a judgment.

Article 10 Termination of business relations
The bank reserves the right to terminate at any time and without notice its business relations with the client and in particular to cancel all advances either promised or made. In such circumstances an immediate refund of all advances will be required, subject to any contrary agreement.

Article 11 Saturday taken to be a public holiday
In all dealings with the bank Saturday will be treated as a public holiday.

Article 12 Swiss law and courts
All the client's legal relations and powers of attorney with the bank are governed by Swiss law. The place of execution of all acts, the place for proceedings for clients resident abroad and the

Figure 1 *continued*

place whose jurisdiction covers any proceedings whatsoever is Geneva, the place of the bank's head office. The bank does, however, reserve the right to commence an action in the client's place of domicile or before any other court or competent authority.

Article 13 Alteration of the general conditions
The bank reserves the right to amend the general conditions at any time, subject to advising the client by all appropriate means. In the absence of a written objection lodged within one month, the amendments will be considered as having been accepted.

DEPOSIT REGULATIONS

Subject to any special arrangements, these deposit regulations are intended to set out the conditions for the safekeeping and administration of shares and other valuables, which services are made available by the Secret Bank of Geneva for its clients.

The bank is prepared to keep all share certificates and similar documents in an 'open deposit' while valuables and similar objects are kept in a 'sealed deposit'. The bank may however refuse a deposit without being required to give any reason for this.

GENERAL RULES

Article 1 Reference to General Conditions
The Bank's General Conditions will apply to all deposits, particularly as concerns the jurisdiction of the Swiss courts.

Article 2 Safekeeping
The bank undertakes to keep the deposits which are entrusted to it carefully and in a safe place.

Article 3 Withdrawals
Subject to discharging the bank of its liability, the client may require the return of all or part of his deposit during the normal hours of business. The bank may also require the withdrawal of the deposit at any time.

Article 4 Statements
The bank will provide the depositor at least once a year and generally at the end of the year with a statement including as precisely as possible a description of the share certificates and other valuables in its safe-keeping. The deposit statements will be considered as having been accepted if they do not give rise to an express objection within four weeks of dispatch. The express or tacit acceptance of the statement implies an acceptance of all the items in it and of the bank's charges.

Deposit statements cannot be transferred, nor can they be used as security.

Article 5 Joint deposits
If several depositors have established a joint deposit, they are jointly responsible to the bank for any sums which may become due.

Article 6 Insurance in transit
In the absence of specific instructions from the depositor, the bank will insure all movements of shares and other valuables at the depositor's expense for an amount usually deemed appropriate and of a type which the bank takes out on its own account.

Article 7 Secrecy
In accordance with the federal law on banks and credit institutions, the bank departments and its staff are required to observe the strictest secrecy concerning the bank's relations with its clients.

Article 8 Custodial dues
Fees are charged according to a scale fixed by the Swiss Bankers Association. Subject to informing the client, the bank reserves the right to modify the rates at any time.

If securities are deposited with a correspondent of the bank, the correspondent's fees will be charged to the client. The client may also be charged for any special services or additional fees, as well as carriage, telephone, telex and other disbursements.

Article 9   Amendments to regulations
Subject to advising the client by any appropriate means, the bank reserves the right to amend its deposit regulations at anytime. In the absence of a written objection lodged within one month, the amendments will be treated as having been accepted.

OPEN DEPOSITS

Article 10   Safekeeping
The banks keep clients securities separate from its own. Except where other arrangements have been specified, the bank keeps securities in collective deposits over which the depositor has co-ownership rights in proportion to the number of securities which he possesses. The numbers of deeds are not supplied to the depositor except where specifically requested.

The bank reserves the right to have documents of title belonging to its clients kept in safekeeping by the bank's correspondents: subject to the provisions of article 11.

Article 11   Overseas deposits
Except where otherwise specified, the bank will entrust documents overseas to the care and under the administration of one of its usual correspondents according to the local terms of business. These documents will be in the bank's name but will be on the depositor's account and at his risk.

Article 12   Administration
The bank undertakes, without requiring a formal instruction from the depositor to:

(a) bank or negotiate at the best rate all interest coupons, dividend payments and refunds of maturing bills or other securities;
(b) check all publications available to the bank — without assuming any responsibility for so doing — for details of any new drawings, renunciations, conversions, subscriptions, amortizations and cancellations of securities;
(c) renew dividend coupons and exchange temporary certificates for permanent ones.

Over and above these, the bank will — on receipt of express instructions from the depositor given in sufficient time — undertake:

(d) operations to convert the portfolio;
(e) supplementary payments on shares which are only partially paid;
(f) collection of interest on mortgages and other securities as well as protesting such documents and obtaining the proceeds;
(g) the exercise of or sale of rights to subscribe to a share issue. In the absence of contrary instructions given by the depositor within the time-scale fixed by the bank, the latter will sell subscription rights at the best going price.

Article 13   Monies received
Money received by the bank is credited to an account in Swiss francs unless the bank has received specific instructions at the appropriate time.

SEALED DEPOSITS

Article 14   Delivery of deposits
As a general rule a sealed deposit should be provided with a declaration of value; the wrapping should carry the depositor's exact address and should be sealed with wax or lead in such a way that it is impossible to open it without breaking the seals.

The sealed deposit is given to the bank against a specific receipt which bears the signature and where possible the seal of the depositor.

Article 15   Contents
Sealed deposits should contain no items or materials which are subject to spontaneous

Figure 1 *continued*

combustion or are dangerous or in any way unsuitable to be kept in a bank. The depositor will be responsible for any failure to observe this rule.

The bank reserves the right to require the depositor to prove the nature of the items deposited.

Article 16 Insurance
The depositor may insure the articles in his deposit, using the bank as a broker if he wishes, by signing an insurance agreement relating to the deposit.

Article 17 Withdrawal and responsibility
When withdrawing the articles the depositor must ensure that the seals are intact.

Any damage to the articles must be proved by the depositor. Except in the event of serious negligence on the part of the bank, it does not assume any responsibility for damage suffered by the articles; in any event, its responsibility is limited to the declared value. The bank specifically denies any responsibility arising from a deterioration of the deposit's condition as a result of the atmospheric conditions under which it was kept or as a result of movements requested by the client.

The release note signed by the depositor when withdrawing the articles frees the bank from all responsibilities.

---

clause 1 'Opening of an account'. Given that the reason for opening the account is not primarily secrecy, Jean Muller's address will appear in clause 5. In this case since Mr Muller wants to be able to withdraw cash over the counter he will complete a sample signature card which will be the sole means available to the cashier of recognizing his signature. Such a facility would not be available to the holder of a numbered account since he must remain anonymous to the cashier who should not be able to make the connnection between the 'coded' account and its holder.

If, in addition, Mr Muller wants his account to be managed by the bank, he will sign the 'Special clauses completing the agreement for the opening of a current account and a deposit' (Figure 2). Of course the contract and its postscript will carry Jean Muller's proper signature if he wishes to confer very wide powers to the bank.

This system of running accounts is almost identical to that operated in other countries and it is only when Mr Muller wishes to open a numbered account that Swiss banking practice takes on its more refined aspects, even if the classic deposit arrangement is already covered by extensive banking secrecy. Furthermore, if Mr Muller is acting as a 'nominee', that is he is lending his name to a client or a friend (a perfectly legal practice in most Anglo-Saxon countries), or is acting under the terms of a 'fiduciary' agreement (a similar arrangement under Swiss law) may content himself with this type of account if he has no other problems in this area. It is on the contrary the friend or client of Mr Muller who should beware of the risk of such an arrangement of which the bank is ignorant; if a Swiss bank is involved it would refuse to open the account if it thinks the person in whose name the account has been proposed is not the beneficiary, or that the beneficiary would not comply with the criteria laid down in the Swiss banking convention. However, it is worth pointing out that despite all requirements for bankers to use extreme caution which may appear in banking conventions, there is no banker in the world who is capable of knowing the identity of the true depositor if it is not revealed to him.

Figure 2

SECRET BANK OF GENEVA LTD.

Geneva

(Named account and deposit and management authority)

Special clauses completing the agreement for opening a current account and a deposit

Management of a named current account and deposit

Completing the agreement for opening a current account and a deposit made on 1 October 1982 between the undersigned depositor and the Secret Bank of Geneva, the depositor gives to the said bank the authority to manage his account and deposit on its own without any special instructions.

In addition to the operations indicated in article 12 of the Deposit Regulations (see Figure 1) this management authority includes specifically the right to change the composition of the portfolio, to sell shares and currency, to place available capital and to commit shares in the event of a reorganisation.

The bank is not authorized to withdraw entirely or partly the depositors credits with itself, to pledge them as security or to charge them otherwise nor to contract loans.

The bank will have the right to take any measure which in its opinion is in the interests of the depositor and the latter confers to the bank for these purposes the widest possible powers. In the exercise of its mandate the bank will act to the best of its ability; that is to say with the same measure of care which it applies to its own affairs — it does not assume any other responsibility.

The authority conferred by this agreement will not be affected by the death or legal incapacity of the depositor and will remain in force until they are revoked in writing.

Geneva, 1 October, 1982

Secret Bank of Geneva Ltd.   Depositor:

PS   By way of qualification of the third paragraph above, the said depositor authorizes the Secret Bank of Geneva to undertake 'margin' operations on his account within the normal limits of the bank's operations, as well as to undertake stock exchange contracts according to normal stock exchange practices.

Geneva..................   Depositor:

2. Mr Muller wants to open a numbered account for reasons of discretion

The principle of a numbered account is to have current transactions performed by the junior employees of the bank, not under the client's name, but under a code (in this case a number),* in such a way that the employees remain ignorant of the identity of the account holder to which the operations relate.

This does not imply that the account is anonymous but simply that the name of the holder is known by a limited number of people, who are normally the bank director and the account manager.

The account manager is generally someone fairly senior within the bank who has management oversight of a collection of numbered accounts. The account manager is the only person, other than the bank director, who has access to the

---

*This can be a series of letters (see, for example, Chapter 35).

files relating to bank accounts which are normally kept in the bank's safe and which give the identity of the true account holder. Access to the safe is restricted to the director and the account managers and each account manager is restricted to a group of files indicated by a number code which is common to the files under his management.

So if M Jean Muller's file is entrusted to an account manager called Aller, for example, the file will be numbered 10-101 which breaks into 10 (account manager number 10—Mr Aller) and 101 (indicating that it is the 101st file under Mr Aller's control).

Of course this kind of internal numbering procedure varies from one bank to another and the numbers or groups of numbers can be replaced by other coding systems.

In the event of the death, resignation or illness of the account manager it is the bank director who undertakes the management of the clients until a new account manager is appointed.

Finally as a further security measure when the director or account manager goes into the bank's file safe he must sign a dated card and give details of the file which he wishes to consult and he is allowed to examine only one file per visit.

The internal control systems may be regarded as exaggerated or futile but they should be seen in context, and it should be appreciated that it is thanks to the fastidious internal controls imposed by Swiss bankers that are prevented most violations of banking secrecy which arise not from dishonesty but from a casual attitude on the part of those on whom weigh the obligations of professional secrecy.

THERE IS NO SUBSCRIBER AT THAT NUMBER...

Where this obligation is carried out in an intelligent way it can bring about some situations which any businessman who is not familiar with the situation would find very surprising. For example, if Mr Dupont wants to transfer for whatever reason a sum of x dollars to Mr Muller whom he knows or suspects has an account with the Secret Bank of Geneva, the bank must accept the money but say: 'Mr Muller is not one of our clients and we can accept the transfer only subject to investigation'.* In between the bank will have contacted Mr Muller to find out if he will accept the transfer and thereby reveal indirectly the existence of his account even if it is 'coded'. If the bank cannot contact Mr Muller its professional duty would be to hold the transfer in suspense or to return it in the absence of instructions. This is the reason why, if Mr Muller wishes to receive a transfer to his account, he will give purely and simply the name and address of the bank and the number of the account,†

---

*This procedure, as childish as it is in fact effective in most parts of the world, is the result of the creative minds of the Gestapo agents when they started playing at Father Christmas.
†Or the pseudonym under which the account is held — see below.

Figure 3

SECRET BANK OF GENEVA LTD.
Geneva

AGREEMENT FOR THE OPENING OF AN ACCOUNT AND DEPOSITING SECURITIES

The contracting parties,
of the first part   Jean MULLER
                                                                                (the depositor)

    Nationality: Swiss
    Residence: 1, Banking Haven Square
of the second part
                           Secret Bank of Geneva Ltd.   at Geneva
                                                                                (the bank)

agree as follows:
1. Opening of an account
The bank will open an account in the name of
                                    10 — 101
under the normal terms of business except if specified otherwise in writing.
2. Opening a security deposit
If the depositor gives into the bank's keeping any share certificates or other items of value, the bank will hold these under the same name as the account.
3. Joint account and joint deposit
If there are several co-holders they are responsible jointly and severally for the obligations towards creditors on the account or deposit, in conformity with article 150 of the Federal Code of Obligations. As a result each co-holder will have the right to dispose freely of part or all credits in the account on his sole signature; at the same time he will be authorized to increase, reduce or charge the securities deposited or even withdraw all the shares and securities deposited. This rule may also apply to a co-holder or co-holders in the event of the death or legal incapacity of one of the co-holders. In the event of the death of one of the co-holders, the other co-holder or co-holders will preserve the sole rights to dispose of the credit on the account and the securities which have been deposited. In carrying out its obligations to one of the co-holders the bank will have satisfied equally its obligations towards the others. The co-holders may substitute by common agreement one or more representatives to operate the account, but the mandate can then only be withdrawn by common agreement.

    In the absence of instructions to the contrary, the bank will have the right to place in the deposit or account any securities or sums of money which it receives in the name of one of the co-holders.

    If the co-holders are married they give each other unrestricted power to dispose of the assets in the joint account or joint-deposit; the wives give express permission to their husbands to act, where the situation passes beyond the normal day to day administration of the conjugal property.
4. Accounting
In the absence of specific instructions the bank will credit the depositor's account with dividends and other income arising from the securities deposited with the bank and will enter on that account all items which arise in respect of the depositor. As far as possible, and in the absence of alternative instructions, the bank will credit all receipts in currencies other than that in which the account is held to the account.
5. Correspondence
All correspondence will be:
*sent regularly to: KEPT BY THE BANK

*held by the bank and sent *only when requested, *once a quarter, *once every six months, *once every year to

*delete as appropriate

Correspondence sent to the address indicated or retained in accordance with the instructions given will be considered as having been dispatched to the depositor. The latter retains the

Figure 3 *continued*

responsibility for all the consequences losses and damages which may result from the application of his instructions concerning the dispatch or retention of correspondence.

6. Applicability of General Conditions and Deposit Regulations

The contractual relations between the depositor and the Secret Bank of Geneva, and in particular the relevant laws and competent courts, are further set out in the General Conditions, which relate to current accounts and other business transactions with clients, and Deposit Regulations. Copies of these are attached hereto and form part of this contract.

Subject to special agreement the bank refuses any obligation to take action without a specific mandate.

7. Special arrangements

Geneva, (date)

The Bank
Secret Bank of Geneva

The Depositor
(Usual signature)

---

which will itself be sufficient indication to allow the bank to credit it with the money offered.*

What now would be the procedure for Mr Muller to open a numbered bank account?

It is the form given in Figure 1 which would be used, but it would be filled in differently, as in the example shown in Figure 3. If at the beginning of the contract the name is still Jean Muller, it changes to a number later, for example 10-101, but his true signature must still be given at the end of the agreement.

By comparison with Figure 1, if the bank and the client take the matter seriously there will be no address for correspondence but rather the instruction 'to be kept by the bank' will replace that in the part dealing with correspondence.

This precaution which dates from the times of the Gestapo still preserves its usefulness in some cases and it will serve a purpose and illustrate the point to mention the pleasant trick played by the IRS a few years ago in Miami, Florida.

To understand the point it is necessary to know that an American citizen, being free of any kind of exchange control, can quite legally keep all or part of his assets in Switzerland. His only liability is to declare the income which he derives from them so that it can be included in his tax computation. At the same time, of course, no Swiss bank would have the bad taste to send its overseas clients a bank statement (even on a numbered account) in an envelope which indicated that it had come from a bank. On the contrary, when statements are requested they are sent in plain envelopes and even the recipient's name and address are written by hand.

---

*It is the author's opinion, and that of the most worthy Swiss professionals, that the banker would be wrong to accept the transfer if in addition to the account number and the bank address the account holder's name also appeared on the transfer advice.

SOMEONE WITH A BIG FAMILY

Given that the mail is sacrosanct in the United States the IRS were prevented from checking any correspondence coming from Switzerland even if they did suspect a certain number of people of failing to declare income in their Swiss bank accounts. The IRS therefore had all the envelopes arriving from Switzerland photocopied over a fairly long period and then passed the photocopies over to handwriting specialists equipped with a computer. This team discovered that some Miami residents had an extensive Swiss family since in certain cases the same Swiss person wrote to 30 different American cousins. The IRS published its findings and at the same time sent to the American 'cousins' a demand that they should complete a sworn declaration that they had no Swiss bank accounts whose income had not been reported to the IRS.* In a parallel move the IRS also contacted all the potential taxpayers and offered an out-of-court settlement if they should decide voluntarily (?) to file an amended return . . . .

This example shows some of the practical problems if not exactly of banking secrecy at least of managing it. There are others. For the numbered bank account the General Conditions are the same as those for a normal account, but there are one or two other differences: firstly the banks who take secrecy seriously will not sign an agreement which permits the account holder to withdraw cash at the counter. Certainly some marginal banks will accept this as long as the number which is used as a signature corresponds to that on the cashier's records. In effect the banker wants to protect his client even from the bank's own cashier who would be able to connect the number with the account holder's face (especially if the latter is well known), but the bank also wants the client's affairs to be followed by the account manager. Therefore it is the account manager who should see the client in his office, and if cash is to be withdrawn this should be done by the account manager under his own signature.

Then a second agreement is generally signed under the heading 'Special agreement completing the contract for opening an ordinary account and deposit'. This appears as Figure 4, and has as a possible variation the management agreement which appears as Figure 5. It is intended to indemnify the bank against any risks arising from the use of this system. The bank's responsibility is similarly protected for accounts under pseudonyms.

---

*To understand this action it is necessary to understand Anglo-Saxon law where an accused person can be called as a witness in his own case and very heavy penalties can be imposed if he fails to tell the truth. This type of trial based on evidence contrasts in principle with that of Roman law based on the conviction of magistrates where it is accepted that the defendant may well not tell the truth as part of his defence . . . to each if not his own truth, then at least his own means of arriving at the truth!

Figure 4
SECRET BANK OF GENEVA LTD.
Geneva

Current account or deposit
under a number or pseudonym,
to be signed by using the
number or pseudonym

SPECIAL CLAUSES WHICH QUALIFY AN AGREEMENT FOR THE OPENING OF A CURRENT ACCOUNT AND DEPOSITING SECURITIES

The administration of an account or deposit under a number or assumed name

This agreement is in amplification of the agreement relating to the opening of a current account and security deposit signed on 1 October 1982 between the undersigned depositor and the Secret Bank of Geneva Ltd.

General conditions

The depositor recognises as being addressed to him any correspondence sent to him in accordance with the above agreement but bearing the number (assumed name).

All risks and all consequences arising from the fact that the account and deposit are designated by number (assumed name) are borne by the depositor. The numbered account (account under an assumed name) must not be used for commercial transactions.

Signature by means of a number or assumed name

As far as the bank is concerned, the depositor will sign by using the number (assumed name) of the account or the deposit, which he will write by hand, in full, in the same form as the specimen signature placed on this agreement. The depositor, however, reserves the right to use his normal signature. These rules are also extended to apply to anyone exercising a power of attorney on behalf of the depositor. The bank may require the use of the depositor's normal signature instead of the agreed number or assumed name for certain documents, in particular acknowledgements of statements on the current account or deposit.

The depositor recognizes as valid and as committing him fully all instructions and acknowledgements as well as all correspondence and all vouchers which carry the agreed number or assumed name in the place of his normal signature or that of his agents. The depositor will ensure that the number (assumed name) will be kept secret by his agents as well as himself and will be responsible for the consequences which can result from the use of the number (assumed name) by him or his representatives.

Geneva, 1 October, 1982

Secret Bank of Geneva Ltd.

The Depositor:
Agreed signature:
Normal signature:

Figure 5
SECRET BANK OF GENEVA LTD.
Geneva

(Account and security deposit under a number
or assumed name to be signed by number or
assumed name, and management agreement)

SPECIAL CLAUSES WHICH QUALIFY AN AGREEMENT FOR THE OPENING OF A CURRENT ACCOUNT AND DEPOSITING SECURITIES

1. Management of an account and security deposit under a number or assumed name

This agreement is in amplification of the agreement relating to the opening of a current account and security deposit signed on 1 October 1982 between the undersigned depositor and the Secret Bank of Geneva.

General conditions

The depositor recognises as being addressed to him any correspondence sent to him in accordance with the above agreement but bearing the agreed number (assumed name).

All risks and consequences arising from the fact that the account and the deposit are designated by number (assumed name) are borne by the depositor. The numbered account (account under an assumed name) must not be used for commercial transactions.

Signature by means of a number or an assumed name

As far as the bank is concerned, the depositor will sign by using the number (assumed name) of the account or the deposit which he will write by hand, in full, in the same form as the specimen signature placed on this document. The depositor, however, reserves the right to use his normal signature. These rules are also extended to apply to anyone using a power of attorney on behalf of the depositor. The bank may require the use of the depositor's normal signature instead of the agreed number or assumed name for certain documents, in particular acknowledgements of statements of the current account or deposit.

The depositor recognizes as valid and as committing him fully all instructions and acknowledgements as well as all correspondence or other vouchers which carry the agreed number or assumed name in the place of his normal signature or that of his representatives. The depositor will ensure that the number (assumed name) will be kept secret by his representatives as well as himself and will be responsible for the consequences which may result from the use of the number (assumed name) by him or his representatives.

2. Bank management authority

The depositor places on the bank the responsibility of itself managing his account and security deposit without specific instructions. In addition to the operations indicated in article 12 of the deposit regulations this management authority includes specifically the right to change the composition of the portfolio, to sell shares and currency, to place available capital and to commit shares in the event of a reorganisation.

The bank is not authorized to withdraw either entirely or partly the depositor's assets with itself, nor to pledge them as security or to charge them otherwise nor to contract loans.

The bank will have the right to take any measure which in its opinion is in the interests of the depositor and the latter confers to the bank for these purposes the widest possible powers. In the exercise of its mandate the bank will act to the best of its ability; that is to say with the same measure of care which it applies to its own affairs — it does not assume any other responsibility.

The authority given by this agreement will not lapse on the legal incapacity or death of the depositor, but will remain in force until revoked in writing.

Geneva, 1 October, 1982

The bank:
Secret Bank of Geneva Ltd.

The depositor:
Agreed signature

Normal signature

PS   By way of qualification of section 2 above, the said depositor authorizes the Secret Bank of Geneva to undertake 'margin' operations on his behalf within the normal limits of the bank's operations, as well as to undertake stock market contracts according to normal stock exchange practices.

Geneva..................

Depositor:
Normal signature

3. Mr Muller is frightened and wants an account under another name

Accounts under false names were created as a result of fear, to be the last variation on numbered accounts.

Often the depositor has wanted to take away with him — to protect himself against the banker — a receipt giving the details of the amount which he has deposited and the number or code used for his account.

This procedure has the disadvantage that in some cases it has led to depositors being put under either moral or sometimes physical pressure after being searched by the police of the country in which they are unfortunate residents, the authorities having assumed that they are indeed the owners of the numbered accounts.

GONZALES THE PHANTOM BECOMES MR MULLER'S REPRESENTATIVE

A Swiss banker therefore thought of the idea of replacing the numbered account system with an ordinary name, so the code given to Mr Muller's statements by the Secret Bank of Geneva is replaced with the name of some non-existent person, 'Gonzales' for example. The advantage of the system is that the statement appears to the eyes of foreign authorities to belong to someone else, and the person carrying it can say that he is doing so on behalf of his friend Gonzales (who will of course never be found, since even the worst political regimes find it difficult to handcuff a phantom).

The risk in theory is that there is a real Gonzales who might learn by some ill chance of the existence of an account in his name at a particular bank and then might claim it. But that risk is non-existent because in such a case the bank would rely on its agreement with Mr Muller and say that the account was not with the same Mr Gonzales.

Of course there remains always the practical risk that someone close to Mr Muller could imitate the Gonzales signature and have a sum of money transferred to his own account held under a number or assumed name. But this risk is inherent in every classic bank account, and moreover as such an act would be a breach of common law, the bank which had received the money could not maintain banking secrecy towards Mr Muller's bank.

In fact Mr Muller's interest in having an account under an assumed name has diminished slightly because he will avoid crossing any frontiers with a bank statement from a Swiss bank, even if it is in someone else's name. In reality Mr Muller is going to use another procedure, again one developed by the Swiss bankers, and one whose aim is not only to protect him but also his future heirs — which is often another motive for using bank secrecy.

Mr Muller is going to mix together the principle of an after-death power of attorney with the use of an open safe in another bank.

AN INSTRUMENT WHICH WILL NOT HAVE ANY EFFECT UNTIL THE MOMENT IT SHOULD BE REVOKED

The 'postmortem' power of attorney is, from the point of view of Swiss law, one of the most debatable and dangerous practices of the country's banks. This consists of giving power of attorney over an account to a person whom the account holder wishes to benefit from the account, but stipulating that the power will take effect only on the death of the holder on presentation of proof of death, giving rise therefore to the description of a 'postmortem' power of attorney.

Most Swiss jurists, however, agree that such a stipulation is not valid in Swiss law, quite apart from any cases where the stipulation is nullified because foreign laws are applied under the terms of the Swiss rules for resolving international conflicts of civil law. Whatever the case, this procedure involves certain dangers and is generally rejected by the more established professionals. Nonetheless when it is used the problem is how to preserve the proof of the existence of the postmortem power of attorney so that it is available to its beneficiary. The question is important because a similar procedure is used in connection with a more 'normal' system.

POSTMORTEM INSTRUMENT AND SAFE DEPOSIT BOX

The more 'normal' system could consist of a number of different processes suggested by practical considerations but which all have the characteristic of being less open to debate than the simple postmortem instrument.

Generally speaking the most popular systems are the following:

1. A joint account between Mr Muller and Mrs Muller (?) which provides that during Mr Muller's lifetime withdrawals can only take place under their joint signature or Mr Muller's sole signature. But on the latter's death Mrs Muller (?) would operate the account on her sole signature. This system is close to the postmortem power of attorney, but has the major difference that the concept of a joint account is accepted in most legal jurisdictions.
2. Straightforward provisions in a will in favour of the intended beneficiaries. This system has the advantage of being the most simple in as much as it takes account on the one hand of the legal realities and on the other of the lack of rights of succession to assets situated in Switzerland for a non-resident. The potential disadvantage is where the provisions of the will do not correspond to the Swiss laws which apply to testamentary dispositions and the law stipulates provisions which have not been applied.*

---

*Certain countries with Roman law require that a proportion of the estate is held for close relatives and this cannot be avoided even if the person making the will wishes to do so. This proportion, which varies according to the degree of kinship and number of relatives, is known as the hereditary reserve.

In either case the depositor (and future deceased) wants to maintain proof of his assets and his wishes as far as concerns the Secret Bank of Geneva. He has two possibilities: he can take away with him the receipt for the securities he has deposited and his copy of the agreement and put them in a safe-deposit box in another bank, or he can put the agreement in a sealed envelope and give it back to his account manager at the Secret Bank of Geneva. The bank would then add to the statement on Mr Muller-Gonzalez's assumed name account a note saying 'sealed envelope number x' and the date on which this was put in the bank's safe. This second possibility only takes the problem a stage further since the statement itself should then be kept somewhere safe . . . .

A SAFE WITH NO KEY — OR ALMOST THE LAST STAGE IN CONFIDENCE

Mr Muller is therefore going to open a safe deposit at another bank where he will lodge (for the benefit of his heirs rather than himself) the proof of his arrangements with the Secret Bank of Geneva using the system which he has chosen. Again there are two problems to deal with—the key, and the postmortem arrangements.

When a safe deposit is opened the bank records the identity of the person opening the safe deposit and notes on its file the exact instructions for opening the safe—or alternatively refers to another document which is itself kept in the bank's safe. The curious thing is that the same problem as before presents itself both as regards death and as regards the key given to the person hiring the safe-deposit.*

A PARTICULARLY VICIOUS CIRCLE

In the case of death the situation has already been examined and is no different. But as far as the key is concerned the Swiss have created a system which is worth its weight in gold (to whom?). The renter of the box, to avoid crossing a frontier with the key in his possession, gives it back to the safe-deposit service. They in turn prepare most carefully another file for leaving something in the bank's general safe deposit; they prepare a stiff envelope festooned with wax seals, sign and ask the hirer of the box to sign jointly.

Then the procedure changes, depending on which bank you use. In the most conservative banks the cashier will want to give the depositor a receipt, which, if he accepts it, would require that he open an infinite series of safe deposits in the same way to contain the receipts of other banks! Otherwise the final

---

*The usual international banking practice is that a safe-deposit box rented from a bank can be opened only with two keys. One is held by the person responsible for the safe-deposits who verifies from the file the right of the person to open a particular box, and the other is given to the person renting the box.

element of confidence comes into play and the hirer accepts that the cashier keeps the receipt in his drawer for the key which is deposited in the general safe . . . .

This is one of the reasons why the most important 'consumers' of banking secrecy also utilize the 'indirect instruments of banking secrecy'.

6 The indirect instruments of banking secrecy

In the usual sense the concept of banking secrecy is a legal concept which derives from professional ethics in the same way as the professional discretion of a doctor or a lawyer. A general study which was limited to the kind of secrecy which relates to a banker's professional discretion and in particular his relations with the public authorities would have left out one of the fundamental accessories of pure banking secrecy in its larger meaning (that is, anonymity), that is the legal institutions which are currently used in banking operations to increase the degree of secrecy.

At one extreme it would be possible to imagine a country in which there was no banking secrecy at all but where there was equally absolutely no bar to the use of foreign legal institutions which would confer complete anonymity on their 'beneficial owner' (the effective owner in this sense). Thus the actual banking operations themselves would be officially totally open in that country while the beneficiary of the transactions could remain quite unknown — which in some cases would be considered quite sufficient and perhaps even better than the classic form of banking secrecy.

Such structures are also currently to be found, giving a form of double security, as the legal owners of accounts in their name in countries which have substantial banking secrecy. These instruments vary according to their legal origins, that is to say the legal structure under which they were formed.

Naturally if these vehicles are to be useful they must not in their own right attract large taxes so they are generally the forms used in tax havens. From the point of view of anonymity there exist three basic types of structure:

1. Structures with local exchange control and private agreements. These are generally to be found in the Anglo-Saxon type of tax haven (the Bahamas, Singapore); secrecy is guaranteed but the identity of the beneficial owner appears at two points:
   (a) for exchange control purposes where the Central Bank wishes to check that he is not a resident;
   (b) in the trust agreement (which corresponds more or less to a nominee arrangement which is legal in English law) which establishes the true ownership of shares registered in the name of one or more other people with whom the trust deed has been created.
2. Structures with no local exchange control but private agreements. These derive from laws of the same nature as those of Switzerland, and Liechtenstein

is the main proponent. In the absence of exchange control the name of the beneficial owner appears only in the 'fiduciary' agreement (which is close to a trust or nominee arrangement but legal in Switzerland)—there is obviously no Central Bank wishing to be sure that the beneficial owner is non-resident.

There too secrecy may be broken in the extremely rare case where the fiduciary agreement is brought to the attention of third parties.*

3. Structures which really are anonymous. These exist in a country which has no exchange control and where all the shares are issued to bearer without any guarantees being required from the administrators—which would necessitate some trust agreement. A country where even the local professionals who formed the company do not know the identity of their client, but know only a foreign lawyer giving instructions. This case which is practically ideal from the point of view of anonymity obtains in particular in Panama.

These systems grant anonymity only as regards the ownership of shares and it remains for the beneficial owner to protect himself as regards the apparent owners who are going to open one or more accounts in the name of the legal entity which they represent and are going to carry out the banking transactions. It is appropriate that we should examine the functioning of these accessories of banking secrecy by looking at a few examples.

STRUCTURES WITH LOCAL EXCHANGE CONTROL AND PRIVATE AGREEMENTS

As we have indicated these are tax haven companies of the Anglo-Saxon type. If our roving depositor wishes to utilize a structure of this sort to open an account in a country giving the maximum bank secrecy, what steps should he take and at what level would his identity appear?

If we take the example of Jersey which is still relatively recent but has become a classic, the entity he would use would be an investment company which would be both non-resident and tax exempt. This company would be outside the exchange control net† and would pay an annual flat rate tax of £300‡ irrespective of its profits and without being required to file accounts with the authorities.

---

*This is precisely the misfortune which befell an important political figure in a country with severe exchange controls. As a result of an indiscretion which was as surprising as it is rare, he had the shock of seeing his fiduciary agreement published in a major satirical paper. It is also true that the harm was limited since such an indiscretion can only relate to shares registered in the name of the nominees whereas many shares were in the bearer form and held in the safe deposit of a Swiss bank to which the authorities in the owner's country of residence have no access.

†In fact exchange controls have not been applied since 24 October 1979 although the basic legislation remains in force.

‡For more details of this kind of company see Edouard Chambost's *Using Tax Havens Successfully*.

A real beneficiary who is really non-resident

Before the suspension of British exchange controls the Island of Jersey was part of the old sterling area (made up of Great Britain and the 'scheduled territories'). The establishment of a non-resident investment company was therefore subject to the approval of the Jersey authorities who were acting on behalf of the Bank of England (if a trading company was proposed, this required approval directly from the Bank of England). In order to give their approval the authorities had to be sure that the beneficial owner was not a British resident and was not therefore attempting to avoid the exchange controls to which he was subject. In this kind of system the approval is requested by the lawyer ('solicitor') who has been instructed to form the company and who in principle checks himself that the beneficial owner is not resident, and moreover asks him to sign a declaration that he is not acting on behalf of someone else.

The name of the actual beneficial owner will therefore appear twice: (*a*) in the files of the solicitor (bound by professional secrecy); (*b*) in the files of the Jersey authorities who are assuring the Bank of England that the beneficial owner is non-resident.*

The company is then formed and shares issued to subscribers in the manner appropriate to this kind of company. The shares are normally subscribed for by solicitors working in the same practice as the one who formed the company. It will be necessary to create a series of trust documents to protect their true owner and to enable him to exercise his rights. There too, although this is an agreement between private individuals and will not be published, the name of the true beneficiary can be traced through these documents.

In order to benefit from the status of a tax-exempt company it must have amongst other things a management which is not British—in practice that means that at least two thirds of its management should not be resident in Britain.

There too, if the beneficial owner does not want to appear officially as a director, he must enter into special agreements with two administrators who are not resident (a fiduciary agreement with Swiss residents perhaps) and his name will appear in these agreements.

These several reasons which have the result that the name of the true owner appears at least four times have had the result that this kind of company is used infrequently (which is not the case with the trading companies where the desire for secrecy is not the main motivation). On top of that Jersey does not have any double tax treaties which would reduce the withholding taxes charged by foreign tax authorities on earnings derived from the assets of such companies. The island is therefore in competition with Liechtenstein and Panama which can offer more secrecy.

---

*The example of Jersey has been pursued, despite the lifting of British exchange controls, because of the significant nature of its institutions.

STRUCTURES WITH NO LOCAL EXCHANGE CONTROL BUT PRIVATE AGREEMENTS

These instruments have the advantage over the earlier ones that the name of the beneficial owner does not appear anywhere in the records of an official body or anyone to whom such powers have been delegated.

Do you have confidence in my trust?

One of the most commonly used vehicles is of an Anglo-Saxon type. Unknown in countries which do not use 'common law' (apart from Monaco and Liechtenstein) it forms part of a branch of law known as 'equity' and requires some explanation of its workings because it is to be found both holding assets directly and holding the shares of companies which themselves hold assets. This creation of Anglo-Saxon law is an agreement whereby person B, the trustee, is entrusted by person A, the settlor, with some assets, the trust property, to be held on behalf of person or persons C, the beneficiaries. This triangular scheme is as follows (Figure 6):

Figure 6 Normal trust

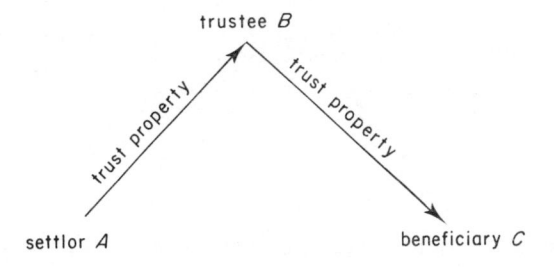

This is the basic scheme for a classic trust and is created by an agreement known as a 'Trust deed'* signed by the settlor and the trustee which, in its classic form, would stipulate that the assets (trust property) should be held by B for the benefit of C during his life. C is described as the 'life tenant'.† It is normal practice for the trust to be established for the life of C-1 (which could in fact be a group of people) and then C-2, if the trust has not been created for charitable purposes (in Britain there is a rule which prohibits trusts in perpetuity).

In general the rules for trusts vary according to the country, which, given that there are 30-odd countries which have 'common law' and about fifty

---

*This agreement is usually called a trust deed or a settlement in Great Britain and its former colonies; in the United States it is known as a trust-instrument.
†In this type of trust the life tenant may only enjoy the revenue of the property during his lifetime. A modern form of trust allows the trustees to distribute a part of the capital as well, but that is described as a 'discretionary trust'.

American states, leads to 80 different sets of legislation which are both the same and different and sometimes with conflicting provisions.* For example, in Britain only the beneficiary can sue for execution of a trust arrangement, while in most American states the settlor can also do it. More seriously, there are some underlying assumptions which differ: in Great Britain the settlor cannot revoke the trust except where this is specifically provided in the agreement, whereas in most American states the agreement can be revoked except where the deed specifically provides otherwise.

Discretionary trusts

Of course life would be too simple if the matter stopped short at that stage, and the settlor could slide round the process and reappear amongst the trustees.

The discretionary trust is one where one of the trustees has the power to decide which amongst several people will receive the benefit of the trust property. The system looks like this (Figure 7):

Figure 7 Trust with right of decision

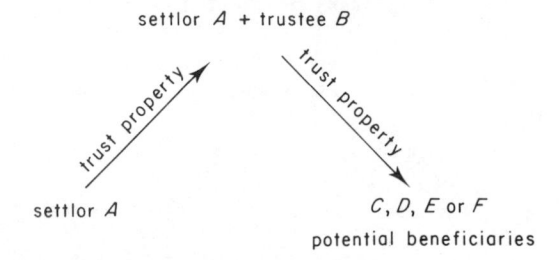

settlor A + trustee B

settlor A ——trust property——> C, D, E or F
potential beneficiaries

The British tax authorities are less compliant and refuse to accept this system. They introduced clauses in 1969 which revoked most of the advantages of a discretionary trust.

A disguised trust

When the system slips even further, the settlor, A, is very often also the beneficiary, C. In effect this is the method used to hold ordinary shares in the name of a nominee. In this system the beneficiary C is the owner A acting as settlor, from which derives the now-familiar Anglo-Saxon concept of the beneficial owner. For the Anglo-Saxon lawyer this would be the reverse of the previous example described by an English solicitor Thomas Crawley as 'nudity clothing itself against fiscal licentiousness'; here the trustee is called a 'bare trustee'.

---

*Which without any doubt adds considerably to the difficulties and risks of error for the professional adviser.

This scheme (Figure 8a), which in reality would be a very curious trust indeed in terms of Anglo-Saxon law, is never used in this form, but it can be done in effect by leaving blank the third part of the arrangement (Figure 8b):

Figure 8 *Beneficially owned trust*

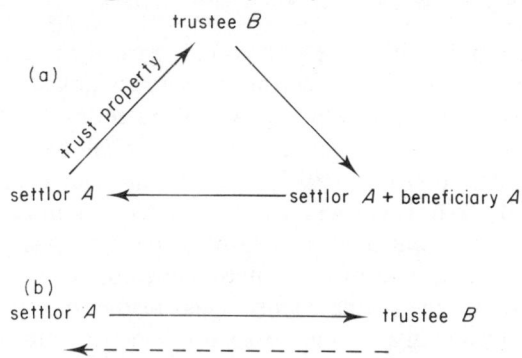

(a)

trustee *B*

trust property

settlor *A* ← settlor *A* + beneficiary *A*

(b)

settlor *A* ⟶ trustee *B*

In certain countries where banking secrecy is not permitted, the governments have also sought to prevent the application of professional secrecy by lawyers and with the benefit of a whole range of laws designed for this purpose have made them testify under oath about their clients' business.*

Faced with the rigours of government legislation the lawyers had only their creative imaginations to help them — and produced the tasty fruit of the 'alternative trust' (Figure 9). In this kind of scheme the settlor *A* is also to be found amongst a group of persons *C* from whom at a given moment the trustee must select a beneficiary. If there is a separate agreement between the trustee *B* and settlor about this choice, the lawyer is ignorant of it and can swear quite freely that to the best of his knowledge his client is not the beneficiary of the trust.

Figure 9 *Simplified alternative trust scheme*

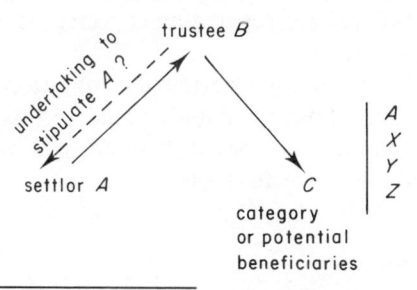

trustee *B*

undertaking to stipulate *A*?

settlor *A*   *C*
category
or potential
beneficiaries

A
X
Y
Z

---

*This essentially Anglo-Saxon procedure has been replaced in certain Roman law countries by the indictment of lawyers for complicity in criminal acts accompanied by seizure of the lawyer's files. The case is investigated by an examining magistrate who is also investigating the client. The case against the lawyer is swiftly dropped, but he has been robbed of his professional secrecy, by the seizure of his files if not by the necessity to defend himself. This process was used in Italy against a well-known company lawyer and resulted in . . . apologies from the Ministry of Justice.

Such a scheme would not stand up in a court hearing and certainly not against cross-examination. It does not stand up against the question: 'Is your client a possible beneficiary of the trust?'

Alternative trusts

For this reason a more sophisticated structure is created and can be excessively complicated (Figure 10). In this scheme trustee B is linked with a group of 'sub-trustees' who will decide which group of potential beneficiaries will in fact benefit from the trust. For his part the settlor will have an undertaking from the sub-trustees that they will stipulate group X of beneficiaries which represents A, A-1, A-2. There will also be a letter of renunciation of rights from A-1 and A-2 in favour of A. If the roving depositor has not explained to the lawyer who set up the trust that he appears in group X, the laywer is able to swear under oath that the roving depositor has neither directly nor indirectly (and it can be expressed in any other tense) any beneficial interest whatsoever.

Figure 10 *complex alternative trust scheme*

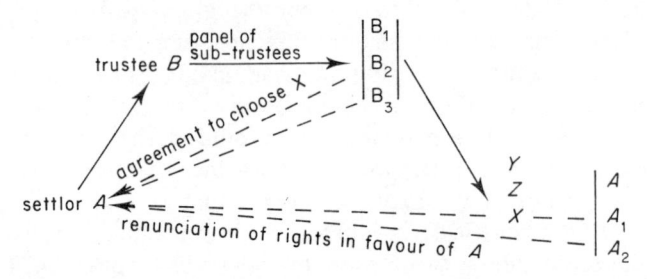

Ultimately if A replaces X-A with a completely anonymous Panamanian company, he will have a further guarantee of secrecy since A-1 and A-2 will be unaware that A and the Panamanian company are the same effective person. One might also wonder in many cases why he did not go directly to another country where professional secrecy and bank secrecy still have some meaning — 'These English are mad!'*

In fact the Anglo-Saxon imagination did not stop at the complicated alternative trust scheme whose mechanics would become useless if laid bare. At the risk of giving Roman law specialists some nightmares the Anglo-Saxon lawyers also invented the 'protected trust'.

A protector for virtuous trusts

If you understand neither the scheme nor the explanations which follow it will be because you are perfectly normal. If on the other hand you understand the

---

*In fact Anglo-Saxons seem to have the same dislike of bearer shares which Roman lawyers have for trusts.

scheme in less than an hour you have been trained in Anglo-Saxon law — but if you should disappear, are you sure your heirs have the same knowledge?

To look at the evidence in the scheme for the protected discretionary trust (Figure 11) it is the 'protector' who is the real beneficiary of the investments shown in the lower part of the example — that is share portfolios, property holdings and active trading companies which are themselves held by holding companies. The advantage of the scheme is that the 'protector' never appears as the owner in the strict legal sense, and could in any event be replaced by a Panamanian company.

The disadvantage of such schemes, apart that is from their high cost both for formation and also for subsequent maintenance, is their extreme

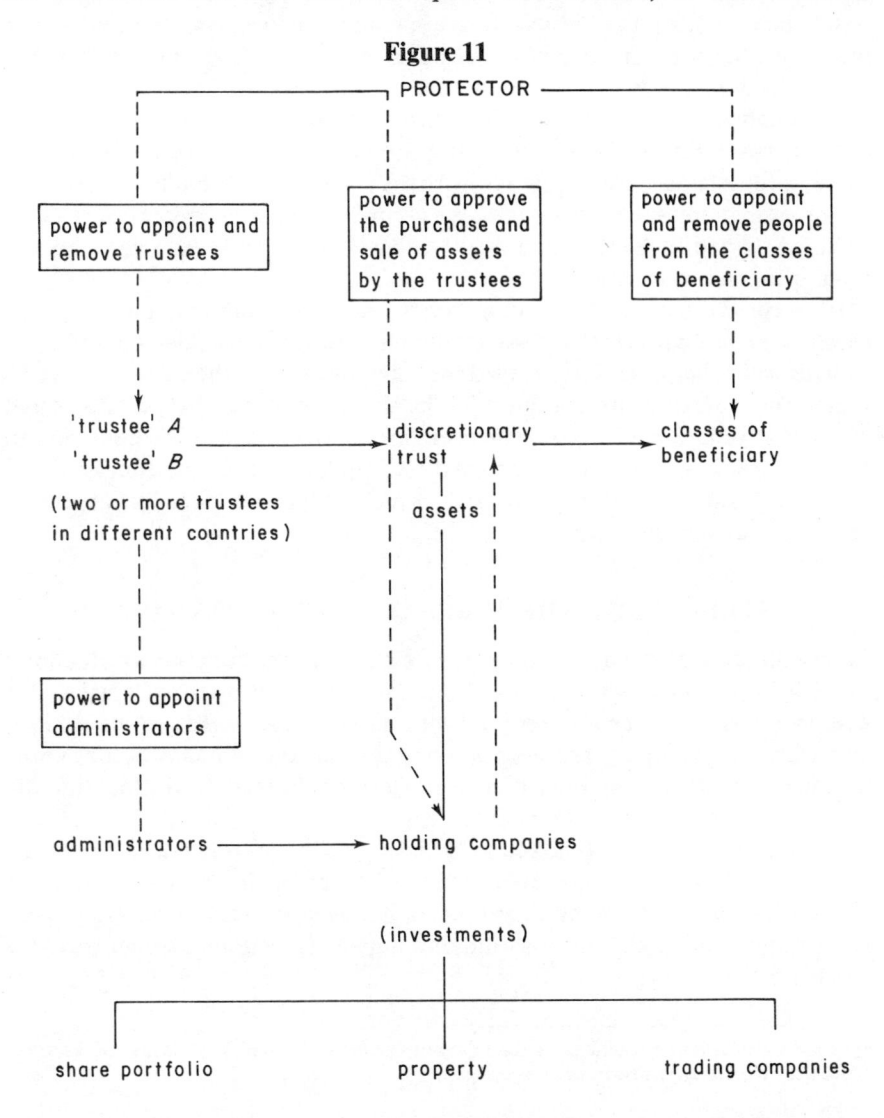

Figure 11

complication although their excesses seem to satisfy some lawyers and their clients. There are other vehicles similar to the Anglo-Saxon trust, of which the most popular has been the Liechtenstein foundation (*Stiftung*) which lends itself very well to a family arrangement and no doubt also owes part of its success to the attraction of its name.

Some scarcely charitable foundations

The foundation is a permanent transfer of property, the result of which constitutes a disctinct legal entity with a name, an object and an internal organization to realize the transfer. The true founder, who can also be the beneficiary, enters into a fiduciary agreement with a local lawyer,* and it is at this point that his name appears—evidently much less frequently than in the case of the Jersey investment company.

Although the foundation was held to be an ideal vehicle for a long time, today it has a major disadvantage: it costs nearly as much to maintain as a mistress (on a modest scale that is), perhaps some $250 a month or more, and on top of that any service over and above simple maintenance costs extra. This situation is one of Switzerland's current problems and is to a large extent holding its success to ransom.†

It is chiefly thanks to banking secrecy and the stability and technical excellence of its bankers that Switzerland has enjoyed a considerable influx of capital, which has practically tripled the external value of the currency over 15 years. The scale of charges applied by the service industries has, in the virtual absence of inflation, changed little over this period, but their effective cost to the foreigner has been multiplied by three. Under these circumstances many roving depositors have turned towards vehicles which are both less expensive and afford greater secrecy.

STRUCTURES WHICH REALLY ARE ANONYMOUS

In the full sense of the definition these are forms where the state which allows them does not know who is using them, where the user does not appear in a written agreement (even a secret one) with those who have created the vehicle, and where ultimately the professionals who formed the company do not know the identity of their client since there is no denying the truth of the fact that the easiest secret to keep is one you don't know!

These companies have renewed their links with the original meanings of the French *societé anonyme*, and evolution has brought an improvement in so far as the fact that not only the shareholders but even the real managers remain anonymous. The model for this kind of company is the Panamanian *sociedad anonyma*.

---

*For more details about foundations see Edouard Chambost's *Using Tax Havens Successfully*
†Liechtenstein uses the Swiss franc as its currency.

The Russian dolls of international finance

This type of company is constituted with shares issued to bearer (generally 500 shares without any nominal value) and with administrators who at the same time that they sign the formation papers provide an undated resignation (for a European lawyer this procedure, although not unusual, leaves an unpleasant taste, and certain Panamanian lawyers prefer to replace the undated resignation with a promise to resign—also undated!).

The Panamanian refinement of the technique consists of providing a decision made by the administrators to give executive powers in relation to the company to Mr _____ (the name is left blank).

Thereafter the administrators enjoy an annual fee which although respectable is still well below that of Liechtenstein and they continue to appear officially on the Panamanian Commercial Register without having any idea of what use is being made of the authority which they have conferred. (You need nerves of steel to be an administrator in Panama* even as a nominee!). The only problem for the user is whether he should take the risk of entering his own name on the blank executive powers or whether to put someone else in—in which case he would have to put his name to a fiduciary agreement! And there again, just as you are on the point of getting the key in the lock, comes the final choice between risk and confidence, if indeed confidence is not also a risk.

In practice Panamanian lawyers will not accept the use of this practice except where a foreign lawyer executes a 'hold harmless' agreement in their favour. Although in some cases they may accept the system without their foreign lawyer signing—in which case his name must be worth its weight in gold!

7 The Rolls-Royces of banking secrecy

The problem for banking secrecy when it comes to the public authorities, be they local or foreign, arises from the intervention of the authorities between the repository of the secret (the banker) and the master of the secret (the client) which at a certain point leads to a conflict of interest. This conflict arises when the pressures exerted by the authorities, either officially through regulations or legal cases, or unofficially through threats of withdrawn licences or public enquiries, become such that the bank may find it necessary to sacrifice the client's interest in favour of its own. Of course at this stage there is also the probable bad publicity arising from a failure to preserve secrecy which must be taken into account, even for an isolated incident.

This conflict of interest has several aspects; for example, a local bank which belongs to a much bigger local organization would be much more responsive to pressure exerted on its head office than could possibly be the case for an organization which was simply a local bank.* On the other hand, a bank which was heavily committed to tax haven operations could well accept the loss of one of its subsidiaries in one tax haven and thereby protect its clients in that haven, the reputation of the banking haven and the reputation of the bank in other havens. This was probably the reasoning behind the withdrawal of the Bank of Nova Scotia's licence by the Bahamian government because of 'bad publicity' for the Bahamas as a banking haven created by the US government.†

In this hard-fought tennis match to which the public authorities and the banks have committed themselves with the judiciary as umpires, the roving depositor who uses the direct instruments can find himself involved as the ball —and in some matches the ball can be lost! And to pursue the sporting metaphor the roving depositor who uses the indirect instruments is in the position of the racquet—rarely lost but occasionally broken. Under these conditions why doesn't the depositor think of taking one further step and through a legal device himself grasp the racquet and enter into a competition where he will have the right to serve the balls?

The vehicle for this competition, which is the Rolls-Royce of banking secrecy is known as an 'offshore captive', a term that perhaps requires explanation!

---

*See Chapter 26 on the British Virgin Islands.
†See Chapters 11 and 31 on the United States and the Bahamas.

FREE CAPTIVES

A captive bank plays its role as bank purely for one physical or legal person or group of people.* This system has an additional advantage in that it allows a group while financing itself to take advantage, within the limits of proper banking ratios, of the multiplying effect of money.

This simple process can lead to fortune or to bankruptcy, depending upon the quality of management, events in general and also pure chance. In simple terms it works like this.

Let us suppose that three people, A, B, and C, each have $100 which must cover their current expenditure and savings. These three wish to avoid having their money stolen or to risk losing it, so they place it with X, the banker, who will look after the money, take care of their payments when instructed, and give them cash for current payments when they want it. The banker's gamble is that all three depositors will not want to use their money at the same time and that there will always be $100 or $200 in the bank. On this assumption the bank can lend $100 or $200 to another person, D, who will pay the bank interest which represents the bank's profit. The borrower could even be A, B, or C if it should happen that one of them needed more than the $100 deposited.

If in our example the bank keeps $100 to meet A, B, and C's payment needs out of total funds deposited short term of $300 and lends $200 on short or medium term, it would be said to have a 'reserve ratio' of $100 or one-third. It may consider that this ratio is not sufficient and keep $200, in which case it would have a reserve ratio of two-thirds. The reserve can be kept in different ways. In the case of the two-thirds ratio for example, one third might be deposited with another bank and the rest invested in property (the place where the bank does business, for example). In this case the bank would still have a reserve ratio of two-thirds but a liquidity coefficient of one-third. These ratios are arrived at either as a management decision on the bank's part or are specified by the local banking laws or the central bank.

Looking at the overall position of our example, there were $300 in circulation before any money was deposited wiht the bank. If the bank uses a one-third reserve ratio and lends $200, the total amount of money in circulation becomes $500. The increase of $200 is created entirely by book entries in the bank. According to the economists this increase in the amount of money in circulation (the money supply) is a source of inflation since it allows demand to increase relative to the supply of goods and services which in a free economy means that unsatisfied demand will lead to an increase in prices. It is for this reason that many countries, amongst their monetary control measures, assign to their central bank the right to set ratios in order to be able to vary the money supply by changing the ratios.

---

*The same idea is used in insurance where subsidiaries cover the risks of the group which controls them. They are also known as captives.

Returning to our example, if *A*, *B*, and *C* are companies which belong to *X* who also controls bank X, the captive bank can act as a bank and fulfil the treasury requirements of the subsidiaries. Furthermore, if bank *X* is resident in a tax haven it can realize a profit from the interest it charges to other members of the group—an expense that is deductible in the subsidiaries for tax purposes, but free of tax in the tax haven.*

INTEREST AT WHOLESALE PRICES

A further advantage—and not a minor one—offered by a captive bank, whether offshore or not, is access to the interbank money markets and also the additional negotiating power as far as interest is concerned to be gained by grouping together the finances of the whole group. For example, if bank *X* which controls companies *A*, *B*, and *C* needs more financing than it can create through its own internal activities, it will be able to negotiate a loan from another bank on the interbank market. It will be charged interest at 'wholesale prices' but can charge retail rates to *A*, *B*, and *C*.

The differences in interest rates or commission charges can be minimal in terms of percentages but when the overall sums involved are large, the value of these differences can also be great. An apparently negligible difference of a quarter of a point (0.25 per cent) on a 12-month loan† for $10 million represents $250 000, in other words a good deal more than the cost of setting up a captive bank.

Quite apart from the advantage of access to the interbank market, the credit created by the bank and the interest due to the bank will escape the exchange control net to which companies are or can be subject and therefore represents a guarantee against capital being locked in and the losses which can result from that.

'OFFSHORE' FINANCIAL PLATFORMS

In most cases a bank created for these purposes and taking only group deposits will exclude any local deposit-taking in the place where it is based. Such an overseas activity is described in financial circles as 'offshore', that is taking place outside a country's borders. One of the advantages of the offshore bank by comparison with a bank which does take local deposits is that in general the regulations controlling it are more flexible because the credit created by the bank cannot have any influence on the local money supply. The offshore bank will probably have a less rigorous set of rules and lower reserve requirements than one which takes money locally. On top of that the cost of a licence (that is to say the right to act as a bank and therefore to create paper credits) is

---

*A few countries prohibit the direct use of this mechanism when *A*, *B*, and *C* are subsidiaries and multinational companies or groups therefore make use—with the help of banking secrecy—of back-to-back loans which obviate the 'subsidiary' relationship. The rates charged are also often restricted to market rates applicable in the subsidiary's country.

†Such financing on the interbank market is often much shorter term but is generally renewed.

normally much lower since the bank is not entering into competition with the local banks and not therefore taking anything out of the community.*

HEAVY RESERVES

The size of reserves required for an offshore bank is extremely important to the extent that it can add a heavy burden to the costs, which are calculated in quarters of a percentage point.

If we return to our example with A, B, and C and bank X with three deposits of $100, and let us assume that the reserve requirement is one-third or $100. If the $100 must be deposited with the central bank and no interest is paid on it, there is a loss of $10 if the interbank rate is 10 per cent and therefore if bank X is not to make a loss on the $300 deposited by A, B, and C it must lend out the remaining $200 at 15 per cent to arrive at interest of $30. At that rate the bank would not have made any money to cover its own expenses and would even then be running at a loss.

One of the last points to consider is that of withholding tax deducted at source on the interest paid by companies A, B, and C when these borrow from their captive bank X. In most cases X will be situated in a tax and banking haven which will not have double tax treaties with the countries where A, B, and C are resident. Consequently when group companies borrow money from X they must deduct from the interest payable to x a sum which will vary between 5 per cent and 30 per cent. The scheme works where A, B, and C are part of the same group and where the interest represents a deductible item locally, the overall cost is less than it would otherwise have been.

The problem can also arise in reverse, particularly when it relates to an offshore bank which is not captive. In this situation the banking haven may itself impose a deduction on interest paid by the bank for money which it has needed to borrow on the money markets. In that case a withholding tax at source, even of so modest a rate as 5 per cent, would eliminate offshore activities more certainly than a 50 per cent tax on net profits.†

Our examination of offshore banks will rest there, since they do not form the focus of this study, but are only one of the aspects of the Rolls Royce of banking secrecy—even though offshore banks do exist in financial centres which are not banking havens (which would not prevent them from functioning but would put them outside part of the financial market and make their use as captives impossible).

PAPER BANKS

The ideal for a captive offshore bank would be formation not in a country with flexible requirements but rather in a country which had no banking

---

*Since the right to create credits can 'go to your head' financially, it is generally subject to licensing, rather like the sale of alcohol whose effects are both similar and different.
†John Chown and Thomas Kelen, *Offshore Investment Centres* (see bibliography, page 292).

regulations whatsoever and allowed any kind of financial fantasy. Such 'flexibility' sometimes has disastrous consequences. The world of international finance is not full only of dynamic businessmen; this world, like all others, has its share of black sheep who are international swindlers. The creator of the Bank of France 'Ltd.'* carried on business for a long time issuing, amongst other things, bouncing cheques in countries where the issue of such a cheque did not in itself constitute a crime. Into the same category must surely be put the owner of the Bank of Sark.†His offices were in fact in Guernsey at a time when that island did not have strict banking rules and he seems never to have been arrested despite a considerable number of swindles.‡ As for the proper Bank of France which was founded by Napoleon, that was hardly more respectable when it opened: 'its nominal capital was 30 million francs but its founders only put up 2 million'.§ It was worthy of the most dangerous banking haven.

These banks, which anyone can form for about $5000, are ordinary commercial companies which include the word 'bank', in one language or another, in their name. Their value as banks is no more than that of the paper on which the word is written, hence the expression 'paper bank', which can be rather more dangerous in the hands of the unscrupulous than a paper tiger. It is for that reason that none of the countries where a paper bank can be formed are indicated here—a Rolls Royce should not have a Volkswagen engine! If the roving depositor has reached the point where he can take the role of the player, then it is preferable that the game should take place on a proper grass court and not on some handy field.

The financial captives game is only possible if the rules of the game are respected. The game is played in offshore banking havens which, in order to eliminate the black sheep in the form of paper banks, have become a sort of private club which impose their own admission requirements. As in all private clubs admission is restricted to those who comply with the requirements and sometimes even requires a form of members' vote.

THE RULES OF THE GAME

If an offshore captive bank is to be formed to fulfil a group's financial needs, to be done satisfactorily there are a number of conditions which should obtain, although each of these need not necessarily have the same strength as a motivation.

1. First it is necessary that the offshore captive be formed in a banking haven which enjoys good banking secrecy.
2. The ratios required should not impose too heavy a burden on financing.

---

*It was a different European central bank followed by 'Ltd.'
†One of the Channel Islands.
‡See *Dirty Money*, cited above.
§Philippe Simonnot, *Banquiers, votre argent nous interesse* (Grasset, 1979).

3. The banking haven should not impose a withholding tax on interest paid by the bank if recourse is had to the interbank market, or the withholding tax should not impose too great a burden.*
4. The local exchange control regulations (if there are any) should not stand in the way of the creation of the investment† (that is, the exchange control which relates to the bank itself, not to the accounts within the bank‡) nor to the eventual liquidation of the bank, or realization of the investment.§
5. The countries in which the captive bank is going to carry out its financing operations should permit loans from foreign sources (only rarely prohibited) and not impose a withholding tax on the interest payable by the local borrower at a rate which is incompatible with the local tax situation‖ unless it is possible to use another financial institution as a conduit or a screening company in another country which would allow the use of double tax treaties. ☆
6. The true owner of the offshore captive (the 'beneficial owner') must be able to remain anonymous. This condition is less than ideal because most established banking havens want to know precisely who is the beneficial owner. A more realistic way of expressing this condition would be that the the beneficial owner, known to the authorities in the banking haven, should be able to preserve his anonymity as regards other countries. ★
7. The banking haven in which the offshore company is formed should also be a tax haven or at least a country in which the maximum rate of tax is acceptable and which does not impose any substantial withholding tax on dividends.
8. On a financial level the threshold for access to a captive bank must be reached. In simplistic terms, the operation must save more money than it costs. It is after all a question of creating a real bank, with offices and employees, even if not many, rather than a 'paper bank'. This is perhaps

---

*In fact the lender on the interbank market will want to receive x per cent; if this rate is reduced by a withholding tax, the notional rate will be increased prorata to achieve the net rate of x per cent. It is therefore the borrower who pays the withholding tax levied on the lender.
†This can be done by forming a company or by buying an existing bank of this type (in which case you should observe the established banking rule: 'look out for any skeletons in the cupboards').
‡Exchange control in any given country often differs between that applied to the financial transactions of non-residents (often very liberal if not non-existent) and that applied to a direct investment (the control of investments by non-residents is not only economically justified but can be quite sensitive).
§Realization in this context is defined as liquidation of the investment and distribution of the proceeds or release of the control which gave the bank captive status.
‖A rate is incompatible if the interest is not allowed for the purposes of local taxes, or if the limitations applied are exaggerated.
☆The details of how such companies are operated are given in *Using Tax Havens Successfully*, cited above.
★In practice there are no international agreements in existence which deal with this subject. On the contrary, companies (even those with offshore activities) are generally regarded as being due protection, even in some cases backed up by criminal penalties (this would be at the limit of the interaction of two separate areas of legislation: that concerning bank secrecy and that concerning industrial espionage).

the most difficult condition to be precise about, since circumstances differ from one financial group to another and furthermore there are no published statistics on this point.

Only a negative definition can be given: it seems unlikely that an offshore captive would be of interest to a group whose annual financial costs were less than US$1 million; and even that limit is misleading when the decision to launch such a venture is made in anticipation of a future situation (for example where a business group foresees future development).

If these conditions may be described as the rules of the game and the roving depositor decides to play, he still needs to be admitted to the 'club' and to do that he needs to comply with the rules of admission.

THE RULES OF THE CLUB

Of course the rules change in some details according to which haven is chosen, but for offshore captives the following rules are generally applicable:

1. There must be another bank behind the offshore bank—or at least the real owner of the captive must take on at a senior level a banking professional whose respectability and professional references are impeccable.
2. The captive must have the required minimum capital.
3. The captive must observe the ratios fixed by local law or by the local central bank, if there is one.
4. The captive must pay the appropriate scale of licence fees.
5. The bank's activities must conform to those normally expected of an offshore bank, failing which its licence may be withdrawn, and in some cases it is required to confine its activities to transactions with 'clients' whose names were specified at the time the licence was granted.
6. The bank's activities must actually take place, following the normal course of business (in order to avoid the use of shell companies).*

The offshore captive banks, having accepted the rules of the game and also complied with the rules of the club, become and remain the most sophisticated structures of banking secrecy. An analysis of captive banks, haven by haven, would represent in itself a major work—which would be likely to bore most readers. So in order to avoid overburdening this book and duplicating the details given in examining individual havens, this section gives only the results of such a study without the detail. In order that this analysis can be used in a practical way, it is presented in the form of comparative tables in which offshore banks are compared based on formation in the havens where they are most frequently to be found. These tables appear in Chapter 41.

---

*A shell company is a legal vehicle without any real activity: in this context it is close to being a 'paper bank'.

When a captive bank is set up in a banking haven and indirect investments are used for holding accounts (which are themselves protected by banking secrecy) the financial mechanisms of a group can become entirely indecipherable and even in extreme cases technically impossible to penetrate. If the screening is in fact absolute and in such an instance a political grain of sand for example upsets this precise clockwork, the owner of the money deposited in the system can sue for his money back from a bank—which in fact he owns but is unaware of this small detail. On the face of it this is the misfortune which befell the Algerian government (see Chapter 9) following on the introduction of a grain of sand by Mohamed Khider which led to his death. And it is true that the machinery worked with precision because it was a Swiss movement!

8 Banking secrecy at the time of death

Since the creation of a separate inheritance for his family is often one of the main motivations of the roving depositor, the question of the account holder's death possesses an inordinate interest. Even if the bankers involved have no great desire to explore the question, it is quite probable that there are some accounts which stand without inheritors because the heirs are unaware of the existence of the accounts and because the banks have not been given sufficiently precise instructions—which they would make a point of honour of observing.

MORAL OR PHYSICAL PERSON

On the subject of the indirect instruments of banking secrecy we have seen that an account may be opened by an individual—as a physical person—or by a moral person, that is a legal entity which belongs to him. Legal entities of course do not suffer from physical death, so the death of their owner moves the problem to a different area, rather than resolving it.

Direct instruments of banking secrecy and death

The apparent danger of secrecy, particularly for a numbered account or one in an assumed name, is that the heirs do not know the code. But this is not a real danger* because this system was designed primarily to ensure protection within the workings of the bank and the owner of the account is known to the bank's management. The procedure to be used would therefore be the same once the identity of the bank itself is known.

In the examples reviewed in this chapter we shall work on the basis of an account with a Swiss bank, while bearing in mind that the system and the normal practices are very similar, if not identical, in another banking haven.

The heirs or the executor of the estate would need first to prove their own standing and the fact of the account holder's death before having any rights to information. Quite logically they should do this by following the law which

---

*Although widely and unsparingly used by false prophets who wish to pretend that they have been disinherited by the ignorance of the right code. Mostly they are confidence tricksters who are trying to win sympathy while creating false credit—with the kind help of ingenuous journalists.

applies under the 'conflict' rules* and produce translations which have been attested and legalized together with certificates of custom.

In practice most banks would be satisfied with a death certificate and a letter to the bank from either a Swiss lawyer† or one known to the banking authorities. One of the difficulties if the bank and branch are not known arises from the fact that not only must the head office of each bank be asked for information but also every branch—a procedure which is both awkward and expensive. If the letter and death certificate draw a positive response it may be that in reality the problem is only just beginning.

It should be noted, by way of a preliminary remark, that the bank will normally give only the current situation of the account and would oppose any attempt by the inheritors to trace past transactions which could for example throw up debatable acts of generosity. The current situation is generally defined as that existing at the time of the last statement approved by the account holder.‡ It is here that a thorny problem of international law crops up, a problem which is too often ignored during the account holder's lifetime. When the roving depositor opens the account he has an irritating tendency to believe that the anonymity which is extended to him allows him to make any dispositions which he likes. He never thinks that his plans may come into conflict with the so-called inheritors' reserve system, given that the law applicable to his account contains this provision and there exist inheritors who would qualify to participate in this reserve (the notion of an inheritors' reserve does not figure in most Anglo-Saxon legal systems).

In most cases the banker would attempt to carry out his client's instructions, but the problem is to know whether he can be legally obliged to breach banking secrecy as a result of a court ruling, for example in favour of 'reserve' inheritors when the law applicable to the estate allows for a reserve.

It seems that most Swiss courts have a tendency to consider that the right to bank secrecy passes to the heirs, and in particular any qualifying as reserve inheritors. This principle applies with the diplomatic qualification that the right to secrecy is passed on only as far as concerns inheritance and the question remains open 'to the extent that the deceased had expressly required the banker to maintain secrecy, even as regards the heirs, concerning facts whose nature was strictly personal.'§ 'In practice there are many people who during their lifetime have some regard for their posthumous reputation and wish to take certain secrets to a grave which as we all know is not always silent.'§

---

*This is the international system of civil law which determines which jurisdiction applies when several are in conflict in a particular situation. The system would be quite simple if each country had the same rules of conflict but it has to be admitted that often there is conflict between the rules of conflict and law *A* refers you to law *B* which refers you to law *A*. This particularly vicious circle is called a double referral. The question is so simple that lawyers may be found in every country whose speciality is international civil law.
†Maurice Aubert: 'Transfer of a bank account upon death', *Tax Planning International*, **5** (1), **January** 1978.
‡This, for example, is the rule adopted by the Luxemburg Banks Association.
§Maurice Aubert, cited above.

It is not possible in the course of such a brief study to analyse all the legal situations which can arise and their eventual effect on banking secrecy. Such an analysis would in any event duplicate Maurice Aubert's work. We shall simply note that a number of legal systems, and in particular those of France and Switzerland, provide that the law which should apply to the disposal of estates is that of the deceased person's last residence. This of course then creates the problem of the validity of the form used for the will (should it comply with the correct form in the country of last residence or in the country where the will was made?) and the problem of the basis for the provisions, that is whether the dispositions themselves are valid. The danger of having a separate Swiss will is that it might be considered to be a revocation of an earlier will under the law applying at the time of death and thus cause a global distribution of the inheritance which was not intended. Another problem which often occurs in practice is that of instructions left with a bank in case of death: do they constitute a will or not? For a lawyer, on this evidence, the answer is yes,* although it may not have been evident in the mind of the roving depositor. There is one detail which creates a fresh doubt: the 'postmortem' instrument.

A 'postmortem' instruction equates to a will

If the owner of an account gives an instruction which is valid during his lifetime, the instruction would in principle remain valid even after his death, unless it was withdrawn by his heirs. If on the other hand the instruction is a 'postmortem' one, that is it only takes effect on the death of the account holder, it would normally be considered in Swiss law as being a will. In any event, a bank would be extremely cautious in the case of death since if it is legally in the wrong in following instructions it runs the risk of having to pay twice.

Indirect instruments of banking secrecy and death

Viewed strictly this question might appear to be outside the scope of an examination of the banking havens; but in reality that is not the case since the indirect instruments are currently in use in banking havens and the problem of the death of their real owner occurs just as frequently as does the problem of the death of an account holder who is a physical person, even if legally speaking there is no change of owner of an account in the name of a legal entity.

Situation obtaining on the death of the beneficial owner of a legal entity in an environment where there is exchange control and private agreements

From the point of view of local exchange control there is no difficulty for an

---

*Maurice Aubert, cited above.

investment company based on the Anglo-Saxon type of tax haven when the heirs are non-resident. But of course the problem becomes much more delicate when one or more of the heirs is subject to local exchange controls. The ideal situation is that the beneficial owner, in order to avoid these difficulties, should avoid using a legal entity which would be subject to the same exchange control as would be one of the presumptive heirs.

As for private trust or fiduciary agreements the situation there becomes no simpler either when the law under which the inheritance will be administered does not have this type of agreement,* or perhaps is aware of this kind of arrangement obtaining in another country but lacks the ability to apply it since local judges do not have sufficient knowledge of the form. Of course, the trust agreements may have been balanced with blank share transfers, but in that case the legality of the process is perhaps more open to question in the country whose laws apply to the company. Moreover this procedure makes named shares in effect bearer shares, implying that there may have been some impropriety in the beneficial owner's approach from the start. It would be much better to have used a legal entity based on a tax haven which allows the issue of bearer shares.

Situation obtaining on the death of the beneficial owner of a legal entity in an environment where there are private agreements but no exchange control

There will of course be no problems arising from the incidence of exchange controls outlined above, but there will be the same difficulties in respect of trust or fiduciary agreements. In the case of the Liechtenstein kind of trust — which is held to be a marvellous vehicle as far as Anglo-Saxon style exchange control systems go — there would in particular be a considerable problem given to a judge under Roman law if the arrangement were to be attacked by a minor who considered that he had been deprived as a result of it.

Situation obtaining on the death of the owner of a truly anonymous entity

On the face of it this is the most simple situation since bearer shares can be transferred by a simple hand movement! In fact it may be simply passing on the problem of an account in the name of a physical person to a safe-deposit opened in the name of the same person, with the account or accounts opened in the name of the company whose shares are kept in the safe-deposit; both of these are movable assets in the legal sense. The difficulties and problems of the account opened directly in the name of the deceased person return in the same way, with one or two extra administrative subtleties such as how to change the decisions of the administrative council if that power was vested in the dead man.

---

*Which is the case in most countries that have adopted Roman law, including France, but excluding Monaco. You must adapt according to your market, and there are many wealthy Anglo-Saxons in the principality!

To sum up these observations, banking havens can involve, and do so quite often in the case of death, serious difficulties in the legal area which might often end up before the courts.

Since the Swiss have the delicacy not to impose any taxes on the estates of non-residents held there, lawsuits are actually fairly rare since they risk drawing attention to an estate which is taxable in the country where the heirs are resident. Things are normally dealt with in a civilized manner — except when one of the claimants to an estate is resident in a tax haven which does not levy any taxes on inheritances deriving from overseas for example, and considers that he may be entitled to a reserved part (as would be the case for Monaco). There would then need to be a little hard negotiation (the layman might call it blackmail) and often the legal practitioners have to arrange some rough justice — but it is really quite measured for the inheritors since it is only the tax authorities who are really deprived of their share. If such a situation serves as a comment, it should not be used as counsel if the roving depositor wishes to avoid arousing at his death spiritual feelings between his relatives which have nothing to do with souls.

9 Banking secrecy and politics

If banking secrecy is in itself a plentiful source of dubious stories, its mixture with politics reaches surrealist heights in terms of the allegations made by apparently serious people. The FLN (Algerian National Liberation Front) fighting fund, the Negus treasure, the spoils of South American despots, and more recently the Shah of Iran's fortune, claimed by his 'successor': the stories abound! They have one point in common, though, all these fortunes have passed through a banking haven at one time or another. They also share a common result: they have all disappeared. People draw conclusions which differ according to their political persuasions; one will say: 'the banks have kept it all', while another will whisper with a conspiratorial air: 'believe me, I have the most reliable sources . . . he got the money out . . . .'

Given all these stories and surrounding allegations it seems worth explaining in more detail what actually happened in one affair where banking secrecy was entangled with politics.

THE ANATOMY (AUTOPSY?) OF A 'POLITICAL' AFFAIR

In order to follow a wise rule which states that the reader should always be on an equal footing with the author, it has been necessary to use an example which appeared before the courts in such a way that the mechanics of the operation can be seen from the proceedings and would at the same time not only be comprehensible but also demonstrate an interesting point for the reader.

The story chosen also has another specific interest: by observing the political events and the various banking procedures the reader will understand both the difficulties and the refinements of a banking haven's laws and the importance of the details when opening up a bank account — a procedure which should be considered as anything but a pure (and simple) formality.

It is for these reasons rather than any others that there follows an analysis of the events which ended with the disappearance, both physically and legally of the FLN fighting fund.

Since the facts are complicated they have been set out in the form of a table (Table 1) and as the notes are also extensive they have been placed at the end of the table. Although this has been set out as simply as possible it still remains complicated and involves some technicalities. So any reader who would rather pass over such a problem should stop at this point and move directly to the general conclusions following the asterisks on page 90.

Table 1 Analysis of the events and proceedings involved in the deposit, disappearance and non-recovery of the FLN (National Liberation Front) fighting fund

Dates of events		Details
In Algeria	*In Switzerland*	
19 September 1958		The FLN gives funds to an executive committee, the GPRA
19 March 1962		Representatives of the FLN sign the Evian agreement with France
June 1962		The FLN creates a provisional political bureau to operate until a government is appointed by a proper assembly
3 July 1962		Algerian independence proclaimed
	7 August 1962	X^1 who is Secretary-General of the political bureau and solely responsible for the finances of the FLN, commences effective management of the finances
	18 October 1962	X, in his own name, opens an account with the Banque Commerciale Arabe SA at Geneva (referred to as 'BCA'). The account is divided into several subaccounts: US dollars, sterling and French francs. Amongst all the important aspects of this commencement of a legal relationship with the bank, the subsequent proceedings brought out two fundamental points: 1. Under the heading of 'remarks' which appears after the signatory's signature it stated: The person in whose name the account is held acknowledges receipt of the General Conditions of business of the Banque Commerciale Arabe SA.[2] These conditions specify in article 5: 'the legal relations between the client and the bank are regulated by Swiss law. The place of execution and the legal jurisdiction for everything which concerns the account are the place where the bank's headquarters are situated.'[3] 2. Not only did X open the account in his own name but he also signed the form twice, firstly as the person solely authorized to dispose of the account, and the second time at the bottom of the form as the person in whose name the account was held. X also gave as his address: Political Bureau, Villa Joly, Rue Franklin-Roosevelt, Algiers, but this appeared under the heading 'address for correspondence'.[4]
	18/19 October 1962	'C', apparently a prominent member of the FLN, deposited US$ 2019 000 and US$ 999 000 and the BCA gives a receipt to X 'we are crediting *his* account'.[5]

Table 1
continued

Dates of events		Details
In Algeria	*In Switzerland*	
April 1963		X resigns from his post as Secretary-General of the FLN but remains a member of the political bureau and shows a willingness to retain his financial responsibilities
10 September 1963		The Algerian constitution comes into effect and the FLN which is described in article 23 as the sole founding party of Algeria takes on public responsibilities. As far as Algerian law is concerned, the FLN's finances become the property of the Algerian Republic
	11 July 1963	Y, who is X's successor as Secretary-General of the FLN describes himself in a letter addressed to the BCA as 'the sole person legally entitled to dispose of the funds and revenues of the FLN'.
	13 December 1963	The director of the BCA receives an undated letter signed by Y which asks him 'to authorize monsieur X to dispose of the assets deposited in his name at your bank', this 'authorization cancels the earlier demand made by myself that the assets should be blocked'.[6]
		X refuses to put the FLN funds at Y's disposal and claims that he does not intend to present accounts until the General Meeting of the FLN which is planned for the spring of 1964.
	3 March 1964	X changes the account opened in his name with the BCA into a numbered account and specifies that this will function under the signature 'BP 510' written out in letters.
	?	X asks the BCA to stop addressing correspondence to Algiers and instead to keep it at the bank.
	31 March 1964	The total assets of account BP 510 amounted to Swiss francs 41 953 509.[7]
16 April 1964		The FLN general meeting takes place and the central committee appoints a new political bureau which does not include X. Z is made responsible for finance.
8 June 1964		Y, who is President of the Algerian Republic and Secretary-General of the FLN gives an order requiring Z 'to take charge of all sums of money handed over by X' and ultimately 'to freeze all credits held by X with all financial organizations and banks'.[8]
	12 June 1964	Z arrives at Geneva for a meeting with administrator A at BCA.[9]

84

Table 1
continued

Dates of events		Details
In Algeria	*In Switzerland*	
	15 June 1964	Zouhair Mardam Bey, the administrator by BCA, accepts that the 'term' account BP 510 shall become a 'call'[10] account provided that all claim is renounced to interest arising after 1 April 1964.[11]
	18 June to 1 July 1964	X withdraws the equivalent of 41 796 046.40 Swiss Francs or 99.56 per cent of the account, which is apparently dealt with by Zouhair Mardam Bey. X will say that the transfer was made secretly to the account of opponents of the FLN led by Y!
	22 June 1964	Starting on this date four numbered accounts are opened at the BCA by one or more unknown clients.
	2 July 1964	Zouhair Mardam Bey maintains that he had his first meeting on this day with Z who says that he has come to take over the FLN's funds.

6 July 1964: A series of legal procedures starts in Switzerland. It would be too demanding to provide all the details, but a number of significant events need to be mentioned in order to understand what was happening.

Dates of events		Main details
External	*Legal*	
	6 July 1964	Y and Z put down an action in the name of the Algerian Republic for a breach of trust against X and the BCA administration.
	6 July 1964	The Swiss Bailiff's office notify BCA of a civil sequestration order which has been made on account BP 510 by Z. The order causes a balance of 157 561.60 Swiss francs[12] to be revealed.
	7 July 1964	A criminal sequestration order is granted by the examining magistrate dealing with the case.
	8 July 1964	The civil order is lifted to be replaced by the criminal one.
4–25 August 1964		The four numbered accounts opened from 22 June are definitively closed down.
	3 November 1964	The examining magistrate appoints an expert to discover in particular whether the bank could have made any cash payments to X with effect from 18 June. The magistrate also issues an order requiring Zouhair Mardam Bey to hand over to the expert the files relating to the four accounts.
	?	Zouhair Mardam Bey, entrenching himself

Table 1
continued

Dates of events		Main details
External	Legal	
		behind banking secrecy, refuses to supply the files to the expert. He refuses to accept even an examination whose object would be limited to verifying the existence of the accounts while respecting the anonymity of their owners.
	?	The magistrate charges Zouhair Mardam Bey with obstructing authority, concealing evidence required by the courts and bearing false witness.
	30 December 1964	The expert delivers his report and concludes that: (*a*) up to 6 July 1964 the bank was in a position to cover X's withdrawals; (*b*) with effect from 22 June 1964 the creation of four numbered accounts (not brought forward in the bank's books) avoided a loss of interest(!); (*c*) it was impossible to know if the transfers made from these accounts were real or fictitious.
	28 October 1965	The examining magistrate issued an order which would allow the criminal sequestration on account BP 510 to be lifted.
	11 March 1966	In the absence of any objection to the magistrate's order, the criminal sequestration order is lifted.
3 January 1967		X is assasinated in Madrid.
	6 January 1967	The Attorney General files the criminal action against X brought as a result of the complaint lodged on 6 July 1964 by Y and Z.[13]
	14 February 1967	The Attorney General also files as having no further outcome the proceedings against Zouhair Mardam Bey, his guilt having apparently not been established.[14]
	10 July 1967	The affair passes into the civil courts since the criminal actions will not be pursued any further having been filed as being without outcome. The democratic peoples' republic of Algeria and the FLN jointly issue a writ in the court of first instance at Geneva against the Banque Commerciale Arabe SA and Zouhair Mardam Bey for payment of 42 796 100 Swiss Francs.
	2 February 1971	The Court of First Instance at Geneva rules that the defenders should pay the Republic of Algeria the sum of 39 246 851.80 Swiss francs with interest at 5 per cent from 10 July 1964.[15] The Court takes the view that

Table 1
continued

Dates of events		Main details
External	*Legal*	
	2 February 1971 *continued*	the FLN alone was the depositor from the point of view of BCA and X acted only as a representative. The repayment granted as a result of the bank's error was the amount determined by an expert as being in the account on 12 June, 1964 (the date of the meeting between Z and the BCA administrator).
	15 June 1973	The Court of Justice of the Canton of Geneva, hearing the defendants' appeal, confirms the judgment of the Court of First Instance.
	1 July 1974	The Federal Court[16] accepts the petition of the defendants, annuls the decision of the Court of Justice of the Canton of Geneva and rejects the demand of the Republic of Algeria.

(1) The principal protagonists in this affair are going to be Mohamed Khider, now dead, assassinated, and who were the others? — the Swiss civil court does not give them numbers, but the text of the public decree (ATF 100 II) describes them as X, Y, and Z. The author will respect their anonymity and leave it to the reader to look up the order.

(2) The reader might be interested to return to the chapter on the direct instruments of banking secrecy and in particular to the sample documents (which are not reproductions of documents issued by the BCA). Most countries in the world use clauses of this type which are often not read and even occasionally printed in a language not known to the account holder. Such clauses correspond in terms of the application of law, to the rules of international civil law in most countries and are usually taken to be contractual in their nature (and therefore known to the client) if the reference to the clause is sufficiently legible to attract the attention of the signatory.

(3) The court which is territorially competent. In international civil law court A may be territorially competent to apply the law of country B to deal with a dispute which has been brought before it (which is not to say that the question does not pose its own problems — it is already difficulty enough to understand the law of your own country!)

(4) The ultimate judges will not see in this detail anything other than a simple note of correspondence.

(5) The ultimate judges will see from this (amongst other items) that the FLN could not have been unaware that the account was in X's name.

(6) There are several possible explanations for this letter. One that seems reasonable is that Y thought X was about to give his agreement for the transfer of the funds and it was therefore necessary that X should be in a position to give instructions. If this explanation is right, it is surprising that Y did not have the transfer instructions at the same time to avoid any subsequent change of mind. Another hypothesis is possible: the FLN might have had some payments to make and X could have refused to countersign Y's instructions, demanding as a point of honour that he have complete freedom to run the account and present his accounts subsequently to his peers. This would seem to coincide with X's later attitude and would also have given him a negotiating advantage within his party.

(7) The equivalent at the time of 47 407 455 French francs (a large part of the funds had been collected from Algerian workers in France) or of US$ 9 674 990, a sum which represents a considerable exchange gain had the receipts been transferred in Swiss francs, quite apart from the interest. In fact account BP 510 was divided into several accounts: US dollars, Swiss francs and sterling.

Table 1
continued

---

(8) The ultimate judges deduced from this order, created by the instruction of 8 June 1964 that only X could dispose of the funds. Otherwise the FLN could have revoked X's mandate directly with the BCA.

(9) We should note that this was not Zouhair Mardam Bey with whom X normally dealt. There are apparently no details available as to what took place at this meeting, but logic suggests that the object of the meeting was to convey to the bank the nature of Z's mission.

(10) Which would permit immediate withdrawals.

(11) This should not be seen as collusion between X and Zouhair Mardam Bey with the bank profiting by not having to pay 45 days' interest, but rather the price of renouncing the term account status. (It would be interesting to know the terms of the deposit, 2 months? 3, 6, 12? Given this transaction it would logically have been 2 or 3 months.)

(12) The small difference appearing between the position at 31 March 1964 and the withdrawals made between 18 June and 1 July, given the renunciation of interest from 1 April, may arise from an exchange difference (after deduction of — commission?)

(13) In most modern systems of criminal law the death of the person accused of a crime will cause the automatic cessation of the action being brought by the magistrate, civil servant or government lawyer (according to the country) without distinguishing as to whether the action was brought on the initiative of the authorities or a private individual. Most legal systems provide that the state representative may refuse to institute criminal proceedings brought by an individual and that proceedings if brought do to an extent engage the responsibility of the individual and may lead to damages and interest (or even a criminal penalty) if they are not upheld. Apparently France is the only country which, through a hole in its legal code, permits one individual to cite another before a criminal court without having to submit a case to the authorities. The rules of this procedure require the person cited, provided the facts as stated indicate he risks a penalty of 2 years' imprisonment or more, to appear personally without the choice of being represented by a lawyer — although he can be assisted of course.

(14) Seen from outside this decision seems much more regrettable — not to say debatable — than the previous one. It has the advantage or disadvantage (depending upon your point of view) of avoiding a public debate which could have been most instructive.

(15) The FLN, for its part, was dismissed from the case on a technical point since Switzerland had recognized the state of Algeria which in terms of its own civil law had succeeded to the FLN.

(16) The principle on which the federal court operates is to play to an extent the role of a third level of jurisdiction and to issue a decree in terms purely of the law, based on the facts established by the cantonal court (which is therefore the final court as regards facts). In the Swiss system, if the federal court cancels a ruling and returns the case to the canton, it can do this only for reasons of law. The federal court cannot ask the canton to re-examine the facts except if it needs further clarification in order to test the legal solution which it has adopted. It can, of course, demand that the canton re-examine the facts where the federal rules of evidence have been violated or where there has clearly been a mistake.

We have just seen how, through a labyrinth of facts and legal proceedings the FLN's war chest evaporated both physically and legally (the FLN's recourse to the bank having finally been rejected by the federal court) — a fortune which, given that it came from subscriptions from members and sympathizers, did apparently belong to the FLN. What judicial analysis could have led through these facts and proceedings to take the federal court to this decision? That is what the following paragraphs will try to explain. The author attaches more importance to explaining the spirit of the decision and the reasons for that than he does to the analysis of the legal details in all their ramifications — that is more properly the province of the Geneva lawyers.

The reasoning of the federal court, although it is not explained in exactly this way in their decision, takes the following broad lines:

1. Was X the account holder or had he opened it on behalf of the FLN under the terms of some agreement which the bank should have observed?
2. Given that the bank was not unaware that the money really belonged to the FLN, was it able to accept instructions from X?
3. Should the existence of a dispute between X and the owners of the money have led the bank, in blocking the assets, to oppose X's instructions?

Of course, in reaching its decision the federal court could only follow the function for which it exists and re-examine the decisions of the lower courts under a system very similar to that which the Algerian court of appeal would have used had it been competent to deal with the case.

An account opened by someone with full powers

Leaving aside the detailed events (X's signature in the contract as account holder, Y's subsequent instructions to Z on 8 June 1964 asking for the eventual freezing of 'X's assets') the contract for the opening of a bank account is incontestably subject to Swiss law (specified in one clause of the agreement and in accordance with legal customs). The federal court, following the cantonal court, excludes the possibility of a fiduciary agreement — non-existent in French law (on which Algerian law is based) and concludes that it is a question of 'direct representation'.*

Swiss law considers that in questions of representation the applicable law is that of the country where the representation takes place. In this case therefore it is Swiss law and article 32 of the civil code applies; in particular section 2 states:

If at the time a contract has been agreed the representative has not made himself known as such, the person represented cannot become a direct debtor or creditor except where the other party to the contract should have inferred from the circumstances that a representative relationship existed or where he is indifferent as to which of the two he is dealing with.

The law is quite clear and we have seen from the facts that there is no doubt about these points. If, on the other hand, X had exceeded his powers in his relationship with the FLN, that raises the question of Algerian law which the court had not refused to apply since it had accepted an action on behalf of the Republic of Algeria as the successor under Algerian law to the FLN.†

---

*The distinction is seemingly quite subtle in Swiss law and not even always clear to Swiss lawyers. Furthermore it is not likely that the existence of a fiduciary agreement would necessarily have changed anything.
†It should be noted that at the time when the transfer of rights took place under Algeria's internal laws, the Swiss government had already 'recognized' the new Algerian Republic (in the sense of international law). It is not certain that the outcome would have been the same under different circumstances and that the internal transfer would have been admitted.

Safe legal cover—a 'third party open account'

It is certainly far from clear that this legal cocktail (Algerian law applying to relationships between X and the FLN, Swiss law applying to relations between X and BCA, Swiss law applying to relations between BCA and the FLN and concluding that there was no relationship) was realized by the participants when the account was opened (unless X was particularly well advised . . .) but spurred on by events each of the actors in this political-financial game tried to remove the legal cover of banking secrecy. But in the end the fortune was hidden behind the legal device known in Swiss law as the 'third party open account' under which the person represented (the true owner of the money) had no rights against the bank.

Incorrect use of a third party open account

Any legal institution may be used for an abnormal purpose or be turned away from its intended use, and it is far from certain that when the account opened in X's name was transformed into account 'BP 510' that there was agreement between X and the FLN on its purpose.

When the conditions of article 32(2) of the civil code are not fulfilled, a legal right may still be established by a third party under the terms of article 32(3) if:

. . . an assignment of credit or acceptance of debt which conforms to the regulations controlling these instruments is necessary.

It is clear that no assignment of credit was made between X and the third party, quite the reverse since X changed the account into a numbered one and also asked that correspondence should no longer be sent to Algiers but should be held by the bank.

The question which then arises is to know whether the bank, which could have been unaware at that time of X's political differences, could or should have refused this transformation and whether by not doing so had engaged its own responsibility.

The answer is in the negative. X, enjoying full powers over these funds which belonged to someone else could, as far as Swiss law is concerned, use or change the account as he wished. The real problem arises during the 'suspect' period which starts from 12 June 1964, the date of the meeting between Z and an administrator from the BCA.

Incorrect use—of which the bank is aware—
of a third party open account by the representative

The purpose of this meeting was without doubt the verbal revocation of X's powers. But such a revocation cannot have any effect since under the terms of article 32(3) of the civil code an assignment of credit in favour of the popular

Democratic Republic of Algeria is necessary. One way of proceeding was possible—a civil or criminal sequestration order; both were used but the first order was not made until 6 July 1964 and in the meantime X, using his powers, had 'withdrawn' or had 'transferred to other numbered accounts' nearly all the money (the fact that the expert who had been opposed for so long by the bank was unable to reach a conclusion on this point is in the final analysis irrelevant if, following the argument of the Federal Court, X had full powers over these funds in his dealings with BCA).

It is worth noting that article 479 of the civil code says:

If a third party presents himself as the owner of something deposited, the person holding the deposit is not in any way less obliged to return it to the person who made the deposit, as long as no legal instrument has been lodged with the person holding the deposit or against the depositor.

It is curious that the Geneva cantonal court confirmed the decision of the first court and found against BCA while the federal court said the bank was 'not only able to return to X the disputed funds but was obliged to do so' and had not, in transferring the funds prior to the sequestration orders, contravened its contractual obligations.

*
* *

Any reader who has had the fortitude to follow the last chapter will easily concede (and it is the only thing 'easily' done in that analysis) the absence of any simplicity in the problems considered. It is particularly important for him to remember that the opening of a bank account is generally subject to the local laws where the bank is situated and that the interpretation of that local law, if it is not always clear to local practitioners, is even less so to foreign ones. It will always be in his interest to consult a local lawyer at the beginning and be prepared to learn that the operation planned is not legal—which is often the case.

What actually happened to the FLN 'fighting fund' whose legal disappearance was so well conceived? Many fantastic suggestions have been put forward. In fact the events must suggest that the money was used to buy shares in BCA. So, through the intervention of banking secrecy, the Algerian government was for a long time suing a bank which it was unaware that it owned. It must be an involuntary captive bank!

II
The Common Law Banking Infernos

Now that we have defined the concept of banking secrecy and examined the main methods by which it is used, and their difficulties, it would have been possible to proceed to a comparative examination of the advantages and disadvantages of the banking havens. However, given that banking havens are defined in practice by comparison with banking infernos, it is still necessary to take an overview of the principal infernos in order to understand the advantages of the havens.

Just as in the Christian religion the devil is actually a fallen angel, so it is that the principles and traditions of banking secrecy were born in what are now banking infernos which thanks to departures at the expense of the individual for the profit of the collective have purely and simply degenerated into infernos. Thus it would be impossible to understand banking secrecy in Jersey and Guernsey which have simply preserved Great Britain's statutes if one did not examine the evolution of secrecy in Great Britain. Similarly banking secrecy in the Cayman Islands would be practically meaningless without an examination of the conflicts with the United States that have given rise to the current position.

Finally, in the absence of more general works, some analysis of a certain number of the more important countries would appear to be useful in placing secrecy in its context. For this reason the countries examined follow an evolutionary order in an attempt to find an internal logic—which does not always exist, but which seems more logical than a purely alphabetical order. It has not seemed necessary in looking at infernos to follow a strict plan in relation to each country which would give a direct comparison of faults, but such a plan has been followed for havens. In the construction of a guide, comparative information is only important in terms of selection and it is difficult to imagine a good food guide, for example, taking the trouble to indicate as between two restaurants which it does not recommend that in the first the steak (or the hamburger) is very bad and in the second inedible. Comparisons of good taste can only be made with items of good taste.

In order to make things clearer, the second part examines the 'common law' infernos, that is those whose legal systems are based on the British one, even though, language apart, they have often preserved only that common tradition.

10 Great Britain:
A world celebrity for less than ten pounds

The principles of British Banking secrecy are summed up in a famous legal case: the 'Tournier case'* which began in April 1922 with a dishonoured cheque for £9 8s. 6d. The poor man, called Tournier, signed an agreement with the bank in which he undertook to pay back £1 a week, starting from when he began a new job, for a period of 3 months and in which he gave the address of his new employer. Unfortunately he failed to make one of his repayments and the manager of the bank telephoned his employer to advise him of this situation and beyond that implied that Tournier had issued some substantial cheques to bookmakers.

Anglo-Saxon morality does not take a lighthearted view of such matters and Tournier's employer declined to renew his contract of employment when this expired, because of the bank manager's comments. Tournier sued the bank, and by a series of miracles which could happen only in Great Britain, the banker and two directors of the employer company all admitted the substance of the conversation and the directors confirmed that this was the reason for the non-renewal of Tournier's contract—which proves that in Great Britain at least there are people in important positions who will admit their errors, which is very much to their credit and furthermore in this case has the additional merit of advancing jurisprudence, if not justice.

JURISPRUDENCE IS NOT NECESSARILY JUSTICE

Tournier's action was dismissed at the first hearing but on appeal the court accepted his case against the bank and in their decision set out the principles of British banking secrecy.

The Anglo-Saxon jurists do not appear capable of saying if in the end the courts examined the affair further, after ruling on the basic principle. In any event if poor Tournier did not finally obtain justice he did figure in British legal history for a cheque of less than £10—which after all is a fairly cheap way to achieve a place in posterity. It is true that thanks to the British system of jurisprudence one gains posterity quite easily—such as in the case of the Irishman called Doneghue who is known for having drunk a bottle of ginger ale. After drinking the bottle he found the remains of a decomposed snail in

---

*Tournier v. National Provincial and Union Bank of England, 1924 IKB 461.

the bottom of it (given the taste of ginger ale, no-one will be surprised that he did not notice before finishing the bottle); he took the case to court and was the object of a famous decision of principle through which British lawyers have to stumble while polishing their trousers (or kilts — Scotland which has discovered oil off its coast is looking for, without yet obtaining, its independence) on the seats of the law schools.

In general terms the Tournier decision distinguishes four classic cases in which the banker is 'relieved' of banking secrecy:
1. By order of the law.
2. Through duty to the public.
3. In the interests of the bank.
4. If the client's express or implicit permission has been given.*

Beyond certain peculiarities this classification is normal in countries which are not banking havens and the legal implications and extensions of it do not merit much attention. One may perhaps point out though that the British tax inspectors do not have a general right of examination and cannot seek more than the identities of the true owners of shares† (the use of nominees is allowed in British law and has even become an institution as far as trusts are concerned‡) and the owners of bank accounts which have received annual interest in excess of £15.§ It is also true that if the Inspector of taxes sees that the account holder is not a British resident, he immediately stops his enquiries and files his papers, in spite of all the splendid double tax agreements signed by Britain under which information is supposed to be exchanged. The pound must be supported, and has needed support for a long time.

However, this disposition does not apply (section 353-3) if the owner of shares is resident in a country whose double taxation agreement allows a reduction of the tax withheld at source. This custom is easily explained in terms of allowing the banker to justify himself if questions are put to him by the authorities about the loss of revenue they are suffering.

This limit on tax enquiries may appear surprising but it must not be forgotten that Great Britain has been until recently, after Algeria, the country with the highest direct taxation and also one which does not allow (and will not admit to, according to its system of thinking) any taxation according to external signs of wealth. This perhaps explains why, the United States and tax havens apart, Great Britain has, despite its incredible taxes, more Rolls Royces per square mile than any other country. It is true that one is also surprised to

---

*The judge who handed down this decision was called — with some form of predestination? — Bankes. It is the Anglo-Saxon practice for judges to give a personal opinion, including those with a dissenting opinion not in agreement with the majority view. This system is technically better than and certainly much more courageous than the decisions of anonymous groups and springs no doubt from the fact that the appointment as a judge is the crowning point of a successful career as a barrister, while in most Roman law countries the judges are only civil servants.
†Income Tax Act 1970, section 13 (which replaces section 103 of the 1918 Act).
‡See Chapter 6.
§Taxes Management Act 1970, section 17.

see as many new Mercedes coupés in circulation as one sees in a socialist country like Algeria, especially when that costs as much there as a Rolls Royce in London. In Algeria's case the reasons are different . . . .

UNUSUAL TRANSACTIONS

The protection given by British banking secrecy stops short at 'ordinary' banking transactions (section 414–5) and does not, for example, cover share dealings by a Bahamian company* and for 'unusual' transactions the manager of the British subsidiary of a Bermudan bank can even be asked to give the name and address for all the clients for whom he has acted 'in any way whatsoever and for any kind of transaction'†

This last decision requires some examination since it reveals on the one hand the absence of banking secrecy as regards transactions which may be categorized as 'unusual'; on the other hand it demonstrates a system which may be justified, but which in any event has been used in numerous countries with quite disparate kinds of legislative backgrounds to provide the same result. The defence has been accepted or rejected according to the country.

Take, for example, the following case:

Clinch performed the functions of London representative of the bank N. T. Butterfield and Son Ltd. from November 1964 to November 1970. The bank was based in Bermuda (although it should be noted that Bermuda is a high-ranking tax haven and financial centre, but *not* a banking haven).

Clinch had received a letter from the British tax authorities asking under article 481 of the Income and Corporation Taxes Act‡ for general information about his clients. The matter was disputed between Clinch's solicitors and the authorities, who finally withdrew their request on the basis that it was too general (apparently that would have been acceptable under Canadian law). The request was replaced by a more specific demand on 2 February 1972 which required that Clinch supplied certain information concerning transactions which he had carried out in London for clients resident in Britain. (Put this way the request would probably have been valid in US law.)

The double qualification of 'activity in London' and 'on behalf of clients resident in Britain' is still debatable as to the principle but makes the request seem much more reasonable as far as tax law is concerned. Furthermore the demand was limited to the transactions actually carried out by the bank and to the clients presented to the bank—or to any other person—in order that their transactions might be carried out; it excluded those who had merely been advised.

Doubtless it was for this reason that Clinch, being well advised, attacked the demand not on the basis of the principle or the extent but of the effects.

---

*Royal Bank of Canada *v*. IRC (1972); *CR* 699.
†Clinch *v*. IRC (1974); *QB* 76.
‡Compare with article 231-3 of the Canadian statute (see Chapter 12).

Clinch claimed that he had between 600 and 650 clients' files, 6000 abstracts, 17 minor files and 15 files of memoranda. In these circumstances he estimated that a reply would take not only 5 months to prepare (English law does not stipulate how long a delay is allowed, it only specifies that it shall be no less than 28 days) but to clear out the files he would need both an assistant and a secretary whose salaries would cost £1857 which he had no intention of paying himself.

The argument was strong. Even if Clinch had exaggerated the difficulties and the time needed, it was clear that a substantial amount of work and costs must result from it. Should he have to meet the costs himself when he was not the subject of the inquiry? That seemed unjust. On the other hand, to accept Clinch's argument would be to remove the practical application of a law which although open to question was nevertheless on the statute book, since it would allow anyone caught by it to offer a similar argument which the authorities would be unable to verify.*

THE INVESTIGATORS WILL NOT PAY THE BILLS

The British courts found in favour of the tax authorities, taking the view that it was not a 'fishing' expedition but rather a discreet surveillance and the right to silence would not apply to tax avoidance and even less so to tax evasion. The judge noted that the bank in Bermuda was based in a tax haven, but qualified that by remarking:

I do not use this term in a pejorative sense since any individual has the right to organize his affairs, if he can, in such a way that the tax resulting from the applicable regulations is less than it might otherwise have been.†

The judge's decision was that since Clinch carried out his activities in London‡ he could not ignore English law and even if his claims as to the amount of time and money necessary were well founded (which the judge refused to look into) Clinch should in the normal course of his activities have been prepared for such a request to be made and would have been able to save himself the work, time and money involved.

Furthermore the widest powers exist in the area of exchange control,

---

*This should be compared with a similar problem in France which concerned the customs officials (see Chapter 16).
†As far as one can see the judge in this ruling was referring to Lord Clyde's declaration in 1929: 'No man in this country is under the smallest obligation, moral or otherwise, to so arrange his affairs as to enable the Revenue to put the largest shovel into his stores' (see *Using Tax Havens Successfully*).
‡This detail is particularly important and should be compared with the 'Field affair' (between the United States and Cayman Islands — see Chapters 11 and 32). Presumably the English judge's decision would have been different if Clinch had been operating from Bermuda in the way that Field was working from the Caymans. It is normal, and generally accepted (by the Swiss banks in particular) that banking secrecy does not follow the laws applying at the bank's head office, but those where the bank is trading.

without limits in this case, and a banker may not claim any rights to banking secrecy in the face of the Treasury's rights.*

As far as the bank's interests are concerned—that is the circumstances where a banker may on his own account deny banking secrecy—one particular decision is worth noting since it has the particular merit of fixing one's ideas. This is the famous 'Sunderland affair' where Mrs Sunderland became relatively famous as a result of her charming lack of good faith.†

A WOMAN BEATEN BY THE HORSES

This honourable lady had a cheque payable to her tailor refused by Barclays Bank because there were no funds available in her account. She complained to her husband, telephoned the bank manager to complain to him and then passed the telephone to her husband to continue the conversation.

The bank manager explained that he was not in the habit of granting overdraft facilities on an account whose main use was to pay bookmakers. Mrs Sunderland was not pleased with this reply and sued the bank for breach of professional secrecy. The bank took the view that since Mrs Sunderland had passed the telephone to her husband it was reasonable to assume that her husband knew what the account was used for.

Is it necessary to remark that Mrs Sunderland received her comeuppance in a country where 'gentlemen' are reputed to love horses more than women?

---

*Exchange Control Act 1947, section 34 and schedule 5. The question has become of only secondary importance since October 1979 since, although the Exchange Control Act has not been repealed, controls have been withdrawn as far as individuals are concerned.
†Sunderland v. Barclays Bank Ltd. (1938), *The Law and Practice of Banking*, by J. Milnes Holden; *The Times* 24–25 November.

11 The United States: Justice worthy of the name

In the United States it is not unusual for someone to reveal his annual income after only a few minutes conversation, so that his status may be properly grasped; clearly, therefore, the concept and extent of banking secrecy in such a country will not have exactly the same meaning and importance as in other countries where it is not unusual, after 30 years of close friendship, to be quite ignorant of the income of someone who has been a friend from childhood and with whom one's worst youthful follies have been carried out.

And as unlikely as that might seem in a country which thrives on legal tomes (often quite amazing ones at that) and which has a greater number of bank accounts than any other country,* there does not appear to exist a single book which deals specifically with the question of banking secrecy. More than that, the majority of the major works and encyclopedias of both law and banking appear to ignore the question, which is itself significant. It is of course true on the other hand that an American jurist would be amazed at the extreme lack of literature available in Europe on the question of racial integration; whereas the bibliography alone of the books and articles on this subject on the United States would fill several volumes the same size as this one.

FROM BANKING TO BIGAMY

Banking secrecy does nonetheless exist in the United States—it is afforded twenty lines in volume 10 of the *American Jurisprudence* encyclopedia between 'bank' and 'bigamy'; and then it is not about the protection of the banker, but about his responsibilities in the event that false information is given about the solvency of a client to an interested third party. In that case it concludes that the banker has no liability because he is not providing a service for a reward but rather one which is a matter of courtesy only, since depositors and bank clients are in the habit of directing potential business partners to their bank for information as to their creditworthiness.

Given that an American banker is therefore required to play the role of a public relations man on behalf of his client, it would be difficult to complain that he lacked the necessary reserve when the essential quality of a good public relations man is to put across information.

---

*There were 106 819 465 accounts in being on 30 June 1975.

PUBLIC RELATIONS, YES—BUT ON WHOSE BEHALF?

It is exactly in the situation where a banker had not been sufficiently eulogistic about his client that the concept of responsibility appeared close to the Tournier case in Britain; the American judges said that it was unacceptable that a bank should under any circumstances whatsoever afford itself the liberty of supplying personal details about its clients' accounts. An unbreakable secrecy is one of the fundamental principles inherent in the relationship between a bank and its depositors or clients.*

If, however, the American banker has to be a good public relations man, can one complain at public relations towards the IRS[†]? This question seems to occupy the minds of American jurists rather more, perhaps because a certain number of their clients must be playing the 'April game'.[‡]

APRIL FOOL'S DAY JOKE

Curiously it is on the American banks—on the basis that it is the price of true democracy—that are laid the most rigorous administrative constraints existing in the western world, despite the banking secrecy finally recognized in the Bank Secrecy Act of 1970. However the object of this Act was not the sanctification of banking secrecy, but the creation of a requirement for the preservation of bank files, because according to the introduction an effective fight against crime depends to a large extent upon the preservation and ease of access to details of transactions carried out by financial institutions. It should be understood that by administrative constraints we are not here referring to the red tape used by the Bank of England (despite the motto on its headquarters —Men not measures) and the central banks of the continental countries, but to real obligations, precisely defined and understood as such. In the absence of exchange controls in the United States, in the strict sense of the term, there is a statistical control over certain operations which weighs heavily on the banks and is not without fiscal implications. Any banking transaction with a foreign country having a total value greater than $10 000 and any transfer exceeding $5000 must be notified to a Commissioner of the Internal Revenue, that is to a tax official.§ This minor requirement which seems of secondary importance to anyone living in a country where prior approval from the exchange control authorities is required to pay for even so much as a peanut overseas, is nonetheless resented as a constraint by the Americans.

One of the oddest aspects of the absence of exchange control is that any US

---

*Peterson v. Idaho First National Bank.
†Internal Revenue Service, in other words, the US tax authorities.
‡The US taxpayer is required to send to the IRS by 15 April each year an income declaration which, in the absence of flat rate allowances, allows the taxpayer (including those in paid employment) to deduct certain actual expenses (medical, educational etc.). A number of taxpayers deduct fictitious expenses, gambling that their return will not be picked out by the IRS computer. This is called the 'April game'.
§Subsection B of the law of 26 October 1970 (84.Stat.1114).

taxpayer must append a special form to his annual income declaration if he has had at his disposal outside the United States one or more accounts of any type whatsoever with a total value in excess of the equivalent of $10 000 during the tax year. This obligation applies even if the taxpayer is not himself the owner of the funds but simply a signatory, for example. In that case he must indicate the name, address and tax number of the owner, except where this is not an American, in which case it is sufficient to say that no US citizen has an interest in these overseas accounts. Similar obligations apply to legal entities, depending upon the proportion of shares and voting rights belonging to US citizens. Needless to say details of the name and address of the bank and level of magnitude of the account have to be provided. It is worth noting that the fact of failing to provide this information, or of filing incorrect information, is considered to be a tax evasion even if the assets in question would not have been subject to any tax.

Of course this constraint is a long way from the result of the 1970 Bank Secrecy Act which allows the IRS to obtain copies of microfilms representing transactions carried out by taxpayers, about which the taxpayer remains in ignorance and which the bank is required to have available. It was precisely this aspect of the law which was attacked by American taxpayers on the grounds that it was an invasion of privacy in violation of the Fourth Amendment to the constitution. This argument, rejected by the Supreme Court,* was followed by several federal courts in certain of which it was even stated that in making his transactions known to a third party (the banker) a bank client was supposed to have run the risk that such information would be transmitted to the government.†

Little understood by the Americans, the procedure was known—without ever going so far as to reach the impudence of an administrative summons‡— as a 'John Doe' summons, that is a 'M Dupont' summons, John Doe being to the Americans what Smith is to the English, Dupont to the French and Muller to the Swiss. Despite the American feminist leagues the masculine sense has precedence at the IRS and the summons is known as John Doe and not Jane Doe, or indeed John and Jane Doe.

THE SUMMONSING OF AN AMERICAN MR DUPONT

According to fiscal law the IRS has the power during an enquiry to determine the tax due from an individual to examine all books, papers, files and other documents which might be useful to or necessary for the investigation. This power includes, from February 1977, that of summonsing anyone (lawyer, accountant, banker etc.) who possesses or has in their charge files relative to

---

*United States v. Miller, 98 S.Ct. 1619 (1976).
†Katz v. United States, 389 US 347, 353 (1967).
‡Section 1205 of the law and 7609 and 7610 of the Code.

the individual, and examining them under oath.* However, when the IRS consider that certain transactions have been effected which might have a bearing on the taxation of one or more people, the administration can sign a 'John Doe' summons to be used when the name of the potential taxpayer is unknown. The courts may only authorize the IRS to do this on the understanding that the following three conditions are fulfilled:

1. The summons must relate to research into one person or a group of people.
2. There are good grounds for believing that the person or group of people have not complied with the tax laws.
3. The information required is not available through any other means.

These conditions were imposed by Congress so that the IRS should not use their power to go on 'fishing expeditions' but only under judicial scrutiny in pursuit of a known situation and known facts. For this reason if the IRS wishes to know the name of a person using a numbered account — or any other kind of account designed to hide the owner's identity — it is not obliged to use the 'John Doe' procedure but needs only to know the beneficial owner.

In fact the main battles fought by the IRS have not arisen internally within the United States but as regards foreign countries which have a tradition of bank secrecy (Switzerland) or have created bank secrecy at the expense of the United States (Bahamas, Cayman Islands). The state of mind of the American authorities was exacerbated by the pressures of a sort of anti-banking secrecy MacCarthyism which reached its heights between about 1968 and 1977 and blamed banking secrecy for all the ills in creation.

This state of mind is perfectly demonstrated by the report of a House Committee on Banking and Currency which is worth its weight in exaggeration:

The financial institutions and the secret foreign bank accounts have permitted a proliferation of 'white-collar' crimes; they have been used as financial vehicles by criminal organizations in the US; they have been used by Americans to evade taxes, cause assets to disappear and to buy gold; they have permitted Americans and foreigners to break the laws and regulations of the stock exchanges and commerce; they have served as essential mechanisms in fraud, often against the State; they have been used as the final resting place of profits from the black market in Vietnam; they have acted as a dubious source of finance for amalgamations, share purchases and takeovers; they have permitted manoeuvres designed to turn aside funds intended for defence and overseas aid; and they have served to launder money which is 'hot' or has been obtained illegally.

Such a list of crimes makes you think rather more of scapegoats than bank secrecy, perhaps. But it enables one to understand more easily the passion of the American courts in the Field case on the subject of bank secrecy in the Cayman Islands (see Chapter 32) and the obligation laid by the court on this

---

*A false declaration under oath is very serious in the United States and if someone refuses to take an oath the IRS can oblige them to do so.

bank employee to be a witness, despite the fact that doing so in the United States constituted an infraction of law in the Cayman Islands where he worked and lived, and that he was in any event a Canadian.

A CASTLE AND A BANK

It is worth remembering that Field was cited as a witness during a visit to Miami, Florida and was to be questioned as to deposits made by US citizens with the Castle Bank of Grand Cayman (and the case was extended to include the Castle Bank in the Bahamas).

Field refused to testify and defended himself with the Fifth Amendment of the American constitution, on the grounds that under the terms of Cayman law if he testified he ran the risk of a 6-month prison sentence in the Cayman Islands where he both worked and lived, and pointed out that he was in any event a Canadian and not a US citizen.

This argument was not upheld* on the grounds that the Fifth Amendment had been consistently interpreted as meaning that a person was not obliged to testify if his testimony might show that he had committed a crime and that his testimony might be used against him in a subsequent prosecution.† Such a conflict is easy to understand, but in any event is well summarized in Judge Morgan's opinion given in the same verdict which said that:

> The first and most important factor to be considered is the interest of the States in the case . . . in this case the United States need information about violations of their fiscal statutes. On the other hand the Cayman Isles need to protect the right to bank secrecy established by their banking legislation. It derives, unfortunately, from the position of the Cayman Isles government that any testimony about the bank will constitute a violation of its statutes. The result is that either the interest of the United States or that of the Cayman Isles must be sacrificed.

UNITED STATES v. NIXON

Could it have been otherwise in a democracy which at the height of its system does not even spare its President?

Criminal justice would be without object if decisions were made on a partial or imaginative presentation of the facts. The integrity itself of the judicial system and the public's confidence in it depend upon the laying bare of all facts within the framework of the system for the administration of proof.‡ In the fight between the greatest democracy in the world and some small Caribbean islands, the stronger hand despite all the evidence was not that of the United States, and the Cayman Islands did not react by giving way, but by strengthening its bank secrecy laws. Is this worth further examination?

---

*Decision 76-1739 of the Court of Appeal Fifth Circuit, on the appeal by Field against the decision of the South Florida District Court.
†Counselman v. Hitchcock 142 US 547 563 (1892) and more recently Couch v. United States 409 US 322 327 (1973).
‡United States v. Nixon 418 US 683 709 (1974).

12 Canada:
Forests without secrets

A former British colony, independent since 1931, Canada is predominantly Anglo-Saxon and a federation. It is therefore not surprising that banking secrecy follows the principles stemming from British common law. This was precisely the view taken by the Ontario High Court of Justice in 1939 which issued the following ruling:

> The protection given to documents in the bank's possession seems to find its origins not in an express provision of the banking laws but in an implicit contract; Tournier v. National Provincial and Union Bank of England . . .*

This origin is also confirmed by the Canadian Banker's Association which says: 'the relations between a banker and his client in Canada are subject to common law'† and follow the doctrine which considers that banking secrecy is 'an implicit part of the contract between the banker and his client'‡ and furthermore saying 'it has been established for a long time that a bank is required to keep secret the affairs of its clients.§

With such a background based on the confirmation in Canadian law of the Tournier decision and the British tradition of secrecy, Canada could, like other common law countries which have not lowered their standards in the judicial sense, have become a haven of banking secrecy of the highest order.

It was not to be, and the principle of secrecy was totally set aside as far as tax is concerned by statutory requirements and to this day article 231-3 of the income tax act states:

> For any purpose connected with the application or execution of this act, the minister‖ may, by registered letter or by a demand communicated to an individual, require from any person:
> (a) any information or any additional information, including an income tax return or a supplementary return, or
> (b) the disclosure, or disclosure under oath, of any books, letters, accounts, invoices,

---

*Kaufman v. McMillan, 9 July 1939, Dominion Tax Cases 499-46 (234).
†The Canadian Bankers' Association, PO Box 282, Toronto (letter of 1 November 1977).
‡Falconbridge: *Banking and Bills of Exchange*, 7th edition, page 291.
§J. Milnes Holden, *The Law and Practice of Banking*, Pitman, Volume I, pages 63-64.
‖The revenue minister who is an administrator rather than a political minister.

statements (financial or otherwise) or other documents, within a reasonable time—which may be stipulated.*

In parallel to this and also as far as concerns exchange controls, the Treasury may require a banker to provide all information known to him, or under his control, in order to ensure the application of the law or to detect evasion.†

Given such blanket legislation it is inevitable that disputes should arise as to its interpretation, particularly in respect of the extent of its boundaries. This is particularly the case in as far as it had already been adjudged that a bank was required, on the simple request of the Commissioner of Inland Revenue, to prepare and file a list giving the name and address of everyone for whose account the bank had received revenue relating to certain categories of shares registered in the name of the bank or one of its 'nominees' or held by the bank as trustee or as security or simply at the request of the beneficial owner.‡

CANADIAN SNOW VERSUS SWISS SNOW

The first major conflict of principle arose between the Attorney General of Canada and the Canadian Bank of Commerce, concerning one of the latter's clients: the Union Bank of Switzerland.

Under Anglo-Saxon procedures it falls to someone who is the subject of a subpeona to challenge the summons. In the Canadian procedure therefore, a banker wishing to oppose an investigation by the tax authorities contests the basis of the investigation and its extent. The authorities demand that they should be given (under the terms of article 126-2, now 231-3) all the files relating to transactions between the Canadian Bank of Commerce and its client the Union Bank of Switzerland for a given period. The Canadian bank took the matter to the courts on the one hand to seek for the affair to be adjudged as improperly based and on the other hand to be released from any liability to be fined for not obeying the summons. It seems from the judgments and statutes examined that the action was brought as a test case—that is a case based not so much on the desire to frustrate the authorities in this individual demand but rather to establish a legal position which would determine the future interpretation of the statutes, a 'precedent' the existence of which is fundamental to common law.

---

*This is the text of the current Income Tax Act, Chapter XV, article 231-3 SRC 1970-71-72; it repeats the text of the earlier statute (Chapter 148, article 126-2, SRC 1952) which was itself derived from a 1918 Income Tax Act.
†Subsection 34 of the 1947 Exchange Control Act.
‡Attorney General v. National Provincial Bank Ltd., 44 TLR 701 (1928). This decision was made under the terms of article 103 of the 1918 Act (see first note above).

LEGAL DECISIONS AND THE LAW OF GRAVITY

In common law systems judges' rulings are particularly important because in principle they would bind judges in future cases which dealt with the same facts. One may also say, to paraphrase Guizot (a French politician), that just like injuries they follow the law of gravity—they are most serious if they come down from a great height. In systems of jurisprudence which do not follow common law, magistrates are not bound by decisions of superior courts—it is true that they make their decisions without attribution!

The application of physical laws to judicial processes results in procedures whose essential features include neither simplicity nor speed. In the Canadian Bank of Commerce case, the Ontario court decided in favour of a 'strict' interpretation of the law:

It is a fundamental rule of interpretation that when a passage in an act requires interpretation, the ordinary and normal sense of the words should be used, even if the result of doing so would appear to be severe, arbitrary, oppressive or even contrary to an established legal rule.

Article 126-2 is clear and unambiguous and may be summarized as follows: 'the minister may, for *any* purpose connected with the application or execution of this act, require *any* individual, *any* information and so on.*

The Canadian Bank of Commerce appealed against the decision but on 13 December 1961 the Ontario Court of Appeal handed down a judgement† confirming the earlier decision, although with one dissenting view.‡

THE GOLDEN RULE

The appeal court's confirmation was based on what it called the 'golden rule' of Lord Wensleydale, which states that words should be taken in their common and grammatical meaning unless absurdity, misunderstanding or incongruity reach a level which convinces the court that the intention could not have been to use the words in their ordinary sense. The golden rule had already been relied upon in a precedent set by Judge Anglin.§

It is interesting to think that with one vote going the other way Canada could have become a banking haven for non-residents in the same way as other common law havens. The judge who gave the dissenting opinion considered that article 126-2 did not apply because the Union Bank of Switzerland was not a Canadian resident for tax purposes and was therefore under Canadian tax rules only taxable on the proportion of its income which may reasonably be deemed to have arisen from its activities conducted in Canada or business

---

*Court Decisions 61 *DTC* (Dominion Tax Cases) 1265 (author's italics).
†Court Decisions 62 *DTC* 1014.
‡A dissenting opinion is one given as a personal opinion by one of the judges sitting in the case.
§Price Bros and Co., and the Board of Commerce of Canada (1919-20) 60 *SRC* 256.

transacted there, and the authorities were not seeking proof of the proper application of that rule.

FISHING FOR TAXPAYERS

The dissenting judge decided therefore that the affair amounted to a 'fishing expedition' by the tax authorities, which was not legal. Although, had this opinion prevailed in the Appeal Court, the Canadian Attorney General would not have failed to lodge a further appeal. In fact an appeal was made by the Canadian Bank of Commerce but the Canadian Supreme Court gave a confirmation, pure and simple, of the Appeal Court's decision on 25 June 1962.*

WALL STREET IS NOT A WALL BETWEEN THE SNOW AND THE PALM TREES

The action over article 126-2, already by then article 231-3, was extended to a Canadian Bank normally subject to US jurisdiction. The New York branch of the Royal Bank of Canada was obliged to hand over the papers concerning a transaction carried out in New York between a Canadian resident and some Bahamian companies.† The fears expressed by Mr Westwood about foreign banks based in the British Virgin Islands (see Chapter 26), of which one of the most important is a Canadian bank, are far from owing their origins to simple pessimism.

Such generosity with information might lead one to wonder whether it did not include international fiscal help, with which Canada is not mean because of its many treaties designed to avoid double taxation. The text of article 231-3 does after all say it is for 'the application and execution of this act'.

This question has not yet been dealt with by the courts, although the Canadian tax authorities have let it be known that they might be prepared to exercise their prerogatives whether or not Canadian taxation was at stake. This occurred in a dispute in the United States with the Bank of Tokyo which concerned similar provisions in the IRS Code. Canada indicated that it might be prepared to effect an exchange of information in this case.‡

---

*Court Decision G2 *DTC* 1236.
†In the court's favour it should perhaps be noted that it is not unlikely that the US courts would have reached the same decision on the case, if it had been tried according to New York state law.
‡See *The Reach for Information*, a report prepared by David C. Nathanson for a conference organized in 1978 by the Canadian Tax Foundation.

13 South Africa:
A black future for bank secrecy

South Africa is the main white country in black Africa—this curious situation is true both as far as economics are concerned (everyone knows it) and as far as history is concerned (fewer people know it and nearly all pretend not to). The country was cultivated originally by Dutch colonists, the Boers, well before the arrival of the first black Africans. The cultivation of the land has made it one of the richest countries in the world and certainly the richest in Africa; the black Africans there, despite apartheid, have a higher standard of living than any other Africans. The British, after a bloody war (in the course of which they invented concentration camps), took common law there in their army boots, although it was accepted only on tiptoe! If the general principle of banking secrecy seems to have been more or less accepted, when it comes to exceptions to the rule the outlook is sombre.

BANK SECRECY GOING BACK TO ABRAHAMS

Amongst the major countries with an Anglo-Saxon tradition, South Africa is the exception to the rule of acknowledging the existence of the principle of banking secrecy and accepting without debate the legal precedent of the Tournier case (see Chapter 10). In 1904, foreseeing the future a South African author wrote that a book on South African banking law would probably be no more than a restatement of an English book.*

The first and only court ruling relating to bank secrecy goes back to Abrahams;† the irritating part of it is that Abrahams existed in 1914 but the decision had no element of presentiment in it. In this case Abrahams was attacking not the bank but an employee of the bank named Burns. Justice Searle who heard the case gave the opinion that he was inclined to think that the bank was responsible for making good the actual damage caused to the client if the state of his account had been disclosed without sufficient reason. The same judge was explicit in pointing out that he did not wish to examine the question of whether the banker was bound by any obligation to observe secrecy.

This decision is 'the only South African court ruling in the area' according

---

*George T. Morice, 'The law of banking in South Africa', *South African Journal*, 1904.
†Abrahams v. Burns 1914, CPC 452.

to L. C. Mather and D. B. Knight, themselves the authors of the only published work in South Africa which mentions bank secrecy.*

Although the decision in the Tournier case has not actually been taken up in South African jurisprudence, general opinion holds that the case is notwithstanding the source of a legal obligation to observe secrecy, but not having the strength of precedent within the common law system. In particular this is confirmed by Mazaham who says: 'When South African law is silent on a point of practical banking law, the courts would not hesitate to apply English law'.† The points clearly established within South African jurisprudence are that if the secrecy of an individual's bank account has been violated, that person may take action against either the employee or the banker where they have been negligent. However, there is an important distinction between English law and South African law in as far as the plaintiff must be able to show that he has suffered actual damage, as a South African court would not be able to offer nominal damages.‡

South Africa has instituted a very strict exchange control in order to limit the export of capital by its residents as a precaution against the black problem —a measure which has only increased the flight of capital. But of course bank secrecy disappears under these conditions and article 19-1 of the regulations for the control of exchange transactions states that:

The Treasury or any person authorized by the Treasury may require any individual to make information available to anyone whom the Treasury or anyone authorized by the Treasury considers necessary for the application of these regulations; and any person with either general or specific authority for this purpose may enter the home or places of work of anyone who has been specified and examine any books and documents belonging to him or under his control.

This text extends so wide in terms of powers conferred on Treasury agents that it needs to be read several times in order to understand its meaning, but in the end this becomes quite clear and may be summed up as: 'What the Treasury requires, so also does Heaven'. The only limitation is that Treasury agents are themselves subject to professional secrecy, except towards the Treasury in the execution of their duties, and the courts—and any other conflicting laws.§ As far as tax matters are concerned, the South African is also preserved from bank secrecy by a strict 'apartheid' since the Secretary for Inland Revenue may require anyone‖ to produce any books, accounts or documents in order to obtain complete information relating to all income acquired by a taxpayer.☆ And more than that, the same statute includes the possibility of questioning anyone under oath, with penalties for obstruction.

---

*L. C. Mather and D. B. Knight 'The law of banker and customer in South Africa'.
†Mazaham 'Bank secrecy in South Africa' (opinion).
‡Pharrel S. Wener 'Principle of banking secrecy'.
§Article 20 of act no. 29, 1914 on the Reserve Bank.
‖South African lawyers seem to think that it is self-evident that this must include banks.
☆Article 14 modified by act no. 58 on income tax, 1962.

Most generously, this same piece of legislation stipulates that tax inspectors are obliged to observe professional secrecy—but this does not hold good towards officials of a foreign tax service with which South Africa has a treaty.

SOUTH AFRICAN AND
CANADIAN INTERPRETATION COMPARED

A number of tax treaties make provision for the exchange of information 'at the disposal' of the country's tax authorities. South African jurists take the view that the country's tax authorities would be exceeding its rights if it were to seek information through existing tax statutes for a foreign tax authority. The existing statutes apply in their normal context to the income of South Africans and not therefore to that of non-residents—which is exactly the reverse of the position taken by the Canadian administration in a similar situation (see Chapter 12). But it is true that the South African view was expressed by lawyers who are also taxpayers, and not by the tax authorities. One thing may be a guide to another before the courts of the countries have ever actually given a decision on the subject.

14 Australia:
A country which goes beyond reasonable bounds

Australia was also a recipient of common law, and the principle of the Tournier case is admitted as a basic rule so that it can be broken the more effectively by the tax legislation and court decisions as time goes by. Australia has very tough exchange controls (see Chapter 35 on Vanuatu) and is not any more relaxed in its approach to bank secrecy when it comes to fiscal matters. The Commissioner of Taxation has very wide powers to require any person, taxpayer or not, to give him whatever evidence he may require, or to appear before him or any official nominated for this purpose, to give information about his/her own income tax return, or that of another person, and to produce any books, documents or any other papers whatsoever in his/her keeping or under his/her control.*

BEYOND REASONABLE BOUNDS

It is perhaps not without justification that Anglo-Saxon lawyers who are accustomed to some rather crude legislation consider that the Australians go beyond the limits of Anglo-Saxon 'fair play'. In fact, the tax commissioner may require that the information or proof offered should be given under oath, either verbally or by affidavit and for these purposes the official nominated by the Commissioner can administer the oath. For the professional adviser who has already had such dealings the procedure is not without interest, since one must take the oath standing up in front of a tax inspector, with one's hand on a bible held by the inspector.

That would perhaps be an interesting idea to use in Italy—the clergy would certainly find their counterpart in the confessional. The Italian inspectors and taxpayers may perhaps lack the same sense of fair play, but they certainly have an excellent sense of the ridiculous.

Clearly with such statutes and principles, the brakes applied in the courts need to be examined closely.

AN OATH ON THE BIBLE BUT LIES ON PAPER

In one decision the courts ruled that a banker's diary is an ordinary book of

---

*Article 264 of the Income Tax Act.

the bank's (and thus a banking document in the sense of an account book) and should therefore be produced to the court.*

After such a decision an ordinary lawyer might have considered it impossible to do better. But that was not the opinion of a tax inspector who asked that the diary of a bank branch should be brought in evidence in order to prove the acquisition of a property by the taxpayer, a client of the bank. It was suggested that the client had discussed the price with the banker and the details of the conversation had been noted in his diary. The bank's client opposed the tax commissioner on the grounds that the conversation had not taken place and that the diary was not admissible in evidence.†

The court took the view that the diary came within the definition of 'bank books' but that 'any notes of any sort made by a banker in whatever books he might use in the normal course of business are only admissible as proof of the truth of the notes'.‡ Which leads one to believe that in Australia one must swear on the bible but anything written need not be true.

THE KANGAROO POUCHES OF THE AUSTRALIAN BANKS HOLD NO SECRETS WHEN THERE ARE DUPLICATE KEYS

Another interesting point in Australian precedent, and one which has not been brought up in any other country, is the question of duplicate keys to safe deposits held by the bank. Generally access to safe deposit boxes is restricted to two keys both of which are needed to open the box and must be used simultaneously. One key belongs to the bank and the other is given to the person who is renting the box. The disadvantage of the system is that if the client loses the key the box has to be forced, which is an expensive exercise. In order to avoid this problem some banks have developed the practice of retaining, with their client's consent, a duplicate of his key while at the same time entering into an agreement not to use the key.

So the problem was put to the High Court in Australia—could the fiscal authorities require a bank to open one or more boxes with their duplicate keys despite the bank's contractual obligation *not* to use the key? The Court took the view that the obligations imposed by statute§ were greater than those imposed by contract, and the bank should use its duplicate keys if a statutory demand was made to do so.‖ The lesson here is—never leave duplicate keys around!

---

*Revenue *v.* William Bacon and Co. Ltd. *NZLR 228 (1969) (New Zealand)*.
†This defence would seem to suggest that the conversation took place and was compromising, which does not seem to be admitted by the Australian lawyers. (In the same way French lawyers are silent on the subject of the report made by a consulting engineer in a customs matter, although this is commented upon by Anglo-Saxon lawyers—perhaps it is easier to talk about one's neighbours than oneself.)
‡L. G. Batten Pty. Ltd., *QW 2* (1962) (Queensland).
§Article 264-1 of the Income Tax Act.
‖Smargon and others *v.* Federal Commissioner of Taxes and others 79, *ATC* 4039 (Australian Federal Tax Reporter: Full High Court of 13 March 1979).

III

The Roman Law Infernos

An overview of the common law banking infernos in Part II has demonstrated how the majority of major countries which use the Anglo-Saxon legal system have 'degenerated' in terms of the protection of the individual expressed by banking secrecy in the face of public authority.

The object of Part III is to show the same phenomenon in the countries which use Roman law. The expression 'Roman law' is not entirely correct and in some cases strains the classification. It is however useful to make the distinction between those countries using a legal code which is entirely reduced to paper and the Anglo-Saxon system based on precedent.

The Roman law countries are much less uniform in their arrangements. In fact the major differences between them and the common law countries is that their regulations may be similar, but they lack a common source.

Certain of the countries which are here classified as infernos might just possibly, like Portugal, have been considered as havens — but any guide implies that a choice has been made and there are false havens which are in fact infernos.

15 The Federal Republic of Germany: The right of might

The Federal Republic does not have any specific laws in the area of banking secrecy (*Bankgeheimnis*) and secrecy derives from the contractual relationship between the banker and his client. However, the principle of secrecy is recognized in law and confirmed by the people whose responsibility it is to control the activities of banking establishments, in particular on behalf of the Federal Bank (*Deutsche Bundesbank*).*

TRUTH ON THIS SIDE OF THE RHINE

The Federal Republic (or West Germany as it is usually called) does not, unlike France, use its customs officials as the means through which it makes a breach in the walls of banking secrecy. In fact there is no exchange control in the strict sense of the term in West Germany, where liberal good sense has triumphed. It is therefore only in the fiscal areas that the major attacks are made on secrecy and in this area as in others, the analysis given by the German lawyers is clear and well organized†which is no doubt due to the mixture of influences found in German law.‡

As a result of this situation the German tax authorities, in the same way as the American authorities, request information from taxpayers which in other countries would be forthcoming through exchange control procedures — either through prior application, or customs officials (France) or from a specialist force of financial investigators (Italy). It is through their tax declaration that details of the creation of overseas businesses or the purchase of overseas interests or shares which comply with certain conditions§ should be disclosed.

---

*According to Swedish lawyers the principle of banking secrecy in Germany is very old and goes back to a law of 1619 which created the Hamburg exchange bank. Article 6 of the statute stated: If anyone asks questions about any other person, the bookkeeper should provide no information whatsoever.

†A major part of the subject matter of this chapter is taken from the brilliant report of Mr Obermuller at a seminar on 'Banking secrecy and its limits' which took place at Basle on 4/5 May 1979.

‡It is possible to suggest that modern German lawyers (who have successfully imitated their American colleagues) make use in an apparently happy symbiosis of both Latin cartesianism (while leaving aside its exaggerations) and the practical law of the Anglo-Saxons. Such a view would of course upset the legal historians — but that is not too important given that they have no contact with the world of business.

§Article 138-2, AO (*Abgabenordnung* — income tax act).

More than that, the German taxpayer has an obligation to explain his business interests overseas and give the authorities all necessary information and provides the corresponding evidence.* Details of overseas partners must be provided and, specifically, what means are used for these activities — indirect (screening company in the middle) or direct.†

It is perhaps because of these heavy obligations weighing on the German taxpayer that the fiscal statutes, banking secrecy aside, are relatively moderate in approach and imply confidence in the taxpayer. There are no 'John Doe' provisions (see Chapter 11 on the United States), and no fishing expeditions (see the different chapters in Part II under common law and also Chapter 16 on France) — or at least not legal ones!

POWERS AND LIMITATIONS

The Fiscal Code exempts from testimony a whole series of people (doctors, lawyers etc.) but not bankers, who are therefore amongst those not protected by professional secrecy, 'which does not mean that they are necessarily obliged to answer all questions put to them'.‡

The Fiscal Code provides two investigation procedures which depend upon whether the object is the determination of the level and composition of the tax (*Besteuerungsverfahren* — assessment procedure) by way of an adjustment or whether it is to detect an evasion (*Steuerfahndung*). In the former the investigation is carried out by the financial authorities (*Finanzbehorden*) and in the latter by a special service set up to investigate tax frauds (*Steuerfahndung*). In either case the authorities have the power to demand and obtain information from third parties, to require disclosure of documents, to visit places of work and to carry out searches.§ However, when there is no evasion involved, the authorities are first required to deal with the taxpayer and any inquiry can only be on a specific point within a short time. Finally, within this kind of enquiry the information requested should meet with several conditions: (1) it must be necessary (the information otherwise not available); (2) it must be in proportion (the demands must not be exaggerated); (3) it must be equitable (it should not involve too great an amount of work or expense for the banker). Within this procedure for correcting erroneous returns, the banker should inform his client immediately of the request made so that the client has the possibility of putting forward a revised return and retaining the benefit of good faith.‖

---

*Article 90-2, AO.
†Article 16-1 *Aussensteurergesetz* — overseas taxes, 8 September 1972.
‡Obermuller, cited above.
§Articles 93-99, AO.
‖This kind of procedure seems restricted, if not to German citizens, then to German residents. A local bank is required — when requested by the German tax authorities, in their turn honouring a request from overseas authorities — to provide the name and address of clients for whom they have acted (this derives from a ruling on a request made by the Swedish authorities to which the superior fiscal court acceded although an adverse judgment had been given in a lower court) (*Bundesfinanzhof, Uorteil vom 20 Februar, 1979*, VII R 16/79: *Der Betrieb*, 8 June 1979).

One should also add to these procedures the possibiliity of a penal case which may be brought by the public prosecutor. Banking secrecy may not be preserved against a court demand and the banker may be called on as a witness (in fact this is often done in writing).

THE JUDICIAL AND FISCAL *'ANSCHLUSS'* OF 1977

In October 1977, following on the publication of a new income tax law, a dozen inspectors entered the Hamburg branch of a bank and seized and took away practically all the documents concerning several categories of accounts (while the practice in the case of tax evasion is that the bank itself looks out documents required and provides photocopies). Such an action without a tax evasion case would be illegal, but the items taken enabled the authorities to discover evasion which they could prosecute, so the *Landgericht* at Hamburg before which the bank brought a case, took the view that as the search had taken place it could no longer be opposed and that the seizure of documents was justified retrospectively by the fact that it had enabled evasion to be detected.*

This was a very sad piece of reasoning which hardly resounds to the credit of the judges who produced it.† A rather more attractive man is the judge from Ohio (see Chapter 31 on the Bahamas) who refused to prosecute an American taxpayer on the basis of documents obtained illegally by the US treasury!

---

*L. G. Hamburg, *NWJ* 1978, 958.
†The Roman/Anglo-Saxon symbiosis in this instance looks rather like a hydra-headed monster and awakens unpleasant memories of German legality.

16 France:
From cash under the mattress to cash vouchers

The majority of French lawyers with an interest in banking law have debated for a long time, and in a manner suitable for a debate similar to that as to the sex of angels, whether a banker's client is protected as far as secrecy is concerned by article 378 of the Penal Code which makes provision for professional secrecy for the benefit of the repositories of 'secrets'. Although the French banker does not appear on the list of 'necessary' repositories, these lawyers believe that apart from civil penalties, criminal ones apply to any banker who violates professional secrecy.

The question is no doubt of great interest in terms of pure law, if the clients do not take into consideration the fact that not only is it one of the countries in which banking secrecy exists the least, but also that the French banker is turned into a professional informer by his legal obligations.

OBLIGED BY THE LAW TO BE INFORMERS

It is doubtless not through their easygoing temperament that French bankers have arrived in this situation. Comparative research shows in effect that in most democratic countries jurisprudence relating to banking secrecy has been composed in part of 'historic' decisions made in cases where a banker has failed to protect his client sufficiently against a third party or against the public authorities.

A foreign lawyer approaching French jurisprudence with a fresh and comparative eye would undoubtedly be surprised to discover that the notable and prominent court decisions are those given in cases where the banker has been unsuccessful in opposing the authorities or has been penalized for not being cooperative enough in terms of informing on his clients. In most cases the banker has been penalized. His courage is praiseworthy. It is a pity in terms of business, since international trade can very well do without French bankers (in France there is no bank secrecy—but then they do not have any oil either).

From the point of view of the law, and to avoid repeating what has already been very well set out by excellent French lawyers* let us recall simply that the absence of bank secrecy in the face of fiscal authorities is a longstanding principle endorsed by the Supreme Court of Appeal (*Cour de Cassation*)

---

*See bibliography, page 297.

since 1887.* It has since then been warmly extended and renewed by subsequent legislation† as well as being further extended by legal decisions — although the Supreme Court has recently interposed the principle of bank secrecy in two decisions made by the criminal courts on customs matters‡ although one of these has been modified. This almost complete lack of secrecy seems to shock nobody in a country where secrecy is not even respected in judicial matters.

IS THERE A PRICE FOR FREE JUSTICE?

If justice is theoretically free in France, the legal authorities in fact are required to make known any instance which gives any indication of a nature which would suggest tax evasion or any manoeuvre whatsoever which has had the object or the result of evading or compromising a tax!§

There is some legal drafting which, without the legislators apparently noticing, is sumptuous in its degree of impossibility. That is certainly the case with the clause requiring 'the legal authorities . . . make known . . . any indication . . . of a nature which would suggest . . . any manoeuvre whatsoever . . . had the result . . . compromising a tax'. Like many repressive French laws, this one sins by its wide excess and presupposes that any judge confronted with a dispute is an economist who will be able to gauge even the unintended results of the case. With such legal drafting it is surprising that you can still find lawyers who are taken aback to discover that most important business problems are settled either by private arbitration or, when there is an international element which permits it, by international arbitration (organized by the international chamber of commerce for example) or before courts in a fiscally neutral country.

It is an interesting fact to note that there have never been any penalties imposed on a judge for failure to cooperate, although there have been many against bankers. Perhaps this springs from the fact that the public ministry is allowed to give details of its files to the tax authorities;‖ unless it is a question of the obligation placed on a litigant to leave the details of his case with the Clerk of the Court at the disposal of the tax authorities for a fortnight following the pronouncement of a decision.✩ It is true that this obligation is reduced to 10 days for minor offences★ — which gives an extra spice to the

---

*Cass. Req. 22 March 1887. In terms of its registration details this decision is frequently quoted by French authors under the wrong reference: 'D 1888-1-32'. The correct reference in order to find it is: 'D 1888-1-277'. Since the incorrect reference is regularly taken up by all the authors, it allows one to think that they have not actually consulted the decision but have contented themselves with the original commentator's wrong reference.
†Article 1991 CGI (*Code Général des Impôts*).
‡25 January 1977 and 30 January 1975.
§Article 1989, CGI.
‖Article 1990, CGI.
✩Article 1898, section 2, CGI.
★Article 1898 section 3 CGI.

situation given that the time during which an appeal should be lodged is also 10 days from the date of judgment.

In effect the person who has been convicted of an offence must leave the documents on his defence file open to the tax authorities during the period which is given him to decide whether or not he will lodge an appeal (who should lodge an appeal? The individual or the tax authorities?). Unfortunately for the poor French banker (no point in even mentioning his client) matters can go a lot further because he is required to volunteer information to the tax authorities about accounts opened, amongst other complicated disclosures of less interest in this instance.

But it is not there that the 'cooperation' of French bankers reaches its zenith. It is in the customs area that they arrive at this peak.

IF YOU DO NOT WORK FOR ME FREE OF CHARGE YOU WILL BE CONVICTED

The customs service in France enjoys powers which are absolutely extraordinary and wideranging in terms of civil law. All it would require would be a few political hooligans at its head and you would have an organization of which the Gestapo in its early days would have been envious. Happily that sort of behaviour does not suit the French character and it is to the credit of the present administration that the fantastic powers given to it are not in general abused. That is no doubt why the 'customs officer' has preserved his image of a pleasant and sympathetic Corsican civil servant even when it is customs agents who are responsible for investigating breaches of exchange control.

In order to perform their duties the customs agents have the same powers as the tax authorities,* which cannot have seemed sufficient to the legislators despite their considerable extent because the customs service has the power to demand 'the disclosure of all papers and documents of any kind relating to operations of interest to the service'†

Anyone who feels that the courts should have been able to erect some barriers against the application of such a statute does not properly understand the French mentality. In the first place, the question of interest was not raised in the courts until very recently, because the expression is well understood by the possessor of cartesian logic.

AUTHORITIES WITH AN INTEREST

It is self-evident to the Latin mind that the authorities (except in the case of a misuse of power) do not act unless they are 'interested', that is unless they have some concern. Furthermore, a banker finding himself obliged to answer one or more questions would find it difficult to make himself judge of the authorities'

---

*Article 455, lines 1 and 2, *Code des Douanes.*
†Article 65, *Code des Douanes.*

interest and reply that the subject was not one which interested them. In the same way it is difficult to imagine the banker replying by demanding that the customs service justify its interest since the posing of questions presuppose that they have an interest. Finally it is impossible to imagine that in the event of a dispute as to the interest the customs service and the banker would wait while some judge or other had made an impossible judgment on the definition of interest. You can only regard it as a bad piece of drafting, unless of course you see it as simply the use of a polite form.

In any event, even if it is only a polite form of words, the statute actually goes very much further, and its interpretation in the courts has been even wider and more accepting. The customs service can in effect act on 'any operation, whether normal or not' and demand 'the production of papers and documents of any kind' which are of interest to the service.*

SAFE-DEPOSITS, BUT NOT SO SAFE

A bank employee was convicted for refusing to prepare for the customs service a detailed list of the safe-deposit boxes in his branch.† However, his lawyers established that if the authorities, which could check the identity of each deposit holder by examining the papers set up when the deposit was taken, insisted that a list which did not exist previously was drawn up, then this constituted additional work and was not covered by the code. The Supreme Court of Appeal confirmed the Agen Court of Appeal which took the view that the phrase 'papers and documents of any kind' included such papers as would allow the identification of those who had rented safe-deposits—papers which the bank was necessarily required to have.

This interpretation reveals an amazing dishonesty, since there is absolutely no legal requirement which obliges a banker to maintain such a list. No doubt the Supreme Court judges thought that a bank 'ought' to keep such a list— taking off from that point there only remains the job of asking lawyers for an alphabetical list of clients with addresses and so on.

Following hard on the heels of that case, the customs service wanted to investigate a bank at Toulouse where they thought (perhaps not without reason) that improper transfers were being made to Andorra, a nearby banking haven of some quality. There the managing director was convicted on the basis that he was prepared to give any information to the authorities on individual accounts and safe-deposits, but refused to give overall information on all accounts and safe-deposits.‡

WHOLESALE FISHING

A foreign lawyer would be amazed at the volume of the literature and

---

*Article 65, *Code des Douanes*.
†*Cour de Cassation, chambre criminelle*, 30 January 1975.
‡Toulouse Court of Appeal, 29 June 1976.

academic articles on these two decisions. This author defers to the erudition of those writing on the subject, while regretting that amongst all of them there is no explanation of the practical reasons for the interest in the problem (with perhaps one exception, but there one needs to know how to read between the lines).

Why all these court decisions, lawyers' pleas, courts of first instance, appeal judges, and finally a whole supreme court of appeal, to say nothing of all the court officials, clerks, bailiffs and so on when all that was wanted was something which a bank typist could prepare in a few hours at the most (something probably done anyway at some time to invoice out the hire charges and check the payments received). It is certainly not on the grounds of principle, because the customs officers could in any event ask for the details client by client. The true reason for this judicial tournament, in which France is not the only country to get involved, is for the banker the commercial aspects of the affair, and for the customs the effectiveness of the measures. If the customs officials request information on an individual basis the banker may immediately warn his client who will be extremely grateful and may even have time to take appropriate steps. If the information is requested on a global basis the banker cannot warn all his clients without risking a commercial disaster, which may follow in any event if any of his staff is less than discreet. No-one pretends on the other hand that the customs officers are interested in the slightest in the bulk of the list when most of the safe-deposits would yield only the small change of bearer certificates of deposit or the few gold coins belonging to the owner of the corner shop. In fact only one person, or occasionally a few people, are the target and it is precisely to prevent them from being warned that a global list is demanded.

It is exactly the same kind of problem which both the Canadians and the Americans have come upon (leaving aside the legal jargon) and describe as 'fishing expeditions'. Although in this case the details would surprise both American and Canadian readers since in the cases mentioned the banks had been nationalized (and were therefore controlled by the state), the customs officers are of course state employees and the judges are also employed by the state—what kind of game is this?' an American would ask. Although if he asked a Russian the man would probably not understand the question because such a thing would seem normal to him.

THE SUPREME COURT DETERMINES THE SIZE OF THE NETS

The customs service, intending to draw their net a little tighter in a particular case, demanded that they be given a copy of a report which the bank had had prepared by a consultant engineer on one of their clients. The bank refused on the basis that the report was a private internal document which could not be said to be included even implicitly in the documents mentioned in the Code. Following on the conviction of the bank officials at the initial hearings and also on appeal there was much discussion about the issue. Some writers even suggested that the information would not have been required to be communicated had it been verbal* but as it was written, then the customs had a right to it!

The Supreme Court of Appeal was quite restrictive in its decision by comparison with its attitude in the case of the list of safe-deposits in 1975. The bank's position depended upon the fact that customs may only require presentation of 'papers and documents which the profession concerned is legally or necessarily obliged to maintain'. The Supreme Court developed the game of 'hide and seek' by quashing the original decision on the basis that 'the documents demanded must relate to normal or abnormal activities within the competence of the customs service' which was not the case as regards the consultant engineer's report.†

According to French procedure, the Supreme Court cannot actually decide a case, but has to refer it back to another Appeal Court. In the interval before the case was reheard Professor Michel Vasseur published a remarkable commentary on it, which is worth quoting here:

The decision makes it quite clear that the customs service does not have the right to demand any written document whatsoever and nor does it have the right to oversee all aspects of the relationship between a bank and its clients . . . the court to which the case has been referred, and in general all judges meeting similar circumstances in the future, will be obliged to discover if the engineer's report was made in relation to past or future operations carried out by the bank with the client, and not only that, but also whether these operations were in the field of international commerce or of financial dealings overseas, the only ones which enter into the competency of the customs service.

He added moreover, with a degree of clairvoyance, that it would remain with the bank to decide on the relationship between the documents demanded and the question posed and this would not be an easy matter. He added:

A vague motivation in which the customs service limited itself for example to declaring that it was undertaking investigations into improper transfers of currency or valuables with a foreign country would not be sufficient. For under such a pretext the customs officials could continue to demand any documents whatsoever. It is not sufficient for the customs service to indicate in very broad terms the reason for its request and in respecting the legal forms quote these. The law and the liberty of the individual should not be dealt with in broad terms.‡

Finally, this author cannot resist the pleasure of quoting Michel Vasseur's opinion which would also have served as a conclusion to this chapter: 'Any reduction in banking secrecy which corresponds to an increase in the powers of

---

*Oddly enough these writers seem to forget that giving evidence (under oath) also exists in French penal proceedings (although of course, it is possible that the French put less value on that than the Anglo-Saxons).
†*Cour de Cassation*, 25 January 1977.
‡Nor the evidence on exchange controls.

the authorities will through its very nature increase the lack of favour shown to France as a centre of international finance'.*

Unfortunately for the French banking system the principle was not upheld (though this decision may have been justified on the facts of this case); a new appeal was brought in and the court did not follow Michel Vasseur's view (decision of 11 June 1979). In France the judges, even those in the Supreme Court of Appeal, are civil servants: they have a training neither as lawyers nor as bankers. It is not certain that they were aware of the unfortunate effects of their decision in the international field and the financial consequences which may be counted if not in thousands then certainly in hundreds of millions of dollars. It is a great pity that a decision based no doubt in law can have such a negative effect, particularly when Lebanese bankers had just established themselves in Paris and were beginning to affect business.

One point which has not been brought up before the courts (although it has been raised in Great Britain) is the situation where a definite additional work burden is demanded of the bank: who should absorb the cost, the bank or the public authorities? Perhaps one day a statute will require that such research (simple to conduct, if one is frank) carried out for the authorities should be invoiced to those hiring the safe-deposit boxes? On a commercial level there is no need to worry: banks and financial institutions are forbidden to make public the official scrutiny to which they are subject†—they should not act in any case!

In such a situation and faced with such powers, how would the banks explain the presence of bearer certificates of deposit which are often used as security for loans which are much larger than the balance sheet of a business would justify, and which, even when their existence is certain, seem never to be checked by the tax authorities?

THE AUTHORITIES ARE OBLIGED TO PROTECT
A 'LEGAL EVASION'

As far as bearer certificates of deposit are concerned, such enquiries would kill the goose which lays the golden eggs: the recycled money which has escaped income tax but will pay a withholding tax on the (very modest) interest paid by banks to the person depositing the money. It may be used to guarantee an overdraft on which interest is charged (this time at a very high rate) providing a difference which generally represents a rather comfortable margin for a bank which is in addition not running any financial risk. It could of course be that some diligent inspector was not aware of this 'economic' aspect of things and might want to take matters further—but such an instance should not happen

---

*The French reader will find this compares well with comments by Swiss and Bahamian officials and will be surprised to realize that there are French lawyers capable of doing anything other than commenting on their favourite academic's response to another academic, while those American lawyers advise the major companies.
†Decision no. 66-81, 15 January 1966.

because, according to an answer given by the Minister of Finance, details of transactions in gold and bearer certificates of deposit (hence their anonymity) may not be given to agents of the tax authorities*—there is very little banking secrecy, certainly no oil, but maybe one or two interesting ideas . . . .

---

*Question no. 10593 put to the Minister of Finance in parliament: *JO* parliamentary debates, National Assembly, March 1974 p.1277 with further details on 10 August 1974, p.4048.

17 Italy:
A 'guardia di finanza'—*something less than civil*

A myth, as tenacious as it is false, circulates in business circles and sometimes Italian business circles at that, to the effect that Italy, if not a banking haven, at least offers some kind of temporary asylum for money. Even though this may have been true once, and article 47 of the constitution states that 'the republic encourages and protects savings in any form', recent developments have brought about a complete change. The legal system and case-law of banking secrecy in Italy share a way of reasoning which is unfortunately to be found all too often in Latin countries.

AN ITALIAN SALAD

In the first instance there is, properly speaking, no statute which truly creates banking secrecy, but rather various departures or legal qualifications of statutes from which the principle of banking secrecy may be derived. In the second instance there is no specific law removing banking secrecy in the face of the public interest, but in various other statutes a series of departures are to be found which qualify the earlier departures and create an infuriating maze, which seems to give much annoyance to Italian lawyers who are not slow to criticize the present situation.

As regards the first instance the departures from statutes read like a catalogue: first there is the banking statute which stipulates, while dealing with the procedure to be followed in the event of a bankruptcy 'the commissioners will provide the court with a list of creditors . . . so that disputes may be resolved . . . but without providing details to the litigants so that banking secrecy may be protected'*; one should also note, particularly in the context of departures from departures, the regulations creating a right of control for the benefit of those making direct contributions to credit organizations which are published under the heading: 'Departures from banking secrecy'.†

All the other statutes are either put forward as the basis of banking secrecy, or are wholly disputed as such by Italian lawyers. The main ones are contained in the following regulations: those requiring professional secrecy to be observed by officials of the Bank of Italy in respect of their duties in checking

---

*Article 78 of the banking law.
†Article 35 of the DPR, 29 September 1973, no. 600.

the activities of the banking sector;* clause in the criminal code which relate to professional secrecy;† an obligation arising out of established custom‡—an element which the Supreme Court has supported§—or a duty to correct.|| As an Italian lawyer notes with a degree of humour 'all these elements are acceptable since there is absolutely no provision within the legal system which expressly establishes a duty to maintain banking secrecy.' ✩

DEPARTURES MADE USE OF BY OPPONENTS

This indigestible legal salad does sometimes seem to have been welcome food to the Italian tax authorities as well as to the authorities whose duty it is to apply the exchange control laws who work in collaboration with the tax officials or on their behalf, and are known as *guardia di finanzia*—financial police. As far as these qualifications and departures are concerned, the situation is made even more complicated by the mixture of their old legal system and new measures which clash with each other and create an even more complicated picture according to whether their origin was fiscal or financial and whether the point at issue qualifies as a criminal one or not.

However, let us look directly at the results of all this which are:

the financial police co-operate with the tax service to obtain and discover information which may be used to confirm income and control violations of the tax laws; they act on their own initiative or at the request of tax officials—and may demand that credit institutions or the postal authorities . . . provide after a specified time period of not less than sixty days a copy of accounts held with the taxpayer together with any and all details relevant to the account, including guarantees given by third parties. ★

It seems that such an investigation does not require the prior approval of the state prosecutor nor is it subject to any prior evidence of crime, which has the absurd result of giving these officials more authority to be exercised on their own initiative than would be the case in a criminal investigation. Which is enough to say that these measures are not to the taste of the local lawyers who agree (agreeing once does not make it a habit) that it must be a drafting error, specifically in the clauses which extend the provisions to cover not only financial but also fiscal matters. Contrary to public opinion there does not seem to exist any obligation,* or indeed any prohibition if the inquiry is

---

*Article 10 of the banking law.
†Article 622 of the criminal code states: 'Anyone whatsoever who, through his employment, situation, profession or art possesses a secret and reveals it, or uses it for his own profit or the profit of another shall be liable if his act harms anyone else, to a prison sentence of up to 1 year or to a fine of between 12 000 and 200 000 lire'.
‡Article 1374 of the civil code.
§Supreme Court, 1st civil chamber, 18 April 1974 FI; 1975, 1, 74 with a complete note by Di Amato.
||Article 1165 of the Civil Code.
✩Luigi Alibrandi, 'Main elements of banking secrecy' a conference organized by the Turin Savings Bank and the National Centre for Legal Studies (CIDIS) Turin, 5-7 May 1978.
★Articles 32, 33, and 35 of Decree 600, 29 September 1973.

started by a magistrate, to advise the person whose affairs are being investigated, who is sometimes wounded . . . .

Furthermore the officials of the Italian Exchange Control Office have, at the same time as the financial police, the power to inspect material through the banks,* from whom they may demand (the banks are required to respond) any necessary information and specifically their registers, books, documents and correspondence. Curiously enough the Italian Exchange Office is given under the latest legislation which increased its powers less extensive powers than those possessed by the financial police who can deal at the same time with taxation matters.

This development of banking secrecy does not suit the banking and legal professions at all who take the view that banking secrecy may be removed by the simple act of informing on someone: 'a tendency which leads to a progressive discrediting of private savings which might otherwise be a self-generating source of wealth'† and 'an involuntary addition to the damage arising from many quarters and affecting private savings, which is the sole means in this poor country of financing productive activities—and unfortunately some which are not productive'.‡

However the Italian socialist party does not seem to share this opinion, and they put forward in March 1982 a draft bill which would give tax inspectors direct access to banks' files and the right to confiscate any documents which they felt merited this. The bill did not stop short there, either, it gave both tax inspectors and police the right to search premises without the prior approval of a magistrate.

---

*Article 3 of law no. 159, 1976.
†Pietro Nuvolone, Conference on bank secrecy, 5–7 May 1978.
‡Fabio Ziccardi, Conference on bank secrecy.

18 Denmark:
The king wore no clothes

With much humour, Peter Alsted,* a Copenhagen lawyer, says: 'to speak of both Denmark and banking secrecy in the same breath invariably makes one think of Hans Christian Andersen's story: *The Emperor's New Clothes*. In this story two rogues tricked an emperor who liked dressing well by pretending to weave cloth which could be seen only by intelligent people. The ministers, the people and even the emperor himself went into raptures about the clothes until a child shouted out 'But he's got no clothes on!' when everyone finally realized that the emperor was naked and the two rogues had disappeared. Although in theory the term 'bank secrecy' is in itself quite clear, in practice it is if not impossible then certainly very difficult to discern in the world's oldest kingdom, as far as exchange control and taxation are concerned.

Every bank has the obligation not to give to its clients information about other clients, nor to give such information to any physical or moral person. This obligation which creates a relationship of confidence between the bank and its clients extends to all bank employees at all levels within the bank. Nonetheless it is true that despite this obligation the bank is authorized to give information about the solvency of individual clients. As far as the controls imposed by the public authorities go, then the accepted rule is that banking secrecy must give way to the public interest.

The same principle applies to investigations made for tax purposes, to the application of exchange control laws and the obligation to give evidence; to sum up, therefore, it is possible to say that in the face of enquiries from the authorities there is nothing bar the imagination between a banker and his client. Any bank, savings institution, exchange bureau, lawyer or any person or entity receiving deposits of money or valuables is required to give the authorities detailed information about, amongst other things, the owner of the assets and to do so not only on demand, but in certain cases spontaneously. These wide requirements do not apply only to clients resident or domiciled in Denmark, but also to non-resident foreigners.

---

*The 'serious' parts of this chapter are an almost literal translation of a study of the subject made by Mr Alsted for this book. There exists practically no published information on this subject, even in the Danish language (although one humorist has remarked that it is not so much a language as a kind of throat infection).

THE LITTLE MERMAID,
AN ALARM SIGNAL AS MUCH AS A SIREN

If the principle of banking secrecy is set out in the commercial banking law[*] and backed up with legal sanctions which duplicate those of the criminal code, this is doubtless only so that they can be the more effectively set aside by the tax code. The law on fiscal control completely removes even the principle of banking secrecy.[†]

In the terms of that law the banks, savings institutions, cooperative societies, bankers, exchange bureaus, lawyers and anyone receiving money or valuables to be administered in a professional capacity, or carrying on business as a lender of money, are obliged at the request of the tax authorities, to provide any information about a named person as regards money deposits, loans or safe-deposits. The authorities may require the seizure of any loan or cash deposit, or assets held in trust or income produced by these, as well as information on the movements on accounts, cheques drawn and deposited, and security or guarantees given for loans or overdrafts.[‡]

The same persons and organizations, on whom this responsibility to reply rests, are required to supply systematically to the authorities[§] details of the interest credited to the accounts of depositors during the previous year together with details of the date on which it was credited, the total in the account at the end of the year, and the name address and registration number of the account holder. Beyond that a similar report is required on accounts closed during the previous year.

SOMETHING ROTTEN IN THE STATE OF DENMARK...

The advertisements which have appeared in the international press on behalf of Danish banks are not totally misleading. The adverts were offering to accept 'protected' term loans with annual interest at between 12 and 14 per cent payable in Danish krone.[||] The rates were all the more interesting in as far as they were exempt from deduction of withholding tax at source. The deposits were limited to a maximum of 200 000 krone[☆] per person, or about US$ 40 000.

Where the publicity was less than frank, if not actually misleading, was on the question of 'protection'. In fact bank accounts belonging to non-residents are subject to the same scrutiny by the tax authorities as those of residents— Scandinavian socialist egalitarianism requires it. This fact would be irrelevant if the Danish authorities had the same attitude to double tax treaties as the

---

[*]Article 54 of law no. 122, 2 April 1974 on commercial banks.
[†]Law no. 496, 19 September 1975 on fiscal investigations, amended in particular by law no. 286 of 9 June 1977.
[‡]Article 8-G of law 496.
[§] Article 8-H of law 496.
[||]It was something which embarrassed the financial institutions of the other countries at the time of the advertisements.
[☆] Without the possibility of going from bank to bank.

South Africans (see Chapter 13). But it seems on the contrary that their attitude is much closer to that of the Canadians (see Chapter 12)—whose weather is also more comparable.

When opening an account with a Danish bank, not only do they demand their client's passport but also their tax number in their home country.* Given that, the Danes have an extensive network of treaties which provide for automatic exchange of information (notably with the other Scandinavian countries and Germany and France) that promises to give a few white hairs to any roving depositors who have forgotten their civic virtues in the face of the siren . . . .

---

*Most Latin countries have not yet adopted this system. But they should not worry, it will certainly arrive before long.

19 Japan: Kamikaze depositors

Banking secrecy in Japan does not derive either from a legal code or from case law which establishes and defines its principles on the British method. Nevertheless a banker's obligation to preserve secrecy is not considered to be only a moral obligation but rather a legal one which springs from the contractual relationship between the bank and its client and from commercial custom. However, a banker does not appear on the list of those subject to professional secrecy.* The first legal decisions relating to banking secrecy in Japan occurred as a result of the exchange of (erroneous) information about clients. This practice of exchanging information, called *shinyo-shokai*, is the subject of an interesting practical regulation which is worth mentioning in view of its individuality, even if the problems of exchanges of information between banks are not the subject of this book.

REGULATED *SHINTO-SHOKAI*

Exchanges of information over the telephone have not been used since 1952 and banks use a formula established by the National Federation of Bankers' Associations which takes the particular form of reproducing at the bottom of the paper the sentence: 'It has been decided that a frank exchange of information should be made in the spirit of an exchange and will not give rise to subsequent legal action to prove responsibility or for breach of professional secrecy'.

This last part of the sentence is in itself very revealing: the Japanese bankers are mutually dispensing with the right—which, in any case, they do not have since it is not the *banker* but the *client* who has a right to secrecy. Japan appears to be a long way from the role of the 'Switzerland' of the Far East, the more so because a significant number of statutes lift banking secrecy, particularly as far as tax is concerned. The tax inspectors may, if it is necessary in their investigation, ask questions and inspect books and documents relating to the affairs of anyone who is under an obligation to pay money or deliver goods to a taxpayer, or on the other hand has the right to obtain payment or delivery from a taxpayer.†

---

*Article 134 of the Japanese criminal code.
†Article 234, para 1, line 3 of the income tax code.

AN EASTERN INFERNO?

A Japanese lawyer, Mr Kawamoto, basing his views on a number of court decisions,* describes as follows the rules covering the conduct of the Japanese tax authorities: the right to examine exists only if the information supplied by the taxpayer is insufficient and uniquely within the limits of what is necessary; investigations must be carried out within the bounds of reasonableness and good sense, taking into account both the private interests of the bank and the objects of the inquiry; due account should be made of the bank's interest. A new banking law is currently in preparation, but this is not expected to include any regulations which impinge upon banking secrecy.†

Mr Hiroshi Kawai, a Tokyo lawyer, remarked:

although it is recognized in Japan that secrecy is an obligation for the banker, legislation to cover banking secrecy is only embryonic. This situation derives from the fact that the country whose law is based on codes (and therefore more Roman than common law) the absence of any basic rules seems therefore to have been the cause of this late development.

It should be pointed out though that this tardy development in a country which seems to have a limited secrecy has not prevented the development of a strange and rather singular banking device, which is the 'sealed account', a device which is examined in detail in Chapter 40 on banking loopholes.

---

*Shizuoka District Court (9 February 1972), Supreme Court (22 November 1972 and 10 July 1973), Tokyo High Court (25 March 1975, judgment on the decision of the Shizuoka District Court of 9 February 1972).
†A commission appointed by the Ministry of Finance has prepared a report on financial institutions which advances a new code.

20 Portugal:
Secrecy born of excess

The events of 25 April 1974, in their nature and through their excesses, have profoundly altered the structure of Portugal. At the moment there exists not a single academic study nor a court decision relating to banking secrecy since the events which some people call a 'revolution'.*

Banking activities, which had been essentially private, were nationalized — apart from the foreign banks. Until 25 April 1974 banking secrecy had been observed as a generally accepted custom but the disorders had their followers within the banks and the publication of banking information in the newspapers concerning individuals who were the subject of political 'investigations' became the rule.

This type of behaviour could not be sustained indefinitely and led to the organic law of 15 November 1975, articles 63 and 64 of which put forward the principle of professional secrecy while leaving to 'higher authority' the job of deciding whether members of the council of administration or bank workers could 'reveal facts or information the knowledge of which came through the exercise of their employment'.

This law proved insufficient and another was published: decree 729-F/15 of 22 December 1975, of which article 7 stated:

Members of management committees, the rest of the workers and members of control committees may not in terms of the law reveal facts or events the knowledge of which derives from their work.

In the same vein article 8 of the law freed the same people from any obligation to bear witness in a court because of professional secrecy. The Portuguese, after committing quite enough stupidities, had realized that they were just about ruining their country, although stopping short of turning their holiday villages into concentration camps, and the Council of Ministers decided: 'Banking secrecy and ethics will be assured in the defence of the interests of any depositor whatsoever',† and banking secrecy in terms of the respect of its principle was given criminal penalties.‡

---

*The author wishes to express his particular gratitude to Mr Antonio Pires de Lima — a Lisbon lawyer — thanks to whose detailed study the preparation of this chapter was possible. His study, written in Portuguese, has been the object of a somewhat 'free' translation which may explain the lack of respect which may be noticeable in some of the remarks.
†Resolution of the Council of Ministers, 9 January 1976.
‡Decree-law 475-76, 16 June 1976, modifying article 290 of the criminal code.

A CLIMATE OF CONFIDENCE

At the moment the situation in Portuguese banking secrecy is regulated by the decree-law of 9 January 1978* whose preamble is very explicit as to the legislature's intentions: 'taking the view that the reconstruction of the country involves the establishment of a state of confidence in banking which will permit the return of capital . . .'.

This decree establishes the general rules of Portuguese banking secrecy and stipulates in particular, as far as those responsible are concerned: members of the administrative committees, management committees or any other body as well as all employees of credit institutions may not reveal or profit from secrets which they have obtained exclusively through the performance of their duties.†

The extent of secrecy is fixed by the same statute which says:

The elements which are particularly required to be kept secret are the names of the clients, deposit accounts and the movement on them, banking transactions realizing exchange operations or other financial operations, authorizations for operations in hand and any other aspects of current transactions as far as concerns the inspection of credits by the Bank of Portugal.‡

Breaches of banking secrecy as defined by this decree are punished (apart from disciplinary and civil actions) by the terms of Article 290 of the Criminal Code§ which provides for imprisonment of up to 6 months.

AN UNKNOWN BANKING HAVEN

As far as the protection of the client is concerned, the limits to professional secrecy would not cause any embarrassment to a Swiss or Cayman Islands banker since apparently the only exception is as follows: 'an exemption concerning facts or relations between the client and the credit institution cannot be given except by an authorization given by the client to the credit institution.'‖

In such conditions the travelling depositor could legitimately wonder whether he had not encountered the most perfect banking haven, surpassing even a Panamanian numbered account since there is apparently no limitation on Portuguese banking secrecy even for criminal matters. It is precisely there that the system sins through its excess. In a country where the institutions have been thrown over, it is well worth examining the practical situation as opposed to the letter of the law.

---

*Decree-law no. 2 *Diaro da Republica* (official gazette) 9 January 1978, carrying the text of a decree signed on 2 December 1977 by Mario Soares.
†Article 1 of decree-law 2/78 modifying line 'A of para 1 of the Constitution'.
‡Article 2 of decree-law 2/78.
§Article 3 of decree-law 2/78.
‖Article 2-2 of decree-law 2/78.

A LEGAL PROVISION DOES NOT MAKE A HAVEN

At a practical level the statutes seem hardly to have entered into force. Mr Pieres de Lima, a Lisbon lawyer, was recently before a Portuguese court where he quoted this decree-law (on the subject of a bank witness); the ministry objected and said that it was only necessary to ask a bank for the information and it would be given—a sad statement for a lawyer on the practicality of the law. At a higher level this law has already created some difficulties: certain banks have refused to answer police questions relating to some criminal matters,* and if the bank union agrees on the legitimacy of the law† the Bank of Portugal will emphasize its terms and has already prepared a project for modifying the text.‡

Clearly the present situation is difficult to support, particularly as far as criminal activities are concerned. The police have made it known that if banking secrecy 'is now correctly invoked to justify the silence of the banking authorities . . .'§ some changes will have to be brought in. Currently, as far as legal provisions go, Portugal is the most perfect banking haven; at the same time its neighbour, Spain, has published a law organizing disclosure.

To classify a haven as an inferno is very unfair, but in a guide one must be a guide and this haven has not entirely dispelled the traces of sulphur fumes. Let us wish it luck as the country, like its inhabitants, gain one's sympathy, but it is highly unlikely that the situation will long remain in its present state.

---

*In fact the law should be changed at this stage because it is unthinkable to impose banking secrecy in the face of criminal aspects of common law—although it is difficult to define what constitutes common law in a country undergoing political traumas.
†Release no. 6/78 of the Bancarios do Sul e Ilhas.
‡Note from the Bank of Portugal, 4 April 1978.
§Release from the police authorities, 24 February 1979.

21 Sweden:
Socialism without penalties

Nothing makes Sweden particularly disposed to be a banking inferno. In fact as early as 22 September 1668 the decree which established the kingdom's State Bank specified: 'No-one should have the effrontery to attempt to gain information about someone else from the books, but if that should happen the book-keeper should give no information whatsoever on the subject'.* Identical provisions were included in the articles of the *Skandinaviska Kreditaktiebolog* at Gothenburg and the Royal decree on private banks of 12 June 1874 states: 'The situation of individuals with the bank must not be revealed to the public'. After several restatements of the law in subsequent legislation, the text which is currently in force has simply repeated the old requirements and stipulates: 'the situation of any individual with a bank must not be revealed except for a compelling reason'.† In interpreting the current position the Swedish jurists, and Mr Lennart Moller (a Stockholm lawyer), seem to take the view that the important part of this text is the expression 'without a compelling reason' and that the law applies to the authorities in so far as they may be deemed to be part of the 'public'.

SCANDINAVIAN COMMONSENSE

In the main the Swedish lawyers seem to recognize the value of banking secrecy and Pr Hakan Nial has said:

... banking secrecy would certainly not have survived so obstinately through the ages if it had been sustained solely by the private interests of the banks' clients. The explanation of its vitality is to be found in its importance for its proper function of giving instructions to banks. An essential condition for banks to fulfil their important role within economic and social life is in the final analysis that they enjoy the confidence of their clients. But a precondition for having confidence in someone is that they should be capable of keeping the secrets which are confided to them. If our banks were to fail in this way, one would have to anticipate that a measure of savings would look elsewhere—that it would be lodged with foreign banks, or individuals or hoarded ....

Such observations, deeply true, would not seem out of place at a conference

---

*Article XXXII of the decree which according to Pr Hakan Nial was based on the statute establishing in 1619 the Hamburg Exchange Bank.
†Article 191 of the law on banking operations of 31 March 1955.

of Swiss or Cayman Isle bankers, the more so since the author (who is considered to be a great specialist on the subject in his own country) adds:

Hostility towards banking secrecy which appeared for example in Nazi Germany and other countries where a dictator has tried as far as possible to put business and other activities under the control and direction of the state, can hardly be a wise and considered expression of what is best for economic health and public opinion.

THE SWEDISH REALITY

The reality in Sweden does not follow these fine sentiments as far as *taxerings-revision* is concerned—tax revision being a modest name for tax inspection. Where the tax authorities are carrying out an investigation, neither the banker nor the taxpayer can claim banking secrecy on a client's transactions.* Such investigations can of course lead the tax officials to discover operations which the taxpayer would have wished to keep secret which do not in themselves constitute infringements. Most countries deal with this problem by imposing professional secrecy on tax officials.†

The Swedish taxpayer, through the income tax court, may ask that certain documents are not subjected to investigation on the basis that he wishes to keep their contents secret or that particular circumstances dictate that such documents are not communicated to any other person.‡

This procedure applies to normal tax inspections and is quite different from the 'fishing expeditions' which also exist in Sweden and also pose problems similar to those encountered in other countries.

FISHING FOR THE HAPPY SALMON

There is a Swedish expression which is quite impossible to translate, but which means a salmon who is both happy and smiling. It is doubtless this kind of fish—not large, but certainly luxurious—which forms the object of the fishing expeditions mounted by the Swedish tax authorities in the form of summonses addressed to bankers and, in one particular case, a demand which was addressed to one bank and asked for details of 78 clients. This operation is not a new one and although based on an old piece of legislation (it was dealt

---

*Articles 56–58 of the tax statute 23 November 1956 (TF).
†Such a procedure does not on the face of it seem to be too reassuring since if there are categories of people for whom professional secrecy is part of their vocation (doctors, lawyers), professional secrecy—even that imposed by law—is certainly not the prime vocation of income tax officials. In reality, rather curiously, the system seems to work very well, and if one takes France as an example, it is quite surprising to see the quality of professional secrecy observed by the officials of the tax service. This would seem to prove after all that on an individual basis human beings are much more responsible than some pessimists would have you believe and are quite capable of taking on obligations for which they do not have a vocation. The quality of professional secrecy observed can sometimes itself lead to excesses since in the case of an extended investigation, the French officials sometimes go so far as to ask for documents and information which they have no right to demand or to obtain.
‡Article 56–4 (TF).

with definitively in 1929) is still valid since the terms of the old statutes have been taken up in more recent ones.

The principle is that the tax authorities may address a summons to any bank in respect of any taxpayer who is 'suspected of having provided incomplete or incorrect information' and may ask for:

1. The amount of his credit balances.
2. The position of his account at a specific date as far as credits are concerned.
3. The amount of any revenue from fixed securities.
4. The amount of any debts due to the bank at a given date.
5. The deposits and withdrawals during a given period.*

The bank which received a summons including 78 taxpayers who were clients refused to provide the information on the basis that it was outside the spirit of the law. The bank won in the initial court hearing but had the case dismissed by the Supreme Court.†

Many Swedish lawyers have inveighed against such a decision, but what can they do in a country where 'it is an aberration that parents still have the right to bring up their children after their own convictions'?‡

Furthermore, the reader will not be surprised to know that according to all the private information which the author has been given it is the Swedish people who in terms of the size of their population and average wealth have the greatest deposits in the banking havens—in the country of drugs it seems not everyone has yet lost his head!

---

*Article 39-1 and 39-3 (TF).
†Record of the Supreme Administrative Court, 1929 p.218. The decision was made by four votes to one.
‡A statement made by Mr Per Garhton, a 'thinker' of the Swedish Liberal party.

22 Some other Roman law infernos

BELGIUM — A WALLOON OR FLEMISH TRANSFER?

This pleasant little country is often the subject of unjustified mockery on the part of its neighbours. An interesting exercise would be to take a version in the same language of the main economic journals and compare them with their foreign peers. As the level of a journal is dictated by its readers, it would soon be seen that some of the more doubtful jokes should be completely overturned.* In terms of banking secrecy Belgium is not Luxembourg and swings between the French and the Dutch systems. There is, properly speaking, no law establishing bank secrecy and the Penal Code (article 458) deals only with those in whom secrets are confided through their position and concerns only doctors, lawyers etc. Banking secrecy does, however, exist in its own way in civil contracts and constitutes a tradition, even if that is set aside for the tax authorities — or rather, according to a rather hypocritical procedure, 'at the request of the taxpayer'.

In fact although the banks are required to supply information to the tax authorities automatically and often quite logically, this does not include the possibility of the tax officials asking for information directly from a bank. However, the taxpayer is required to give the authorities all documents necessary for making the assessment at their first request and on pain of having a forced assessment imposed (articles 221 to 224 of the tax code). In a situation where the taxpayer is contesting an assessment (but *only* in this case) the authorities may make inquiries from the banks without the taxpayer's approval (article 275 of the tax code). The banks are obliged to respond, again in these limited circumstances, or face a fine of between 200 and 10 000 Belgian francs (article 335 of the tax code).

---

*Belgium has always been a trap for the French who, with astonishing chauvinism, assume that Belgian statutes are the same as the French. The example of the bankruptcy of the Central-Belgium Bank (see *Trends*, 22 November 1979) showed precisely the opposite as far as certificates of deposit or gold collateral are concerned because the Banking Commission published a directive in 1977 under whose terms 'financial agents are required to mention the guarantees given by their clients within the loan agreements which they issue'.

SPAIN — THE BANKING BULLFIGHT HAS BEGUN

It is difficult to give an opinion on the Spanish situation, on the banking bullfight which might not have to be changed after a few more passes of the cape. Spain has never been a tax haven although the Franco administration delicately avoided asking rich strangers who lived in Spain for some income tax returns although they were subject to Spanish income tax laws. The regime of Juan Carlos is still finding itself, while at the same time making sure it does not lose the tourist goose which lays the golden eggs. It is no doubt within the context of this awkward equilibrium that one should see the creation of a law establishing a wealth tax on non-residents having assets in Spain: a law restricted to individuals and not applicable to companies, with the result that the opulent properties all held in the name of some Panamanian or Liechtenstein entity will escape the tax while the small tourist flat bought with a loan on the Costa Brava will qualify for the tax (which to the Spanish resident seems an extremely modest and healthy tax).

As far as banking is concerned, Spain is interesting from certain points of view and an English lawyer had no qualms about publishing in a professional magazine an article entitled: 'Spain: a banking sanctuary?' Banking secrecy is now regulated by a 1977 law which, by comparison with the US banking secrecy law, does more to remove banking secrecy than reinforce it.* If you add to this brilliant legal initiative a terrible reputation for professional incompetence (carefully maintained by competitors) it is not a bullfight, it is a massacre.

FINLAND — THE END OF THE EARTH
BUT PERHAPS IN THE SPRINGTIME OF BANKING SECRECY

The classification of Finland amongst the banking infernos may be the greatest injustice done by this book. But any form of classification necessarily contains some form of injustice. Finland should ordinarily appear within the 'other banking havens' category but the author's feelings and the difficulty of obtaining information have resulted in the country not yet entering into the category of banking havens, as long as any serious doubt remains as to its true position.

The principle of banking secrecy is established by article 43 which states:

(Bankers) are obliged to keep secret whatever they may learn through their business of the economic position or the professional and commercial secrets of their clients or of anyone else. Banks are not authorized to give information except to the legal or police services in pursuance of a criminal inquiry, or to any other body authorized in law to obtain such information.

---

*The regulations removing banking secrecy specifically as far as tax is concerned were published as section VIII of the 14 November 1977 law and entitled: 'Banking secrecy and collaboration with the tax authorities'.

The problem posed by such a piece of legislation is the definition of 'any other body authorized in law' and it is this definition which determines the scale of the exercise. And it was on this question of the scale of the exercise that the Supreme Court gave an interesting decision in 1974 when it refused to allow the tax authorities to set aside banking secrecy and obtain information about transfers made on an account. But it is also true that the tax authorities did not put forward any valid reason as to why they wanted this information and the decision of the court was only made on a three-to-two majority!

MEXICO — BANKING SECRECY
WHICH IS WELL BRONZED BUT NOT WELL MUSCLED

Banking secrecy in Mexico finds its principal source in article 105 of the law of 3 May 1945 which states in particular:

Deposit-taking institutions may not give information concerning deposits and other operations except to the depositor or donor or beneficiary, to their legal representatives and those who have the power to dispose of the money or to intervene in the transaction....

On the basis of such a law, correctly interpreted by the local courts, Mexico could be a banking haven of high quality, the more so because article 210 of the criminal code (law of 13 August 1931) punishes anyone who steals a professional secret, and article 211 of the same code increases the penalties if the person carrying out the crime is himself a professional.

Alas! the Mexican's sombrero has a hole at the bottom (or the top) and lets in the light of the authorities. The same article 105 which creates bank secrecy also provides that the banker is relieved of it in certain cases, notably including the tax authorities.

NORWAY — FJORDS WITH NO SECRETS

Banking secrecy exists in Norway and is established by the law of 24 May 1961 in which article 18 stipulates:

The management, employees and auditors are held to professional secrecy as far as anything which they may learn of in the performance of their duties which pertains to the bank's situation or that of its clients or that of another bank or any clients of the other bank, except where they are under an obligation imposed by this law or any other law to give such information....

Once again the roving depositor finds himself confronted with a recognition of the principle but with exceptions to it which go as deep as the country's fjords. Furthermore the shareholders of the banks have been deprived of their control which has been taken over by the state — although they have also been given the option of selling their shares to the state.

THE NETHERLANDS — ACCOUNTS WHICH
THE AUTHORITIES ENTER LIKE WINDMILLS

Professional secrecy exists in the Netherlands and the failure to observe it is punished by law, according to article 272 of the Criminal Code. The problem is that this protection is restricted to 'necessary repositories of secrets' and Dutch lawyers and local authorities seem to consider that a banker (as opposed to a doctor or a lawyer) is not a 'necessary repository'.

The result is, therefore, according to some, that there is no form of banking secrecy in the face of the tax authorities, but the authorities very seldom exercise their rights in this area. The author is obliged to admit that the explanations given to him on the subject in the Netherlands have also seemed rather confused, but they all have one common element which is that the Netherlands is not a banking haven!

This situation seems all the more curious in that by its methods of playing hide and seek with the Netherlands Antilles, the country has created one of the most sophisticated tax havens in the world. Is there something else there which has been hidden? The specialists do not think so, but who has not seen a specialist make a mistake? Or at least, specialists do not make mistakes, they revise their opinion in the light of new circumstances!

IV

The Traditional Banking Havens

It was necessary to take an overview of the different banking infernos because havens are the more readily defined by comparison with the infernos which form the majority of countries at the moment. Parts IV and V analyse the main banking havens existing today, and in order to facilitate a comparison of the various havens and their attributes, the same scheme has been followed for each chapter. Needless to say the relative importance of each part of the scheme are not the same. The scheme to be used is as follows; it will permit the reader, if he so desires, to make a more detailed comparison based on the practical comparison tables at the end of the book.

I The country and its components
Geographical, historical and economic situation
Population, stability, communications and legal system
II The currency
III Exchange controls
Non-residents
Interest paid to non-residents
Residents
IV Banks and the banking system
V Banking secrecy
General outline
Legal basis and penalties
VI Instruments of banking secrecy
Direct
Indirect
Bearer
VII The practice of banking secrecy and foreign economic powers
Exchange control
Taxation
VIII International agreements likely to undermine banking secrecy
General agreements
Specific agreements
IX Banking secrecy and the financial market
Blind market for non-residents*
Official non-resident market
Back-to-back loans
X Personal comments

---

*Translator's note: There is no direct English translation which effectively renders the French *marche anonyme*, so to avoid repeating a lengthy paraphrase I have adopted the rather clumsy 'blind market', which should be taken as referring to the terms and conditions which would obtain in a situation where the depositor's identity (and therefore country of residence) is not revealed, and he does not therefore qualify for any reliefs which might otherwise result from the application of double taxation agreements.

Part IV analyses banking havens defined as 'traditional havens', because of the complete absence of formal statutes and pursuit of a tradition of secrecy, or maintenance of case-law or other laws which have established banking secrecy, and the absence of laws which diminish secrecy (Jersey and Guernsey, Luxembourg, British Virgin Isles etc.). Part V analyses 'Banking havens through choice'—that is countries which have deliberately become banking havens by enacting legislation to this end (Bahamas, Cayman Islands etc.), or those countries that have produced legislation with the same effects but which have simply strengthened an existing tradition (Switzerland, Liechtenstein).

23 Andorra: The Middle Ages of bank secrecy

I THE COUNTRY AND ITS COMPONENTS

Geographical, historical and economic situation

The co-principality of Andorra extends through three valleys in the Pyrenees comprising 460 square kilometres of territory, between France and Spain. The co-principality's autonomy goes back to an agreement signed by France and Spain on 8 September 1278 (and known as the *pareage*) which placed the territory under the joint authority of the head of the French state (which inherited the rights of the Comte de Foix) and the Bishop of Urgel, who between them share the duties of 'co-princes'.

The local economy is based principally upon tourism, which is encouraged by the sale of goods free of taxes and duties.

Population, stability, communications and legal system

The population of approximately 27 000 inhabitants, of whom about 8000 live in the capital (Andorra la Vella), consists of 7000 Andorrans and the remainder are 90 per cent Spanish and 10 per cent French.

The legal system smacks very much of the Middle Ages and is based on a mixture of ancient Catalan law with Roman and Canon law. The political situation is stable; the travel communications and post, telex, and telephone systems are all satisfactory.

II THE CURRENCY

The co-principality has no organization for issuing currency and its budget is calculated in Spanish currency, the peseta:

$$1 \text{ peseta} = 100 \text{ centimos}$$
$$100 \text{ pesetas} = \text{Swiss francs } 1.91 \text{ (May 1982)}*$$
$$100 \text{ pesetas} = \text{US\$0.89}$$

---

*The currency rates will be quoted in Swiss francs for each banking haven. This currency, despite international fluctuations in other currencies in relation to it, is one of the best points of reference because of the relative stability of its international purchasing power. By way of further information the value will also be given in US dollars at the same date. These are only approximate values relating to those ruling in London on 17 May 1982. Since rates are constantly changing these are given as an indication only.

In the total absence of exchange controls all forms of currency are in theory usable for local transactions, but in practice current transactions are made in French francs or pesetas.

III EXCHANGE CONTROL

The issue can be resolved without distinguishing between residents and non-residents: there is absolutely no form of exchange control.

IV BANKS AND THE BANKING SYSTEM

There are six banks in Andorra, of which the major ones are Spanish in origin. In the overall the banking system is both efficient and careful, despite the agreeable apparent casualness of the Catalans and in no way shares the commission charges and delays in transfers which are practised by Spanish banks whose only other significant attribute is inefficiency. The banks are normally open from 9 am to 1 pm and from 3 pm to 5 pm and are closed Saturday afternoon and Sunday.

V BANKING SECRECY

General outline

To suggest a general basis for banking secrecy in a country which lives by commerce (derived originally from a word meaning contraband) and has no commercial code, is to run something of a risk. However, it is in fact possible but is based, like all Andorran rules, on internal principles close to secrecy. The bankers when questioned point out that the co-principality has never had any need of rules since it has never been the object of any attempt to breach secrecy along the lines of the Gestapo in Switzerland.

Legal basis and penalties

There is no legal basis: it is simply a question of Andorra having always respected banking secrecy, except in one local case. There was one court decision in a case involving Morocco and Switzerland. The Andorran judge lifted the veil of banking secrecy for one specific piece of information, but ordered as part of his decision that once the information had been given the bank's files should be quite simply destroyed. In the absence of law, there are no legal penalties for the non-observance of bank secrecy.

Although this aspect of the question does not form part of this book, it is quite interesting to review banking secrecy between husband and wife: the Andorran woman, enjoying Catalan law, is completely emancipated as regards any husband (Swiss ladies should be jealous!) and the question of banking secrecy between husband and wife is exactly the same as between strangers.

As for the hypothetical situation of an eventual legal conflict between husband and wife of different nationalities whose last place of residence was Andorra, any suggestions made by a foreign lawyer to his Andorran colleagues give the impression of such incongruity as to be completely ignored by the local practitioner.

VI INSTRUMENTS OF BANKING SECRECY

Direct

Andorra is familiar with not only numbered accounts but also accounts in false names.

Indirect

In the absence of any exchange control foreign legal entities are perfectly acceptable without any of the restrictions existing in Switzerland, and the identity of the beneficial owner can remain secret.

Bearer

These do not exist.

VII THE PRACTICE OF BANKING SECRECY AND FOREIGN ECONOMIC POWERS

Banking secrecy is granted irrespective of residence as there are no exchange controls.

Exchange control

The breach of an economic regulation in another country would not appear to cause an Andorran judge to raise banking secrecy. The rule suggested is that in principle secrecy may not be lifted by an Andorran judge except in a criminal matter and then only on condition that the crime would be considered as such in Andorran law, which would certainly not be the case for exchange control. But there is apparently no evidence of a court ruling in this area.

Taxation

Banking secrecy seems complete.

VIII INTERNATIONAL AGREEMENTS LIKELY TO UNDERMINE BANKING SECRECY

In principle Andorra is not in a position to sign any international agreements since it does not have an international identity. Neither is it party to any signed by France or Spain, although it is not unknown for some, such as the Geneva convention on authors' rights, to be extended. There are not, on the face of it, any such extensions of a general or specific nature which are likely to affect banking secrecy.

IX BANKING SECRECY AND THE FINANCIAL MARKET

Non-residents' market, blind and official

In the total absence of exchange controls, local direct taxation and double taxation agreements, there is no need to create a distinction between the official market and the anonymous one.

The rates of withholding tax at source are as follows:

> bank interest   nil
> dividends   nil

The question of dividends is ultimately only of secondary importance since there are few large Andorran companies and investments made in Andorra are more usually in the property market,* and the banks play an important role because the investments are often made by a company officially controlled by a bank. In such a case only the company appears on the property register in the valleys and the beneficial owner is protected by a private *fiducia* agreement (a system similar to the Swiss fiduciary agreement and similarly derived from Roman law).

The true owner does not therefore appear and may, to use the expression of the valleys, 'play the Andorran' (appear to be poor). The example is indeed set by the banks themselves who 'play the Andorran' far more than their foreign counterparts. The branch of one of the biggest banks in Andorra la Vella is a discreet little shop, which, once you have passed through the entrance is transformed into sumptuous offices, built within the neighbouring buildings.

Back-to-back loans

There is no legal or fiscal obstacle to their use. The only problem is a psychological one and springs from the fact that Andorra, a true banking haven, is not an important international financial centre. Any financing beyond the immediate Spanish and French provinces risks giving the impression of being a back-to-back loan, even if it is genuine.

X PERSONAL COMMENTS

A number of professional people suggest that Andorra acts as a conduit for capital leaving France on its way to Switzerland. This seems unlikely to be true

---

*Although apartments are sold by the square metre, land is sold by the square 'pem', a local measurement equivalent to 20 square centimetres.

for two reasons: firstly because French capital has no need to pass through Andorra to get to Switzerland and secondly because once capital has been transferred to Andorra there seems scarcely any point in suffering the disadvantages of Switzerland—at the worst time of negative bank interest charged on deposits in Swiss francs owned by non-residents, the Andorran banks were going so far as to pay interest in Swiss francs!

According to French bankers (jealous in this case) the Andorrans were able to do such things because of major property development in the principality which allowed them to make guaranteed loans at rates going up to 18 per cent, as at the best time in France. It is sad to think that during the 'good times' in France the banks never had the idea of paying interest on credit balances. They hide from this issue behind the facile excuse of rules which do not permit it, following the principles and procedures of their Swiss colleagues, while forgetting of course that they are the people who make the rules and could therefore change them if they had the least desire to do so.

The development of banking in Andorra is not, however, solely related to banking secrecy, but also to the attitude of the Spanish bankers who have encouraged a certain number of investments in Spain to be made through Andorra, and also some flows in the opposite direction. This tendency has good chances of expanding since the introduction of the Spanish law suppressing bank secrecy as far as fiscal matters are concerned (17 November 1977). So much the better for the Andorran bankers—their success has come from their own efforts, but it is agreeable that they should also, like the Swiss, profit from the mistakes of their neighbours.

24 Bahrein:
The Offshore Banking Units (OBUs) of international finance

I THE COUNTRY AND ITS COMPONENTS

Geographical, historical and economic situation

Bahrein is an archipelago of 33 islands in the Persian Gulf which lie within a sort of harbour formed by the coast of Saudi Arabia and Qatar. They have an total land area of 620 square kilometres.

After the departure of the British, Bahrein hesitated between joining a federation with Qatar and the other Emirates and also internally between a parliamentary democracy and the traditions of the Koran. The latter seems to have succeeded, given that there is a Sheik as head of state and his younger brother is prime minister.*

Oil extraction is the main source of revenue but there is also important activity in the areas of a dry dock service, banking and fishing for the giant prawn.†

Population, stability, communications and legal system

The population of 260 000 people is essentially urban and is based mainly at Manama, the administrative capital, which has 90 000 inhabitants and is at the northern end of the main island which is also called Bahrein. This island is linked by a motorway bridge to two neighbouring islands: Muharraq, where the international airport is sited, and Sitrah, where there is a refinery. There is a project in hand to construct a causeway linking Bahrein to Saudi Arabia, 30 kilometres away; this is estimated to cost about US$ 750 million.

The legal system is based on local usage and in general terms the Koran, to which has been added British common law. Traditionally this has been accepted in commercial matters.

The political situation is stable, despite the fact that the National Assembly,

---

*Sheik Isa ben Sulman and Sheik Khalifah ben Sulman al Khalifah. The Khalifah family has ruled Bahrein since 1783, having taken over from the Persians, thanks to the British.
†This activity, almost part of the folklore of the Gulf, brings in about $7 million annually.

elected in 1973, was dissolved in 1975 and has not met subsequently. The telephone and telex systems are excellent when they are not fully occupied.

II THE CURRENCY

The local currency is the Bahrein dinar, issued by the Bahrein Monetary Agency* whose objects are to organize the issue and circulation of money in the State of Bahrein and its foreign exchange.†

Since 1978 it has been based on a fixed exchange rate with the US dollar:

>1 Bahrein dinar = 1000 fils
>1 Bahrein dinar = Swiss franc 5.16 (May 1982)
>1 Bahrein dinar = US$ 2.64

There is no form of exchange control and all currencies can circulate freely. The currencies of the neighbouring countries are obviously the ones most commonly to be found in cash transactions: Saudi Arabia (Saudi rials), Kuwait (Kuwaiti dinars) Arab Emirates (UAE dirhams).

III EXCHANGE CONTROLS

There is no exchange control and therefore no need to distinguish between residents and non-residents, except for the offshore banks which may not accept deposits from residents.

IV BANKS AND THE BANKING SYSTEM

The banks operate under the control of the Bahrein Monetary Agency, whose function is in particular to organize and control the activities of the banking sector and control and direct credit in accordance with the objectives and political economy of the state, and to create and develop a financial and money market.

Bahrein has seen an extraordinary development of banking, due in particular to its privileged geographical position in the heart of the 'rich' Arab world. Since the Decree of 1973 created Offshore Banking Units (generally known under the abbreviation OBUs) more than 35 offshore banks have been created and their assets at the end of 1978 were in the region of US$ 25 billion,‡ thereby giving Bahrein a similar value to that of Singapore. It is welcome to see the Arabs, to whom we owe 'algorithmetic'§ and algebra‖ and probably

---

*The Director-General of the BMA is an Englishman, Alan Moore, and is generally considered to be the moving spirit behind offshore banks.
†Decree 23, 1973.
‡'Banking and finance in the Arab world', *International Herald Tribune*, May 1979.
§The algorithms used in the Middle Ages were an invention of the Muslim mathematician AlKhwarismi (or Akarismi) and their name was based on his after 'Europeanization'.
‖This term derives from the mathematics book by the same author whose title was 'Al-Jabr Wa'l Muqabalah', and was also Europeanized.

zero (attributed by some authors to the Arabs), utilizing the instruments which they have created with such success—even if Bahrein's amazing growth comes in part from the sad decline of Lebanon.* In addition to the 35 offshore banks there are 18 local banks.

One of the peculiarities of Bahrein is its hours of business in the banking sector. As a Muslim country its religious holiday is Friday, and banks work on Saturday and Sunday, which enables them to take up from other centres which are closed. The banks are normally open from 7 am to noon and 3.30 pm to 5.30 pm.

V BANKING SECRECY

General outline and legal basis

Normally Bahrein would not appear amongst the banking havens in a direct way because in terms of banking secrecy it is not a haven through deliberate intention and it is difficult to replace the traditional aspect by the creation of offshore banks. Of course the Bahrein bankers are far from being inclined to shout your secrets from the rooftops. In this sense secrecy is part of the commercial custom which is derived from British common law and the Koran which is part of the law, and encourages confidence. But these aspects would be insufficient in themselves to cause Bahrein to be classified as a haven were it not for the Rolls Royces of banking secrecy, the OBUs. And even with the importance of the OBUs† Bahrein would not constitute a haven of banking secrecy were it not for one further fact: Bahrein which is an absolute tax haven is not linked by any bilateral or multilateral agreements which provide for exchanges of information—which does not in itself imply any guarantee but does allow a solid presumption of international discretion.

Bahrein should also have its place in this guide since (it is one of the reasons for its success) used in conjunction with other places, it permits banking activities to take place 24 hours a day, 7 days a week.

VI THE INSTRUMENTS OF BANKING SECRECY

Direct

They are not used.

Indirect

In the absence of exchange controls the use of foreign legal entities presents no difficulties, and the Swiss restrictions do not exist.

---

*It should perhaps be stated though that the banking activity in the Lebanon was more geared to taking private deposits than is that of Bahrein.
†The OBUs have been particularly selected since in practice only an internationally recognized bank or financial group will be given a licence by the Bahrein Monetary Agency.

Bearer

There are none.

VII THE PRACTICE OF BANKING SECRECY AND FOREIGN ECONOMIC POWERS

A country with a secrecy tradition which has not been properly established, and a vocation now incontestably recognized as a financial centre, Bahrein finds the sources of its banking secrecy in the quality of its bankers and the volume of the business now done—renewing therefore the Bank of England's motto 'Men not ideas' before that institution became submerged in its own red tape. Bahrein is not in the position of the Bahamas and Caymans, obliged to avoid disturbing the American eagle too much, and based on that modern source of power, oil, fears no-one except perhaps those who use it since nothing prevents Kuwait or Saudi Arabia from creating OBUs in their own territories, provided that they can find someone to do it for them.

One last problem is that Bahrein is part of the Arab boycott of Israel and prohibits imports from that country (as was also previously the case of Rhodesia), but the boycott is an arm against nature. One last detail which is more a matter of courtesy—it is preferable to avoid mention of things which bring back unpleasant events and sometimes it is necessary to pay attention when choosing a name, or indeed to change a name.*

VIII INTERNATIONAL AGREEMENTS LIKELY TO UNDERMINE BANKING SECRECY

There is no bilateral or multilateral agreement in force which is likely to affect banking secrecy. One small shadow is that Bahrein is a signatory to the Bretton Woods agreement and has been a member of the International Monetary Fund since 7 September 1972.

IX BANKING SECRECY AND THE FINANCIAL MARKET

Blind and official markets for non-residents

In the absence of double taxation agreements there is no need to distinguish between these two markets:

                    bank interest   nil
                    dividends   nil

---

*Thus, for example, when it set up in Saudi Arabia the Banque de l'Indochine et Suez left out the 'Suez' and called itself the Al Bank Al Saudi Al Fransi (Franco-Saudi Bank); but for some unknown reason this bank's OBU in Bahrein is called the Banque de l'Indochine et de Suez.

Back-to-back loans

These present no difficulty. There is a political obstacle as far as Israel is concerned.

X PERSONAL COMMENTS

In the banking sector figures are often an important factor. The assets of foreign OBUs have grown from US $1.5 billion in 1975 to US $23.5 billion in 1978. What more can one say?

25 Hong Kong: The band of three

I THE COUNTRY AND ITS COMPONENTS

Geographical, historical, and economic situation

The British colony of Hong Kong is anything but asleep there on the South East coast of China and its 1000 square kilometres of territory overflowing with Chinese refugees is full of activity. Ceded by China to Great Britain after the opium war of 1842 the island of Hong Kong itself covers only 82 square kilometres, which explains why everything is built very high and why the cost per square metre of land can reach such truly impressive levels.*

Hong Kong is very important as a commercial and industrial centre as well as a seaport, and to this should be added its activity as a not inconsiderable centre and also its tourism which is a second resource.

Population, stability, communications, and legal system

The population of 5 000 000 (of which 98 per cent are of Chinese origin) is growing constantly because of the influx of refugees from 'continental' China and Chinese refugees from Vietnam.† Despite this Hong Kong is with Singapore one of the richest Asian countries (competing with Japan) in terms of income per head, even after taking into account a population density 20 times that of its neighbours.

The legal system is that of British common law together with local laws. The telecommunications are remarkable.

II THE CURRENCY

The local currency is the Hong Kong dollar which, having been attached to sterling, was then tied to the US dollar but was finally floated free after the effective devaluation of the dollar in 1974:

---

*The record for all categories was reached by the Tsim Sha Tsui site which reached a price of HK$ 400 million for a 1380 square metre site—about 271 000 French francs per square metre.
†This exodus does not seem to have harmed Hong Kong since the rate of population growth was estimated in 1979 to be 12 per cent instead of 6.4 per cent.

HK $ 1 = 100 cents
HK $ 1 = Swiss francs 0.34 (May 1982)
HK $ 1 = US $0.17

Curiously enough Hong Kong is apparently the only country in the world where the privilege of issuing banknotes is not restricted to the central bank but is given to three commercial banks: Hong Kong and Shanghai Banking Corporation, Chartered Bank, and the Mercantile Bank of India. There is not in any event a Central Bank, which may have something to do with the fact that the Hong Kong dollar is more than 100 per cent covered by the monetary reserves.

III EXCHANGE CONTROL

There is no form of exchange control.

IV BANKS AND THE BANKING SYSTEM

The main characteristic of the Hong Kong banking system is that there is no system in the strict sense of the term—which is a confirmation of the principle that a well-run country does not need constraints. 'Liberalism' is not in Hong Kong synonymous with 'anarchy' and the banking law gives the Commissioner of Banking the power at any time, with or without prior notice, to inspect such books, documents or transactions which might seem necessary to him* but is in doing so subject to professional secrecy determined by the same banking law,† except in the case of a criminal act or liquidation of a bank.

There are 108 banks in Hong Kong‡ and more than 200 financial institutions (finance companies) which play a role similar to that of banks and are also subject to inspection by the Commissioner.§ The banks are generally open from 10 am to 3 pm during the week, 9 am to noon on Saturdays and closed on Sundays.

Hong Kong is not a haven as regards the Rolls Royce of banking secrecy. In fact, even if since March 1978 the authorities have been granting new banking licences, the conditions required are rather draconian and, apart from the fact that the recipient must already be a bank in another country which affords reciprocal arrangements, the assets must exceed 3 billion dollars—really a solid gold Rolls Royce.

---

*Banking Ordinance, Cap. 155 section 15.
†Section 13.
‡As at 1 June 1979.
§Deposit-taking Companies Ordinance (Cap. 328, section 31A).

V BANKING SECRECY

General outline

Hong Kong has not created a financial and banking environment based on secrecy. This absence of legislation in a country which is intelligently managed by remarkable people seems difficult to explain. The situation arises from two factors: firstly Hong Kong received an injection of Anglo-Saxon law, which has led to the use of trust deeds (that is indirect instruments) and then the absence of exchange controls has permitted the development of companies run by 'nominees' without having to indicate the beneficial owner to any central bank.

These possibilities would themselves have been insufficient to make Hong Kong a banking haven, even if they had not been the dominant factor in the place. Given that Hong Kong has taken in the practice of common law, the principle of the Tournier case (see Chapter 10 on Great Britain) is applied and the value of this principle grows in relation to the very few exceptions in the case of the non-resident.

Legal basis and penalties

As the legal basis is simply British common law, the principles of bank secrecy rest with those of the Tournier case and the only penalty is that of civil damages.

Secrecy extends to all bank employees, even after they have left the bank.*

VI INSTRUMENTS OF BANKING SECRECY

Direct

Numbered accounts are not normally used in Hong Kong, nor apart from exceptional cases are accounts under false names.

Indirect

These are the normal area for banking secrecy, without the Swiss restrictions. It is particularly important that the Swiss restrictions should not exist because if the bank knew the beneficial owner the local tax authorities (Inland Revenue) could obtain information from the bank (although that is unusual). The same thing applies to the Independent Commission against Corruption.

VII THE PRACTICE OF BANKING SECRECY AND FOREIGN ECONOMIC POWERS

It is certainly not the powerful neighbour, known in Hong Kong as 'continental China', which finds protection in Hong Kong's banking secrecy.

---

*This is based on questionnaires, but one bank noted that it is difficult to prove.

In fact the Chinese, a people who are both practical and commercial, are far from neglecting the possibilities offered by Hong Kong to carry out trade which could not be officially approved.

Exchange control

In the absence of exchange control in Hong Kong the reservations which applied for a long time to the Channel Islands, the Bahamas and the Cayman Islands do not have any point. Certain cautions have already been given as far as the United Kingdom is concerned although they do not have any legal basis.

Taxation

Although banking secrecy may not be interposed with the tax authorities for the collection of local taxes, this point is relatively unimportant in as far as Hong Kong is also a tax haven and only business realized in Hong Kong or by Hong Kong residents is taxable (and then at moderate rates).

VIII INTERNATIONAL AGREEMENTS LIKELY TO UNDERMINE BANKING SECRECY

General and specific agreements

There are no general agreements likely to prevent banking secrecy. Nonetheless it should be noted that as a dependent territory of Great Britain the Bretton Woods agreement applies to Hong Kong in the same way as it does to the Cayman Islands and British Virgin Islands. There are no specific agreements.

IX BANKING SECRECY AND THE FINANCIAL MARKET

Blind and official market for non-residents

In the absence of any double taxation agreements there is no need to distinguish between these two markets.
    The common rates of withholding tax are as follows:

                       bank interest   nil

(but if the rate of interest is greater than a variable market rate specified by the Inland Revenue there is a withholding tax of 15 per cent for individuals and 17 per cent for companies not subject to Hong Kong taxation)

                       dividends   nil

Back-to-back loans

They are used locally and do not present any particular difficulties.

X PERSONAL COMMENTS

Although the accent is not placed on banking secrecy in Hong Kong and the Rolls Royce of banking secrecy is difficult to use, the place is very interesting because it brings together the different functions of banking haven, tax haven, commercial centre and financial centre. What more can you ask?

26 British Virgin Islands: Banking virginity still preserved

I THE COUNTRY AND ITS COMPONENTS

Geographical, historical, and economic situation

The 60 islands which make up the British Virgin Islands (more commonly known in its abbreviated form: BVI) lie about 80 kilometres to the west of Puerto Rico. Historically a part of the Leeward Islands, the BVI separated from them (while remaining a British colony) and have established links with the American Virgin Islands, from which they are separated only by the Sir Francis Drake Channel which is about 5 kilometres wide.

Population, stability, communications, and legal system

The population is about 10 000 of which 9000 live in the main island of Tortola which also includes the capital Port Town and is connected to the neighbouring Beef Island by a bridge.

The legal system is based on British common law and has also received some case law from the Leeward Islands on tax matters. Local measures complete the pleasant mixture. The political situation is stable. Communications, post, telephone, and telex systems are all satisfactory.

II THE CURRENCY

The BVI adopted the US dollar in 1962:

> US $1 = 100 cents
> US $1 = Swiss francs 1.95 (May 1982)

There is no local issuance of notes, even of a theoretical nature like Panama. Only the US dollar is used, which has brought the BVI closer to its American neighbours.

III EXCHANGE CONTROLS

There is no reason to distinguish between residents and non-residents, given the absence of exchange controls. It is precisely this absence of controls, rarely to be found in the Caribbean, which makes the major difference between the BVI and the Bahamas and Caymans.

IV BANKS AND THE BANKING SYSTEM

There are a dozen financial institutions (trust companies and so on) of which four are international banks: two local, one Canadian and one British are the only ones with licences for local activities. Prior to 1972,* and in the absence of banking legislation, anyone could form a company including the word 'bank' in its name and having this kind of activity.† The banks are now regulated and receive licences to operate either locally or offshore. The banks are open from 9 am to 2 pm from Monday to Thursday; from 9 am to 2 pm and then from 3.30 pm to 5 pm on Friday. They are closed on Saturdays and Sundays.

V BANKING SECRECY

General outline

This comes within the classic situation of the Tournier case (see Chapter 10 on Great Britain) with a theoretical limitation since the BVI are not a 'no tax' haven but a 'low tax' haven—which also explains the existence of double taxation agreements and the parallel agreements for exchanges of information with certain countries (the BVI and Netherlands Antilles are two favourite bases for investment in the United States because of the treaties which exist between these countries).

As the English put it, you cannot have your cake and eat it, and the existence of local taxes allows the Commissioner of Income Tax to ask the banks for information on all loans and deposits relating to anyone liable to the (moderate) taxation due on income in the BVI. In such a case the bank could not insist upon banking secrecy. However, as Mr N. Westwood, a specialist lawyer in Tortola, remarks: 'to the best of my knowledge such a procedure has never resulted in information being provided by a bank.'

Legal basis and penalties

Legal basis: the legal basis is British common law and in the opposite sense the power of investigation given to the Commissioner of Income Tax implies precisely by imposing a limitation that banking secrecy exists.

---

*Banking Ordinance, no. 17, 1972.
†The Anglo-Saxons call this kind of bank a 'paper bank'—which has no connection with the Chinese expression of a 'paper tiger' meaning an ineffectual enemy—except in as much as the expression signifies a bank which exists on paper only and has no real activity. By comparison a 'captive bank' has a real activity but this is limited to working within the group which owns it.

Penalties: in the absence of a law there is only civil action. Apparently there have never been any cases.

VI INSTRUMENTS OF BANKING SECRECY

Direct

Curiously there exist neither numbered accounts nor ones under false names. Local bankers nonetheless have let it be known that for an important client such an arrangement would not be impossible.

Indirect

There is no obstacle to their use, which is even to be recommended because of the powers of the Commissioner of Income Tax and the existence of the double taxation treaties.

Bearer

They do not exist, despite the absence of exchange controls.

VII THE PRACTICE OF BANKING SECRECY AND FOREIGN ECONOMIC POWERS

Banking secrecy is not the primary virtue of the BVI but it is an element which exists and of which particular note should be taken as far as the Caribbean is concerned, because of the absence of exchange control.

Exchange control

It is particularly in this area that banking secrecy is most certain since in the absence of local exchange controls the equivocal principle of double incrimination which applies in other Caribbean havens does not apply here.

Taxation

This is the area in which secrecy is the least pressing since at least on the local level it does not exist but which poses a problem in terms of conflict between different laws and then, as we shall see, because of existing international treaties.

VIII INTERNATIONAL AGREEMENTS LIKELY TO UNDERMINE BANKING SECRECY

General agreements

There are none. However, as a British colony the BVI enter into the category of dependent territories of the United Kingdom when it comes to international matters and in this sense the Bretton Woods agreement applies to them.

Specific agreements

A number of double taxation agreements signed by Great Britain have been extended to include the BVI. These treaties have been signed by the following countries: Denmark, United States, Norway, Japan, Sweden and Switzerland. Oddly enough there is not actually any treaty in force between Great Britain and the BVI—the last one expired in 1972 and its successor is still under negotiation.

These treaties provide for exchanges of information which are applicable therefore in terms of the powers enjoyed by the Commissioner of Income Tax, that is within the limits of matters affecting local income tax.

IX BANKING SECRECY AND THE FINANCIAL MARKET

Blind market for non-residents

This is obligatory for residents of countries which have signed double taxation agreements with Great Britain that have been extended to the BVI and wish to remain anonymous. In the absence of agreements, the common rate of withholding tax applicable to non-residents (in the fiscal sense) are as follows:

bank interest   nil

This rule has applied only since 1978 and on condition that the interest is paid at normal commercial rates.

Dividends   nil

Since 1978.

Official non-resident market

The treaties signed by Great Britain and applicable to individuals or companies considered to be fiscally resident provide for the suppression of or diminution of withholding taxes. Some withholding taxes can under certain conditions be treated as a credit against local taxes.

Back-to-back loans

There is no particular obstacle nor special difficulties in the blind market.

X PERSONAL COMMENTS

Because of the absence of local exchange control it seems that the BVI may have a certain future in the banking sphere in the Caribbean. In the light of the experience of the Bahamas and Cayman Islands, Mr Westwood is prudent to note:

We do not have any treaties providing for the exchange of information in respect of foreign exchange controls nor affecting banking secrecy, although the foreign banks with branches here may be subject to enforcement measures in their countries of origin or that of their main base.

Such a fear would seem to be well founded as far as Canada is concerned (see Chapter 12). Perhaps it would be desirable for the BVI to provide itself with the appropriate legislation before any conflict with the United States? Such a solution seems very unlikely since the BVI would be extremely reluctant to lose the benefit of the treaty linking it with the United States.

27 Jersey and Guernsey: A new card up one's sleeve

I THE CHANNEL ISLANDS AND THEIR COMPONENTS

Geographical, historical, and economic situation

The Channel Islands consist of Jersey, Guernsey, Alderney and Sark. Only Jersey and Guernsey are used as banking centres. Covering an area of 140 square kilometres, Jersey lies to the north of the French coast and of the two main islands is the one nearest to France, being about 20 kilometres from Mont St Michel. Jersey and Guernsey have been autonomous within the framework of the British Isles since the Middle Ages and the two islands, which once (and particularly so during Cromwell's reign) were rivals are united in their activities as tax havens to which may be added that of banking havens. Jersey and Guernsey both joined the Common Market at the time of Britain's admission, while maintaining their fiscal independence.*

Population, stability, communications, and legal system

The population, Anglo-Saxon in origin, is 126 000 of which 72 000 live on Jersey (whose capital is St Helier) and 54 000 on Guernsey (whose capital is St Peter Port).

The legal system is based on the ancient customs of Normandy together with British common law, to which have been added the decisions of the states of Jersey and Guernsey.

II THE CURRENCY

The currency in current use is the pound sterling together with pounds issued by Jersey and by Guernsey. The two last have parity with the pound sterling and circulate freely on the two islands, but they are not convertible in foreign exchange terms except into pounds sterling.

> 1 pound sterling = 100 new pence
> 1 pound sterling = Swiss francs 3.55 (May 1982)
> 1 pound sterling = US $1.82

---

*Protocol no. 3 of the treaty of accession, signed under the terms of, and in application of, article 227 of the Treaty of Rome.

III EXCHANGE CONTROL

Jersey and Guernsey were part of the 'Scheduled Territories',* that is countries listed in an appendix to a document—in this case the Exchange Control Act which created Bank of England restrictions, until its suspension on 24 October 1979.

This statute, which was outside the competence and the authority of the two states (as for that matter a number of other international matters which are reserved to the United Kingdom), was applicable in all its details immediately after it had been put forward by the Bank of England, which was at the same time the only body authorized to give consent for operations to take place when they were required.†

Although it would normally be considered a disadvantage for a tax haven, the inclusion within a zone subject to severe monetary controls seems in fact to have been an advantage in the case of Jersey and Guernsey because of their fiscal independence.

Transfers with the United Kingdom were not subject to controls because they were part of the same monetary zone and a number of UK residents used the islands either as residents or through an intermediary company, given that the maximum rate of tax for residents and companies who are not exempt is 20 per cent, which is much less than that payable in the United Kingdom. The freedom of transfer also avoided the dollar premium,‡ providing further economies since this has at times reached as much as 50 per cent.

The system does not seem to have created any substantial problems for non-residents who enjoyed complete liberty in retaining foreign currency and transferring it, but its suppression will certainly cause some new activities.

IV BANKS AND THE BANKING SYSTEM

Jersey and Guernsey have experienced in the last 15 years a considerable growth in banking and finance and beyond that Guernsey (no doubt in competition with Bermuda) has started to specialize in captive insurance companies, which cannot be used in Jersey.

There are currently about 50 banks and financial institutions in being, of which 30 are on Jersey. There has been since 1967 (Jersey) and 1969 (Guernsey) a serious technical control on the creation of banks, but there is no system along the lines of the Swiss one.

---

*The Scheduled Territories comprise: United Kingdom, Channel Islands, Isle of Man, Republic of Ireland and Gibraltar.

†The government of Jersey was delegated the power by the Bank of England to authorize in its place the creation of non-resident investment companies, provided that a resident bank would check and certify that the beneficial owner was not a resident of the United Kingdom or the Scheduled Territories. Direct approval was still required for trading companies.

‡A fictitious operation which demands that US dollars be bought and sold at a predetermined—and unfavourable—rate which was supposed to relate the amount of foreign exchange available for these purposes to the demands made.

The banks are open from 9.30 am to 3.30 pm from Monday to Friday and closed on Saturday and Sunday.

V BANKING SECRECY

General outline

This falls within the British type of common law (see Chapter 10) but without the series of exceptions which cause Great Britain to be classified as an inferno.

Legal basis and penalties

Jersey and Guernsey do not have any statutes on banking secrecy nor any penalties which might apply to it. In practice some banks, inspired by the example of their Swiss colleagues, make their employees sign contracts which require secrecy.

There is no legal basis other than the case-law of the Tournier decision and a very limited amount in the local courts. In fact, even in a case of bankruptcy in the face of tax debts, which occurred in the Taylor case (see below), the authorities preferred to withdraw their demand rather than risk a new decision on the principle.

Some explanation, however, would be appropriate on the Taylor case, since the position of the Jersey Attorney General is very revealing and one must be satisfied with that in the absence of a court decision.

Harold Taylor moved to Jersey in 1968 where he became a resident and had his domicile (in the Anglo-Saxon sense). The UK Inland Revenue subsequently examined his tax affairs and came to the conclusion that 'errors' in earlier tax declarations had resulted in an underpayment of tax of £190 000. The Inland Revenue asked the High Court in London, in 1976, to pronounce Taylor as bankrupt on the grounds that he had left England in order to defraud his creditors (in fact, contrary to the allegations made by the Revenue, they were the only creditor). Taylor opposed this on the basis that it was an attempt to make the United Kingdom's taxes applicable in Jersey, but this argument failed and he was pronounced bankrupt in 1977. The British Official Receiver (an official responsible for winding up the affairs of bankrupts) immediately brought an action before the Jersey courts so that property and valuables held by Taylor in Jersey could be handed over to him.* Taylor argued that such a demand constituted a flagrant attempt to execute a foreign fiscal debt. On his side the Official Receiver made it clear that he was an officer of the High Court and not some agent of the British tax authorities, and he was therefore

---

*Under the terms of articles 122 and 233 of the 1914 Bankruptcy Act, the High Court can require any other British court which is competent to give assistance to the Official Receiver to place in his hands the property of a bankrupt.

carrying out his duties on behalf of the High Court and not Her Majesty's tax authorities.

It was at this point that the Jersey Attorney General intervened and said in particular:

That it is necessary to distinguish between public and private debts . . . . That between Jersey and the United Kingdom there are two quite separate and distinct tax systems. That the recovery of a debt due to the Inland Revenue is the recovery of a fiscal debt due to a foreign power . . . . That the Jersey courts are not competent to judge, directly or indirectly, a case for settlement of a fiscal debt of another country . . . and concluded that the Royal Court should use its discretionary powers to reject the demand made.

The affair did not come to court, and was settled outside, according to local lawyers in a way which was to the advantage of the former taxpayer.

VI INSTRUMENTS OF BANKING SECRECY

Direct

It is possible to use numbered accounts, but those under false names do not exist.

Indirect

All foreign legal entities are accepted without any check on their beneficial owner. Investment companies which qualify as exempt and non-resident benefit from bank secrecy. Until the suspension of exchange controls the name of the beneficial owner had to be revealed to the authorities even if they considered the information as being confidential. As non-resident trusts do not benefit from the concession that withholding tax is not charged on interest paid by resident banks to non-residents, it is better to avoid legal entities which may fall into that category and limit oneself to the classic form of company.

Bearer

These do not exist and in any event the principle, incompatible with what was for a long time a strict exchange control, does not permit of a practical assessment.

VII THE PRACTICE OF BANKING SECRECY AND FOREIGN ECONOMIC POWER

Banking secrecy varies according to taxation and exchange control.

Exchange control

There was no banking secrecy for United Kingdom residents and those in the Scheduled Territories until the suspension of exchange controls.

According to the local lawyers the breach of some economic regulations of a foreign country would not cause banking secrecy to be lifted on a non-resident's account, although there is no case-law on this point. This could not in any event happen without the authorization of the courts, but their decision is a lot less certain than the local professionals would have it. In fact in the face of a regime with severe exchange controls, the principle of double incrimination comes into play, since the breach in the foreign country could also constitute a breach in Jersey or Guernsey.*

Furthermore, if the country making the request offered reciprocity, that is would lift banking secrecy on receipt of a similar demand from Jersey or Guernsey, it is difficult to see what reason the local court would have to oppose their request, apart that is from the unwelcome nature of a request which would undoubtedly cause publicity that would discourage depositors. It is very probable that the absence of case-law springs from out-of-court settlements.

It is worth noticing that in the Taylor affair (it did not concern exchange control, but the principle was the same) although the bank vigorously opposed the demands of the British tax authorities, it did nonetheless block Taylor's accounts, although leaving him sufficient income to live comfortably. Under these circumstances there are good reasons for making a settlement when a case might last 10 years or more.

Taxation

In the absence of agreements, except with the United Kingdom, secrecy seems complete for non-residents and even for residents as far as exchange control goes with countries not linked directly to Jersey and Guernsey (Republic of Ireland, Isle of Man and Gibraltar).

VIII INTERNATIONAL AGREEMENTS LIKELY TO UNDERMINE BANKING SECRECY

General agreements

According to local lawyers, there are none likely to affect banking secrecy. It should, however, be noted that Jersey and Guernsey as part of the United Kingdom come into the category of dependencies and in that way are subject to the Bretton Woods agreement.

Specific agreements

There is an agreement between Jersey and Guernsey, signed in 1952, to avoid double taxation between the islands, and a 1956 agreement with the United

---

*The exchange control provisions have been suspended, not repealed.

Kingdom. Both provide for exchange of information, but limited to matters within the competence of each tax authority. On the face of it therefore it would not permit Guernsey, for example, to supply information to the United Kingdom for use by a third country which had made the request under the terms of a double tax treaty with the United Kingdom.*

IX BANKING SECRECY AND FINANCIAL MARKET

Blind market for non-residents

It is available to anyone except residents of the United Kingdom, Jersey and Guernsey. Non-resident trusts are excluded.

In the absence of double tax treaties the rates of withholding tax are as follows:

bank interest   nil

There is an extra-statutory concession made by the tax authorities on condition that the recipient is non-resident and has no income derived from Jersey. (This latter condition does not have a Guernsey equivalent, apparently.)

dividends   nil

There is no withholding tax on dividends paid by an exempt company to non-resident shareholders (there is no tax on this kind of company).

Official non-resident market

This is the United Kingdom, or alternatively, Jersey for Guernsey and vice versa. The agreement with the United Kingdom specifically excludes dividends. In effect, companies which are not exempt are taxed at the rate of 20 per cent on profits, the same as residents are taxed on income. Residents receive a credit for this tax but this does not benefit UK residents.

Back-to-back loans

There is no obstacle to this device.

X PERSONAL COMMENTS

The reputation of Jersey and Guernsey as banking havens has perhaps been damaged, even if the islands are undoubted tax havens and financial centres, but it is also a question of a different approach.

---

*There is a double tax agreement with France for activities in the fields of marine and aviation activity.

It is more in the economic field that the greater doubts exist, given the absence of statutory secrecy and the legislative remainder of the exchange control provisions which might permit the application of the principle of double incrimination.

The roving depositor who wanted to use Jersey or Guernsey notwithstanding would find it worthwhile to use the indirect instruments of banking secrecy, whose use is made easier by the suspension of exchange control—easier in practice, however, the principle is unaffected.

28 Luxembourg:
The blue blood of banking secrecy

I THE COUNTRY AND ITS COMPONENTS

Geographical, historical, and economic situation

Luxembourg is situated in western Europe, between France, Belgium, and Germany. It has a surface area of 2586 square kilometres, and it is a member of the European Community.

The country was created in 1815 at the Congress of Vienna as a member of the German confederation but the Grand Duchy became independent in 1890. It signed a customs and economic union with Belgium in 1921, to which Holland was admitted later the same year, and which is known as Benelux.

Steel manufacture and the mining of iron ore are the main base of its economy, but the financial sector is also very important.

Population, stability, communications, and legal system

It has 350 000 inhabitants, all of a similar Franco-German extraction; 77 000 live in the capital, also called Luxembourg. The legal system is based on the 1804 French civil code. The political situation seems stable and the communications, posts, telephone, and telex systems are excellent.

II THE CURRENCY

The legal tender is the Luxembourg franc which has a fixed parity with the Belgian franc:

$$1 \text{ Luxembourg franc} = 1 \text{ Belgian franc} = 100 \text{ centimes}$$
$$100 \text{ Luxembourg francs} = \text{Swiss francs } 4.49 \text{ (May, 1982)}$$
$$100 \text{ Luxembourg francs} = \text{US } \$2.30$$

The currency is controlled by the Belgian-Luxembourg Institute (BLEU). The Belgian franc circulates freely in Luxembourg and is accepted everywhere in practice.

III EXCHANGE CONTROL

Non-residents

They escape completely from exchange controls and can have accounts in any currency they wish.

Interest paid to non-residents

There is no statutory limitation nor any withholding tax on interest paid to non-residents, and interest may be freely withdrawn from the country.

Residents

There is a sort of double exchange market to which they are obliged to submit, but the system is simple and, subject to a premium, gives free access to capital markets.

IV BANKS AND BANKING SYSTEM

Curiously enough the Luxembourg people do not themselves seem to know exactly how many banks there are in their country: the figure quoted varies between 94 and 108 depending upon the author and the source of information (and taking into account the branches of foreign banks). There are nine banks of Luxembourg origin.

The banking sector employs 7000 people, actually about 10 per cent of the working population, which is a very substantial figure. Control of the sector is exercised by a Bank Control Commissariat (Commisariat au controle des banques). The banks are normally open from 8.30 am to 1 pm and from 1.30 pm to 4.30 pm, but closed on Saturday and Sunday.

V BANKING SECRECY

General outline

As in most countries it can be raised in the event of a dispute between the bank and its client, and in the event of a breach of criminal law overseas which would also be considered to be criminal in Luxembourg, but only within the strict limits of these circumstances. When it comes to the 'spirit' of the law concerning non-residents and banking secrecy in the face of tax matters and exchange controls, an explanation should be left to a prominent Luxembourg professional whose introduction is worth its weight in francs:*

---

*M Albert Dondelinger was President of the Executive board of the International Bank of Luxembourg.

In popular parlance banking secrecy is the antidote to tax investigations. It is here that people's hearts and minds come into conflict and collide with each other, depending upon whether one has a 'little something' or not. I should not deny that there are also some idealists. Happily!

But there is reality, even if it may be lacking in dignity and sense: economic reality which would be horrible if one were not able to deflect it a little and which can become terribly human. There are some facts which are much more important than many grandiose sentiments. There are those people who have too much money to let themselves be caught; those who have a little, but not enough to escape to the Virgin Isles or the Antilles or the Canal side; and then those who have only the time and means to spend exactly what they earn, and consider that to be little enough.

I have always been struck by the fact that practically any measure which is brought in to provide fiscal justice hardly ever touches those it was meant to catch. On the contrary the most severe countries make themselves bleed: their economies become anaemic, capital escapes. I remember reading that in reply to a parliamentary question during a time of monetary troubles in his country M Giscard d'Estaing admitted that even if he put Gendarmes at one metre intervals round the boundaries of France, nothing would prevent the escape of capital if there were no confidence in the country.

All things considered, is it not better to react as Camus did when he said that if pimps and thieves were constantly decried everywhere, then everyone would forever be protesting their honesty—something which above all should be avoided.*

Legal basis and penalties

This is based on a gentle mixture of case-law and various specific statutes, as well as the notable requirement for officials and employees of the State Savings Bank to declare 'guilty' facts. Although this requirement does not apply to private banks, most Luxembourg lawyers agree that it is observed by them.

In any event there was not until very recently any general statute whose non-observance would be punished by the courts, although certain authors—generally not Luxembourg nationals—took the view that article 458 of the Criminal Code (medical secrets)† applies to banking secrecy.

Their view seems to have been confirmed by the Luxembourg legislators in article 16 of the law of 23 April 1981 which states:

as an extension to article 458 of the Criminal Code which will prohibit the administrators, members of supervisory and management boards, management and other employees of entities defined in article 19 of this law [i.e. Luxembourg banking concerns] from revealing secrets which they have learned in their professional capacity.

---

*Certainly a very personal comment! If the sentence attributed to President Giscard d'Estaing provides evidence of lucid analysis and good sense, the Luxembourg interpretation of Albert Camus may be a different matter.
†Article 458 states: Doctors, surgeons, health officers, pharmacists, midwives and any other person who learns secrets by virtue of their profession will be punished for revealing such secrets, except in evidence before the courts or where the law obliges them to reveal the secrets . . . .

VI INSTRUMENTS OF BANKING SECRECY

Direct

The use of numbered accounts seems to be relatively widespread but less common than in Switzerland. Accounts under false names do not seem to be used in practice, even though those banks who were asked seemed in favour of the system.

Indirect

Foreign legal entities seem to be perfectly acceptable without the Luxembourg bankers in fact requiring any proof of the beneficial owner's non-resident status.

Bearer

This sort of account does not exist.

VII THE PRACTICE OF BANKING SECRECY AND FOREIGN ECONOMIC POWERS

Banking secrecy seems to be a concept treated very favourably as far as non-residents are concerned.

Exchange control

It does not appear that a breach of another country's economic regulations would lead to a removal of banking secrecy, even though there is some form of exchange control locally. There is no court decision on this point.

Taxation

Although certain regulations specify that banking secrecy may not be imposed in the face of the tax authorities (particularly as far as making a return is concerned), these regulations do not seem to be applied in practice — and have not given rise to any court decisions even about direct taxation. The local lawyers complain about the absence of any precise legislation to deal with this matter, but are agreed notwithstanding that banking secrecy does exist in this area, particularly for non-residents.

VIII INTERNATIONAL AGREEMENTS LIKELY TO UNDERMINE BANKING SECRECY

General agreements

Luxembourg observes the European Legal Cooperation Agreement signed in Strasbourg on 20 April 1959.* However, Luxembourg's approval is qualified with several reservations, including one that the Grand Duchy reserves the right not to accept a request for help when it relates to an inquiry or proceedings incompatible with the double infraction principle.

Furthermore the Agreement itself stipulates in article 2 that help may be refused if it relates to fiscal contraventions. The result of all this is that Luxembourg can in fact act as it wishes, and there is no reason to think that it would act contrary to its own interests.

Luxembourg is one of the founder members of the IMF and signed the Bretton Woods agreement on 31 December 1945.

Specific agreements

Luxembourg has signed and ratified double taxation agreements with eight countries but the benefits (or disadvantages?) of these treaties have been withheld from holding companies — which makes Luxembourg a tax haven for this kind of entity.

One of these agreements, signed with Belgium and the Netherlands in Brussels on 5 September 1952, deals with reciprocal help in the recovery of tax debts. This treaty was ratified in the Grand Duchy by a decree of 24 December 1955, whose opening sentences are: 'We, Charlotte, by the grace of God Grand Duchess of Luxemburg, Duchess of Nassau . . . etc.' This law seems to have more than one point of interest — even if, according to Luxemburg lawyers it does not operate in practice.

IX BANKING SECRECY AND THE FINANCIAL MARKET

Blind market for non-residents

There is no political constraint which would cause a non-resident to avoid this country or require him to drop his anonymity in order to benefit from double taxation agreements applying because of his nationality or residence. In the absence of a double-taxation agreement the withholding rates are as follows:

bank interest	nil
dividends	15 per cent

---

*Ratified by Luxembourg in its law of 21 July 1976 (Memorial A 1976 p.727).

Official non-resident market

Treaties signed with Austria, United States, Ireland, Netherlands, or the United Kingdom provide for a reduction of withholding tax where the recipient is a resident of these countries.

Back-to-back loans

There is no obstacle to their use and this is encouraged by the fact that the absence of withholding tax on the interest paid to the non-resident on the sum guaranteeing the loan makes the cost of the whole operation not unacceptable. The bank's margin is negotiable, but a deposit of US $1 million in that currency would probably cost a difference of 1 per cent to compensate for the inclusion of the sum in the bank's balance sheet.

X PERSONAL COMMENTS

Luxembourg and Belgium form parts of the same (simple) system of exchange control under which banking secrecy is very limited in Belgium but very well established in Luxembourg. The cynics would conclude from that that Belgian capital escapes through Luxembourg; that may be true, but it is not sufficient to account for the prosperity of the Luxembourg banks. In fact the place has become much more sophisticated from a banking point of view because of the quality of its bankers. In this sense, and above all if banking secrecy continues to be applied and even institutionalized, Luxembourg would appear to be one of Switzerland's most redoubtable competitors—despite its membership of the European Community.

29 Isle of Man:
An isle of man for the businessman

I THE COUNTRY AND ITS COMPONENTS

Geographical, historical, and economic situation

The Isle of Man represents the strange juxtaposition of being the last country in Europe which still birches its inhabitants and also the tax haven which has most recently whipped up its banking sector. An old Viking colony, the island was incorporated into the United Kingdom in 1765 and is today in a situation analogous to that of Jersey and Guernsey. It lies in the Irish Sea, equidistant from Scotland, Ireland and England and has a surface area of approximately 330 square kilometres. Its economy is just being developed, having for a long time been wholly dependent upon tourism, and they are seeking to attract back those Manxmen (the correct designation of the islanders) who have migrated.

Population, stability, communications, and legal system

The population is about 60 000, and the capital is Douglas, which is in the southern part of the island. The institutions are based on survivals from the Middle Ages; the parliament is called Tynwald and has two chambers. Communications exist but in fact are not that easy with continental Europe. Telephone, telex and post systems are reasonably satisfactory.

The legal system follows in a general way that of British common law, onto which are grafted local laws.

II THE CURRENCY

Legal tender is the pound sterling and the pound issued by the Manx government—which is at par with sterling but is not convertible externally into any other currency:

Sterling £1.00 = 100 new pence
Sterling £1.00 = Swiss francs 3.55 (May 1982)
Sterling £1.00 = US $1.82

III EXCHANGE CONTROL

Like Guernsey and Jersey (which chapters contain the appropriate details), the Isle of Man was part of the 'scheduled territories' prior to the suspension of exchange controls in Britain, and the explanations provided for Jersey and Guernsey also apply to the Isle of Man.

IV BANKS AND BANKING SYSTEM

The Isle of Man has been the scene of considerable development in the banking sector recently and there are currently 39 banks active there, employing according to the most recent statistics (1976) 1173 people and controlled under the 1975 Banking Law.*

The reasons for the development of the Isle of Man as a banking centre are similar to those which brought about the development of Jersey and Guernsey, but unlike them, it is impossible to form a bank if the owner is not already established as a bank.

Banks are normally open from 9.30 am to 3.30 pm from Monday to Friday and are closed on Saturday and Sunday.

V BANKING SECRECY

General outline

The general position is that of British common law (see Chapter 10) without the British exceptions which cause that island to be included in the banking infernos.

Under the terms of the 1975 Banking Act the Treasurer of the Isle of Man has the power to make investigations, although this does not apply to those banks which are members of the London Clearing House and their subsidiaries, nor to members of the London Accepting House Committee. Control of 'exempt' banks, those carrying on an offshore activity, is in the hands of the Bank of England. 'This control includes the power of investigation and search, and that of seizure of books and accounts, but does not permit of the examination of the affairs of individual clients. Information gained in this way may not be divulged.'*

Legal position and penalties

The legal basis is that of the Tournier decision which provides a 'very persuasive' precedent, according to Cain and Sons, advocates in Douglas, although no court decision has ever been obtained on the island on the

---

*Banking Act 18 March 1975, which received Royal Assent on 16 April 1975 and was published by Tynwald on 20 May 1975.

question of banking secrecy. In the absence of any statute, there are no penalties provided, other than, as in the Tournier case, damages and interest.

VI   INSTRUMENTS OF BANKING SECRECY

Direct

There is no obstacle to the use of numbered accounts or those in false names, but in practice they are not used.

Indirect

Foreign legal entities are accepted without inquiry as to the beneficial owner. The use of local legal entities is certainly a possibility, but the problems created by this are similar to those in Jersey and Guernsey, and as in most indirect schemes, a foreign legal entity is a worthwhile precaution.

Bearer

In the same way as Jersey and Guernsey, and for the same reasons, bearer documents are not currently used.

VII   THE PRACTICE OF BANKING SECRECY AND FOREIGN ECONOMIC POWERS

The situation is similar to that of Jersey and Guernsey.

VIII   INTERNATIONAL AGREEMENTS LIKELY TO UNDERMINE BANKING SECRECY

Again the situation is identical to that in Jersey and Guernsey.

IX   BANKING SECRECY AND THE FINANCIAL MARKET

Blind market for non-residents

This is available other than to UK residents, and has been so since 1955. In the absence of double taxation agreements, the rates of withholding tax are as follows:

bank interest	nil
dividends	20 per cent

(but no withholding tax is levied on dividends from a non-resident company)

Official non-resident market

This exists as a result of a treaty with Great Britain which has been in force since 1955.

Back-to-back loans

There is no obstacle to the use of this device.

X PERSONAL COMMENTS

An undisputed tax haven, the Isle of Man wishes to become a banking haven and in particular to attract captive banks. Wanting to attract captive banks but restricting their formation to existing banks is a strange procedure which seems more like trying to sell a Rolls Royce in a pedestrian precinct. The Isle of Man is, however, in business.

30 USSR:
See no evil, speak no evil, hear no evil

I THE COUNTRY AND ITS COMPONENTS

The USSR has no need of further explanation, but the USSR as a banking haven is an unusual enough idea to warrant a little clarification, which can usefully be given in the place of a description of the country.

One should not confuse a Soviet bank in the USSR and a bank outside the USSR and under Soviet control, such as the BCEN (Narodny Bank) in Paris. It is of only secondary importance to note, for example that the Wozschod Handelsbank of Zurich offers numbered accounts; it offers even more than that—it offers Swiss banking secrecy, because although it may be under Soviet control, legally it is subject to Swiss banking law in the same way that the BCEN is a French bank.

There could also be a certain conflict between banking secrecy and the possibility of opening a numbered bank account. If it is true that 'the Soviet State creates conditions in which the individual may grow happily and freely . . freedom of speech, freedom of the press, freedom to hold meetings and make processions and demonstrations in the streets',* banking secrecy—which is available only to non-residents for deposits in foreign currencies—has not been created in order to protect the individual.

It has been created to meet the need of the USSR for foreign currency and as a result finds its legal basis in that need, since in currency problems the end justifies the means. How can such a system be politically acceptable to the Soviet workers? It is very simple—they know nothing of it, since if information is free, facts given to the press must be presented in the correct legal context so that no information will damage the Soviet state.

It is therefore for those reasons that the roving depositor will find the Soviet Union offers a high standard of banking secrecy, provided that his deposits are not counterbalanced by any embarrassing political activities on the part of the depositor; a benevolent neutrality is warmly recommended before journeying to the frozen north.

II THE CURRENCY

The legal tender is the rouble, which is not convertible. The daro-rouble, derived from foreign currencies and restricted in use to the purchases made by

---
*P. Romachkine, 'The current state of Soviet law' in *Principles of Soviet Law*, Moscow.

the *apparatchiks* in the shops reserved for them, was officially discontinued in 20 December 1975, but a similar system has allowed the *apparatchiks* to increase their purchasing power by 650 per cent.*

> 1 rouble = 100 kopecks
> 1 rouble = Swiss francs 2.73 (May 1982)
> 1 rouble = US $1.40

(The rates are very different on the unofficial market)

III EXCHANGE CONTROL

Non-residents

They escape exchange controls, but as there are no convertible roubles, they can only hold deposits in foreign currencies. The import and export of roubles is forbidden.

Interest paid to non-residents

There is no legal limitation and interest may be exported freely.

Residents

It is useless to examine the rights which they do not have.

IV BANKS AND BANKING SYSTEM

Vladimir Oulianov, perhaps better known under the name of Lenin, wrote: 'as the State Bank has offices in all the factories, it is already nine-tenths of the Socialist machinery . . . it is in a way the bones of the Socialist system'. This line of thought perhaps explains the extreme centralization of the Soviet banking system (which does not in any event permit of private banks). The system is very simple: the Gosbank plays the role of central bank and issuer of currency, the Stroibank operates as a normal commercial bank for the people and makes loans, the State Savings Bank collects people's savings and the Vnechtorgbank looks after international financing and the secret deposits of non-residents. The bank is normally open from 9 am to 1 pm and from 2 pm to 6 pm, but closed on Saturday and Sunday.

V BANKING SECRECY

General outline

Banking secrecy does not appear in Soviet statutes in the strict sense of the term, but rather it enters into the wider area of Soviet legality which covers

---

Pick's Currency Year Book (see bibliography, page 292).

decisions made by government bodies, in this case a decision that the Vnechtorgbank should offer banking secrecy.

However, all accounts, even straightforward current accounts, offered to non-residents are protected with banking secrecy without the need for depositors to have numbered accounts, which in reality are a technical protection against junior employees of the bank as in all countries. Article 10 of the general conditions for opening a bank account (type A) of the Vnechtorgbank says: 'The bank observes secrecy on all accounts opened'.

As far as numbered accounts are concerned, the Vnechtorgbank makes no secret of their existence, quite the reverse. In its publicity material distributed under the title of *The Foreign Trade Bank of the USSR* the following points are set out:

1. The USSR Foreign Trade Bank accepts foreign currency funds from non-residents to be held in current or deposit accounts.
2. Foreign currency sums deposited in these accounts, as well as interest accruing on the funds, are free of any tax charges.
3. The funds may be transferred abroad on demand of the account holder. As far as numbered accounts and deposits are concerned, the bank guarantees not only the preservation of secrecy as to the state of the account and any transactions carried out through the account, but also as to the identity of the holder of such an account.

Curiously enough this information appears in a box above a cartoon which shows three people: one is covering his mouth, another his eyes and the third his ears. After the gnomes of Zurich, the monkeys of Moscow? It is to be hoped that the picture is not a warning to travellers . . . in the absence of a caption, an interpretation must be justified.

Legal basis and penalties

The legal basis is the principle of Soviet legality. There are no formal penalties and given that the bank is part of the state, it is difficult to see how there might be any.

The Soviets, without perhaps appreciating it, are today confronted with a problem which is found in the capitalist countries, which is not surprising since they copy capitalist structures in their international relations. The USSR published new legislation which imposed a 40 per cent tax on the net profits of foreign legal entities trading in the USSR, and a sliding scale of tax (depending upon category) for individual income derived from the USSR.*

Since the Soviet concept of legality does not concern itself with the principle of laws not being retroactive, the new tax system applied not only from 1 July 1978 (which would be normal, as each country has the right to raise the taxes

---

*Decree of the Praesidium, 12 May 1978 and executive 'Instruction'.

to which its citizens consent) but would also be retroactive for 2 years and would apply on an individual basis to such cases as were agreed between the Finance Ministry and the Foreign Ministry.

This piece of legislation which is pernicious in that it is retroactive, is also unclear, a burden and infinitely dangerous.

Unclear

First of all there is a degree of ambiguity between the remarks of the Vnechtorgbank which suggest that all interest credited to anonymous accounts is free of tax charges, and the text of the 'Instruction' which says that: 'all foreign persons are not subject to income tax in the USSR on interest paid on accounts and loans opened or deposit made with Soviet credit institutions'. The ambiguity arises from the fact that if one takes a restrictive interpretation within the context of the Soviet banking system the Vnechtorgbank is not strictly speaking a credit organization. It seems that the interpretation is not clear and the Soviet drafters should have referred to the actual banking practice.

A burden

The principle of exemption from tax on bank interest only applies to depositors from countries which give reciprocal benefits to Soviet citizens.*
Such a formula does not go well with numbered accounts and is scarcely compatible with their principle.

Infinitely dangerous

This is rather more serious. In practice, most users of numbered accounts in Moscow are people who have some professional or commercial involvement with the USSR. However, we have seen that in certain unspecified cases they may become taxable retrospectively, according to the whims of two ministries, those of Finance and Foreign Affairs. In such an abnormal situation, it might be possible or even normal that the person being plundered might be inclined to understate his profits, since he could not have foreseen the tax when working out his original price and profit margin. Could he then rely upon the secrecy of his numbered account? The matter is far from certain, given that the administration has wide powers of investigation† and the procedure for them is that fixed by the Ministry of Finance, with no further details given!‡

---

*Article 29, line 2 of the Instruction.
†Article 29 line 2 of the Instruction.
‡Article 30 of the Instruction.

VI   THE INSTRUMENTS OF BANK SECRECY

Direct

Numbered accounts present no problem since they are even suggested in the publicity. Accounts in false names are feasible.

Indirect

Their use is feasible, even though it might seem surprising that a Panamanian company should have an account in Moscow. However, the Vnechtorgbank, to be certain of the political situation, would want to know the identity of the real owner.

Bearer

They do not exist apparently, and for reasons of political safety their adoption is unlikely.

VII   THE PRACTICE OF BANKING SECRECY AND FOREIGN ECONOMIC POWERS

The USSR, unlike the Bahamas or Cayman Islands and perhaps even to a lesser extent Switzerland, has no need to fear American sanctions for two reasons. Firstly the balance of power is not the same as with a small country; and secondly it is unlikely that a large number of US citizens have numbered accounts in Moscow and so such accounts would represent an isolated phenomenon which is unlikely to affect US Treasury statistics.

Exchange control

Despite the existence of local exchange controls, a breach of another country's exchange controls does not seem likely to bring about a lifting of banking secrecy, but of course as far as can be ascertained there exists no case-law on this matter.

Taxation

According to the authorities no exchanges of information are allowed on numbered accounts.

VIII INTERNATIONAL AGREEMENTS LIKELY TO UNDERMINE BANKING SECRECY

General agreements

There are none. It is worth noting as well that the USSR is not a member of the International Monetary Fund.

Specific agreements

There do not seem to be any agreements likely to affect banking secrecy.

IX BANKING SECRECY AND THE FINANCIAL MARKET

Blind market for non-residents

There is no reason to anticipate in the context of the Soviet economy the difficulty of withholding tax on dividends, and as far as bank interest goes subject to the qualifications already explained, there is normally no withholding tax for those whose countries do not impose one.

        bank interest nil (provided there is reciprocity)

Official non-resident market

There are a number of treaties to avoid double-taxation.

Back-to-back loans

There are a number of geographical and political obstacles to their use.

X PERSONAL COMMENTS

Until the introduction of its clumsy 1978 measures the USSR would have seemed a very interesting banking haven. What confidence though can a roving depositor have in a country which publishes fiscal measures that are retroactive on an individual basis—and which might therefore decide tomorrow, if the whim occurred, to publish retroactively the names of all those holding numbered accounts or to tax them with a retroactive negative interest on the basis of a 'personal' assessment? It is all a matter of taste and if there are plenty of people who like a fish served when scarcely cooked, why not those who like the Soviet *nouvelle cuisine*?

V
Banking Havens
which have chosen their vocation

Sometimes vocations chosen late in life are the most sincere, and their novelty sharpens and strengthens them.

It was to fight against the Gestapo that Switzerland, a country with a tradition of secrecy, finally felt the need to make a law on banking secrecy, not only to protect its clients, but also its bankers and its bank employees, against the actions of foreign powers.

Such motives led the Bahamas and the Cayman Islands to want to protect their clients from American agents of the IRS, and even 'obliged' the Cayman Islands to strengthen their laws which the American courts (having weighed the balance of the economic interests of the two countries) deliberately decided to violate.

Generally speaking, it is apparently the 'threatened' countries which have been led towards a 'stronger' vocation when simple tradition would have been enough.

Certainly every rule has its exceptions, and Nauru (an island in the Central Pacific) had no tradition; it is true that if Nauru does have a law, Nauru has still only one bank!

It is also most often in countries with a vocation that laws on offshore banks have been created which, when they are captive, are the Rolls Royce of banking secrecy. They will be briefly compared in Part VI since we have decided, in this way imitating the most serious banking havens, to eliminate from this work the 'paper banks' which are nothing more than the radiator cap on the Rolls Royce.

31 The Bahamas:
Nothing but the sea is transparent

I THE COUNTRY AND ITS COMPONENTS

Geographical, historical, and economic situation

The 700 islands making up the 'Commonwealth of the Bahamas'* are situated between Haiti and the southwestern tip of Florida.

The Bahamas, which had been a British colony since 1717, became independent on the 10 July 1973, but within the Commonwealth, and the Queen of England is still head of this parliamentary democracy.

The economy is based mainly on tourism, including fiscal tourism. Banking activity has become the secondary industry of the country.

Population, stability, communications, and legal system

The population of 240 000 inhabitants (140 000 of which live in New Providence where Nassau, the capital, is located, and 20 000 in Freeport on Grand Bahamas Island) is composed of 80 per cent blacks and 20 per cent whites.

The basis of the legal system is British 'common law' complemented by local laws drawn up before and since the colonial period.

The political situation continues to be stable and is strengthened by the developing banking activity.

II CURRENCY

The currency is the Bahamian dollar linked to the American dollar on the basis of fixed parity:

        1 Bahamian dollar = 100 cents
        1 Bahamian dollar = US $1.00
        1 Bahamian dollar = Swiss francs 1.95 (May 1982)

---

*This is the correct name of the country, having been previously known as 'The Colony of the Bahamas Islands'.

III EXCHANGE CONTROL

The Bahamas were part of the 'scheduled territories' until 1973 when they pulled out, and are now subject only to the Central Bank of the Bahamas, which plays the role that the Bank of England used to perform.

The Bahamian system of exchange control is largely inspired by the old British system and makes a distinction between both individuals and corporate bodies as residents and non-residents.

Non-residents

Non-residents escape all exchange control and can hold accounts in any currency without restriction except for Bahamian dollars (unless authorization is given by the Central Bank). Investments, even real estate, are subject to prior authorization and justification of a transfer of currency at the official rate. The re-exportation of the dividends and the result of the liquidation of the investment is then authorized and guaranteed, but can only take place by conversion into the currency whose transfer permitted the initial investment and at the official rate on the day of transfer.

The definition of 'non-resident' is complicated by a stay on the island, and the banking traveller should consult a local lawyer. In general, permission to stay granted for less than 1 year corresponds to the status of non-resident, but other conditions may arise in the case of professional activities, even for foreign companies.

Interest paid to non-residents

There is no obstacle to this, and no withholding tax at source.

Residents

Residents are subject to a strict exchange control and can only hold their assets in Bahamian dollars which obviously cannot be credited to a non-resident's account nor to the non-resident account of a temporary resident.

Temporary residents

A special case is that of temporary residents defined as the residents of another country working in the Bahamas and whose initial work permit was granted for 1 year or more. In this curious system, they are treated as Bahamian residents with regard to the Bahamian dollars produced by their work, and cannot hold an account in convertible Bahamian dollars; on the other hand, they are considered as non-residents with regard to their other assets, which are freely convertible and transferable. The balances of these 'mixed' accounts of non-residents in Bahamian dollars can be transferred periodically as can their balance on departure, after prior authorization.

IV BANKS AND THE BANKING SYSTEM

There are approximately 350 Bahamian and foreign banks and financial institutions in the Bahamas, and it is safe to bet that without the government's policy of 'reorganization', there would be many more. More than 2000 people, 90 per cent of which are Bahamian, representing 7 per cent of the working population, are directly employed in the banking sector, which for 1978 meant that salaries amounted to 500 million dollars. Baswell Donaldson, governor of the Central Bank, has said: 'The Bahamas have probably produced more bankers and financiers per head of population than any other country in the world'.*

The reality is that the Bahamas have in fact become one of the most important financial centres in the world, and this situation has not arisen simply because of its banking secrecy, but rather as a result of restrictions imposed on American banks. Nevertheless, without banking secrecy, this activity would not have developed.

The total amount in deposits of non-residents, in August 1978, came to more than $100 billion, a figure, according to some calculations, comparable to the deposits in Switzerland.†

As for the market in Eurocurrency, the Bahamas are now in second place, after London, representing 9–10 per cent of the world market.

A form of control of the banking system is organized by the Governor-General who has the power, when a bank cannot or seems not to be able to meet its obligations, or else seems, in his opinion, to be conducting its affairs in a manner contrary to the public interest or the interest of its clients or creditors, to require an audited financial statement.‡

In the event that the financial statement does not appear to be satisfactory, the licence permitting the banking activity may be revoked.

Furthermore, the Central Bank may require information of banks and financial institutions and all their directors or employees (in a prescribed form and within a set period) judged by it to be necessary for the exercise of its functions.§ The local courts possess a similar power.§

On the other hand, any

administrator, director or employee of the Bank [in this context the Central Bank of the Bahamas] who divulges any information obtained in this manner to any person other than a person authorized by the Bank or a tribunal, or permitting access to any other bank or document relating to the affairs of any financial institution or trust company by any person not authorized by the Bank or a tribunal to this effect, will be committing a

---

*Mr Donaldson is not being absolutely straightforward. This is obviously why he says 'probably'. He knows full well that the Cayman Islands with a bank for every 60 inhabitants compared with one for every 514 in the Bahamas holds an unbeatable record.
†*Financial Times*, 20 April 1979.
‡Article 7 of the law on banks and financial institutions, 1965.
§Articles 33-1 and 35-1 of the 1974 law on the Central Bank of the Bahamas.

breach of the present law, and is liable in this case to a fine not exceeding 2500 dollars or to imprisonment not exceeding 2 years.*

The banks are open from 9.30 am to 3 pm and on Fridays until 5 pm and are closed on Saturdays and Sundays.

V BANKING SECRECY

General outline

As a former British colony, the Bahamas 'received' British jurisprudence from the 'Tournier judgment' (*see* Chapter 10) but added to it an appropriate complementary legislative system.

Their attitude, which is similar to that of the Cayman Islands, is quite contrary to that of the United States (see Chapter 11) and is partially summarized by a speech given by Donald M. Fleming,* the President of a local bank, to the Bahamian Chamber of Commerce who said that:

The secrecy attached to relations and transactions between financial institutions and their clients has been another factor essential in the attraction of financial business . . . . Any lessening of this guarantee would harm the interests of the Bahamas, and any strengthening of it would bolster them.

This judgment relating to a banking haven that also holds an international financial position makes an interesting comparison with an opinion voiced by Mr Alfred E. Sarasin, President of the Swiss Association of Bankers:‡

The Swiss financial position is not a product of banking secrecy. But if it did not exist, our country would no longer be a serious competitor in the international competition between the financial centres of the world.

This attitude is not directly limited to the one law on banking secrecy, but also concerns the procedures which would weaken it indirectly by means of treaties on double taxation providing for the exchange of information (the Swiss mind is very similar in this respect; is it not said that the Bahamas are the Switzerland of the Caribbean?)

The United States has exercised direct and indirect pressures for the signing of such treaties, specifically with Switzerland, the Bahamas and the Cayman Islands.

---

*Article 35-3 of the 1974 law on the Central Bank of the Bahamas.
†One might suppose that Mr Fleming, who had previously been Minister of Finance in Canada, President of the International Monetary Fund, and President of the International Bank for Reconstsruction and Development, is fully aware of the problem about which he speaks and that he did not lose his clarity of mind when he became President of the Bank of Nova Scotia Trust Company (Bahamas) and made a speech about it in 1977.
‡Speech given at the Bankers' Day in the Kursaal in Berne, 22 September 1978 (*see* Chapter 38).

The Swiss, following their usual tactics, have avoided direct confrontation and have preferred to negotiate, thus gradually depriving the treaty of its substance before finally signing it to satisfy the honour of the American eagle.

The Bahamians, like the Cayman Islanders, forgetting the traditions of British diplomacy, have had direct confrontation with the United States, and Mr Fleming stated that:*

> The pressure to draw up treaties on double taxation with the US and other countries with which the Bahamas have close relationships would become almost irresistible. Exchange of information relating to the taxpayer would follow. This sacrifice of secrecy would cause the Bahamas to lose a good part of its attraction for the foreign investor.

Legal basis and penalties

Legal basis: this results from the 'Tournier judgment' and article 19-1 of the 1965 amendment introducing banking secrecy into the 1909 law on banks which stipulates:

> Except for the execution of his obligations or the exercise of his functions, in the application of this law or under legal obligation to a competent tribunal of the colony† or in the application of other laws, no person will be obliged to divulge any information relating to the affairs of a bank or to the affairs of a client of the bank, that was acquired by him in the execution of his obligations or in the exercise of his functions, within the framework of the present law.

This text, which is much narrower in scope than the one in the Cayman Islands strengthening the scope of banking secrecy, appears to be sufficient without going as far as the Cayman legislative excesses (*see* Chapter 32).

Curiously enough, the same year the Bahamian legislature thought it insufficient and revived in article 10 of the *Banks and Trust Companies* rules a text that was practically identical by adding penalties that were identical to those envisaged in the 1965 amendment to the 1909 law.

This needless repetition (the first law also relates to trusts) might be seen to demonstrate the desire to strengthen the principle of banking secrecy.

With typical British humour Anthony Thomson, a Bahamian lawyer, specialist on banking questions, comments laconically‡ that such a need was not glaringly obvious.

Finally, Bahamian jurisprudence has drawn up laws to cover the situation where a bank becomes insolvent, a situation not specified in the law, and extends banking secrecy to the liquidator of a bankrupt bank.§

---

*The wording is in the conditional tense because Mr Fleming is advancing a hypothesis which, to him, is absurd, about the introduction of some form of taxation on revenue.
†When this law was published, the Commonwealth of the Bahamas was still a British colony.
‡*Bank Secrecy in the Bahamas*, June 1978.
§Judgment of the president, Leonard Knowles 10 March 1977, in the 'Nassau Bank and Trust Company Limited affair', I (*BLR*), 1977, p.1.

Penalties: besides civil damages arising from the Tournier judgment and the possible revocation of the licence permitting banking activity, there exist criminal penalties.

Anyone contravening the clauses of section one of this article* will have committed a breach of this law and will incur a penalty not exceeding £1000† or a prison sentence not exceeding one year, or both.

VI THE INSTRUMENTS OF BANKING SECRECY

Direct

Numbered accounts and accounts held under a false name exist in the Bahamas, but bearer accounts are unknown.

Indirect

Swiss reservations do not apply to foreign legal entities. Although this might be possible if the legal entity is classified as non-resident, it is not advisable to use local legal entities because of the complexity of local exchange control and the high cost of their maintenance. Despite the complexity and severity of local exchange control, the authorities of the country do not seek to know the identity of the beneficial owner of entities opening a bank account. Severity does not necessarily imply 'blindness' and it is in a good banking haven's interest not to look for what it is best not to know, for, as a Bahamian financier has remarked: 'banking secrecy is egalitarian: it puts good and bad fellows . . . on the same footing.‡

Bearer

These are non-existent.

VII THE PRACTICE OF BANKING SECRECY AND FOREIGN ECONOMIC POWERS

One fundamental element in the Bahamas, as in the Cayman Islands, is that although banking secrecy is far from being the object of internal attack, this does not apply to external attack, which comes particularly from the United States.

---

*In both laws banking secrecy is the object of subsection one of this section.
†The Bahamas was still a British colony (dependent on Jamaica) at the time of the publication of the two laws and the currency was still the £ sterling and not the Bahamian dollar.
‡Oliver P. Gibson, January 1978.

Exchange control

In this area hovers the old ambiguity of Jersey and Guernsey, which is encountered again in the Cayman Islands, an ambiguity that is due to a local exchange control and the principle of double incrimination.

Apparently no decision has been given by the Bahamian courts on the question of lifting banking secrecy for the benefit of a foreign power, and the only existing decision has been an injunction on the Central Bank of the Bahamas, made by a Bahamian court, requiring it to reveal to the court if a particular person had a 'beneficial interest'. The Central Bank complied, which might constitute a troublesome precedent.*

Although strictly speaking not a question of exchange control, the Bahamas have had several confrontations with the United States, in connection with the Castle Bank affair,† relating to the holding of assets abroad by Americans, and not declared to the IRS (*see* Chapter 11).

The operation, mounted by the IRS first of all under the poetic code name of 'tradewinds' and then 'project haven', had ended in the seizure at Miami airport of the attaché-case of a bank employee in which was found a list of 300 Americans holding secret accounts at the Castle Bank† in the Bahamas.

The mechanism that permitted this 'magnificent catch' was examined by a judge in the State of Ohio, in connection with P who was accused of having concealed $440 000 in this way.

An analysis of the facts showed that the IRS agents, having perhaps seen too much television, imagined themselves to be cowboys, and after putting pressure on a bank employee had bribed him.

Judge Manos of Ohio refused to consider the evidence obtained in this way, and for this reason released the offending taxpayer, condemning in an 'opinion' running to 29 pages the IRS procedures:

> The activities of the government agents were outrageous. They plotted, organized, and finally acted contrary to the Constitution of the United States and the laws of Florida, knowing full well that their conduct was illegal. It is vital to point out to all similar-minded individuals that criminal acts carried out on behalf of the government will not be tolerated in this country and it will never be permitted for such actions to bear fruit.‡

Although the 'cowboy' operation was stopped at this stage in the United States, such was not the case in the Bahamas, where the licence of the Castle Bank was revoked because of bad publicity!

---

*Corporate Bank and Trust Company Limited affair, decision no. 334, 1975.
†The Castle Bank has become particularly famous in the modern history of banking secrecy, and it was in connection with the Castle Bank (this time the Cayman Islands branch) that the 'conflict' between the United States and the Cayman Islands came about, over the 'Field affair'.
‡The European reader will no doubt be puzzled by such a judgment on facts which probably would have gained a promotion for their author in most European countries and a bonus, or even a percentage, to the informer described by this judge as 'corrupt'!

Taxation

The absence of taxation in the Bahamas is closely linked to banking secrecy, and it is highly improbable that direct taxation will be instituted. The maintenance of tax-free status is considered to be one of the most important elements in the financial development of the Bahamas. 'It follows that any material change in the taxation structure,* or even the suspicion of such a change, would withdraw from the country its main attraction for foreign financial affairs.'†

VIII INTERNATIONAL AGREEMENTS LIKELY TO UNDERMINE BANKING SECRECY

General agreements

There are none. However, it should be noted that, after their independence, the Bahamas joined the International Monetary Fund on 21 August 1973. The applicability of the so-called Bretton Woods agreements dates from then.

Specific agreements

The problem raised by Anglo-Saxon banking havens, such as Jersey, Guernsey and the Cayman Islands does not apply because of the independent status of the Bahamas which are not signatories to any agreement on double taxation providing for exchange of information.

IX BANKING SECRECY AND THE FINANCIAL MARKET

Blind market and official market for non-residents

In the absence of agreement on double taxation, and indeed of taxation, there is no reason to distinguish between the official market and the blind market. There are no geopolitical obstacles. The rate of withholding tax at source is therefore as follows:

bank interest	nil
dividends	nil

Back-to-back loans

This practice is common and there is no obstacle to it.

---

*It would be more correct to say 'in the absence of taxation structure'.
†Donald M. Fleming (quoted above).

X PERSONAL COMMENTS

A British humorist described it as the 'bikini bank' . . . and why not? Bankers estimate that in addition to the considerable income from tourist currency, bank visitors annually spend $5 million in accommodation expenses, which represents 1 per cent of their local real estate investments, and an estimated $500 million in Bahamian stocks.

It would be in the Bahamian interest to avoid the ambiguity relating to infringements of exchange control. A future with a blue sky over a blue sea . . . and yet, there is a little cloud on the horizon.* Some American bankers and experts envisage the creation of a sort of 'free banking zone' in New York, in which the banks could deal only in Euromoney transactions. And like the Bahamian banks, the American banks operating in this zone and this sphere of activity would be exempted from taxes and would not be bound by ratios between loans and deposits.† But this is only a little cloud, because one fundamental aspect would be lacking . . . banking secrecy.‡

---

*New York has recently experienced a rather amazing development in banking. In 1972 there were 53 foreign banks representing 17 million dollars of assets, whereas in 1979 these figures had risen respectively to $125 and $80 million (*Financial Times*, 'A bigger role for New York', 21 May 1979).
†The suppression of ratios for 'offshore' transactions is subject to the approval of the 'Federal Reserve Board'.
‡This also seems to be lacking in the island of Guam, which is beginning to be used by American bankers for 'syndicating' offshore loans.

32 Cayman Islands:
A strong banking castle

I THE COUNTRY AND ITS COMPONENTS

Geographical, historical, and economic situation

Situated about 590 kilometres to the south of Miami and about 320 kilometres to the north-west of Jamaica, the Cayman Islands have a total surface area of 159 square kilometres divided between three islands: Grand Cayman (with the capital Georgetown), Cayman Brac and Little Cayman.

The Cayman Islands were administered by Jamaica until 1972, which was itself a colony under English administration, but when the latter became independent the Cayman Islands decided to stay as a British colony which was perhaps not the 'direction of history' but seemed to best represent the interests of its inhabitants.

The economy is based on tourism, particularly fiscal and banking tourism.

Population, stability, communications, and legal system

The population of approximately 13 000 inhabitants is composed of 20 per cent European, 20 per cent black and 60 per cent of mixed race.

The judicial system is based on British 'common law' to which local laws have been added, particularly in banking matters.

The political situation is stable.

Communications, post, telegraph, telephone, and telex systems are excellent (because of the number of banks and their activities, the telex line density per head of population is the highest in the world).

II CURRENCY

The currency is the Cayman Island dollar which is linked to the American dollar on the basis of a fixed rate of exchange: 0.833 Cayman Islands dollar to the American dollar, or 1.20 US dollars to 1 Cayman dollar.

EXCHANGE CONTROL

Until 1973 the Cayman Islands were part of the 'scheduled territories' in the old sterling zone and therefore subject to British exchange control. The

Cayman Islands now have their own system of exchange control which, having been inspired by the British system, classifies both individual and corporate bodies as either Cayman residents or non-residents.

The 'controller of exchange' in the Cayman system plays the role that the Bank of England played in the British system before exchange control, particularly in approving the creation of Cayman legal entities qualifying for non-resident status. Cayman and foreign banks operating in the Cayman Islands play the role of approved intermediaries.

Non-residents

These escape all exchange control and can therefore hold accounts in the currency of their choice without restriction.

Interest paid to non-residents

There is no legal limitations and no deduction at source. In any case, there is no form of taxation in the Cayman Islands, which derive their income from customs duty fixed at 20 per cent.*

Residents

These can only hold their assets in Cayman dollars and transfer operations are subject to prior authorization with the possibility of a prior guarantee to re-export when investments (including real estate) have been made in currency by non-residents who subsequently become resident.

IV BANKS AND THE BANKING SYSTEM

There are more than 220 Cayman and foreign banks in the Cayman Islands, and their number is constantly increasing. The Cayman Islands hold the world record, since this means that there is a bank for every 60 inhabitants.

The Bahamas and the Caymans have largely displaced London's primary position for transactions in Euromoney, since these two countries agree in estimating the total operation of the Cayman Islands to be $48 billion for 1976.

Control of the banking system and the banks is exercised by the inspector of bank and trust companies, who is himself subject to banking secrecy.

---

*This almost exclusive source of revenue explains, though does not justify, the cavalier attitude of the local customs officers who have caused spectacular bouts of hysterics among the wives (legitimate or not) of roving depositors when passing through the Immigration Office. On arrival at the airport, the roving depositor receives a blanket which is spread on the ground and on which the customs officers tip the entire contents of his luggage in order to facilitate their search. The blanket is then returned with its contents, and the empty baggage separately . . . . A curious welcome for 'flying' travellers who are often bearers of 'floating' capital, which has discouraged more than a few from having their Cayman residence built with their capital.

The banks are normally open from 8.30 am to 1.00 pm and on Friday afternoons from 4.30 to 6.00 pm.

V BANKING SECRECY

General outline

In this country which inherited British 'common law', banking secrecy has its beginnings in the Tournier judgement (*see* Chapter 10), but it has been more than considerably strengthened by a law in 1966 by which, following on the conflict with the United States (*see* below), the penalties were very seriously increased by a new law of 13 September 1976.

This new law, which is extremely wide and severe in its penalties, makes the Cayman Islands, as far as the statutes are concerned, the very peak of banking havens.*

The Cayman state of mind in response to Judge Morgan's 'opinion' in the 'Field affair' (*see* Chapter 11) is perfectly summarized by the financial secretary's statement about the strengthening of the Cayman law:

Concern was expressed in 1976 by the financial community about an affair in which a foreign financial institution, based in the Cayman Islands, was the object of a foreign government enquiry.
 The origins of this affair come from the continual enquiries into the operations of tax havens by the major powers. The problem of these countries is that their tax laws can be violated by nationals using the possibilities offered by tax havens. Our point of view is that financial activity is a very important part of the local economy and we must therefore continue to welcome investors who choose to conduct their affairs in the Cayman Islands. Those who do business abroad must be assured that their activities do not violate the regulations of other countries. It must be clearly stated that a tax infringement in other countries is not an infringement in the Cayman Islands . . . .

Legal basis and penalties

Legal basis: there are two bases, resulting from both a contractual obligation and the case law of the Tournier judgment,† and from article 10 of the 1966 law on banks and trust companies, amended by the law of the 13 September 1976 known under the name of the Confidential Relationships (Preservation) Law.

---

*The extremely severe nature of this law caused several professionals to think, at the time of its appearance, that the British governor (the Cayman Islands are still a colony) could, for the first time, utilize his right of veto. This pessimistic opinion has had no consequences.
†There is even an explicit stipulation in the law of 13 September 1976 where, curiously enough, article 5 says: 'No clause in the present law is supposed to depart from the regulation put forward by the Tournier judgment. To the author's knowledge, a clause such as this is the only existing one in a law of the country relating to established jurisprudence. The procedure, which has the merit of simplicity, should perhaps be retained; it is true that it emanates from a country and a system where the law is made by legal practitioners and not by civil servants who, as soon as they are appointed to office, do their utmost to wipe out the work of their predecessors.

This distinction is interesting, for the law on confidential relationships, in article 7, anticipates that no action can be started without the agreement of the attorney general, which could therefore leave the client without civil protection (damages and interest) at the level of a violation of confidential relationships that the attorney general might refuse to pursue.

Secrecy, according to the legal definition, extends to:

all confidential information relating to business or professional matters, that begins in or is brought into the islands, and to any person entering at any time, or outside the islands in possession of such information.*

The definitions of persons receiving confidential information are so wide that it is possible to arrive at strange results; thus it is stipulated, for example, that in addition to the categories of persons usually protected by professional secrecy in most civilized countries, the following are also included:

... real-estate and insurance agents, currency dealers, commercial representatives and advisors entering or not entering into the preceding categories, whether or not they are licensed or entitled to act in such a capacity . . . .†

In such circumstances, and given that people could commit some breach of it in a country which they have never visited, for acts that are not illegal in their own country, one can understand that this law is a redoubtable weapon, and that, it is for this reason, that it cannot be invoked without the agreement of the Attorney General.

The bankers in the Cayman Islands who are tempted to play the public relations role for their clients, like their American counterparts are seriously advised to avoid the publicity, since the law stipulates:

In order to avoid all suspicion, it is specified . . . that a bank giving credit references concerning one of its clients, without his prior agreement, is guilty of an offence . . . .‡

Penalties: in addition to the civil damages defined by the Tournier judgment there are penalties which are applicable not only to persons in violation, in the strict sense of the 'confidential relationship', but also to those who have attempted, offered or threatened to divulge secrets, or have obtained or attempted to obtain confidential information not intended for them.

The penalty is a fine of up to 5000 Cayman dollars or a prison sentence of up to two years, or both.§

Anyone who, in violating the confidential relationship by divulging information has received or solicited for himself or another any reward incurs

---

*Article 3-1, law of 13 September 1976.
†Article 2 (same law).
‡Article 5, law of the 13 September 1976 (and without prejudice to a stronger additional sentence for violation of professional secrecy of another kind).
§Article 4-1 (law of 13 September 1976).

double the preceding sentences, the confiscation of the consideration, and, furthermore, a fine equivalent to the consideration.*

Anyone in possession of a professional secret who uses it for the benefit of himself or a third party, without the agreement of the holder, incurs the preceding sentences and the profit resulting from any related transaction is considered as compensation.†

Anyone who is himself a professional who has committed any one of the three types of infringements, will have a double sentence.‡

VI THE INSTRUMENTS OF BANKING SECRECY

Direct

Certain banks operate numbered accounts, but accounts held under a false name seem to be unheard of. In fact, following good Anglo-Saxon practices, bankers suggested instead a trust agreement (indirect instruments), which in the Cayman Island presents none of the tax disadvantages existing in the Channel Islands.

Indirect

Foreign legal entities are accepted without the reservations applicable to Switzerland.

VII THE PRACTICE OF BANKING SECRECY AND FOREIGN ECONOMIC POWERS

Banking secrecy is a fundamental element in the Cayman Islands and there is every reason to think that it will continue to be vigorously defended in order to continue to attract banks and their clients.

Exchange control

Until now there seem not to have been any decisions made to deal with problems of foreign exchange control, since the conflicts with the United States were related to taxation. The United States, however, treated certain clauses as if they were similarly applicable to exchange control.

As in the Bahamas or Singapore, and in the absence of a legal decision or a law on this point, the existence of a local exchange control raises the concern about the possibility of applying the principle of double incrimination.

---

*Article 4-2 (law of 13 September 1976).
†Article 4-3 (same law).
‡Article 4-4 (same law).

In applying the recently published law on 'confidential relationships (preservation)', no information relating to the account of a client or an open user of any institution in the financial community can be divulged to anyone. If a foreign government is making an enquiry into an affair relating to a crime which is not a tax crime, and one in which the government of the Cayman Islands is required to assist in providing specific information, the law states that such a demand for information should be made through the intermediary of the local police to the governor on executive council.* Such a demand would be examined if the alleged infringement, having been committed in the Cayman Islands, was also an infringement according to Cayman laws.†

A 'reassuring' declaration that is in fact much less so than its author would have wished. Clearly optimists will say that the demand 'would be examined', but some investors do not like 'examinations', and would perhaps prefer a banking haven where this risk, even though slight, is actually non-existent.

Taxation

There is no need to deal with this question because it is regulated in a totally favourable way.

VIII INTERNATIONAL AGREEMENTS LIKELY TO UNDERMINE BANKING SECRECY

General agreements

The Cayman lawyers seem to dodge this embarrassing question. The Cayman government has acted wisely in keeping the status of a British colony which apparently brings only advantages, but it should not be forgotten that Great Britain is party to a certain number of treaties providing for exchanges of information and it is logical to consider them as applicable to a colony. The response of English jurists is far from clear: such treaties are applicable only if this is stipulated, and such stipulations do not seem to exist . . . .

In any case, it is generally agreed that there is no problem.‡ Whatever the position, as a British colony, the Cayman Islands, like the British Virgin Islands, are categorized as a country 'dependent' on the United Kingdom and the Bretton Woods agreement is applicable to them.

Specific agreements

The problem arises again in the same way, but with less serious consequences. however as a result of the extension of the Anglo-American treaty to Jamaica in 1959 (at this time the Cayman Islands were dependent on Jamaica) a

---

*The executive council is composed of seven members responsible for the day-to-day administration. Locally it is known as the 'Ex. Co.'.
†Statement made by the finance Secretary of State, V. G. Johnson (quoted above).
‡This statement seems to be supported by the status of different treaties extended by Great Britain to the British Virgin Islands (see below).

Treasury department decision had to be made excluding the Cayman Islands from the extension to Jamaica.

English jurists reply that this is precisely because the treaty provided for an extension to a colony (Jamaica was, at the time, a British colony). The explanation seems logical and apparently there is no treaty signed by Great Britain providing for exchange of information that extends to the Cayman Islands.

IX BANKING SECRECY AND THE FINANCIAL MARKET

Blind market and official market for non-residents

There are no geopolitical obstacles to using the Cayman Islands. There is again no point in distinguishing between the blind market and the official market in the absence of any local taxation and any agreement on double taxation. The rate of deduction at source is therefore as follows:

                      bank interest   nil
                      dividends   nil

Back-to-back loans

There is no obstacle, this is common practice.

X PERSONAL COMMENTS

It is not without good reason that there is now one bank for every 60 inhabitants in the Cayman Islands. To be sure, banking secrecy is not an sufficient condition but it is nevertheless a necessary condition, and this is well understood locally. The great modern conflicts in banking secrecy have occurred between the United States and Switzerland, and between the United States and the Cayman Islands and the Bahamas. Each country has had its own method: the Swiss, who are more traditional, negotiated, thus practically depriving American claims of any substance, agreeing to sign a treaty granting them what, in any case, they give to all other countries; the Caymans countered by legal force by strengthening (excessively?) their legislative system. They are obsessed by the American problem, and have, purely and simply, forgotten the rest of the world and its problems of exchange control. This is an unfortunate forgetfulness which it would be easy to rectify; after the legislative orgy of the new law on banking secrecy, a few additional lines would not have been a problem, or would they? It is difficult to reproach foreign countries for maintaining exchange control when the exchange control of its own country is visibly worse than that of neighbouring countries.

33 Hungary:*
Liberty—for floating capital

I THE COUNTRY AND ITS COMPONENTS

The reader will certainly be surprised to find Hungary singled out as a banking haven, and especially since this country is waging an ideological war against 'decadent capitalism', and the *Magyar Posta* (the Hungarian Post Office) has issued stamps bearing the following inscription: 'You who hide in the shadows, propagators of false tidings, counter-revolutionaries, tremble!' next to an armed soldier pointing at the reader.† Usually, banking havens issue much pleasanter stamps.

If the roving depositor stops short at the particularly bad official propaganda, he will be committing a serious error of judgement. Hungary, despite 50 000 Russian soldiers stationed on its territory, exudes the discreet perfume of the bourgeoisie. After the bloody experience of Budapest, and the tragic Czechoslovakian repeat, the Hungarians, who have remained in commerce through atavism, have understood that they had to act flexibly, and they get closer to the free world through business affairs, a situation which is much more viable and very much less embarrassing for the neighbouring bear who is not very sympathetic to the humour of street demonstrations.

Since the logic of this book requires that the main traditional or vocational havens should have sufficient stability, it would have been abnormal to dismiss Hungary on the grounds of a stability whose origin and effects do not make for unanimity, but one which certainly seems to exist, and, moreover seems to have a promising evolution.

For obvious reasons there is no need to spend further time introducing Hungary.

---

*Because of the lack of any other documentation on banking secrecy in Hungary, almost all of this chapter is based on a very detailed questionnaire that the legal service of the National Bank of Hungary filled out and sent to the author, and on an exchange of letters intended to clarify answers given in this questionnaire. The author wishes to thank the National Bank of Hungary and its personnel for their efficiency and intelligent cooperation which might serve as an example to certain central banks in better-known banking havens who might well take lessons from this country.
†According to certain unverifiable information, this stamp would be affixed only on letters intended for 'dissidents'; in any case the author's correspondence with the National Bank of Hungary did not require any, since the letters were stamped mechanically.

II CURRENCY

The currency is the forint which on the 1 August 1946 replaced the old pengoe on the basis of 1 forint for 400 000 quadrillion pengoes (a record difficult to beat in the devaluation stakes!).

    1 forint = 100 filler
    100 forints = US $2.91
    100 forints = Swiss francs 5.69 (May 1982)

III EXCHANGE CONTROL

Hungary is a country with a very strict exchange control, so strict that the non-resident can export currency only if it has been declared on entry into the country. As for the export of local currency (one would have to be mad), this is limited to 400 forints.

Non-residents

Despite this strict exchange control on the circulation of cash, non-residents enjoy the greatest freedom on the circulation of currency through the banks. The forint seems not to enjoy the prestige of the Swiss franc; there is certainly no negative interest nor any similar system.

Interest paid to non-residents

There is no obstacle.

Residents

Comment on their status has no point except that it should be noted that they have practically no rights, which will come as no surprise to anyone.

IV BANKS AND THE BANKING SYSTEM

The key organ of the banking system is the National Bank of Hungary which also deals with private business. An interesting sign is that branches of foreign banks have opened, and 'offshore' banking activities could be on the horizon . . . where is the world going to? The National Bank of Hungary is open from 8 am to 12.00 noon and from 1 pm to 4 pm, closed on Saturdays and Sundays.

V BANKING SECRECY

General outline

The Hungarian legislature made no mistake in defining its goals and the situation of the country when it published in 1977 a law modifying the civil code,* a law that was drawn up with a certain finesse since the clauses instituting banking secrecy are derived from it. It would have been politically unthinkable to publish a text that was blatantly modelled on article 47 of Swiss law on banks. Hungarian professionals no doubt thought that foreign professionals, being well able to read would understand them and that the text would not create local difficulties nor disturb too much the neighbouring bear who, in fact, does the same thing without officially saying so.

The Hungarian lawyers should be reassured, the message has been received, the proof being this present chapter.

LEGAL BASIS AND PENALTIES

Legal basis: banking secrecy is dealt with in various clauses relating to savings accounts, one of which specifies:

With regard to monetary deposits made by private persons within the framework of a bank account agreement, the regulations governing savings accounts are applicable.†

So what are these clauses relating to savings accounts? The answer is very clear:

Savings accounts are secret. No information concerning the details of these accounts can be given without the prior agreement of the depositor or his legal representative . . . .‡

The simple juxtaposition of these texts is revealing: the one follows immediately after the other, just to make sure that the message is not lost . . . ! Similarly, the exceptions are revealing:

The bank is nevertheless obliged to inform the courts (or notaries) on their demand in the case of a judgment pronouncing confiscation, or establishing an obligation to compensate for damage in favour of the State, or in case of litigation in respect of the deceased holder of the savings account.§

This is a particularly restrictive text; in fact, one must logically conclude from it that the banker, even in the case of a judicial decision (except one given on behalf of the state) or of confiscation pronounced by a Hungarian judge, is bound by banking secrecy, which is a very rare situation (like coded accounts in Panama (*see* Chapter 36).

Furthermore, the Hungarians consider that banking secrecy applies not only to all bank employees, but also continues to apply after their departure from the bank.

---

*Civil code of Hungary, law no. 4, 1959, modified by law no. 4, 1977.
†Article 535, paragraph 2 (modified) Hungarian civil code.
‡Article 534, paragraph 1, Hungarian civil code (modified).
§Article 534, paragraph 2, Hungarian civil code (modified).

Finally, in the case of a national bank of a socialist country, the possibility of bankruptcy is legally inconceivable.*

Penalties: there are no penal sanctions for violation of banking secrecy but the bank is financially responsible for any loss caused.

VI THE INSTRUMENTS OF BANKING SECRECY

Direct

Numbered accounts do not exist but accounts held under a false name can be used.

Indirect

There is no obstacle to their utilization and the bank does not seek to know the identification of the 'beneficial owner'.

Bearer

Bearer savings accounts can be opened, or those under a pseudonym.†

VII THE PRACTICE OF BANKING SECRECY AND FOREIGN ECONOMIC POWERS

Hungarian banking secrecy for the time being goes unchallenged by all other countries. Up to the present time it seems to be very little known, or even completely unknown, abroad.

VIII INTERNATIONAL AGREEMENTS LIKELY TO UNDERMINE BANKING SECRECY

General agreements

There are none. Furthermore, Hungary is not a signatory of the Bretton Woods agreement.

Specific agreements

Agreements signed by Hungary, even with Eastern bloc countries, do not provide for exchange of information in matters of taxation or exchange control.

---

*Even if that is not the case for a State.
†Details of this method do not seem readily available.

IX BANKING SECRECY AND THE FINANCIAL MARKET

Blind market for non-residents

The question of dividends is of little interest, since we are dealing with a socialist economy; on the other hand, bank interest has tax withheld at source, and the rate is not always clear or straightforward.

Official market for non-residents

The rate or rates may be reduced on the official market for non-residents by the use of double taxation agreements, but also, curiously enough, because of the nationality of the depositor (if it is not a bearer savings account), by the application of a clause of Hungarian tax law which states:

Exemption from general tax on revenue: the foreign citizen whose tax exemption is assured by international treaty or a reciprocity within the limits fixed by this treaty or by the practice of this reciprocity.*

The result is that because of their nationality, account holders are exempt from any deduction at source on interest if the situation is the same, treaties apart in the country from which the account holder comes.

In this respect, the situation for the major countries is as follows:†

1. Countries that do not withhold tax at source on deposits of non-residents in any currency:

    Austria, the Dutch West Indies, Saudia Arabia, the Bahamas, Bahrein, Belgium, the Cayman Islands, Chile, Denmark, the United States, Finland, Greece, Hong Kong, Kenya, India, Ireland, Iceland, Israel, Italy, Kuwait, Liechtenstein, Lebanon, Liberia, Luxemburg, Morocco, Monaco, Holland, Singapore, Sweden, Tunisia.

2. Countries that withhold tax at source on deposits of non-residents, held in their national currency:

    Canada 25 per cent; Italy 18 per cent.

3. Countries that withhold tax at source on deposits in any currency. The rates are modified in very special cases:

---

*Decree passed by the Council of Ministers, no. 42, 1971, concerning general taxation on revenue (paragraph 2/i/b).
†The comparison of these rates is interesting even for the reader who would not be interested in Hungary. They are therefore given in some detail.

Cuba 6 per cent; South Africa, Haiti 10 per cent; Portugal 11.2 per cent; Australia 10–20 per cent; Indonesia, Mexico, Japan (from 1 January 1980, previously 35 per cent) 20 per cent; Spain 24 per cent; Brazil, France 25 per cent; Paraguay 30 per cent; Great Britain 33 per cent (33/67 of 52 per cent); Switzerland, Rhodesia 35 per cent; Egypt 38.05 per cent; Ecuador, Nigeria, Peru 40 per cent; Pakistan 50 per cent.

Although it is clear that the countries which come into the third category are subject to the application of normal Hungarian rates of withholding tax on interest earned by the nationals of these countries in Hungary, there is some doubt about the countries in the second category. In this case, should one take it that normal Hungarian rates apply to Canadian and Italian nationals or, on the other hand, that deduction at source applies only to deposits in convertible forints? Juridical logic tends to conclude that the second solution is correct.

Back-to-back loans

In theory there is no obstacle to their use, which might legitimately come as a surprise to some authorities as far as direct investments are concerned.

X PERSONAL COMMENTS

Hungary: the Switzerland of socialist havens? Such a comparison would be totally misplaced; first of all, it takes several generations to make a Switzerland, and, secondly, Hungary is certainly not the Bahamas! But perhaps one day? In the meantime Hungary already offers substantial possibilities that are not to be found in most countries, and the quality of cooperation of the National Bank personnel is encouraging in the extreme. Furthermore, there are apparently well-founded rumours circulating about a joint enterprise having to be created in Hungary between western European banks and the National Bank of Hungary.*

---

*This information does not come from the National Bank itself.

34 Liechtenstein: A Swiss transfer

I THE COUNTRY AND ITS COMPONENTS

Geographical, historical, and economic situation

Situated between north-eastern Austria and south-western Switzerland, the principality of Liechtenstein extends over 160 square kilometres.

It was German as a result of the treaty of Verdun in 843, became an autonomous principality in 1434 and, after a customs union with Austria, it turned towards Switzerland at the end of the First World War and became a constitutional monarchy under the terms of a constitution of 5 October 1921.

The local economy is not very substantial, and is based on fiscal tourism. Liechtenstein might, in some senses, be considered as the tax haven of Switzerland with which it has been linked by a customs and monetary union since 1924.

Population, stability, communications, and legal system

The population is of approximately 23 000 inhabitants, mainly of German origin, and the capital is Vaduz.

The legal system reflects the history of Liechtenstein which, until the First World War, applied Austrian law. As a result of its union with Switzerland, Liechtenstein did not receive Swiss law in the way that the Commonwealth countries received British common law. Liechtenstein proclaimed its own civil code called PGR,* which is certainly strongly influenced by certain Swiss statutes and, furthermore, various laws on banks copied from the Swiss systems as at 1971.

The result is that if a foreign banker wants to make enquiries for example about powers of investigation in banking matters between, say, husband and wife, he has to know:

1. the Austrian law as it was before 1914.
2. Swiss banking law and jurisprudence from 1914 to 1971.
3. The Liechtenstein laws in effect from 1914 to 1971.

---

*Personen und Gesellschraftsrecht =: LGB (*Liechtensteinisches Landeesgesetzblatt:* official Liechtenstein journal, 1925, 4. Law governing persons and societies, 20 January 1926.

4. Finally, Liechtenstein jurisprudence and laws since 1971—a fine Liechtenstein salad.

The political situation is a model of stability.

Communications, post, telegraph, telephone, and telex systems are excellent.

II CURRENCY

Since 1924, legal currency is the Swiss franc* representing 100 rapen, i.e. centimes:

$$1 \text{ Swiss franc} = 100 \text{ rapen} = 100 \text{ centimes}$$
$$1 \text{ Swiss franc} = \text{US } \$1.95 \text{ (May 1982)}$$

III EXCHANGE CONTROL

There is no exchange control in Liechtenstein. In any case, since Swiss regulations apply, the same observations about a disguised exchange control are valid (*see* Chapter 4).

In practice, the Liechtenstein banks apply the regulations of the Swiss National Bank, but with more flexibility than the Swiss banks. This was particularly true at the time when negative interest was introduced, and even provoked protests from the Swiss bankers.†

IV BANKS AND THE BANKING SYSTEM

Liechtenstein has three banks: the Liechtenstein *Landesbank*, the *Bank in Liechtenstein AG* and the *Verwaltungs und Privat Bank AG*.

The oldest is the Liechtenstein *Landesbank*, founded in 1861, which officially has the role of Central Bank, but because of the monetary union with Switzerland in fact plays the role of cantonal bank.

The banks are normally open from 8 am to 12.00 noon and from 1.30 pm to 4 pm, and are closed on Saturdays and Sundays.

V BANKING SECRECY

General outline

As a Liechtenstein lawyer says '. . . banking secrecy in Liechtenstein took the form of common law . . . . In fact, even before the promulgation of the law,

---

*Law relating to the introduction of Swiss currency, 26 May 1924, *LGB*, 1924-28.

†However, it would be incorrect to claim that Swiss restrictions are not observed in Liechtenstein. In fact, the profits of the *Landesbank* fell in 1977 by 2.6 million Swiss francs, and the experts are in agreement in attributing this loss to Swiss restrictions on deposits. Bankers have certainly not suffered this loss gladly which, however, will make no one weep, since despite this loss the profit was still 50.6 million Swiss francs, and the total assets of the bank have increased by 214.2 million (*THR*, May 1979). Is the conclusion of the experts conclusive? Let us leave to other experts the problem of concluding!

Liechtenstein banks habitually observed secrecy about the assets of their clients. It is therefore not as if ... there had been a "legal vacuum".'

Legal basis and penalties

Legal basis: the professional secrecy of the banker has its basis not only in Liechtenstein common law, but in a certain number of clauses, some of which, for the jurist, smack of the classification of common law regulations typical of the Middle Ages: this is the case of the *handeln nach Tren und Glauben* regulation (to act according to allegiance and the law),* and clauses relating specifically to common law.†Because of such clauses the principle of the civil responsibility of the banker applies. This principle is also mentioned in article 32 of the internal regulations of the Liechtenstein *Landesbank*.

In addition to these legal bases there is article 47-1-B of banking law which, while not explicitly using the term *bankgeheimnis* (banking secrecy), nevertheless states very clearly:

Anyone who, as agent, bank employee, auditor, or auditor's associate, civil servant or employee of its secretariat, intentionally fails to observe professional secrecy, and anyone who incites or attempts to incite others ... will be punished.‡

The most remarkable thing in this text is perhaps the numbering: no doubt impressed by the Swiss law on banking secrecy of 8 November 1934, the Liechtenstein legislators wished to adopt the same numbering of articles and, in both laws, it is article 47 which is devoted to banking secrecy.

Penalties: in addition to financial penalties resulting from the application of Liechtenstein Civil Code, article 47 on banking law provides for a fine which could go up to 20 000 Swiss francs and a term of imprisonment going up to 6 months, or both.

VI THE INSTRUMENTS OF BANKING SECRECY

Direct

As in Switzerland, numbered accounts or accounts held under a false name may be used.

Indirect

There is no obstacle of any kind to the use of foreign or local legal entities.

Furthermore, since the Liechtenstein banks are not party to the Swiss agreements on the *obligation de diligence*, the beneficial owner can remain unknown.

---

*Article 2, *PGR*.
†Article 39, *PGR*.
‡*Bankengesetz* (law on banks), 21 December 1969, *LGB*, 1961-63.

Bearer

Apparently these are not used. It is true, bearing in mind the local legal arsenal of indirect instruments, that there is not felt to be a pressing need for other measures.

VII THE PRACTICE OF BANKING SECRECY AND FOREIGN ECONOMIC POWERS

Breach of a foreign economic statute does not permit banking secrecy to be broken, but, contrary to a myth that is as false as it is widespread, Liechtenstein does not knowingly give shelter to funds of criminal origin, and when 'a removal of banking secrecy seems to permit the clarification of the facts . . . the banker can not legitimately invoke professional secrecy'.

On the question of certain Liechtenstein legal entities being used as indirect instruments of banking secrecy, and particularly the *anstalt*, the author had previously mentioned the rejection of legal access resulting from two decisions made respectively by the Brussels court of Appeal in January 1975, and the Venice court of Appeal in April 1975, in two non-tax matters on the grounds* that the *anstalt* would be a one-man company and that no-one would plead by proxy. Such a situation was clearly dangerous for banking, and perhaps even more so than for tax, and the author had considered that these decisions were 'legally debatable'.* This opinion must have been shared by the Belgian superior magistrates' court who quashed the decision (the result in Venice is not known but if an appeal was lodged, it logically should be the same).

Exchange control

Banking secrecy is total.

Taxation

Banking secrecy is guaranteed. Its protection is even assured by the tax statutes, article 9–3 specifying:

Total tax secrecy applies concerning taxes that have to be paid by holding companies, resident companies, and persons subject to tax on income not coming from employment.†

VII INTERNATIONAL AGREEMENTS LIKELY TO UNDERMINE BANKING SECRECY

General agreements

Apparently none exist that are applicable.

---

*See *Using Tax Havens Successfully* (anti-tax haven measures), cited above.
†'Steuergesetes', *LGB* 7, tax law, 30 January 1961.

Specific agreements

Liechtenstein signed an agreement with Austria on 5 November 1969, that was ratified on 28 January 1971, and which retroactively came into effect on the 1 January 1969. This agreement does not allow for exchange of information and, in any case, is not therefore likely to affect banking secrecy.

IX BANKING SECRECY AND THE FINANCIAL MARKET

Blind market for non-residents

There are no geopolitical obstacles or constraints.

The basic rates of withholding tax are the following in the absence of any treaty:

bank interest	nil
(3 per cent on deposits of more than 1 year)	
dividends	4 per cent

Official market for non-residents

Within the framework of the treaty signed with Austria, deduction at source is limited to 3 per cent (which was the rate in effect at the date of signature).

Back-to-back loans

There is no obstacle to this and it is common practice, carried out more competitively than in Switzerland where a deduction at source of 35 per cent is applied to interest paid to non-residents, in the absence of any agreement on double taxation.

X PERSONAL COMMENTS

Even the most pessimistic auguries prefer to remain silent about Liechtenstein since it is extremely difficult to imagine that the situation of this country and its banking secrecy could evolve in an unfavourable way.

35 Vanuatu:
Secrecy springs from exemption

I THE COUNTRY AND ITS COMPONENTS

Geographical, historical, and economic situation

This group of 13 islands constituting the 'Condominium of the New Hebrides' is situated in the south-east of the Pacific approximately 2000 kilometres from Sydney, Australia.

Under joint British and French administration since 1914, the New Hebrides had prepared for their independence and the two administrative powers had agreed to it.

The two local political parties are both moderate and apparently multiracial. The economy is geared towards fiscal and banking tourism.

Population, stability, communications, and legal system

There are 85 000 inhabitants, of which 76 500 are of Melanesian stock. The biggest island is Espiritu Santo, but the capital is situated in Port-Vila, on the island of Efate.

The basis of the legal system is threefold: British common law for the legal entities which opt for the Anglo-Saxon system, French law for those legal entities which opt for French law. In addition to these two systems there are local laws as well as British laws applicable on the 1 January 1961, and French laws that relate in general to New Caledonia. It is certain that with independence, the Anglo-Saxon legal system, which is greatly superior in business law to the French system (which is a pale, bad imitation of German laws with regard to companies), will continue to be used and that the French laws will keep the value (without the quality) of ancient Norman customs in English law.

II THE CURRENCY

There were theoretically two currencies in circulation: the franc and the pound sterling. Between the theory and practice there is a very serious margin since, in practice, the franc was not the French franc but the 'Pacific franc', issued by the overseas issuing institute, which did not have the same value as the French franc; on the other hand, the pound sterling was no longer actually in circulation and, since an exchange of notes in 1935, had been replaced by the Australian dollar which is linked to the American dollar but which, having been freed from it (in order to devalue all alone, like a grown-up currency) was tending, in its turn, to be replaced by the French franc, which, it must be remembered, was not really French but 'New Hebridean'. To simplify matters, although representatives of the two administrations gained the power in 1935 to establish jointly the internal rates of exchange, the rates were fixed by the internal banking market.

Apparently Vanuatu has provided itself with a new currency—the vatu.

$$100 \text{ vatu} = \text{Swiss francs } 2.01 \text{ (May 1982)}$$
$$100 \text{ vatu} = \text{US } \$1.03$$

III EXCHANGE CONTROL

There is no exchange control in Vanuatu, and accounts can be held in any currency. Neither is there any obstacle to the payment of interest to non-residents, nor any deduction of tax at source.

IV BANKS AND THE BANKING SYSTEM

The absence of a Central Bank has been no obstacle in the early days of Vanuatu as a banking haven since it has chosen from the start the Rolls Royce of banking secrecy.

Curiously enough, banking secrecy is linked to the 'offshore' banks which are called 'exempted banks', and must also be non-taxable 'exempted companies', because of their 'offshore' activity.

At the moment there are nine banks performing 'local bank' activities, and 37 'exempted banks'.

The resident commissioner* could call for the general examination, or inspection of specific points of the books or affairs, but he was then subject to banking secrecy as are any such persons nominated by him.

One of the nice legislative points is that a company formed in another country can transfer its base and its activities to Vanuatu, and vice versa, without the procedure being considered as constituting a new company.†

The banks are generally open from 7.30 am to 11 am and from 1.30 pm to 3 pm and closed on Saturdays and Sundays.

V BANKING SECRECY

General outline

There was no banking secrecy worthy of this name in the French part of the legislative system.

---

*The highest representative of the British administration. The representative of the French administration had only the right to look at French entities, which were generally carefully avoided.
†With the exception of a certain number of clauses relating to safeguarding the rights of minority creditors and shareholders.

In the Anglo-Saxon part, in addition to the jurisprudence received as a result of the Tournier judgment (*see* Chapter 10), the law on local banks was silent on the question, with one (enormous) exception which stipulates that a financial institution is not obliged to provide accounts or information to the resident commissioner relating to any client.

Banking secrecy reached out to its full extent when applied to an account opened in an 'exempted bank' which is itself an 'exempted company'. First of all, it is important to define what is an 'exempted company'. An 'exempted company' is a company whose activities are 'offshore', and whose administrative council meets at least once a year outside Vanuatu.* The 'exempted company' is itself protected by secrecy whatever its activities (banking or otherwise), and violation of its secrecy is punished by a fine of up to 1000 Australian dollars or 1 year's imprisonment.†

The 'exempted bank' is an 'exempted company' that has received a banker's licence for 'offshore' activity.

Legal basis and penalties

Legal basis: the legal basis of banking secrecy is not to be found in the 17 September 1970 law on banks, but in company law which states:

With the exception of the exercise of its functions, within the framework of the present regulations, or of a legal requisition by a competent court of the New Hebrides, for the application of the present law or any other law applicable to Her Majesty's subjects in the New Hebrides, or for the examination of government accounts, no person will have to give to any other person or entity any information whatsoever . . . during his employment or after such employment has come to an end.‡

Banking secrecy extends to any litigation in which an exempted company is involved and which has to be examined in the council chamber, and includes also the auditors of the accounts of these same companies.

One of the difficulties of the system applied to banks as far as the clients of the bank are concerned is precisely that a bank, if it has an 'offshore' licence only comes within the scope of the law on banking secrecy if it functions according to the system of exempted companies. This formulation seems to be redundant, but in practice may be dangerous for, according to a director of a local financial company: 'It must be mentioned that a company with a licence as an exempted bank is not necessarily itself an exempted company.§ It is, then, only after being assured that an 'offshore' bank is also an exempted company, that the roving depositor will benefit from this protection.

Penalties: apart from the possibility of a licence being cancelled the reception by local jurisprudence of British common law and the jurisprudence

---

*This is a less restrictive definition than the one used in Jersey or Guernsey.
†Article 416, company law, 1971.
‡Article 416-3, company law, 1971.
§S. R. Tatham, Opinion, November 1977 (Investors' Trust Ltd.).

of the Tournier judgment poses the principle of indemnification. Furthermore, for accounts opened in exempted banks whose activity is the work of an exempted company, the penal ties of company law apply:

Any person who contravenes these clauses will incur a fine not exceeding 1000 Australian dollars, or an imprisonment of not more than 12 months, or both.*

VI THE INSTRUMENTS OF BANKING SECRECY

Direct

The banks do not offer the facility of numbered accounts or accounts held under a false name, although there is no obstacle to their use, since a Swiss bank in Vanuatu offers these same services.

Indirect

There is no obstacle to their use, either local or foreign.

Bearer

There are none.

VII THE PRACTICE OF BANKING SECRECY AND FOREIGN ECONOMIC POWERS

Unlike the violent legal attacks of the Americans against Bahamian and Cayman banking secrecy, the powerful Australian neighbour seems to have limited itself to legislative attacks against Vanuatu which has restricted its activities as a tax haven, without excessively harming its activities as a banking haven, perhaps even indirectly benefiting it, so great is the temptation of the forbidden.

It is by means of exchange control (Australian exchange control, since Vanuatu has none) that the Australian authorities have tried to isolate Vanuatu (when it was still the New Hebrides).

In fact Australia has established a list of 18 tax havens (with certain omissions) from which Australian individuals or corporate bodies cannot borrow or lend money, buy or sell shares, land, property, rights relating to shares (except by going through an Australian exchange agent), pay author's royalties or similar royalties, or provide services.†

One might think that the inclusion of the Vanuatu in this prohibitive list would have been sufficient attack. This is not so, and in addition to these

---

*Article 163-5, company law, 1971.
†Modification in the law on banks, 23 December 1974.

general measures there are specific measures relating to Vanuatu whereby no Australian individual or corporate body can enforce any agreement relating to any money or property in Vanuatu, or any contract, agreement or arrangement to which a resident of Vanuatu is party. In addition to these prohibitions relating to transactions in Vanuatu, there are other minor ones, but also a few exceptions and one particularly, for an Australian bank, of completing in Australia local transactions carried out in Vanuatu—business, even banking business, must not be discouraged!

VIII INTERNATIONAL AGREEMENTS LIKELY TO UNDERMINE BANKING SECRECY

There are no general or specific agreements likely to affect banking secrecy. There are, furthermore, no agreements relating to double taxation, Vanuatu being a complete tax haven.

IX BANKING SECRECY AND THE FINANCIAL MARKET

Blind and official markets for non-residents

In the absence of treaties, there is no reason to distinguish between the official market and the blind market. The rates for withholding tax are the following:

bank interest	nil
dividends	nil

Back-to-back loans

There are no obstacles.

X PERSONAL COMMENTS

Despite Australian legislative prohibitions, progress has for a long time seemed to be very favourable, because of the conjunction of banking and tax haven activities, local rates of inflation varying from 6 to 9 per cent, (apart from one point in 1974, when it reached 31 per cent). It is true that there is hardly any competition in this field, geographically speaking: Nauru Island (in the Central Pacific) did not know how to become a banking haven and, lacking in dynamism that springs from the fact that its inhabitants have the highest income in the world (the island is a phosphate mine), has not really promoted its tax haven activities. French Polynesia seems to be sleeping in the shadows of the French civil service, dreaming of an independence that it is financially incapable of achieving through lack of imagination, and because it has already caused the flight of Chinese capital by dreaming up, in the French manner (a brilliant idea of the French civil service—there are several people to congratulate!) the idea of an income tax but on what income since the Tahitians themselves imitate the Chinese?

Vanuatu has suffered a 'difficult' independence, but there is every reason to believe that the effects of this will quickly disappear, thanks to the skill of the local Anglo-Saxon businessmen who have not abandoned the new state.

36 Panama:
A canal for floating capital

I THE COUNTRY AND ITS COMPONENTS

Geographical, historical, and economic situation

Panama is a republic which extends on both sides of the canal that passes through the narrowest part of the isthmus between Costa Rica on the west and Colombia to the east; the canal and the zone bordering it are not, strictly speaking, Panamanian.

Panama was discovered in 1501 by a Spanish lawyer. Until 1903 it was a Colombian district; it then became an independent republic after a musical comedy-style revolution supported by the United States which obtained in perpetuity the concession of the Canal Zone which is 9½ kilometres wide and has a total area of 1077 square kilometres. Like all sentences in perpetuity, this one has subsequently been commuted—for good behaviour—and the Canal Zone should be returned to Panama in the year 2000.*

The economy is based on revenue from the canal (rent for the concession and income from the personnel employed in the Zone), income from the free zone of Colon where a large number of international companies are installed, and tax and banking tourism.

Population, stability, communications, and legal system

The population is approaching 1 900 000 inhabitants, of which 600 000 live in Panama City, the capital, situated on the mouth of the Canal on the Pacific, and 100 000 in Colon, a free port situated on the Atlantic coast; Panama is composed of 50 per cent mulattoes of Indian origin, 40 per cent blacks, and 10 per cent whites.

As far as clever imititation and the judicious choice of models go, Hong Kong tailors and jewellers have only the Panamanian lawyers as serious competitors: the basic legal system is the civil code, company law is based on 'Delaware' law, and the law on banking secrecy on Swiss law. This is not an

---

*Theoretically the Republic of Panama took back the control of the Canal Zone on 1 October 1979, but full sovereignty will not be regained until 31 December 1999 and, until this date, the United States will still control about 40 per cent of the zone where they have their military bases, which is perhaps one of the best guarantees of maintaining the privileges of this country.

insult but a compliment, and a certain number of countries might well avoid mistakes, particularly in tax matters, by studying what their neighbours have done and looking at the results.*

Despite renewed pessimistic statements by certain journalists, the situation is stable and there is a strong chance that it will remain so. The pessimists say that as the United States now has a presence in the two oceans and that the US Navy rarely uses the Canal, the Canal has consequently lost its strategic interest and therefore Panama has lost American protection. This is a very bad analysis of a strategic plan for, according to better-informed sources, it is in the Canal Zone that the United States has installed a ring of nuclear missiles designed to protect (?) South America. It is precisely because of the necessity to protect this ring, the dismantling of which would cost a fortune and might pose problems of relocation, that one can be certain of the political stability of Panama.

Communications, post, telegraph, telephone (satellite communication), and telex systems, approach perfection, perhaps even the sublime.

II CURRENCY

The official currency is the balboa which carries the picture of the Spanish *conquistador* Vasco Nuñez de Balbao. This *conquistador* not only gave his name to the local currency, but also his head, (literally) since he was decapitated. The balboa exists on paper, but not on bank paper, no note having ever been printed. Only the American dollar is in circulation in note form, since a monetary agreement in 1904.†

Coins have been minted in cents and have the same format as American coins:

$$1 \text{ balboa} = 100 \text{ centimos}$$
$$1 \text{ balboa} = \text{US } \$1.00$$

III EXCHANGE CONTROL

For a Panamanian the mere mention of this question is in bad taste. There is no exchange control, even indirectly, nor, consequently, any distinction in this sense between residents and non-residents.

---

*Such is the situation in France which recently considered whether or not to create a capital gains tax. Those who were technically responsible for the project did not consider that at the same period the canton of Zurich, having earlier tried the experiment, had abolished this tax which was not only regressive, but also cost more to raise than it contributed. One can similarly classify the criticisms and fears relating to a wealth tax which, inversely, is dynamic and economically healthy and has nothing to do with 'Marxist plundering' since one of its prime promoters is the Federal Republic of Germany, where not only does it function perfectly well but is reckoned to be one of the best weapons against tax fraud.

France is far from being the only country with such an attitude, and one of the most serious comparisons is that few few countries make comparisons.

†Law no. 84, 1904.

IV BANKS AND THE BANKING SYSTEM

There are at present close to 82 banks in Panama representing 26 different countries and employing about 7000 people. Financial analysts estimate that there will be about 200 banks in 1990. However, the laws relating to the granting of licences are increasingly severe, particularly after the 1974 change* since when licences no longer bear the numbers I–III, but are called respectively: 'general licence' (at present 47 banks), 'international licence' (at present 25 banks) and 'representation licence' (eight banks), which terms are sufficiently clear as not to require explanation.

Licences are increasingly difficult to obtain, since Panama is now seeking to be an international financial centre rather than a banking haven and sees itself as being 'in competition with Hong Kong and Singapore'. It is now no longer possible for *bancos brujos* (magic banks—a Spanish term applied to banks that specialize in 'hot' transactions) to set up in Panama.

Among the unwritten conditions for obtaining a licence, the request must come from 'either a subsidiary company or an affiliated company of a large international bank or that, at least such an institution is in fact the one requesting the licence, even if, officially, the ownership of the bank is in other hands.†

The control of the banking system is undertaken by the Bank Commission, one of whose objectives is to 'strengthen and promote conditions suitable for the development of Panama as an international financial centre'.‡ This Bank Commission possesses wide powers of investigation, but powers that do not violate the secrecy enjoyed by the client.§ In reality, 'the nearest comparison is with the banking laws and the situation prevalent in Belgium where the Bank Commission does not function in practice as a body initiating detailed audits of bank operations, but acts as 'a bureau of statistical control' on the level of the banks' financial results and exercises its control mainly at the level of issuing licences'.∥

At present there are 30 requests for licences in process. The development of banking activity in Panama is shown by the figures: the banks' assets which were estimated at US $1.9 billion in 1972 were, by the end of 1978, more than $10 billion. ☆

The banks are open from 8.30 am to 1 pm and closed on Saturdays and Sundays.

---

*Law no. 93, 27 November 1974.
†International Service Company Inc., Panama (Opinion of A. R. Valdes, 3 May 1979).
‡Law, no. 28, 2 July 1970 (*Journal officiel*, no. 16640, 6 July 1970).
§Law no. 28, 2 July 1970, Chapter IX, 'Banking inspection', articles 62–75.
∥International Service Company Inc., cited above.
☆'Liberal laws create a haven for offshore banking', Panama, 1979 (Special Report, *International Herald Tribune*, February 1979).

V BANKING SECRECY

General outline

'There is absolutely no legal decision to this day, in Panama relating to the interpretation of banking secrecy by the courts in civil matters.'*

This revealing statement contains numerous indicators. First of all, it may be the simple fact that the texts in themselves are clear, but there may also be another explanation. The major conflicts between the United States and the Bahamas, and the Cayman Islands, come from the fact that North American capital is involved, is placed in the banks of these countries which therefore prosper at the expense of 'Uncle Sam'. In Panama, it is more a question of the capital of 'Uncle Gonzales' which is deposited and protected by banking secrecy against the extremely severe laws of certain South American dictatorships from whence it comes. This is true to such a point that Panama hopes to see the expression 'latino-dollars' pass into current parlance, in connection with dollars that come from South America and are deposited in its banks. Finally, it is of little importance that the Supreme Court of Uruguay, for example, does not recognize Panamanian banking secrecy since, in any case, there is little chance that the Panamanian banker 'passes' the funds.

He will be content to leave the risk to the 'passer' (smuggler) a risk which is quite considerable.†

Legal basis and sanctions

Legal basis: Panamanian banking secrecy has its general basis in the clauses of the Civil Code and in article 184 of the Penal Code relating to professional secrecy, and, contrary to the position in Luxembourg, jurists consider that this secrecy applies to the banker.‡

In addition to these clauses of a general nature there are those which, curiously enough, exist only for the *cuentas bancarias cifradas* (numbered bank accounts), a definition of which is given in article 2 of the same law:§

The numbered bank account is a contract by which an individual or corporate body maintains or deposits in a bank either cash, or shares, and in which the bank agrees to

---

*International Service Company Inc., cited above.
†According to specialist bankers, the price of 'passage' is currently at 50 per cent and sometimes, in critical situations, went up to 75 per cent for Latin-American dictatorships. According to these bankers (whose opinion is confirmed by the 'interested' American administration), the rates of 'passage' are the same for 'popular' (for whom?) socialist republics. As always, the extremes meet and if liberty has no price, certainly the freedom of money does have one. For the 'passer' the sanction is death after an interrogation in which the assistance of a lawyer is usefully replaced by a catalogue of instruments and practices recommended by Amnesty International. But one must not be naive, these states and their leaders themselves use Panama, but *for* themselves; for this reason official attacks are always moderated!
‡Opinion of Mr Winston Robles, lawyer in Panama (13 December 1973).
§Law no. 18, 28 January 1959 *'por la cual se dictan disposiciones en relación con cuentas bancarias cifradas'*.

carry out orders for payment of the depositor within the limits of the cash or stocks deposited by him or of the credit having been granted to him, and to observe absolute secrecy relating to the existence of this account, its balance and the identity of the depositor.

The interest which according to the clauses of the account agreement may be acquired by the depositor, forms an integral part of the account for all legal purposes.

Furthermore, the Panamanian legislator feels the need, in article 3 of the same law, to explain the function of cheques and payment orders relating to a particular account, the wording of which in fact only permits numbered accounts, and excludes the Swiss invention of accounts held under a false name, at least as regards the protection of this law, since such accounts would not enter into its definition:

It is not necessary that the name of the drawer appears on the cheques or the payment orders drawn on a numbered current account or on orders for delivery of shares. The bank will be obliged to pay such cheques or payment orders* on condition that the usual signature previously provided by the client and the account number appears on it.

The people concerned, the extent of secrecy and the penalties are indicated in articles 4–6:

The directors, administrators and other employees, nationals or not, of banking establishments who reveal or inform persons foreign to the establishment and to the handling of these accounts any information relating to their existence, their balance or the identity of the numbered account, will be guilty . . . .

It should be pointed out that it is clearly specified that the same persons cannot give any information (under the same sanctions) to the Panamanian authorities or magistrates except in criminal matters on behalf of investigators and magistrates who would then themselves be held to the same secrecy if the information thus obtained does not lead to the solution of criminal acts that are the object of the enquiry . . . . It is difficult to imagine a wider 'cover' without actually admitting the existence of criminal money.

Finally, and perhaps to avoid litigation, it is clearly stated in article 11 that 'all clauses contrary to the present law are null and void'.

As for the powers of investigation of the local fiscal administration, they are, with regard to numbered accounts, limited to the global sums handled by the bank without reference to the details of individual accounts.

In practice, one of the fundamental differences between banking secrecy applied to ordinary and numbered accounts is that, within the framework of normal accounts, secrecy may be lifted by a Panamanian magistrate by applying article 89 of the Commercial Code, whilst in the case of a numbered account, even if the identity of the holder happens to be revealed, a Panamanian magistrate has no legal power (beyond criminal matters) to

---

*And what about the 'delivery' of shares?

order, for example, seizure; if he does order it, this would be ineffective anyway.

Penalties: the civil sanctions are the damages and interest, to which may be added the administrative sanction of withdrawal of licence. The penal sanctions vary depending on whether the violation has been committed in relation to a numbered or an ordinary account.

In the case of an ordinary account, the penalty applicable is a fine of $20-200 and an imprisonment of between 5 days and a month.

For a numbered account, the penalty is a fine of $1000-10 000 and an imprisonment of between 30 days and 6 months, or one of these penalties only.

VI THE INSTRUMENTS OF BANKING SECRECY

Direct

Numbered accounts clearly exist since they are the object of a law. Certain banks accept accounts under a false name, but there is a certain ambiguity surrounding their protection since they do not correspond to the definition of 'coded' accounts. There is reason to believe that this variant would be assimilated along with the numbered accounts if the question had to be settled by the Panamanian courts. Finally, Panamanian banks refuse to open accounts to Panamanian companies under fictitious names, and it is easy to understand why. Since Panamanian companies are, in effect, totally anonymous (*see* Chapter 6*), the fact that they may want to operate under a fictitious name can only serve to hide concerns that are doubtless far removed from a legitimate concern for secrecy and can only harm the good reputation of the bank.

Indirect

'Anonymous' companies certainly can be used in the widest possible sense in the country which is the main supplier of them.

Bearer

These are apparently not used.

VII THE PRACTICE OF BANKING SECRECY AND FOREIGN ECONOMIC POWERS

Banking secrecy for numbered accounts is absolute in all domains, except in criminal cases, and this situation seems to be better tolerated by the United States than the situation in the Bahamas or the Cayman Islands.

---

*See also the chapter 'Panama' in *Using Tax Havens Successfully*, cited above.

VIII INTERNATIONAL AGREEMENTS LIKELY TO UNDERMINE BANKING SECRECY

General agreements

There are none but it should be noted (without the reservations that apply to countries having exchange control) that the Republic of Panama has been a member of the Bretton Woods agreement since 14 March 1946, in its (retroactive) role as founder member.

Specific agreements

Only one exists that is signed with the United States; it limits double taxation in the maritime field, but does not affect banking secrecy.

IX BANKING SECRECY AND THE FINANCIAL MARKET

No geopolitical obstacle exists to the utilization of Panama. Since this country is a territorial tax haven (in other words, taxing only activities carried out within the country), it is important not to forget this detail.

Blind market for non-residents

The basic rates of withholding tax are the following:

bank interest	nil
dividends	10 per cent

(in the case where the company distributing the dividend has a local activity.)

Official market for non-residents

The Republic of Panama signed double tax treaties with the United States and New Zealand, but their use is not relevant for the two preceding categories of income, since the rates provided by these treaties are the same as the basic rates.

Back-to-back loans

These are normal practice and without fiscal obstacles.

X PERSONAL COMMENTS

Development should continue to be favourable, even on the political level despite the predictions of certain alarmists. Certainly the number of banks will increase much less than intended, even though there are at present 30 requests for licences ('one man's loss is another man's gain). Panama will perhaps become, if it is not already, the Switzerland of South America. But a Switzerland under American protection.

37 Singapore:
A bad number for numbered accounts

I THE COUNTRY AND ITS COMPONENTS

Geographical, historical, and economic situation

The Republic of Singapore, in the south-east of Asia, is separated from Malaysia, with which it was politically united from 1963 to 1965, by the straits of Johore which is about 2 kilometres wide.

A former British colony, this island, which used to be marshy, has had an extraordinary economic development due mainly to a political regime which is both strong and liberal. The island has a surface area of about 430 square kilometres and 90 per cent of its population of 2 200 000 inhabitants is concentrated in the capital, also called Singapore.

Thanks to its special geographical position, Singapore has become the primary port in south-east Asia and one of the most important naval dockyards in the world.

Population, stability, communications, and legal system

The population is composed of 75 per cent Chinese, 14 per cent Malay, 8 per cent Indian and Pakistani, the rest being of various races with some Europeans.

The legal system is rather complex since it is largely based on British common law, a shared legislation dating from the time when it was united with Malaysia, and local laws and jurisprudence.

Communications systems of all kinds are excellent.

II CURRENCY

Legal tender is the Singapore dollar which was created on the 19 May 1967. Like the Hong Kong dollar, the Singapore dollar detached itself from the American dollar as a result of its devaluation.

1 Singapore dollar = 100 cents
1 Singapore dollar = US $0.48
1 Singapore dollar = Swiss francs 0.93½ (May 1982)

III EXCHANGE CONTROL

The system of exchange control in Singapore is relatively simple and fairly strange since it is based on the pre-1972 British definition of the scheduled territories. The scheduled territories have singularly diminished since that date and no longer include Singapore which, nevertheless, pretends not to notice this. The result of this amusing situation was that Singapore's exchange control acted just like a sieve until the suppression of British exchange control, which was no hindrance, since to play the pound sterling against the Singapore dollar was for a long time absolute lunacy. Thus, a Singapore resident could freely export unlimited sums of money to Great Britain (old British definition) where, by contrast, this money could only be credited to an 'external account' (new British definition), but then freely go out again to Switzerland (which is of no particular interest in this case). It should be noted, however, that the legality of the procedure was suspect within the framework of the Singapore definition and was not appreciated by the Monetary Authority of Singapore (MAS), the authority responsible for exchange control.*

Non-residents

They escape totally from exchange control and can keep accounts in any currency. But attention should be drawn to the definition of a non-resident. Thus, any resident of the scheduled territories, according to the old British definition, is considered to be a resident in Singapore, and the same applies to residents of Indonesia, the Philippines and Thailand. The accounts of non-residents are 'external accounts' and can only be credited in Singapore dollars through the sale of convertible currency for currencies of the 'scheduled territories'.

Interest paid to non-residents

There is no obstacle.

Residents

The definition of a resident has already been given. Overall, they enjoy great monetary freedom because of high thresholds fixed for authorization. Exchange control in Singapore seems in fact to be a control of investments and to be maintained only through a (dastardly) habit inherited from the British.

---

*With the suppression of British exchange control, the Singapore zone of exchange control includes a zone without exchange control, which is a record! Nevertheless, it is not clear that the authorities will change their legislation.

IV BANKS AND THE BANKING SYSTEM

The banking system is placed under the authority of the MAS which is responsible for the supervision of the Asia Currency Units (ACUs) which are bank divisions with an independent accountability (but under the responsibility of the bank), responsible for the market in Asia-dollars. The MAS does not circulate banknotes; this role is reserved for the BCC (Board of Commissioners of Currency).

There are a hundred banks in Singapore, of which 17 are purely 'offshore'. Singapore has become, in competition with Hong Kong, the financial centre of south-east Asia with deposits of US $30 billion* divided in the proportion of two-thirds in Singapore and one-third in Hong Kong. This disproportion could, furthermore, increase because of the fact that Hong Kong now levies a withholding tax on bank interest above a threshold of interest fixed by the inland revenue, while there is no deduction at source in Singapore. For this reason, Singapore (in competition with Bahrein) is at present taking over part of the financial activities of Hong Kong.

It should be noted that if the MAS uses its power of investigation and surveillance over the banks, its agents are bound to secrecy, and any violation of this is punished by the same penalties as the violation of banking secrecy.†

The banks are generally open from 10 am to 3 pm from Monday to Friday, and from 10 am to 11.30 am on Saturdays.

V BANKING SECRECY

General outline

'There has been no legal decision made in Singapore excluding banking secrecy.' This statement made by Mr Karthigesu, a lawyer in Singapore, is very revealing about the situation in this country which, in terms of banking secrecy, might be summarized as follows: there is no such decision but there could well be one; on the other hand, there *could* be numbered accounts, but there aren't any!

This curious balancing act probably comes from the attitude of the government which wants to be Hong Kong without the vice (we shall leave the responsibility for this statement to its authors, for a good number of reasons), but, above all, the Switzerland of Asia.‡

It is these reasons which led to the 1970 law to replace the 1958 law because it was insufficiently explicit on banking secrecy. It created numbered accounts while entrusting the opportunity for opening such accounts to the MAS. Curiously enough, and doubtless because of the financial hyperdevelopment

---

*Figure given by *The Economist*, June 1979.
†Article 41 of the Banking Act 1970.
‡It is amusing to notice how much this nice little country, thanks to its appreciation of work and freedom, has been able to create a vocation. Are those in Switzerland who denigrate their country and banking secrecy, freedom's accessory, aware of this?

of Singapore, the MAS has never authorized the opening of numbered accounts, since it is true that indirect instruments, and the Rolls Royce of banking secrecy, are used so widely that Singapore has not wanted to introduce bicycles among its rickshaws!

Since Singapore is not hampered by international sensitivities banking secrecy is made mainly for foreigners and used as a shield against foreign authorities.

Legal basis and penalties

Legal basis: the principle of banking secrecy in Singapore is to be found in article 42-2 of the Banking Act of 1970 which says that:

No employee of any bank nor any person who, because of his functions or his employment, has access to dossiers, registers, correspondence or written information concerning the account of any client of the bank, will give, divulge or reveal any information whatever about the operations or details of this client's account to:
(a) any person or bank, company or group of people non-resident in Singapore;* or
(b) any government or foreign organization, unless:
   (i) the client or his representative gives their permission to do so.
   (ii) the client is declared bankrupt; or
   (iii) the information is demanded in order to establish the credit of a client in connection with or relating to an existing or proposed commercial transaction . . . .†

This text is, in reality, much less clear than it may seem at first glance.

In fact, and contrary to most banking havens which define the beneficiaries of secrecy and grant them the protection of the law, article 42-2 does not depart from the general principle, but defines the categories of persons against whom banking secrecy is strengthened. Therefore, it is necessary to distinguish between two categories of situations, not as a function of the holder of the secret, but as a function of the one who would be likely to break it.

Position in common law: for example, the case of an account holder (resident or non-resident) *vis-à-vis* the Singapore authorities or the local banks. The protection is that offered by the Tournier judgment (*see* Chapter 10) since in applying the law of Singapore, British common law is applicable. In this case, for example, the comptroller of income tax has the power to oblige the bank to give information relating to accounts‡ and a tribunal or a magistrate can request such information in a criminal or civil case.§

Position in article 42-2: banking secrecy as presented in the Tournier judgment is reinforced by the conditions set out in article 42-2 with regard to persons as defined in it.

---

*For the application of this idea, article 42-3 of the same law defines as non-resident in Singapore any bank, company or group of people whose 'control and management of affairs is carried on outside Singapore'.
†According to Myint Soe, this text is inspired by article 275 of the Swiss penal code ('The Law of Banking and Negotiable Instruments in Singapore and Malaysia'; see bibliography).
‡Article 65A of the law on taxation.
§Fourth part of the law on evidence.

One point apparently not clarified, but very important, is the compatibility of this text with international treaties providing for exchange of information. The solution is not given even if it seems that in practice the local tax administration yields only the information that it has at its disposal and not that which it is authorized to have. Prudence is necessary when faced with what is merely an interpretation!

The fate of numbered accounts is specified in articles 50–52 of the 1970 Banking Act. These accounts will not be examined here, since they are only of academic interest. In fact, opening one is subject to an authorization by the MAS, which since its creation in 1970 has not authorized a single one.

Penalties: the violation of banking secrecy, in the common law situation, is the sanction of the Tournier judgment, that is to say, damages and interest.

In the situation where common law is strengthened by article 42-2, the violation of banking secrecy is punished by a fine of 10 000 Singapore dollars or a penalty of up to 3 years' imprisonment, or both.

Until now there has been no conviction, based either on the Tournier judgment or on a violation of article 42-2.

VI THE INSTRUMENTS OF BANKING SECRECY

Direct

There are none.

Indirect

They present no obstacle, and are allowed by the banks, without the Swiss restrictions.

VII THE PRACTICE OF BANKING SECRECY AND FOREIGN ECONOMIC POWERS

Banking secrecy in Singapore is an accepted fact which has not particularly attracted the attention of other countries and does not give rise to jealousy.

VIII INTERNATIONAL AGREEMENTS LIKELY TO UNDERMINE BANKING SECRECY

General agreements

Apparently there are none, but it should be emphasized that the Republic of Singapore has adhered to the Bretton Woods agreement since 3 August 1966.

Specific agreements

Singapore has signed double taxation agreements with 17 countries, one of which is Switzerland, and there is one with Italy which has not yet come into effect. In a general way, these agreements provide for exchanges of information, and the ambiguity previously mentioned relates to a large number of countries, but this is relatively secondary in the case of Singapore.

IX BANKING SECRECY AND THE FINANCIAL MARKET

Blind market for non-residents

The rates for withholding tax are the following:

bank interest	nil
dividends	40 per cent

The official market for non-residents

Interest is fairly limited because of the absence of deduction at source on bank interest. At the level of dividends, most agreements provide for a reduction to 15 per cent. It should be noted that dividends relating to certain approved investments in certain sectors are exempted (outside agreements) from deduction at source.

Back-to-back loans

This presents no obstacle and is current practice.

X PERSONAL COMMENTS

Singapore has not put into circulation the bicycles of banking secrecy, i.e. numbered accounts, preferring to reserve its favours for indirect instruments and the Rolls Royces of banking secrecy. In these conditions, the ambiguity hovering over banking secrecy that is confronted by agreements providing for exchanges of information, is secondary. Nevertheless, it is a pity—for whom?

38 Switzerland:*
A currency—even for the blind

I THE COUNTRY AND ITS COMPONENTS

It is almost an insult to try to introduce this country that is already so well known, so we shall limit ourselves to the reminder that this country is a model of stability (*the* model?) and that its communications of all sorts are absolutely perfect.

II THE CURRENCY

The history of Swiss currency could, in itself, justify a whole book, but we shall refrain from giving figures mentioning only that the German deutschmark and the Swiss franc are, amongst the major currencies, the ones that have risen most in value.

This very strong appreciation of the German deutschmark and the Swiss franc provides the basis for the measures taken by these two countries to limit the demand for their currency and, specifically, the negative interest instituted and then abolished on deposits made in Switzerland in Swiss francs by non-residents (besides the fact that, traditionally, deposits in Swiss francs do not earn interest).

$$1 \text{ Swiss franc} = 100 \text{ centimes}$$
$$1 \text{ US dollar} = \text{Swiss francs } 1.95 \text{ (May 1982)}$$

The Swiss franc is used not only in Switzerland, but also in Liechtenstein.

It is to be noted that the wicked gnomes of Geneva (as notorious as those of Zurich) had the delicacy to have the signs on banknotes embossed so that even the blind can recognize the currency. This is an example that foreign issuing institutes might follow at very little expense. However, it is not this procedure alone which has attracted to Switzerland deposits that certain local authors estimated in 1977 to be 300 billion Swiss francs† (of which 60 billion are in

---

*Because of the extreme importance of Switzerland, as much from the point of view of principles as of practice, this chapter contains certain developments in greater detail than was judged necessary for other banking havens.
†U. E. Rumati, *TPI*, **4**, (6), June 1977.

safes or in gold),* and American authors at US $36 billion (to which should be added the contents of the safes).†

If we go over these estimates of deposits: 240 billion Swiss francs, or approximately US $100 billion (Swiss author), i.e. the same estimate as for the deposits of non-residents in the Bahamas in August 1978,‡ or US $36 billion (American author), or approximately three times less, one can ascertain that the most fanciful figures abound on the question, and this is the only serious observation that we shall make on this level.

III EXCHANGE CONTROL

'In Switzerland there exists no form of exchange control.' This type of statement, put about almost unanimously by the best experts is a monstrous absurdity, since these same experts, enclosed within the intellectual circle of the laws of their own countries, start from the classical analysis that an exchange control is defined on the basis of a notion of residence, without even imagining that the converse might be true. How otherwise to explain the negative interest that the Swiss authorities from time to time levy on deposits in Swiss francs of non-residents beyond a certain sum? It is certainly not a question of taxation since the object is not to collect a tax, but to discourage the acquisition of a currency (how otherwise to explain a negative interest of 10 per cent on the deposits of non-residents above 100 000 Swiss francs?).

How otherwise to explain the provisions made in February 1978, then abolished on 25 January 1979 (after a relative drop in the Swiss franc), forbidding the acquisition of shares in Swiss companies in Swiss francs? It is true that this last provision was shaped by the purchase of bonds convertible into shares, the conversion of which the National Bank, under penalty of an expropriation that is apparently contrary to the Constitution, could not suspend.§

**Pick's Currency Year Book*, 1975–76.

†The journal *The Economist* does not hesitate to give a 'high' estimate of US $180 billion ('International banking: a survey', March 1979).

For its part, the equally worthy *Financial Times* estimates the bank deposits (end 1976) at 95.6 billion Swiss francs and those made on fiduciary accounts at 49.2 billion Swiss francs, or a total of 144.8 billion Swiss francs, therefore approximately US $51 billion, to which sum should be added 100 billion Swiss francs deposited in trust outside the financial institutions, the whole coming to a total of US $100 billion. If one adds to these sums 200 billion Swiss francs invested in Swiss securities, or US $87 billion, the total global estimate is US $187 billion ('Switzerland: banks soften their image', 23 May 1979). The Swiss socialist party, which is partisan to suppressing banking secrecy, estimates the 'occult' deposits at 90 billion Swiss francs, or US $36 billion, basing this on the fact that the basic withholding tax (in the absence of a treaty on double taxation) allows one to arrive at this conclusion. Like all the other figures this latter is very debatable since it comes up against 'anonymous' deposits in cases where no treaty exists on double taxation, which is the case in the Arab Emirates.

‡Estimate of the *Financial Times*, 20 April 1979.

§The Swiss federal council, in conjunction with the National Bank, has specifically been authorized, in case of severe disturbances in the international monetary order, to take for the sake of internal monetary politics the exceptional measures that are judged necessary (decree of 8 October 1971, R.S. 941.11, modified and extended by the federal decree of 28 June 1974, R.S. 941.110).

The appropriate phrase here is: Switzerland has an intermittent exchange control that is applied generally, after a certain exemption, to the holding of its own currency by non-residents.*

Non-residents

Except for restrictions on the holding of assets in Swiss francs or investments (even real estate), they totally escape all forms of exchange control.

Interest paid to non-residents

Legislation changes as a function of the monetary market, and, in fact, rather often. The basic principle is that bank deposits are not remunerated and can even incur a negative interest if they are denominated in Swiss francs.†

Payments made to non-residents are subject to a withholding tax which may be reduced by reference to double taxation agreements. One of the characteristics that results from the quest for banking secrecy is that these agreements are rarely invoked for reasons of secrecy and that deduction at source is applied generally at basic rates.

Residents

They are not subject to any constraints.

IV BANKS AND THE BANKING SYSTEM

There are approximately 500 banks, of which 140 are in the canton of Geneva, with more than 4500 bank branches in the Confederation. These banks are bound to provide the Swiss National Bank (BNS) with their annual accounts and, eventually, as a function of the importance of their affairs, interim balance-sheets; they must also respond to questions raised by the BNS on the development of their balance sheet. The foreign banks or those 'in foreign hands' must also give to the BNS information on the affairs that they handle and on their relations with foreign countries. The whole of the information received by the BNS and its employees is subject to banking secrecy.‡ The BNS also has at its disposal a team of independent auditors, one of their activities being to verify the application of measures designed to limit the flow of funds; they are also subject to banking secrecy, except with regard to the BNS for the verification of breaches.§ For the supervision of the banks with regard to the

---

*The negative interest fixed at 2 per cent per trimester (4 July 1972) was raised to 10 per cent (22 January 1975) then reduced again to 2.5 per cent (November 1979) and finally abolished on 1 December 1979.
†This principle was in reality a prohibition which was removed on 21 February 1980.
‡Article 9, paragraph 1 of banking law, and 58 of the law on the Swiss National Bank.
§Article 20, no. 5, of banking law.

clients' risks, there also exists a Federal Bank Commission authorized to delegate an expert to monitor a bank whose creditors seem to be particularly at risk.* The expert appointed has to observe the management of the bank and enjoys the right to unlimited access to the books and files of the bank; he is subject to banking secrecy, and the members of the Federal Banking Commission, to which he makes a report as well as the secretariat of the Commission, are subject to the secrecy of 'function'.† Finally, most banks are members of the Swiss Association of Bankers, although this is not an obligation; nevertheless the Swiss Association of Bankers is sufficiently representative to be a signatory, with the BNS, to the agreement on the acceptance of foreign deposits to which all the Swiss banks finally adhered.

V BANKING SECRECY

General outline

The general framework of banking secrecy in Switzerland has already been defined in Chapter 4; suffice it to say that, according to the principle of Swiss legal ethics, the 'inviolability' of private life does not constitute simply a moral principle, it is also a rule of law, a legal asset (*Rechtsgut*); it is an attribute of personality, and the law protects it (judgment of the Swiss federal Tribunal).

Legal basis and penalties

Legal basis: the professional secrecy of the banker is implicitly contained in articles 27 and 28 of the Swiss Civil Code granting to each individual, or corporate body, protection for the secrets of private life, independent of any contractual relationship. Article 28, 1st paragraph, of the Civil Code stipulates: 'Anyone who comes under an illicit attack on his interests can ask the courts to take action.'

The legal basis of the banker's duty finds a complementary source not only in the contract made with his client, based on the idea of confidence the violation of which is sanctionable by the terms of the general clauses of the *Code des obligations*, but also on the fact that it often concerns him in his role as authorized agent and where the client is 'master of the secrecy', in the sense of article 398 of the same *Code des obligations*, which stipulates in paragraph 3: 'The authorized agent is responsible towards the authorizing person for the good and faithful performance of his contract.'

The federal law on banks and savings banks of 8 November 1934 in its article 47‡ deals with the respect for the banker's duties as stipulated in the

---

*Article 23–4, paragraph 1, of banking law.
†This is no longer related to article 47 of banking law but to article 320 of the Swiss Penal Code.
‡Completed by the federal law of 11 March 1971, modifying the law on banks and savings banks (effective from 1 July 1971).

civil code and the *Code des Obligations*, and sanctions this secrecy by virtue of the *droit pénal administratif*; it specifies:

1. Anyone, who, in his role as member of an organization, as employee, authorized agent, liquidator or bank commissioner, or observer at the bank commission, or as member of an organization or employee of a recognized auditing institution, reveals a secret that has been confided to him or of which he had knowledge because of his responsibility or his employment, will be punished . . . .
2. If the offender acted through negligence, the penalty will be . . . .
3. The violation of secrecy remains punishable even after the responsibility or the employment is finished or when the holder of the secret no longer exercises his profession.

It seems that this text is in itself sufficiently clear as to avoid the necessity for detailed commentary. The obligation to be discreet extends very clearly, not only to contractual relationships, but also to precontractual relationships, even those not followed by action (for example, information provided for a request for a loan which is not followed by a loan), and postcontractual (information on a terminated operation). Furthermore, the attempt is itself punishable.

It appears that the beneficiary of this obligation can renounce it.*

Penalties: the violations of banking secrecy are severely sanctioned in Switzerland. There are three types of sanctions:

1. Administrative sanctions:
   (a) dismissal of the administrator concerned or removal of the employee;
   (b) exclusion of the bank from the Swiss Association of Bankers (article 5 of the statutes);
   (c) withdrawal of the authorization to practice by the Federal Bank Commission (banking law, article 25-5, 1st paragraph).
2. Financial sanctions: there is no distinction made between whether the violation of banking secrecy was voluntary or involuntary, and caused directly or through an employee, the real problem being compensation for the damage.†

The principle of compensation is that the damage must be quantifiable which implies that it is not contingent.

This principle is related to the particular situation of the client, and the judge can reduce, or even abolish, the damages and interest in case of contributory acts of the injured party. This is the case particularly when the client is a foreign resident and contravenes the tax regulations or the exchange control which apply to him.

---

*This question is far from being devoid of practical interest, for certain Swiss banks use the highly debatable practice of making their American clients sign a renunciation of banking secrecy 'in advance'. It is quite obvious that an *a posteriori* renunciation is still more delicate since it can be imposed by an external moral or physical constraint.
†The rather special Swiss system of 'reparation' reminds one of those mixed systems used by insurance companies for dealing with car accidents where the blame is shared. It is not true to say that Switzerland is a large garage for capital which has often moved too fast?

If, following on the violation of banking secrecy, the client incurs a fine or a sequestriation from a foreign power, he will not in principle be able to claim full damages.*

Overall, there are not many decisions relating to the violation of banking secrecy for the excellent reason that 'in general, a settlement is arrived at';† furthermore, even if (as in any bank) indiscretions or mistakes are made, the reflex mechanisms of the professionals in the system immediately catch the 'error' or limit the difficulty. This is the reason and the advantage of the importance of the banking haven tradition compared to the law being created from scratch in a system that does not have the experience.

At present the really significant cases of violation of banking secrecy are when employees or directors of banks, at the time of a change of employer-banker, advise their clients of the change (even in Switzerland, it is better to leave with one's baggage). Normally there should be a trial for unfair competition and a suit for violation of banking secrecy (the new employer-banker being advised of the existence of the clients of the bank where his new employee worked). 'These cases are known in banking circles, but the two banks "arrange" the situation, for any publicity would be bad for the two banks and for the Swiss financial situation as a whole.'‡

3. Penal sanctions (5-year limitation):

(a) intentional violation of banking secrecy (offence): up to 6 months' imprisonment or a fine up to 50 000 Swiss francs;

(b) violation of banking secrecy through negligence (contravention): fine to the amount of 30 000 Swiss francs.

(c) extent: to appreciate the extent of Swiss banking secrecy one needs to understand that the public interest is held to be identical to the State interest which explains why the violations of banking secrecy are automatically pursued by the Public Prosecutor, unlike breaches of other categories of professional secrecy.

This wide conception of the extent of banking secrecy was created originally to counteract

the many attempts of the totalitarian régimes of the time to apply in Switzerland their legislation on exchange control which often ended in seizure, and the appropriation of fortunes placed in your banks by persons pursued for political or racist motives.§

---

*In a particular case, a judgment of 20 January 1933 of the *'Appellationsgericht'* in the canton of Bâle-Ville reduced by half the damage and interest granted to the client.
†Contribution made by Mr Maurice Aubert at the seminar on 'The professional secrecy of the banker and its limits', organized by the International Union and the Swiss Federation of Lawyers, Basle, 4 and 5 May 1979.
‡Contribution of a member of the secretariat of the Federal Commission of (Swiss) Banks at the same seminar.
§Message in the 'Feuille française de la Confederation suisse (Berne)', 1970–71. It is to be remembered that the federal banking law dates from November 1934.

The obligation to be discreet extends not only to the banker, but also to his employees. However, the banker is no longer responsible for them after they have left the bank since the obligation which he is under to supervise them can no longer be guaranteed. Nevertheless, article 47-3 of the federal banking law states that any employee who reveals a secret will be punishable even when he no longer exercises the profession.

In practice, bankers draw attention to this obligation for secrecy in any work contract prior to taking on a bank employee. Similarly, it is reiterated on work contracts that even after the departure of the employee he remains bound by banking secrecy.

Banking law also applies 'by analogy' to the 'offices, branches and agencies of foreign banks'.* For the application of this law the term 'bank' must be understood in the Swiss sense and not in the sense of the definitions given by foreign laws.

The result is that the personnel of these banks are subject to the same banking secrecy.

The definition of organizations classified as banks in Swiss law can easily be verified with the Federal Bank Commission in Berne, which maintains a public list of enterprises subject to bank legislation.

Naturally the branches of Swiss banks abroad are subject to the regulations of the foreign country and not to Swiss banking secrecy.

One of the difficulties of the Swiss legislative system comes from the fact that this state is a confederation of 23 cantons† and that even if there is one single federal legislation there are theoretically as many cantonal legislations as there are cantons.

Certain clauses relating to banking secrecy and, specifically its exceptions, come from cantonal laws, and the same applies to the question of court testimony given by a banker in civil cases. It should be remembered that article 47-4 states that 'the disposition of federal and cantonal legislation decreeing the obligation to inform the authority and to give evidence in justice are set aside (that is are the exception to banking secrecy)'. If federal legislation is clear on criminal matters, the principle being that the banker must testify in a penal affair (in the Swiss sense of the term), if the penal affair is not a financial matter in disguise; in civil cases, and by way of example, the banker is not obliged to testify in the procedural Code of the canton of Geneva, but in Basle he is obliged to do so, and other cantons refer his testimony for the evaluation of magistrates according to the nature and importance of the affair—it would be quite easy to come unstuck in such legal complexity!

Finally, attention should be drawn to the fact that, although Swiss lawyers and solicitors are subject to professional secrecy which is appropriate to them, this is not the case for managers of large funds or business agents, to whom

---

*Article 2, 1st paragraph of banking law.
†There are 23 cantons since the referendum creating the canton of the Jura, whose entry into the Confederation took effect on 1 January 1979.

foreigners often have recourse, who limit themselves to administering their clients' funds without exercising banking activity.* Yet, when they regularly place their clients' funds on their own account or in their own name, they are then taking on the character of a bank and are subject to banking law (a preliminary verification of their registration with the Federal Bank Commission could be a wise measure).

VI INSTRUMENTS OF BANKING SECRECY

Direct

Obviously numbered accounts and accounts held in a false name exist in Switzerland, since it is in this country that they were born.

Indirect

Foreign legal entities are perfectly acceptable, but one of the peculiarities of the agreement and general terms of the Swiss National Bank and the Swiss Association of Bankers is that the beneficial owner must be known.

In fact, it is contrary to the agreement to open and manage accounts and deposits if the true owners are not known, and the banks must require companies domiciled in Switzerland or abroad to produce a written declaration which indicates who controls the company.

The expression 'domiciled company' (*société de domicile*) is a classic Swiss expression, a definition of which is nevertheless given in the agreement: domiciled companies in the sense of the present agreement refers to all establishments, companies, foundations, fiduciary enterprises, etc. which do not exercise a commercial or manufacturing activity in Switzerland, nor use a workforce in any commercial form.

Bearer

There are bearer savings books which, under the terms of the agreement, can be issued only after verification of identity, but are not controlled subsequently (if they are not deposited at the bank) since they are bearer documents. This type of account seems to be largely unknown to non-Swiss people but are in any event only used for very small amounts.

VIII THE PRACTICE OF BANKING SECRECY AND FOREIGN POWERS

There are limits, both internal and external, to Swiss banking secrecy. The current state of thinking, in the light of the experience of using the convention,

---

*Article 1, paragraph 3 of banking law.

is very well summarized by Mr Alfred E. Sarasin* who, speaking of attacks from other financial centres, made a remarkable analysis of the (unfair?) competition from other financial centres where these attacks originate:

The new requirement being formulated now is the total or partial lifting of banking secrecy in favour of foreign fiscal or monetary authorities. The motives for such suggestions, like, for example, international solidarity, seem at first sight comprehensible, but do not bear realistic examination.

The agreements for mutual legal help are there to guarantee that international offenders have nothing to gain from Swiss banking secrecy.

But not all foreign legislation agrees with our sense of right and fairness. There are some states where certain taxes are merely indirect expropriations. Some prescriptions for change of a nationalist nature are not compatible with the principles of our external politics. For Switzerland, it is not possible either to know or apply all the regulations of all the countries.

It is obviously impossible to restrict the politics of the individual to clients from some nations only and to predict that only certain countries, determined in the last resort according to ideological criteria, would have the benefit of mutual legal aid extended to fiscal and monetary matters. This would involve the division of the world into moral and immoral countries on the fiscal and monetary level.† From that point on, the door would be open to all pressures.

The Swiss financial market place is not a product of banking secrecy. But if it did not retain all its value, our country would no longer be a serious force in the international competition between the financial market places. This is understood better abroad than in Switzerland. The origin of some reproaches shows this: the noisiest critics come precisely from countries possessing the most competitive financial centres. The banks there are hardly less discreet than ours, and they are not so diligent in matters of identifying their clients to the point of finding out about—as do the Swiss banks, in conformity with the agreement—the economic interests lying behind their contracting parties.

Liberalism is not licence and Mr Alfred E. Sarasin states also: 'Contrary to errors often spread about, banking secrecy in Switzerland protects neither tax evaders nor criminals';‡ what then are the international limits?

Exchange control

Certainly it is against breaches of economic regulations and particularly the exchange controls of different countries using this type of legal barb, that Swiss banking secrecy is at its most strong.

---

*Speech made by Mr Alfred E. Sarasin, president of the Swiss Association of Bankers, at the Bankers' Day in the Kursaal, Berne, 22 September 1978.
†Certain 'high-taxation' countries, such as Australia and the German Federal Republic, have drawn up an official list of countries considered to be tax havens and have drawn legal implications from it. France followed the same system but, while drawing legal implications, drew up a 'confidential' list (a concern for discretion, legal blunders or hypocrisy?). What would be really interesting would be to see a country like Switzerland publish a list of tax and banking infernos. Unfortunately, Switzerland has better taste, unless it does not find it desirable to publish a list—of its *better* clients.
‡Again one must be clear about the definition of the term evasion, the description of which varies according to the country—in a mistake on this side of the Alps!

This derives mainly from the fact that there is no exchange control in Switzerland and the country mistrusts temporary laws concerning monetary spoliation or imprisonment which appear in other countries, particularly in periods of 'crisis'.

On the other hand, breaches of honest dealing as it is conceived according to Swiss law (a fraudulent bankruptcy, for example) can lead in certain cases to a lifting of banking secrecy. There does exist a special agreement between France and Switzerland concerning bankruptcies.

Taxation

There are subtle distinctions concerning Swiss taxation and corresponding breaches of it depending on whether it is cantonal (there are at present 24 different legislations) or federal taxes that are being evaded, and whether or not the means of evasion in themselves constitute fraud in a commercial context.

The principle in these cases has remained that of double incrimination, which means that banking secrecy can only be lifted if the act of which a non-resident is accused constitutes not only a penal infraction in his country of residence, but also in Switzerland (false bills, etc.).

In such a case, but only in this case, banking secrecy can be lifted, and the international agreements interpreted differently by other states do not receive the same interpretation in Switzerland.

Even in this extreme case, it seems that in practice the lifting of banking secrecy is somewhat of an academic exercise only.

VIII INTERNATIONAL AGREEMENTS LIKELY TO UNDERMINE BANKING SECRECY

General agreements

Switzerland joined the European agreement for mutual legal aid and the international convention on civil proceedings, signed at The Hague in 1905 and revised in 1954.

Specific agreements

Switzerland has signed and ratified a considerable number of double tax agreements, but only five of them have clauses dealing with exchange of information. The first three, signed with Denmark, France, and the German Federal Republic expressly exclude the violation of information, corresponding in actual fact to banking secrecy, without ever mentioning its name, which reduces its field; the oldest, signed with Great Britain, excludes exchange of information relating to commercial proceedings; finally, the agreements signed with the United States bring up particular points which have already been considered (*see* Chapter 3).

IX BANKING SECRECY AND THE FINANCIAL MARKET

Blind market for non-residents

Subject to continually changing clauses relating to non-residents holding accounts or negotiable securities denominated in Swiss francs, there is no geographical obstacle requiring the non-resident to be placed within the framework of an agreement on double taxation because of his residence or his nationality.

The basic rates of withholding tax are the following, in the absence of agreements:

> bank interest   35 per cent
> (but sometimes a 'negative interest' on deposits in Swiss francs at a rate that could be prohibitive.)
> dividends   35 per cent

Official market for non-residents

Like all the big countries, Switzerland has signed a veritable panoply of tax treaties and allowing for reductions in withholding tax in the case where the recipient is a resident of a treaty country.

Certain users of 'domiciled' companies, enjoying a favourable tax regime as such, have wanted to use these as stepping stones* to avoid the deductions at source made by other countries that are signatories of agreements with Switzerland and, judging their anonymity to be covered by the clauses covering banking secrecy for the agreements with Denmark, France and the German Federal Republic, have thought that they could use them with these countries. The rather maladroit operation consisted of mixing banking secrecy with fiscal proceedings which if not debatable are in any event certainly debated by the administrations concerned. This was to confuse banking secrecy with exchange of information on taxes (or rather the absence of taxes) paid by the 'domiciled' company or acting in a fiduciary capacity, and in this way bringing out the economically unreal nature of the company with regard to the Swiss authorities and the absence of any right to the reduction of withholding taxes.

Back-to-back loans

With the exception of the problem of negative interest applicable in certain situations, in cases of transactions in Swiss francs, this is in fact one of the specialties of the country, in competition with Luxembourg.

---

*For companies that are stepping stones and screens, see *Using Tax Havens Successfully*, cited above.

X PERSONAL COMMENTS

It is surprising to find that in a banking haven all bankers sign an agreement on the acceptance of funds under the terms of which they formally agree not to 'lend any active assistance in the transfer of capital outside countries whose legislation has restrictions concerning the placing of funds abroad'.* This is perhaps the price of success or the price of a new virginity, unless it is simply a wise measure with regard to those who disparage banking secrecy who also exist in Switzerland, since it is true that in any country there are false prophets and charlatans who are 'above all suspicion'.

---

*For an excellent commentary on the agreement, see the interpretative study of Mr J. J. Magnin of Geneva.

VI

Other Havens and Banking Loopholes

39 The other banking havens

The principle of a guide is to make a selection. The havens with which we have dealt so far (devoting a complete chapter to each) are all three-star, or more appropriately three-dollar ($$$) havens, while those that are examined in this section are only two- or one-dollar ($$, $) havens.

Following the example of a very well-known guide we shall specify that the number of dollars may be changed as the particular haven develops or international values change. When banking secrecy derives from a political decision, the haven may well gain or lose a dollar simply by changing its government.*

$ LEBANON — IN THE ABSENCE OF A CHEF, IT IS NO LONGER A GOOD KITCHEN

Lebanon, thanks to a highly developed set of statutes and the intelligence of its bankers, was a first-class banking haven. It appears here now only out of a sense of personal sympathy for its diaspora. Lebanon is no longer a banking haven, although Lebanese banks (something quite different) flourish all over the world. Will the Lebanese bankers suffer the fate of the Lombard bankers?

$ MALAYSIA — A MALAISE IN MALAYSIA

Although Singapore broke away from Malaysia, it still has some influence on the country, and following Singapore's 1970 law on banking secrecy Malaysia published its own statute in 1973. The two statutes are not dissimilar, but they are far from being the same. While Singapore concentrated its efforts on numbered bank accounts which the Monetary Authority of Singapore (MAS) has never put into action, Malaysia appears to have forgotten to protect secrecy for ordinary transactions, while at the same time omitting to create numbered accounts. If Malaysia's law does resemble (article 36-2, Banking Act of 1973) Singapore's, it does unfortunately start with the words: 'except with the written consent of the Central Bank . . .'; this makes it clear that with the Central Bank's written permission banking secrecy disappears (the interpretation of Mr Myint Soe), which creates a legal stew it is difficult to sort

---

*Barbados does not appear in this guide, although its Prime Minister has made announcements intended to allow the country to compete with the Bahamas and Moscow with the help of a law as yet unpublished — because it has not yet been written. Is there any point in mentioning a restaurant in a guide when its kitchen has not yet been built?

out. If you add to that something of a reputation for corruption which is suggested by some writers, although difficult to verify, it is unpleasant in principle and the roving depositor risks some indigestion (see also Chapter 37).

$ NAURU — BANKING SECRECY, BUT ONLY ONE MAIN COURSE

The person who likes money and does not know of Nauru is as unforgiveable as the art connoisseur who is ignorant of the Mona Lisa. Nauru (an island in the Central Pacific) is in fact the richest country in the world, as its inhabitants have an average annual per capita income of US $25 000. Given that the island is one big phosphate mine, its physical appearance has little in common with other Polynesian islands, but happily money has no smell. As the supply of phosphate is not inexhaustible, Nauru has been trying to establish itself as a banking and tax haven and its 1975 banking law envisaged banking secrecy reinforced by the absence of exchange controls, taxation and tax treaties.

The disadvantage of Nauru, apart from its isolation in the middle of the Pacific ocean, is that the only existing bank was established on 19 September 1976, and belongs to the state. Nor does Nauru offer direct instruments for banking secrecy. Let us leave the Nauruans for the moment to gain experience of handling their own bank and their own money — or at least, that of their neighbours, since the legal tender is the Australian dollar.

$$ AUSTRIA — WILL THE EAGLE OF BANKING SECRECY FLY AWAY?

According to Austrian lawyers the country has acquired a tradition of banking secrecy since it published on 24 January 1979 (*Official Gazette*, **64**, 20 February 1979) a new law of which section 13 is the equivalent of article 47 of the Swiss banking law: an immediate translation is required. What are the terms of this law, of which section XIII is in fact entitled *'Bankgeheimnis'* (bank secrecy)?

The principle of banking secrecy is established in paragraph 23, line 1 which states:

credit institutions, their shareholders, directors and employees are not allowed to divulge or make known in any way whatsoever the secrets which are entrusted to them exclusively in the context of their commercial relations with the clients to whom they have access . . . .

The main limitation of this principle is set out in paragraph 2 of the same section which withholds banking secrecy in the circumstances described in section 23-2. Amongst these are the classical exclusions such as the case where the client consents, where formal permission must be given in writing, but also 'in the context of criminal proceedings for tax evasion which has been carried out intentionally, but excluding failure to make financial settlements in respect of the fiscal authorities'. It is difficult to know how to interpret this piece of legislation in the absence of any judicial interpretations (and even any commentaries, either official or unofficial).

Austrian lawyers compare the statute with article 47 of the Swiss banking law. Certainly if the text is interpreted in that way it is far from being without interest and such an interpretation is possible. Let us re-examine the text.

First condition for lifting bank secrecy

It must be for criminal proceedings for tax evasion. This condition is not sufficient in itself to be interesting. In practice criminal proceedings could be instituted for no matter what kind of breach of regulations. It is therefore the second condition which is more interesting.

Second condition for lifting bank secrecy

The tax evasion must have been committed 'intentionally'. It is this question of the intention of the evasion in the definition of its extent which creates the problem of comparison with the Swiss law.

If a simple understatement of receipts is taken to be an intentional tax evasion, the Austrian banking secrecy is in no way comparable to that of Switzerland. If on the other hand it is a requirement that the actions which have brought about the tax evasion are themselves criminal (use of false invoices for example), the situation would indeed be comparable.

It is too early to expect commentaries from Austrian lawyers which will depend upon the law. But there is one simple question: is it possible that a major developed nation should transform itself into a banking haven? The answer is certainly yes, particularly in the case of a country like Austria which wishes to be a neutral staging-post between East and West. When Hungary and the USSR have legislation as banking havens, there is nothing unusual in Austria wanting to emulate Switzerland although this is certain to reveal some surprising things about two little valleys called Kleinwalsertal and Jungholz and bearer bank deposits (*Ueberbringer Sparbachen*).

Bearer bank deposits also exist in Switzerland, but they are generally used only by people of modest means. The better-off Swiss and foreigners tend to avoid them because of their several disadvantages: low interest, limit on amount deposited, limitation of one account per person (although this is somewhat academic since they are bearer accounts and it is theoretically possible therefore to open one of these accounts not only *with* each bank but *at* each branch—provided you like travelling).

The advantage of the Austrian bearer deposit accounts is that they use an ingenious system which avoids the Swiss limitations which have diminished the value of the accounts in Switzerland. The disadvantage is that they are denominated in Austrian schillings which is not necessarily going to suit the depositor. This disadvantage disappears in the two Austrian enclaves within Germany, Jungholz and Kleinwalsertal, where the currency used is the deutschmark and accounts can be opened using that currency (the operation of these accounts is dealt with in the section on Kleinwalsertal below).

$$ COSTA RICA — A PASSPORT FOR BANKING SECRECY

'The banks are obliged by law to maintain absolute secrecy on the operations of their clients, except for normal transactions which may be brought to the attention of the Central Bank but are not passed to any other government agency, and specifically not the income tax authorities.'

This statement, made by Dr Humberto Pacheco who is one of the best-known lawyers in Costa Rica, should be treated with respect, even if the statutes on which it is based are not quoted and neither has it been possible to discover them. The banking system belongs to the state except for certain private banks (articles 141–177 of law no. 1644) which cannot take deposits from the public and play the role of captive banks.

Costa Rica offers the roving depositor not only banking secrecy but also another document which is more and more sought after in a world where the governments of certain so-called democratic countries have a tendency to deprive their opponents of this same document. Costa Rica offers a passport against a property investment of at least $30 000 (the transaction actually costs more than double that) plus a deposit of $20 000 with the Bank of Costa Rica and against one's signature (renewable?) on an engagement to apply for Costa Rican nationality within five years. The roving depositor can obtain not only a Costa Rican residence but an authentic Costa Rican passport which is perfectly valid internationally.

Since Costa Rica has the extraordinarily agreeable quality of being the only country in the world which does not possess an army, not only does the passport bespeak a pleasing neutrality but enables one to dispense with a number of visa constraints. It could prove to be a very useful tool for the roving depositor.

$$ KLEINWALSERTAL — BEARER BANK DEPOSIT BOOKS

Accidents of geography sometimes coincide with those of history. In the field of tax havens Campione d'Italia is just such a case, an Italian enclave within Swiss territory on the shores of Lake Lugano. Banking havens also have such situations and Kleinwalsertal, which is a magnificent Austrian valley, is a legal monstrosity within German territory.

An advance piece of Austria in Bavaria, 180 kilometres south of Munich and 80 kilometres as the crow flies from Liechtenstein, Kleinwalsertal (with its 5000 inhabitants in their valley, 16 kilometres long and 6 kilometres wide) can only be reached on German roads because the surrounding mountains prevent communication with Austria. The valley is in fact economically linked to Germany.

By a curious turn of fate the valley was occupied for the first time in 1277 — by Swiss emigrants. After various international problems and an attempt at economic annexation by Germany which only just stopped short of ruining the valley's economy, a customs agreement was made in 1891.

The result of this situation is that the police are Austrian but the customs officials German (at least in theory since there is no customs control on entry to the valley nor police, and the customs post has been quite simply transformed into an inn).

The post and telephone services are Austrian as is also the tax regime, but the currency is German. This valley, which is also a separate commune called Mittelberg has despite its apparent similarity with Campione d'Italia one fundamental difference: Campione d'Italia has no bank while Kleinwalsertal has according to the serious estimate of a Belgian magazine *Trends*, deposits in the region of 70 million deutschmarks — which is quite a good average amount per head for the 2000 inhabitants of Hireschegg, the main town.

A magnificent valley for winter sports, Kleinwalsertal is also a refuge for capital, mostly from Germany but also from Belgium. This is deposited in bearer deposit accounts at the Raiffeisen Bank or the Hypo Bank (whose front door is next to that of the Casino which is in the same building. It is true that the Casino does not open until 5 pm, after the bank has closed, which is useful since their doors are only 3 metres apart and this avoids any mistakes . . .).

A bearer account is of course opened without any proof of identity since the client remains anonymous as far as the bank is concerned. Payments into the account and withdrawals are made in cash (deutschmarks). When the account is opened the client chooses a code name which he handwrites on the agreement, and withdrawals can only be made on production of the deposit book together with the code name (Karl Marx or Robin Hood, perhaps). However no comparison is made between the writing on the agreement and that made at the time of the withdrawal. Anyone who has the deposit book in their possession and knows the right code name can make any withdrawal and sign the receipt for the cash. The deposit book itself — in which all transactions are entered as they are made — carries only a reference number and the description *Ueberbringer* (bearer). The inside cover of the book carries a warning against loss or theft and depending upon the bank but usually at the end of the book, there are the general conditions of use prescribed by the bank which deny responsibility for the client's negligence.

The deposit books also have entered in them by the cashier the rate of interest on sight deposits which was 5 per cent in February 1982. There is no upper limit on the amount which may be deposited; on the contrary, deposits over 50 000 deutschmarks qualify for specially negotiated (and better!) rates of interest.

In such circumstances it is hardly surprising that some Germans prefer such a beautiful valley to Switzerland.

JUNGHOLZ — A BABY BANK HAVEN

Jungholz, part of the Austrian Tyrol in German Oberallgan, is both the most newly born and the smallest of bank havens.

Situated about 160 kilometres south of Munich it is a very beautiful valley and winter sports centre about 12 kilometres long and 10 kilometres wide, has one town which carries the same name and about 800 inhabitants (German skiers and the presently rare roving depositors passing through excluded).

Its legal system is similar to that of Kleinwalsertal (German currency, Austrian police, neither customs nor police controls at the frontier which is indicated only by a discreet sign at the beginning of a magnificent pine forest) and it became a banking haven in March 1981. It was at that time that the Austrian Raiffeirsin Bank opened a small branch whose single employee plays the roles of clerk, manager, and cashier. The bank can actually be found by smell because it is sited in this charming town opposite a farm which possesses an enormous dungheap. This should certainly attract the ecology-minded roving depositors since only money has no smell . . . .

This baby bank haven offers exactly the same services as the banks in Kleinwalsertal, the same bearer bank deposit accounts, the same conditions. The baby has not yet acquired any great renown, and to tell the truth the author discovered it by chance, having taken a wrong turning in the mountains. For those who love discretion it would be difficult to find (let alone imagine) anything better, but things change quickly and the good addresses become well-known quickly.

$$ ST VINCENT — SECRETS IN THE SHADOW OF A VOLCANO

Discovered by Christopher Colombus on St Vincent's day, this group of 17 Leeward Isles is part of the Grenadines, and the main island of St Vincent with 100 000 inhabitants and a surface area of about 388 square kilometres, is unfortunately well-known for its volcano, la Soufrière, which must undoubtedly be the victim of too much local punch. St Vincent has for a long time been one of the rare 'associated states' (as also are St Kitts and Antigua) for which Great Britain takes responsibility for foreign affairs. St Vincent had envisaged becoming wholly independent, but the eruptions of the volcano in April 1979, although not causing any deaths (there were 2000 in 1902), disrupted the economy which is based on bananas and the independence initiative has been postponed. Finally St Vincent joined the Windward Islands Federation (including Dominica, Grenada and St Lucia) amongst whose states the average annual income of St Vincent inhabitants is the smallest at $400 per man.

The legal system is that of common law together with local statutues, including in particular that of 1976 which included a definition of international banks as those having an offshore activity. They are not taxed and there is no withholding tax on interest or dividends paid to non-residents. There is no law concerning the licensing of banks; their establishment has to be negotiated on a case-by-case basis with the Governor. Apart from local banks, there are currently three international banks.

$$ TURKS AND CAICOS ISLANDS — CAPTIVE BANKS AND PELICANS

These islands, which as yet have few tourists by comparison with the Caymans and the Bahamas and their luxuriant vegetation, have been rather denuded. They are both a banking and a tax haven and are situated about 900 kilometres from Miami, to the south-east of the Bahamas. There are four main islands of which the most beautiful is North Caicos. This is also known as Pelican Island because of the presence of large numbers of pelicans, apparently attracted by the surrounding sea and its plentiful fish. The pelicans have become the focus of a tourist development organized by the Pelican Holdings Company.

Formerly a dependency of Jamaica, the Turks and Caicos Islands remained a British colony in 1962 when Jamaica became independent. The legal system is that of common law with the addition of local statutes — including in particular the 1979 Banking Ordinance.

The currency is the US dollar and there is no exchange control. There is no direct taxation nor any withholding taxes. There is no central bank. There are two local banks (and a third planned) which give the Government global figures for their accounts. The annual fee for a banking licence is US $2000 and the licence is given, after investigation, by the Governor. There are no double tax treaties.

40 Banking loopholes
Receiving does not pay—except for bankers

Banking loopholes are opportunities voluntarily offered by a banking inferno in order to give 'warm' money the chance of being recycled back into the local market, thereby avoiding the money being removed to some banking haven or other or stagnating in the form of cash held out of circulation (underneath a mattress, for example). There are various consequences arising from this kind of situation which are common to all markets of this type:

1. Only the local currency is accepted through the loophole (since it has been created precisely for the purpose of avoiding exchange losses).
2. The protection must be more absolute within the loophole than that normally offered by a banking haven (the loophole should allow the recycling of money from tax evasion, therefore something more than 'warm' in its origin).
3. The cost of the protection is higher both as far as the banks are concerned (very low rates of interest) and as far as tax is concerned (maximum withholding taxes, given that the recipient remains anonymous and is placed in the same position as though he were resident in a tax haven).
4. Accounts opened in this way are normally term accounts where a large sum is deposited at the beginning and has to stay with the bank for an agreed period.

What value does this have for the countries which practice it? Let us take an arbitrary example (not far removed from the reality, though) in country A—we should not like to embarrass anyone. The facts are as follows: amount to be invested: $100; rate of inflation within the country: 10 per cent; rate of interest: 6 per cent; withholding tax: one-third.

If the travelling depositor makes such a deposit for a one-year term, he will receive two-thirds of 6 per cent, that is 4 per cent, and will therefore have $104 available after one year. The loss in purchasing power due to inflation was 10 per cent, or $10.40, so at the end of the year he will have $104 less $10.40, that is $93.40: his net loss will therefore be 6.4 per cent. In fact it is not uncommon to see losses derived from this system of about 10 per cent.

BEARER CERTIFICATES AND NET LOSSES

If the roving depositor has given his banker the title to this deposit in order to guarantee an overdraft which is otherwise too great to be covered by his asset position, it is not unusual for such a situation to become perpetual, and if the small amount of net interest received is left in the scheme it has a cumulative effect which after several years will mean that a sum has been lost which is equivalent to the tax that was evaded in the first place.

For the banker on the other hand, the operation is splendid. In practice the banker does not suffer from inflation if he borrows $100 and re-lends $100; it is of no consequence to him if the money is only worth $90 a year later. Normally banking logic says that the bank's profit is the amount of interest received on paper loans made, or the price of the risk. In the case of an overdraft secured by a bearer certificate of deposit there is absolutely no risk but the bank nevertheless charges the normal interest which would be charged on an overdraft with the normal risks. It is not uncommon through this game of interest rates, called the 'interest turn', that the difference received by the bank amounts to as much as 10 per cent simply for having lent a reluctant taxpayer his own money.

For its part the state is satisfied in part by the fact that the money has not left the country and for the rest because it receives some withholding tax on the interest paid to the roving depositor.

In such conditions it is clear that it is much better to be a banker than a tax evader, since the banker quite legally and without any risk profits from the results of the tax evasion. It is a case of legal receiving.

Such an operation constitutes in effect a back-to-back loan, but curiously enough this title is reserved for transactions where there is an international element, which reduces the cost considerable. For example the Luxemburg banks generally ask 1 per cent for such transactions (already a long way from the intranational 10 per cent) as the price of having the money in their balance sheet while the offshore banks in certain banking havens are often content with ¼ per cent. The operation can of course be more costly if the banking haven charges a withholding tax (as is the case in Switzerland) on the interest paid to the depositor by the bank on the money deposited as a guarantee for the loan.

FUNDS WITH FLOATING MORALITY

Curiously enough it appears that the money used in the international field does not generally derive from tax evasion (unless perhaps passage through a banking haven has cleansed it of this original sin). This situation derives from the fact that the international operator, like the international companies, who are not tied down by their attraction to one particular residence or nationality which will hold them in a fiscal vice, generally escape taxation quite legally through the use of tax havens. It is doubtless this difference in origin and degree (the international operator is generally both much more powerful and much better advised than the national) which brings about the difference in rates. Does that mean that all banking loopholes should be avoided?

Not entirely, no: rather that banking loopholes have some interest only if a national loophole is used by a foreigner and there is in some way an international element, particularly in the appreciation of one currency against another. This situation occurs when the roving depositor can make deposits in a currency of his choice and if that increases in value in relation to his own currency, he may not only avoid the effects of devaluation, but also make a profit. This situation can come about when a country permits bearer deposits in any currency, which is the case, for example, in Hungary. On the other hand if a country permits only deposits in its own currency, then this can be interesting if its currency is likely to appreciate. This certainly happened to Japan in the late 1970s. Japan is not a banking haven, but it offers a banking loophole for yen deposits.

MU-KIMEI ACCOUNTS WITH *NATSU-IN*

According to Mr Kawai,* a Tokyo lawyer, the Japanese word anonymous is *mu-kimei* in which *mu* means 'without' and *kimei* means 'written name'. In Japan people naturally use signatures sometimes, but *kimei* does not necessarily mean signature in that sense. It is possible legally‡ to use a written name (not necessarily written oneself, but perhaps typed or printed) with the appropriate personal seal attached (*natsu-in* means seal attached). The Japanese seal used in this case generally represents the family name broken down into Japanese characters and reformed. These seals can also be used to represent a false name. How therefore is the depositor protected and what is the system?

When the account is opened, the name chosen by the depositor is typed and the corresponding seal is attached by the depositor to the agreement for the account, and also appears on the receipt.

Toku-betsu receipts

The receipt is a normal numbered deposit slip where instead of the name of the depositor there appears a gummed stip on which the following characters are printed: 特 別 (pronounced *toku-betsu* which means 'special').

Apart from this detail, the following information is given:

1. name of the bank and number of the receipt;
2. numbers giving the amount of the deposit;
3. date of deposit and date for reimbursement of the sum deposited together with accrued interest. The dating system is unfamiliar to a westerner; for example, an account opened on 28 March 1979 to expire on 28 March 1980 will carry the figures '54-3-28' and '55-3-28', which reading from right to left signifies 28 March 54 (fifty-fourth year of *Showa*, which is 1979);
4. rate of interest to be applied to the sum.

---

*The author is particularly grateful to his Japanese colleague, Mr Kawai, for his detailed explanations of the *mu-kimei* accounts with *kimei-natsu-in*.
†Law no. 17, 26 February 1900.

On the other side of the receipt will be found the general conditions applying to the account.

Seals have their uses

Having opened the account, how will its owner recover his money at the end of the term? The classical system of bearer documents provides that you simply present the receipt. This has the major disadvantage—which often dissuades people from its use—that the receipt may be used by a thief or someone with evil intentions. In the case of the *mu-kimei* account, the bearer of the receipt must attach his *natsu-in* when he appears at the bank, that is he must use his seal, and a comparison of its imprint with that already in the bank's records will allow the funds to be returned.

This solution has first of all the advantage that a seal (even one made in the form of a rubber stamp) is relatively difficult to copy,* particularly when one is not very familiar with the exact original imprint, but of course impossible when the imprint is unknown. This is the case when the account is held under a false name. But of course bearer documents represent a risk and this is increased by the existence of two instruments. However, in practice this is not so—Japanese banks and their clients are not *kamikaze* pilots.

RE-CREATION OF BEARER INSTRUMENTS

The re-creation of lost bearer instruments using *mu-kimei* is possible, but under specific conditions which are printed on the back of the receipt. Sometimes these say only that the procedure for re-creation of lost documents is that 'laid down by the bank': it is worth therefore mentioning general practice, which is as follows:

1. Loss or theft of certificate: the bank will ask the person who has the seal various questions about the details of the receipt (amount of the deposit, date account was opened, date for settlement etc.). If the replies are satisfactory, practices vary from one bank to another: some issue a new certificate, others change the account into an ordinary account. In either case refund of the money is withheld for one month.
2. Loss or theft of the seal: the bank will ask for details of the seal, and if these are convincing will change the account into an ordinary one which, as in the previous situation, would not be available for a month.
3. Loss or theft of both seal and certificate: in this situation the bank's enquiries will be much more rigorous and will bear upon both the receipt,

---

*Of course it would be child's play for a professional forger, but all criminals or similarly ill-intentioned people are not professional forgers.

that is to say the detailed terms of the deposit, and the seal itself. If the bank considers the information it is given to be sufficient, the reimbursement will be made six months after its normal date.

Quite clearly in this last case many difficulties have arisen and given rise both to numerous commentaries and also some occasionally divergent case law.

THIRD-PARTY ACCOUNTS IN SWITZERLAND AND SUBJECTIVE OR OBJECTIVE THEORY IN JAPAN

It is surprising to note that having reached a certain stage of sophistication in banking techniques, countries having completely different legal systems end up facing very similar problems. The problem which has arisen for the Japanese where actions have been brought over certain *mu-kimei* accounts is that of deposits made *natsu-in* where the seal was not that of the owner of the funds and the owner commenced action to obtain the return of his money. It seems that there are no professional contacts between the Japanese lawyers and their Swiss colleagues, but the problems are remarkably close to those of the open third party account and the difficulties which led to the disappearance of the FLN war chest (see Chapter 9).

The problem in Switzerland was whether the bank should, in the case of an open third party account, take instructions from the owner of the funds or the administrator, and if he is in error, in taking instructions solely from the administrator.

In Japanese law the problem is to know whether the funds should be given to the holder of the seal (administrator) or the owner of the funds (if ownership can be demonstrated). The theory in favour of the owner of the seal is known as 'subjective theory' which is the theory upheld by academics, while the 'objective theory' in favour of the owner seems to be upheld by the courts, although not unanimously.

GOOD SENSE DOES NOT HARM THE LAW

Roving depositors should understand that if at a certain level bankers place sophisticated instruments at their disposal, the very sophistication of these demands that they are not put in just anybody's hands. An unskilled depositor should not normally expect any compensation from a bank for errors he has made himself. By way of example, a racing car is a very safe vehicle in the hands of a professional driver, but is highly dangerous in the hands of a 'weekend' motorist. However, there are no laws to prevent a 'weekend' driver from using a racing car. In the event of an accident caused by the driver's ignorance of the vehicle, the 'weekend' driver has no recourse against the manufacturer. The roving depositor should use instruments which his education and ability to understand fit him for; if, for instance he can only drive a mini, he will be wise not to use a racing car—unless he has a professional driver to do the job—or, in the banking field, unless he takes a specialist lawyer with him.

THE JAPANESE STATE AND *MU-KIMEI* ACCOUNTS

Mu-kimei accounts were created at the end of the Second World War by the Japanese government in order to allow the recyling of money from the postwar 'black market' (which seems to have lasted a long time). The authorities were aware that the accounts permitted or even encouraged tax evasion and therefore suspended them, but the need for them made itself felt sufficiently for the system to be reactivated in 1967 despite its disadvantages.*

These 'seal' accounts form, together with classical savings accounts, 'the most stable source of funds for banks and pay the highest rates of interest'. The levels of interest rates fixed by the authorities for all the banks[†] are summarized in Table 2 by reference to the date on which rates came into force and the length of time for which deposits were fixed.

Table 2

Date on which rates fixed	14 Jan. 1974	24 Sept. 1974	4 Nov. 1975	4 April 1977	6 May 1977	26 Sept. 1977	17 April 1978	7 May 1979
Duration of deposit								
3 months	5.25	5.50	4.50	4.50	3.75	3.25	2.50	3.25
6 months	6.25	6.75	5.75	5.75	5.00	4.50	3.75	4.50
1 Year	7.25	7.75	6.75	6.75	5.75	5.25	4.50	5.25
2 years	7.50	8.00	7.00	7.00	6.00	5.50	4.75	5.50

The rates provided in the table are not net for the roving depositor, but gross, since it is necessary to deduct 20 per cent withholding tax—which was increased to 35 per cent for the period from 1 April 1977 to 31 December 1980 —as far as the anonymous Japanese depositor or the foreign depositor is concerned.

Let us imagine a Japanese depositor, operating with yen from 1 January 1975, and making an annual deposit which is automatically renewed until it is finally reimbursed on 31 December 1978. Let us imagine at the same time a foreign roving depositor who is operating from the following currencies: US dollar, Italian lira, pound sterling, French franc, Swiss franc. Given that the deposits can be made only in yen, these currencies were converted into yen on 1 January 1975 and then reconverted back to their original currency to see the result at the end.

---

*Notice from the Director of the Banking Affairs Bureau, 2 February 1967.
†Law of 1947 on the fixing of interest rates.

So that our hypothetical example gives the depositor the most favourable result, he would have chosen a *mu-kimei* account with automatic renewal with consolidation of accrued interest. Certain Japanese banks offer to do this (if they are pushed hard enough). The rates of interest applicable are of course those in force on the 1 January of each year. What then is the result of a 1 million yen deposit? See Table 3.

Table 3

Interest rate	Yen deposit	Interest	Withholding tax	Net income carried forward
1 January 75 7.75 per cent	1 000 000	77 500	15 500 (20 per cent)	62 000
1 January 76 6.75 per cent	1 062 000	71 685	14 337 (20 per cent)	57 348
1 January 77 6.75 per cent	1 119 348	75 555	3729 3 months 20 per cent 19 833 9 months 35 per cent 23 662	51 903
1 January 78 5.25 per cent	1 171 251	61 490	21 521 (35 per cent)	39 969

Situation at 31 December 1978: 1 211 220

What then is the result for the depositor who had operated in currencies? See Table 4.

Table 4

	Cost of Y 1 000 000 bought on Tokyo exchange 1 January 1975	Proceeds of Y 1 211 220 sold on Tokyo exchange 31 December 1978	Increase per cent
US dollars	$3310	$6200	87
Italian lire	L2 150 000	L5 170 000	140
Pounds sterling	£1410	£3060	117
French francs	FFr 14 710	FFr 26 040	77
Swiss francs	SFr 8400	SFr 10 110	20

These are the results from a legal or fiscal point of view, but not from an economic point of view. In fact, each of the currencies would have lost a degree of purchasing power as a result of inflation. The rates of inflation and the loss of purchasing power are given in simplified form in Table 5.

Table 5

Rates of inflation	1975	1976	1977	1978	Loss of purchasing power 1 January 1975– 31 December 1978 per cent
Japan	11.8	9.3	8.2	3.8	33
United States	9.6	5.2	5.9	7.4	28
Italy	17.1	16.5	18.1	12.4	64
Great Britain	24.2	16.5	15.9	8.3	65
France	9.6	9.9	9.0	9.7	38
Switzerland	3.4	1.8	1.7	0.8	8

The net result for the depositor operating in yen or the other currencies gives the position shown in Table 6 after use of a *mu-kimei* account.

Table 6

	Legal/fiscal increase per cent	Loss in purchasing power per cent	Economic gain/(loss) per cent
Japan	21	33	(12)
United States	87	28	59
Italy	140	64	76
Great Britain	117	65	52
France	77	38	39
Switzerland	20	8	12

These calculations are not intended to suggest a particular interest in *mu-kimei* accounts, but rather to demonstrate various points which will permit of a comparison between a truly anonymous placing of funds and placements of other types which are also covered with anonymity. When it comes to banking secrecy, all that glitters is not gold, but actually gold itself is a form of anonymous placing!

41 Conclusion
The true limits of banking secrecy—
or how not to go too far

The true limits to banking secrecy are certainly not legal, since laws change in time (as the result of economic change) and in space (in terms of political frontiers). The true limits are probably moral rules accepted internationally as being the minimum requirements for acceptable human behaviour, and which do not necessarily correspond with any of the sociojudicial structures forming the laws of any given country at any given time. The problem is to discover whether such international principles exist, not at the level of individual states, whose definitions also change, but at the level of the actual constituents without whom there would be no states—the human beings themselves. But even at this stage experience shows that definitions change: for example, the simple trader in 'ebony'* who would certainly have enjoyed banking secrecy from the Florentine bankers, would today probably be rejected by the international community as a slave trader, and no bank haven knowing his business would give him the least protection.

It seems therefore that positive definition is very difficult if not impossible to make and perhaps a negative definition should be attempted. For example, that banking secrecy, which is a form of protection of the individual, should disappear when 'international morality' rejects on a global basis the acts or activity of the individual. Such appears to be the case in kidnappings and ransom demands; but even here some states will extend their political protection and corresponding bank secrecy on the basis not of the act but of its political motivation if that coincides with that of the country concerned.

Where then is the limit? In fact there is none because it is all a question of balance, putting one in mind of Nietsche's clown and tightrope. Clowns or not, all equilibrium comes from a sense of balance.

---

*A polite expression of the time for those selling Africans.

The Traditional Havens (1)

	Andorra	*Bahrein*	*Hong Kong*
Communications	satisfactory	good	excellent
Legal system	Middle Ages	Middle Ages	common law
Currency	peseta (most widely used)	Bahrein dinar	Hong Kong dollar
Equivalent value in Swiss francs (May 1982)	100 = 1.91	1 = 5.16	1 = 0.34
Equivalent value in US dollars (May 1982)	100 = 0.98	1 = 2.64	1 = 0.17
Local exchange controls	no	no	no
Non-resident may maintain accounts in any currency	yes	yes	yes
Number of banks which may be used	6	53	108
Normal opening hours	9 am–1 pm 3 pm–5 pm	7 am–noon 3.30 pm–5.30 pm	10 am–3 pm 9 am–noon Saturday
Closing days	Saturday afternoon and Sunday	Friday	Sunday
Legal basis of banking secrecy	custom	Koranic custom and common law	common law
Banking secrecy and foreign tax authorities	complete secrecy	complete secrecy	complete secrecy (apart from local authorities)
Banking secrecy and foreign exchange control	complete secrecy	complete secrecy	complete secrecy (Great Britain?)
Penalties for violation of secrecy	civil damages	civil damages	civil damages

British Virgin Islands	Jersey and Guernsey	Luxembourg	Isle of Man	USSR
satisfactory	excellent	excellent	satisfactory	excellent
common law	common law	French Civil Code	common law	socialist legality
US dollar	sterling	Luxemburg franc	sterling	rouble
1 = 1.95	1 = 3.55	100 = 4.49	1 = 3.55	1 = 2.73
*	1 = 1.82	100 = 2.30	1 = 1.82	1 = 1.40
no	yes	yes	yes	yes
yes	yes	yes	yes	no
4	50	94	39	1
9 am–2 pm 9 am–3 pm and 3 pm–5 pm Friday	9.30 am–3.30 pm	8.30 am–1 pm 1.30 pm–4.30 pm	9.30 am–3.30 pm	9 am–1 pm 2 pm–6 pm
Saturday and Sunday	Saturday and Sunday	Saturday and Sunday	Saturday and Sunday	Saturday and Sunday
common law	common law	tradition and some statutes	common law	General conditions of State Bank
complete secrecy (apart from local and treaties)	complete secrecy (apart from local and Great Britain)	secret (but treaties in existence)	complete secrecy (apart from local tax)	secret
secret	secret	secret	secret	secret
civil damages	civil damages	civil and statutory	civil damages	no legally structured penalties

The Traditional Havens (2)

	Andorra	Bahrein	Hong Kong
Numbered accounts	yes	no	difficult
Accounts in false names	yes	no	difficult
Foreign legal entities accepted	yes	yes	yes
Identity of owner required	no	no	no
Bearer instruments	no	no	no
Countries with which difficulties may arise	France and Spain — but unlikely	none	China and Great Britain — but unlikely
Treaties providing for exchange of information	none	none	none
Withholding tax on interest in 'blind' market	none	none	none (subject to level fixed by tax authorities)
Withholding tax on dividends paid by local companies	none	none	none
Obstacles to back-to-back loans	only psychological	Israel	none

	British Virgin Islands	Jersey and Guernsey	Luxemburg	Isle of Man	USSR
	difficult	yes	yes	yes	yes
	difficult	no	difficult	no	difficult
	yes	yes	yes	yes	yes
	no	no	no	no	yes
	no	no	no	no	no
	none	Great Britain — but unlikely	none	Great Britain — but unlikely	?
	Denmark, United States, Norway, Japan, Sweden, Switzerland	Great Britain	none	Great Britain	with many countries but with no apparent consequence?
	none	none (under certain conditions)	none	none	none (provided reciprocal arrangement)
	none	none	15 per cent	20 per cent	—
	none	none	none	none	psychological and political perhaps

Banking Havens by Vocation (1)

	Bahamas	*Cayman Islands*	*Hungary*
Communications	excellent	excellent	good
Legal system	common law	common law	statutory code
Currency	Bahamian dollar	Cayman dollar	forint
Equivalent value in Swiss francs (May 1982)	1 = 1.95	1 = 2.34	100 = 5.69
Equivalent value in US dollars (May 1982)	linked parity	1 = 1.20	100 = 2.91
Local exchange controls	yes	yes	yes
Non-resident may maintain accounts in any currency	no	yes	yes
Number of banks which may be used	350	220	1
Normal opening hours	9.30 am–3 pm Friday: 9.30 am–5 pm	8.30 am–1 pm Friday: plus 4.30 pm–6 pm	8 am–noon 1 pm–4 pm
Closing days	Saturday and Sunday	Saturday and Sunday	Saturday and Sunday
Legal basis of banking secrecy	article 19-1 (1965 Act)	article 10 (1966 Act)	article 534, paragraph 1 civil code
Banking secrecy and foreign tax authorities	complete secrecy	complete secrecy	secret
Banking secrecy and foreign exchange control	secret	secret	secret
Penalties for violation of secrecy	damages, fine and/or prison	damages, fine and/or prison	civil damages

Liechtenstein	Vanuatu	Panama	Singapore	Switzerland
excellent	satisfactory	excellent	excellent	perfect
Germano-Roman	common law	civil code	common law	civil code
Swiss franc	vatu	Balboa (US dollar)	Singapore dollar	Swiss franc
—	100 = 2.01	1 = 1.95	1 = 0.93½	—
1 = 0.52	100 = 1.03	—	1 = 0.48	1 = 0.52
no	yes	no	yes	not in the strict sense of the term
yes	yes	yes	yes	yes
3	46 (of which 37 are 'exempt')	82	100	500
8 am–noon 1.30 pm–4 pm	7.30 am–11 am 1.30 pm–3 pm	8.30 am–1 pm	10 am–3 pm Saturday: 10 am–11.30 am	8 am–noon 1.30 pm–4 pm
Saturday and Sunday	Saturday and Sunday	Saturday and Sunday	Sunday	Saturday and Sunday
47-I-B (law of 21 December 1960)	article 416 (1971 law)	article 2 (law of 28 January 1959 (coded accounts)	article 42-2 (1970 law)	article 47 (law of 8 November 1934)
complete secrecy	complete secrecy	complete secrecy	secret	complete secrecy
complete secrecy	complete secrecy	complete secrecy	secret	complete secrecy
damages, fine and/or prison	damages, and criminal if the bank is an exempt company	damages and criminal for coded accounts	damages and criminal for non-residents	damages, fine and/or prison

Banking Havens by Vocation (2)

	Bahamas	Cayman Islands	Hungary
Numbered accounts	yes	yes	no
Accounts in false names	yes	difficult	yes
Foreign legal entities accepted	yes	yes	yes
Identity of owner required	no	no	yes
Bearer instruments	no	no	yes
Countries with which difficulties may arise	Difficulties with United States seem resolved	United States	?
Treaties providing for exchange of information	none	none	not operative
Withholding tax on interest in 'blind' market	none	none	?
Withholding tax on dividends paid by local companies	none	none	—
Obstacles to back-to-back loans	none	none	psychological and political?

Liechtenstein	Vanuatu	Panama	Singapore	Switzerland
yes	yes	yes	no	yes
yes	yes	no	no	yes
yes	yes	yes	yes	yes
no	no	no	no	yes
no	no	no	no	yes
none	Australia	none	none	none
none	none	none	significant number of countries	some countries but limited exchanges
none	none	none	none	35 per cent
4 per cent	none	10 per cent (if there is local trading)	40 per cent	35 per cent
none	Australia	none	none	none

The Rules of the Club for an Offshore Captive Bank in a Haven

	Type of licence appropriate to an offshore bank	Cost of licence initially (US dollars)	Annual fee for retaining licence (US dollars)
Panama	international licence	500	
Bahamas	licence with restricted client list to be given to Minister of Finance. (A general offshore licence is also available, but costs more)	1500 (but note that a work permit for the manager can cost $5000)	1500
Cayman Islands	'Category B' restricted offshore licence: list of clients to be provided. (A general offshore licence is also available but costs more)	6098	6098
Guernsey	normal licence	approximately 2000	approximately 2000
Luxemburg	normal licence	—	—
Switzerland	normal licence	—	—
Vanuatu	'exempt' bank licence	approximately 1000	approximately 2000
Bahrein	offshore banking unit (OBU)	25 780	25 780

Penalty for non-observance of ratios	Waiting period before commencing operations	Have any licences been withdrawn?	Number of offshore licences in existence (January 1979)
withdrawal of licence	provisional licence granted 90 days before full licence. Suspension of trade for any period greater than 6 months causes withdrawal	yes	25 (before the 1970 law there were 274 banks, the number fell to 20 and climbed back to 82)
withdrawal of licence	none	yes	80 (with restricted licences)
—	none	not revealed	150
—	none	not revealed	44
various	none	not revealed	there is no distinction between offshore banks and those operating locally
various	none	yes	there is no distinction between offshore banks and those operating locally
—	none	not revealed	37
—	none	no	35

The Rules of the Club for an Offshore Captive Bank in a Haven *continued*

	Degree of difficulty to obtain a licence: *1 = very easy* *2 = easy* *3 = average* *4 = difficult* *5 = very difficult*	*Existence of a central bank or commission with investigative powers*	*Requirements to provide regular financial reports to the controlling authority*
Panama	5	yes	yes
Bahamas	4	yes	yes
Cayman Islands	4 (more than 20 applications refused recently)	no (but there is a Financial Secretary who performs the same function)	yes
Guernsey	4	yes	yes
Luxemburg	4	yes	yes (strict)
Switzerland	3	yes	yes (strict)
Vanuatu	2	no, but some government authority to examine books	yes?
Bahrein	5	yes	yes

Minimum capital (US dollars)	Payment of initial capital	Requirement for experienced staff or management by foreign bank
250 000	full payment	in practice there must be an internationally known financial institution behind the bank even if the Panamanian unit appears to be in other hands
250 000	full payment (by converting foreign currency)	in practice 'recommendations' are warmly recommended
25 000	full payment (by converting foreign currency)	good references (which will be checked) are necessary as a minimum regarding the bank experience of the general manager and the financial standing of the owner
negotiable (considerable financial independence is required if the bank is not a subsidiary of an international bank)	full payment (by converting foreign currency)	first-class international references are indispensable
approximately 8 million and expected to increase	full payment	the Banking Commission must approve the owners, directors, and management as well as the type of operations planned
approximately 1 million	full payment	the Banking Commission requires that a majority of directors are resident in Switzerland and are of impeccable reputation
—	—	there must be a resident general manager or 'representative'
negotiable (legal minimum is 20 000 dinars)	full payment	criteria identical with those of Panama

The Rules of the Game for Offshore Banks in Banking Havens

	Banking secrecy: tradition or vocation	Owner's identity withheld from foreign authorities	Local control of direct investment and reinvestment	Existence and nature of ratios	
				Reserve ratios	Liquidity ratios
Panama	vocation	yes	none	a permanent reserve of 10 per cent of assets to be held in US dollars (contingent credit)	30 per cent
Bahamas	vocation	yes	Authorization necessary from Exchange Control Department, even for transfer of shares between non-residents	fixed by the Central Bank	fixed by the Central Bank
Cayman	vocation	yes	authorization is necessary but exchange controls are simpler than in Bahamas	none	none
Guernsey	tradition	yes	Bank of England authorization necessary	negotiated with the 'States Advisory Finance Committee'	negotiated with the 'States Advisory Finance Committee'
Luxemburg	tradition	difficult	dealings on the official IBLC market	3 per cent	30 per cent
Switzerland	vocation	yes	none	complicated calculation to arrive at ratio	complicated calculation to arrive at ratio
Vanuatu	vocation	yes	none	none apply to an 'exempt' bank	none apply to an 'exempt' bank
Bahrein	tradition	possible	none	none	none

283

Existence and nature of ratios Sundry requirements	Withholding tax on interest paid to an anonymous lender	Local taxes on operating profits	Withholding tax on dividends paid to an anonymous shareholder
deposits or credits received from the parent company, subsidiaries or affiliated operations and company dividends from an overseas source may not be used in calculating the liquidity ratio	none	none	none
fixed by the Central Bank	none	none	none
—	none	none	none
—	none	flat rate of £300	none
—	none	progressive rates, rising at the upper end to about 50 per cent	15%
in addition to various ratios there are also some restrictions on certain deposits and contractual obligations	35 per cent	varies according to security, reasonable average would be 30 per cent	35 per cent
—	none	none	none
—	none	none	none

Appendix I:
Glossary

Arbitrage	The simultaneous purchase and sale of shares or financial securities between different stock exchanges or money markets whose object is to earn a profit as a result of different prices obtaining in the different markets.
Asia-dollars	US dollars which are deposited in Asia (see also Eurodollars).
Back-to-back loan	A procedure whereby an individual or company deposits money with a bank in one country in return for, and as security for, an equivalent loan from the bank in another country.
Balance of payments	The difference (surplus or deficit) between a country's foreign currency purchases and receipts.
Bancos brujos	The literal translation from the Spanish means 'magic banks'. The expression was used to describe fringe Panamanian banks which specialized in clearing money from doubtful sources. The Panama government, in an attempt to clean up its image, has withdrawn the licences of such banks.
Beneficial owner	An English term which has passed into wider usage and denotes the person who obtains the benefit or profit of a particular entity in reality (substance) rather than the nominee of trustee who may be the legal owner (form).
Black market	A free market forbidden by the state.
Captive bank	A bank established for the sole use of an individual or group of companies, often to escape exchange control restrictions. Such banks are normally situated in tax havens in order to avoid taxation as well.
Carrier	Someone who arranges for the illegal movement of capital or securities from one country to another, generally in return for a percentage of the proceeds. (*See also* Passer).
Clearing	The cancellation or exchanging of debits and credits against one another as between one country and another without any money actually changing hands. Private arrangements of this sort are generally prohibited in countries with exchange controls.
Common law	The Anglo-Saxon system of jurisprudence which according to Blackstone, one of the greatest English judges, is a rule that judgments are bound by earlier precedents when the facts are the same.
Captive insurance company	These are formed by companies or groups to cover insurable risks at the best rates, or to cover otherwise non-insurable risks, but they also serve to handle financial manoeuvres which escape local exchange controls.
Commercial convertibility	Convertibility applied to currency used by commercial concerns for current expenses.
Company of domicile	A Swiss term meaning a company without any real economic activity which is used as a legal device for the purposes of taxation

	or exchange control. Such companies are often based in tax havens; there is a definition of them in the Convention on the acceptance of funds.
Convertibility	The freedom to convert a country's currency without restriction into any other currency without regard to the resident status of the owner.
Depreciation	The loss of value of money in terms of its purchasing power or against other currencies.
Devaluation	Diminution of the value of a currency in terms of other currencies by a national government. The effect of a devaluation is usually to increase exports in as far as the change in relative currency values makes local products cheaper on the foreign markets. It also diminishes the value of external debt where this is denominated in the local currency.
Direct investment	An operation where a person or company which is not resident in a country with exchange controls makes an investment or creates a subsidiary in that country under terms fixed by the exchange control regulations. The investment would usually be required to be financed with external funds either completely or substantially.
Dirty money	An expression which implies that the money has been the subject of tax evasion, or is otherwise illegally obtained.
Double exchange market	A system where a country operates more than one set of rates of exchange according to the type of international transaction to be carried out. It is intended to encourage or discourage specific operations or import and export or to control the flight of capital. Sometimes a premium is payable in one part of the market.
Eurobond	A loan raised by an international syndicate of banks and placed on several capital markets as well as being quoted on the money markets.
Eurocurrency	Operates on the same principle as Eurodollars (*q.v.*) but in any other currency.
Eurodollar	These are simply US dollars deposited in Europe; those deposited in Asia are called 'Asia-dollars'. This market got under way in 1950 and those Americans who deposited funds before that at the First National City Bank in Paris for business or tourism were unaware that they were using Eurodollars.
Exchange control	Restrictions imposed by a country on the holding, use, export and import of currency. The imposition of exchange controls often brings about the flight of capital which would no doubt not otherwise have left the country. This clumsy system is generally the proof of a financially immature government. It should, however, be distinguished from the control of direct investments which is absolutely necessary (even if only for information) in states which are economically at war.
Export expense allowances	This is an export incentive system used by some countries, Italy in particular. The exporter is automatically granted a remission of exchange control requirements and a tax deduction which is generally 10 per cent of the export price and which may be lodged abroad in general, and in a country with banking secrecy in particular, without any real check on justification of the expense. Where Italian companies find themselves in competition with Americans who have a DISC allowance, this deduction may rise to 25 per cent. The buyer and seller generally split the sum.
External debt	Total loans received from foreign sources from a Central Bank.

Financial zone	A group of countries who exchange their currencies according to a fixed system of parities, such as the European Monetary System (EMS).
Fishing trip	An operation carried out by the tax authorities in an Anglo-Saxon country where they examine all the transactions or particular types of transaction carried out by a bank in the hope of finding evidence of tax evasion by contrast with an enquiry in pursuit of a specific tax case where they already have some evidence. In Roman law countries this kind of operation is more often conducted by the customs authorities.
Fixed parity	A situation where the exchange rate of one currency is fixed in relation to that of another, or group of others in the same financial zone.
Floating capital	Capital which is not locked into a particular financial market as a result of exchange controls, but can be moved about the world to take advantage of the best rates available at any given moment.
Floating rate	Currency exchange rate which is left free to 'float' up or down in response to supply and demand. This does not exclude the possibility of the Central Bank intervening to buy or sell on the market in order to move the rate up or down.
Floating rate note	An ordinary bond whose rate of interest is revised regularly according to some independent indicator. Often the revision is 6-monthly and is carried out by reference to Libor (*q.v.*).
Foreign loan	A loan issued by someone outside his own country. Those issued from New York are called 'Yankee bonds' while those coming from Tokyo are 'Samurai bonds' (which does not mean the borrower is necessarily a *kamikaze*).
Free market	Currency market where the rate is solely determined according to supply and demand. It differs from the floating rate in that there is normally no Central Bank intervention.
Fugitive capital	Capital which leaves a country (legally or illegally in terms of local laws) in order to prevent its being blocked or confiscated as a result of that country's exchange controls.
Hard currency	A currency with an international reputation for holding its value which is also generally freely convertible.
Hot money	Money which moves about the international markets seeking the best short-term interest rates combined with minimum risk.
Inland Revenue	British tax authority.
Inflataxation	A combination of inflation and taxation which takes no account of inflation, the two combining to deprive the small saver of value. The word has been coined by the author.
International cash swap	A procedure whereby someone resident in a country whose exchange controls require repatriation of foreign assets when they are sold, arranges for a cash payment in the foreign currency which is then exchanged for currency in a banking haven — on the assumption that the country where the transaction takes place is not a haven. Not to be confused with international currency swaps which are agreed between companies at prearranged rates for a future date as a means of hedging an exchange risk.
IRC	The Commissioners of the Inland Revenue. The body which supervises the machinery of British taxation and hears first appeals on assessments. The same term is used in Canada.
IRS	Internal Revenue Service: the US tax authority.

Kata-kana	A grouping of Chinese characters forming a seal which is used for operating a *mu-kimei* account with *natsu-in* (*q.v.*).
Libor or LIBOR	London Inter Bank Offered Rate: a base interest rate ruling on the London money market and used as a sort of price index for Eurobonds.
Laundering	A process whereby money obtained illegally is recycled through a legitimate business enterprise in order for it to be available for legitimate investment. The term appears to have derived from the 1930s when the American Mafia bought laundries on a large scale because they were cash businesses through which money could be recycled. It is thought that casinos form one modern equivalent.
Monetary area	*See* Financial zone.
Multiple exchange rates	*See* Double exchange market.
Mu-kimei	Literally 'having no written name'. This term applies to Japanese accounts with *natsu-in* (*q.v.*), that is those where a seal is used instead of the name (false or otherwise) of the account holder.
Natsu-in	Literally 'with seal attached'. The word is used in relation to *Mu-kimei* accounts (*q.v.*).
Non-resident or external account	An account held either in a foreign currency or convertible local currency by a non-resident in a country which operates exchange controls. According to the type of controls in use, these accounts are either completely free of restrictions or blocked — which latter is generally the case in newly independent countries, and the expression becomes synonymous with plundering.
Offshore bank	These are banks whose activities are carried out 'offshore', that is outside the country where the bank is actually situated. Such banks are generally not authorized to take deposits from residents and have a 'restricted' licence which is less espensive than a full licence (Bahamas, Cayman Islands, for example). Offshore banks are frequently not subject to ratios, local exchange controls or taxation (if there is any). They may or may not also be 'captive'.
Offshore insurance company	An insurance company formed according to the same principles as an offshore bank (*q.v.*) — it may be captive or not.
Omnibus account	A slang expression used in the United States to mean in particular back-to-back loans arranged to provide laundered money for reinvestment while concealing its true origins.
Overinvoicing	An illegal method used sometimes by importers to move money out of an exchange control country. It consists of obtaining an invoice for imported goods which is above the normal price and arranging for the difference to be reimbursed outside the country. This also involves tax evasion and in some cases a fraud against fellow shareholders, who are in effect being robbed of their profit.
Paper bank	This is a bank formed in a country where there is no legislation restricting the use of the expression 'bank'. It is formed in the same way as any other company and is not subject to licensing or any other controls by the local authorities. In the absence of normal economic activity such banks often deal with rather doubtful business and most banking havens now have legislation designed to eliminate paper banks.
Parallel market	A free market existing alongside an official market.

Passer	The term covers people or organizations who transfer abroad funds or securities out of a country in contravention of that country's exchange controls. They generally take a percentage as a fee. Some writers maintain that this kind of operation is often carried out by some holders of diplomatic passports (*see also* Carrier).
Plundering	A form of international crime to which young 'revolutionary' states take in order to do what others have before them. It usually consists of confiscating or nationalizing other people's assets without compensation. This procedure usually has the opposite effect to that intended and is subsequently replaced in well-administered and viable states by incentives for investment.
Premium	A surcharge sometimes imposed by countries with exchange controls to deter people from using currency destined for purposes which the government wishes to discourage. The system was used in particular in Britain prior to the lifting of controls where foreign currency for investment was held to be a separate market where the price of the currency was determined by a restricted supply.
Printing plates	In this context the plates carrying the impression of a country's banknotes; when a country says 'print more money' this means that a government is issuing more notes than it has the theoretical capacity to reimburse, as a palliative when its management has led it into debt. To use a medical simile, it is the equivalent of curing someone who is ill by administering an anaesthetic.
Resident	A person or legal entity who is held to be subject to a country's exchange control regulations because he is based there. Curiously enough the definition of residence for exchange control purposes can differ from that for tax purposes in the same country and provide a situation from which some advantage may be drawn.
Resident account	An account in local currency belonging to a resident of a country which operates exchange controls. Transfers from such accounts overseas or to a non-resident account are often prohibited or subject to prior authorization.
Revaluation	Opposite of devaluation (*q.v.*).
Screening bank	A procedure by which an investor has a financial transaction carried out by a bank on his account but in the bank's name in order to avoid disclosure. The system, which presupposes a high standard of bank secrecy, is often criticized and carries with it the risk, where the transaction is a large one, of its existence being apparent from the published financial statements of the bank. The United States often criticize the Swiss banks for carrying out such operations.
SDR (Special Drawing Rights)	Created by the International Monetary Fund and based on a basket of 16 currencies, this is a brilliant idea destined to relieve pressure on gold and reserve currencies. It is supported by the IMF's members who themselves nonetheless continue to stock up on gold ingots like the neighbourhood grocer.
Swap	An exchange of one good or value for another: in currency dealing it may refer to an arrangement between two companies carrying on business in each other's currency to ensure an agreed exchange rate in advance. Central Banks also arrange currency swaps privately between themselves to avoid influencing the

	exchange markets by passing currency through the market, or to provide currency for a Central Bank to intervene on the markets.
Tax haven	A country which does not impose any taxes (e.g. Monaco), or has low taxes (e.g. British Virgin Islands), or exempts non-resident companies and individuals (e.g. Jersey), or taxes only local activities (e.g. Costa Rica or Panama), or allows loopholes to remain in their tax legislation (e.g. Netherlands, Luxemburg).
Toku-betsu	Literally 'special': is used in Japan in conjunction with the *mu-kimei* accounts with *natsu-in* (*q.v.*).
Unconvertible	Currency which is subject to restrictions on its use, either by residents or non-residents.
Under the table	Partial settlement of a transaction (illegal) in cash in order to avoid exchange controls or evade tax. Such settlements are generally made outside the banking system except possibly between non-residents through banks in countries where the banking secrecy laws would not be set aside as a result of the illegal nature of the transaction.
Underinvoicing	An internal operation which is the opposite of overinvoicing (*q.v.*).

Appendix II: Bibliography

A bibliography is a working tool. This one does not claim to be complete; it is certainly lacking in some areas since it is impossible to put together a complete and coherent set of published sources on a subject which is both so wide and of course so shrouded in secrecy and where sometimes for that matter only the practice exists. On the other hand, the fact that a particular work has been omitted does not mean that it is lacking in interest. In an attempt to be of practical use the most important works are accompanied by a brief commentary which will enable the reader to place them more exactly in context. With the same object in mind the title of the work and its author are accompanied by the publisher's name and address and the date of publication.

For some countries works of a more general nature are quoted and may cover a number of other subjects or indeed other countries. This arises because they may mention some important information on banking secrecy in passing or because there are no published sources which deal directly with secrecy or the particular aspect of it.

There are no or few references quoted on certain cases. For these the author has been unable to find any original sources and has based his research on works which may have appeared in another language or another country, or the questionnaires which were sent to bankers in these countries and the consultations which he has had with specialist lawyers in those countries. Any specialists themselves looking through here will certainly find publishing gaps for themselves to fill! The scheme of the bibliography is as follows: I General works; II General sources; III Specific sources.

I General works

This consists of various books which bear on one or more aspects of banking secrecy and the means of utilizing it.

II General sources

In a sense this is a contradiction since there are no general sources on the question. These are a chosen collection of periodicals and technical works mostly to do with tax havens. They are only included to the extent that they provide sufficient ancillary information to merit a mention. In most cases specific details provided by these publications in relation to individual countries are also recorded in the analysis by country. Since the use of banking havens normally also requires research into withholding taxes and double taxation agreements a number of international tax publications have also been included, even though such works do not deal with banking secrecy.

III Specific sources

This section provides details of sources country by country, although it should be borne in mind that some of the sources have a very restricted circulation. As far as possible sufficient information has been given to enable the reader to obtain copies of books by referring to the publisher whose address is given or to the author of a paper whose address also appears. The lack of information in some cases derives from the fact that some information was only available in response to questionnaires sent systematically to the banks in the countries concerned or from studies undertaken for this book by specialist lawyers in the countries.

Books are given in chronological order following the date of publication.

I GENERAL WORKS

Le Contrôle des Changes: Hamel, Bertrand et Roblot, 1955, Recueil Sirey, 22 rue Soufflot, 75005 Paris, france.

This book, published a long time ago under the aegis of the French centre for comparative law, has the faults of its qualities. It is a collection of information based on a questionnaire sent to various countries and as such is full of information but lacks any kind of unity. Although it does not, properly speaking, touch upon banking secrecy it is worth mentioning as being apparently the only comparative work available on exchange controls.

Souveraineté et Coopération monétaire internationale: Dominique Carreau, 1970, Editions Cujas, 19 rue Cujas, 75005 Paris, France.

The author studied for a time in the United States which may explain to a degree the quality of his research. Clear, intelligent and very well documented, this is the only book written in French which explains precisely the problems posed by the Bretton Woods agreements. There may be others but one cannot read everything.

All the Monies of the World: Franz Pick, Rene Sedillot, 1972, Pick Publishing Corporation, New York, NY 10006, USA.

This is a more or less complete catalogue of currencies.

Modern African Banking Cases: Alan Milner and Susan Abrahams, 1973, The African Law Reports, Oxford, UK.

This very interesting collection of court decisions on banking matters in black Africa is significant in itself and worth mentioning on those grounds; nearly all banking matters are dealt with except that of secrecy — the reader is left in the dark on this question.

Le Secret Bancaire dans la CEE et en Suisse: Université de Paris I, 1973, Presses Universitaires de France, 108 Boulevard Saint Germain, 75006 Paris, France.

This work was published after a conference in October 1971 and covers only Luxembourg and Switzerland as far as banking havens go. The other countries dealt with are: West Germany, Belgium, France, Netherlands and Italy. Each chapter is written by a different author but follows the same plan. It was seemingly the first attempt at a comparative work but was unfortunately very limited in its geographical spread. This work will be quoted in respect of various countries but subsequent legislation has taken away its relevance in others.

Dirty Money: Thurston Clarke and John J. Tigue, 1975, Millington Books, London, UK.

Annuaire International des Monnaies: J. Tixier, J.-F. Cartier and R.-L. Martin, 1975, Edition numismatique et Change, Louppy-sur-Chée, 55000 Bar-le-Duc, France.

This work is the only French international catalogue of currency. It gives a description and a photograph of the principal notes and brief descriptions of the exchange controls.

Pick's Currency Year Book: 1975-76, Pick Publishing Corporation, New York, NY 10006, USA.
This is the best currency book at an international level. It is a mine of information but must also, taking account of its fabulous price, be a goldmine for its author.

The Numbered Account: Franz Pick, 1976, Pick Publishing Corporation, New York, NY 10006, USA.
An interesting 62-page summary of Swiss numbered bank accounts seen from the American point of view—and sold at the comfortable price of $45.

The Exchange of Information under Tax Treaties: 1978, Report of the 19th technical conference of the centre for inter-American taxation at Curacão, 28 August- 3 September, 1977, International Bureau of Fiscal Documentation, Muiderport, 124 Sarphatistraat, Amsterdam C, Netherlands.
Disappointing: the reader would expect much more from a conference of specialists held in Curacão. Very interesting from a different point of view: the way in which people see governments. Very inconsistent: there are good and bad reports. Interesting from one other point of view: only businessmen chose far away places for their conferences.

Silver (How and Where to Buy and Hold it): (4th edition), Franz Pick, 1978, Pick Publishing Corporation, New York, NY 10006, USA.
In accord with the author's customary biting humour the cover of the book carries the information 'Fifty paper dollars each', which, given the number of pages in the book, makes it nearly a dollar a page—not a bad record. It is true that these are only paper dollars while Pick is thinking in terms of gold and silver. Events seem to have proved though that like insurance the price only seems high at the beginning.

The Management of Foreign Exchange Risk: 1978, collection of 35 articles from various specialists, Euromoney Publications Ltd., Nestor House, Playhouse Yard, London EC +, UK.
This collection of high-quality studies is both very technical and difficult and not therefore sutable for a general reader. The studies look at the accounting and mathematical analysis of exchange cover.

Off-shore Investment Centres: John F. Chown and Thomas F. Kelen, 1978, Banker Research Unit, Financial Times Ltd., Bracken House, Cannon Street, London EC4, UK.
This serious study deals, as its title indicates, with various offshore financial centres, some of which hold themselves out to be banking havens.

La Fuite des Capitaux: Victor Franco, March 1979, Editions Grasset et Fasquelle, 61 rue des Saints-Pères, 75006 Paris, France.
Written by a journalist, this is a non-technical consideration of illegal transfers of money. It makes very interesting reading.

Union des Banques Suisses: Liste des Cours de Devises Étrangères, 1979, UBS Documentation, rue du Rhône, Genève, Switzerland.
This remarkable booklet is published annually and is a useful working tool which provides average exchange rates and a brief summary of the relevant regulations.

II GENERAL SOURCES

Tax publications dealing only in international tax

Supplementary Service to European Taxation: International Bureau of Fiscal Documentation, Muiderpoort, 124 Sarphatistraat, Amsterdam C, Netherlands.
This deals with European taxation and consists of ten loose-leaf volumes which are updated every month. They provide both personal and corporate tax rates in the main European countries and the text (in English) of the main international treaties.

Guides to European Taxation: Volume 1: The Taxation of Patents, Royalties, Dividends and Interest in Europe; Volume 2: The Taxation of Companies in Europe; Volume 3: The Taxation of Private Investment Income; Volume 4: Value Added Taxation in Europe, International Bureau of Fiscal Documentation.
These volumes, used in conjunction with the *Supplementary Service to European Taxation*, make possible a close study of nearly all tax regimes in Europe. They are without doubt the best publication on European taxation and, further than that, the best presented.

Taxes and Investment in Asia and the Pacific: International Bureau of Fiscal Documentation.
This work is separated into two parts. The first gives a survey dealing with both the general economic situation and taxation of the countries covered and the second provides a list of the main tax treaties to which each country is party.

Taxes and Investment in the Middle East: International Bureau of Fiscal Documentation.
An overview, in two volumes, of the economic and tax situation in the Arab countries.

Foreign Tax and Trade Briefs: Walter Diamond, Matthew Bender, 235 E 45th St, New York, NY 10017, USA.
This is a series of practical tables in loose-leaf form. It gives the rates of withholding taxes applicable to all the countries in the world according to the nature of the revenue and the country of destination.

Tax Planning International*: THR Book Centre, Capacity House, 2-6 Rothsay Street, London SE1, UK.
This monthly publication, which was first published in Denmark as *Tax Haven Review* is now produced in Britain. It gives occasional details which are very relevant to banking secrecy but deals in particular with the evolution of US taxation in relation to foreign countries. Originally geared towards tax havens, it seems now to deal more with purely international taxation.

Tax News Services †: International Bureau of Fiscal Documentation, Muiderpoort, 124 Sarphatistraat, Amsterdam C, Netherlands.
A bimonthly review published as a supplement to *European Taxation*, this gives details of the most recent tax developments in the world and more rarely, touches on banking secrecy.

Tax Management International Journal‡: Tax Management Inc, 1231 25th Street NW, Washington, DC 20037, USA.

In the rest of this bibliography references to articles in these publications will be abbreviated as follows:
**Tax Planning International:* TPI (from June, 1976 and *THR* for earlier articles).
†*Tax News Service:* TNS.
‡*Tax Management International Journal:* TMIJ.

This monthly tax review provides details of recent tax developments in the countries of the world and from time to time gives some information relevant to banking secrecy.

Foreign Tax and Trade Briefs: Matthew Bender, 235 E 45th St, New York, NY 10017, USA.
A monthly tax review which also includes from time to time some very interesting economic reviews.

Books and periodicals which deal with tax havens and give ancillary information on banking secrecy

Books

Using Tax Havens Successfully: Edouard Chambost, 1978 (English edition with Thomas Crawley), Institute for International Research, 70 Warren Street, London W1, UK.
It is not purely egotism which motivates the inclusion of the English edition of *Guide des Paradis Fiscaux*; in fact it is much more than a pure and simple translation, since the English solicitor Thomas Crawley has adapted it to make it complementary to the French version and a useful working tool. The roving depositor who wishes to make use of trusts within the context of the indirect instruments of banking secrecy should refer to this work into which a section has been inserted to provide a study of trusts in relation to each of the countries covered. This study has not been included in versions intended for the Roman law countries since practical experience shows that, whatever the technical merits of the device, their use by lawyers not versed in Anglo-Saxon law often results in disasters. (Since there is an exception to all rules, the Liechtenstein lawyers understand the system perfectly and have even made it more sophisticated with the result that sometimes it is the Anglo-Saxons who have difficulties . . . .) If the roving depositor has links or interests in Great Britain he will find it useful to look at the English version in which several chapters have been written with that in mind.

Guida di Paradise Fiscale: Edouard Chambost, 1978 (Italian edition), Franzo Grande-Stevens, Ugo Mursia Editore, Via Tadino 29, Italy.
In the same way, although not to the same degree since this version is much closer to the French original, the Italian reader should refer to the Italian version of *Guide des Paradis Fiscaux* to which certain additional information has been added in relation to Italian requirements. As far as other foreign editions go, they are all direct translations of the original and space does not permit inclusion of their details.

Guide till Skatteparadisen, Edouard Chambost, 1980 (Swedish edition), P.M.U. AB, 561 02 Huskvarna, Sweden.
The Swedish edition of the same book is interesting to the extent that it analyses the situation of the Swedish taxpayer and the measures taken in Sweden. It is, however, published in Swedish, which limits its use in international circles.

Practical International Tax Planning: Marshall J. Langer, 1979, Practising Law Institute, New York City, USA.
This book, which was originally published in 1975 under the title *How to use Foreign Tax Havens*, is the most complete and systematic work on the use of tax havens. Although written by a specialist US lawyer, the book does not limit itself to the perspective of the US citizen. It is a very valuable work which gives ancillary information about tax havens.

Le Nouveau Guide des Paradis Fiscaux: Edouard Chambost, 1982, Editions Sand & Tchou, 6 rue du Mail, 75002 Paris, France.

This new edition of *Guide des Paradis Fiscaux* (from which the English adaptation *Using tax havens successfully* was drawn) is a complete revision of the earlier work. It updates the old chapters and analyses the new tax havens which are still relatively unknown, such as Cyprus and the Turks and Caicos Islands, as well as those which are still completely unknown, such as Saint Bartholomew. The details of each tax haven covered also include a brief comment on the banking system and banking secrecy.

Tax Haven Encyclopedia*: 1981 (last edition), Butterworth and Co. Ltd, 4–5 Bell Yard, London WC2, UK.

This is a loose-leaf book written by lawyers and accountants and covers 22 true tax havens: Netherlands Antilles, Bahamas, Bermuda, Cyprus, Costa Rica, Cayman Islands, British Virgin Islands, Jersey, Gibraltar, Great Britain, Guernsey, Hong Kong, Liberia, Liechtenstein, Luxemburg, Isle of Man, Monaco, Nauru, Vanuatu, Panama, Switzerland. Some of these are also banking havens. The book also deals with some marginal countries.

Tax Havens of the World †: Walter H. Diamond and D. B. Diamond, 1981 (last edition), Matthew Bender, 235 E 45th St, New York, NY 10017, USA.

This two-volume work in loose-leaf form is written by two American lawyers and is brought up to date very regularly. It covers 44 tax havens, or would-be havens (some of which are also banking havens): Andorra, Anguilla, Antigua, Barbados and the Grenadines, Netherlands Antilles, Bahamas, Bahrein, Bermuda, Campione d'Italia, Cayman Islands, Cyprus, Costa Rica, Gibraltar, Great Britain, Greece, Guernsey, Hong Kong, Ireland, Jersey, Jordan, Lebanon, Liberia, Liechtenstein, Luxembourg, Malaysia, Isle of Man, Monaco, Montserrat, Nauru, Vanuatu, Panama, Netherlands, Philippines, Saint Marin, Sark, Singapore, Switzerland, Turks and Caicos Islands, United Arab Emirates, Uruguay, Venezuela, British Virgin Islands.

Periodicals

International Tax Report ‡: Institute for International Research Ltd, 70 Warren Street, London W1, UK.

This newsletter, published fortnightly, gives information in the form of short articles on developments in international tax and contains several interesting articles on countries which have banking secrecy.

The European and Middle East Tax Report §: Institute for International Research Ltd.

This newsletter gives the same kind of information in the same form but with a European focus. Some interesting studies relating to bank secrecy.

Tax Haven and Investment Report ‖: Institute for International Research.

Formerly entitled *Tax Haven and Shelter Report* this is a monthly publication less technically sophisticated than the two publications mentioned above, aimed more at the businessman than the specialist. It also contains useful information on banking secrecy.

---

*References to this book subsequently in the bibliography will appear as *THE* with the name of the author, publication number and year of publication.
These works will be referred to as follows:
†Tax Havens of the World: *THW* with the date of the last update.
‡International Tax Report: *ITR* with the date of publication.
§European and Middle East Tax Report: *ETR*.
‖Tax Haven and Shelter Report: *THSR*.

III SPECIFIC SOURCES

Great Britain

Paget's Law of Banking: Maurice Megraph and F. R. Ryder, 1972, Butterworths and Co., 88 Kingsway, London WC2, UK.
This remarkable book on British law could be considered as the definitive work on the subject.

Sheldon's Practice and Law of Banking: C, B. Drover and R. W. B. Bosley, 1972, Macdonald and Evans Ltd., Estover Road, Plymouth, UK.
The Law and Practice of Banking, Volume 1: *Banker and Customer:* J. Milnes Holden, 1977, Pitman Publishing Ltd., 39 Parker Street, London WC1, UK.
Leading Cases in the Law of Banking: Chorley and Smart, 1977, Sweet and Maxwell, 11 New Fetter Lane, London EC4.

United States

American Jurisprudence, volume 10: *From Bank to . . . Bigamy:* 1963: The Lawyers Cooperative Publishing Company, Rochester, NY, USA.
'IRS uses mail checks to uncover secret Swiss bank accounts': *ITR*, **October** 1975.
General Explanation of the Tax Reform Act of 1976: Joint Committee on Taxation, 1976, Commerce Clearing House Inc., 4025 W Peterson Ave, Chicago, Illinois 60646, USA.
'In the United States Court of Appeals for the Fifth Circuit': *TPI*, June 1976.
'The IRS sharpens its teeth': *ITR*, **October** 1976.
'Government access to bank records in the aftermath of United States *v.* Miller and the Tax Reform Act of 1976': Elaine Block Davies, *Houston Law Review*, **14**, 1977.
'Search and seizure of bank records under the Banking Secrecy Act': Susan M. Knight, *Tulane Law Review*, 1977.
'Tax haven banking in New York': *ETR*, **January** 1979.
'Bank secrecy and its limits': Gordon Isleley, May 1979, a paper given at a seminar organized by the Union internationale et la Féderation suisse des avocats.

Canada

Dominion Tax Cases, 1946: Kaufman *v.* McMillen, 499–46, CCH Canadian Ltd.
Dominion Tax Cases, 1961: Canadian Bank of Commerce *v.* The Attorney General of Canada, 1264 CCH Canadian Ltd.
Dominion Tax Cases, 1962: Canadian Bank of Commerce *v.* The Attorney General of Canada, 1014, CCH Canadian Ltd.
Dominion Tax Cases, 1963: Canadian Bank of Commerce *v.* The Attorney General of Canada, 1236, CCH Canadian Ltd.
Income Tax Act Part XV: Administration and Enforcement: SRC, 1970-71-72.
Banking and Bills of Exchange: Falconbridge, 7th edition.
The Law and Practice of Banking: J. Milnes Holden, Pitman and Sons Ltd.
Dominion Tax Cases 1976: P. B. *v.* HM the Queen, 6334, CCH Canadian Ltd.
'Search and Seizure': Martin L. O'Brien, 1976, Canadian Tax Foundation: Corporate Tax Management Conference.
'Canada on 31st December 1976': 28th annual report on exchange controls, 1977, International Monetary Fund.
'The Canadian Bankers' Association': Legal opinion (legal adviser), November 1977, PO Box 282, Toronto, Dominion Center, Ontario.
Dominion Tax Cases, 1978: P.B. *v.* HM the Queen, 5433, CCH Canadian Ltd.

'The reach for information': David C. Nathanson, 1978, Canadian Tax Foundation, tax conference.

South Africa

The Law of Banker and Customer in South Africa: L. C. Mather and D. B. Knight, Waterlow and Sons.
'South African taxation of investment income of non-residents': Pharrel S. Wener, *TPI.*
'The banker's duty of secrecy': Catherine Smith.
'Principle of bank secrecy': Pharrel S. Wener, May 1979 (opinion).
Bank Secrecy in South Africa: Mazaham, May 1979, Werksman.
'Particulars of the Statutory Law compelling banks to make certain disclosures': Pharrel S. Wener, May 1979, B. Amler, Wener and Co, Cape Town.

Australia

The Law Relating to Banker and Customer in Australia, G. A. Weaver and C. R. Craigie, 1975, The Law Book Company Ltd., 301 Kent Street, Sydney.
Banking Law and Practise in Australia: W. S. Weerasooria and F. W. Coops, 1976, Butterworths Pty. Ltd., 586 Pacific Highway, Chatswood 2067.
'Australian Federal Tax Reporter': March 1979, *New Developments,* 323-3-79.

France

'Le secret professional du banquier, en droit français et en droit comparé': Pierre Gulph, *Revue Trimestrielle de droit commercial,* 1948.
Le Secret des Affaires (Mélanges): Christian Gavalda, 1965; Librairie Dalloz, 11 rue Soufflot, 75005 Paris, France.
Banques et Opérations de Banque: Michel Vasseur and Xavier Marin, 1966. Editions Sirey, 22 rue Soufflot, 75005 Paris.
'Commentaire de jurisprudence': Michel Trochu, 1969, Recueil Dalloz-Sirey, Editions Dalloz, 11 rue Soufflot, 75005 Paris.
'Le secret professional et le fisc': Maurice Cozian, 1970, Etudes de Droit Contemporain, Editions de l'Epargne, 174 Boulevard Saint Germain, 75006 Paris.
Droit bancaire: Rodière and Rives Lange, 1973, Précis Dalloz, Editions Dalloz, 11 rue Soufflot, 75005 Paris.
Droit de la banque: Christian Gavalda and Jean Soufflet, 1974, Presses Universitaires de France, coll. Thémis, 108 Boulevard Saint Germain, 75006, Paris.
'Commentaire de jurisprudence': Jack Vezian, 1975, Recueil Dalloz-Sirey, Editions Dalloz, 11 rue Soufflot, 75005 Paris.
'Commentaire de jurisprudence': Christian Gavalda, *La sémaine juridique,* Editions Techniques, 110 Boulevard Saint Germain, 75006 Paris.
'*Crédit et titres de crédit*': Cabrillac and Rives Lange, *Revue Trimestrielle de droit commercial,* 1975, Editions Sirey, 22 rue Soufflot, 75005 Paris.
Banque (Jurisclasseur commercial: annexes) 1977: Sections 5, 8, 11, 17 *ter*, 30 and 61. Various authors: Michel Cavalie, R. LaClaviere, Christian Gavalda, Henri Rameau, Editions Techniques, 18 rue Séguier, 75006 Paris.
La Responsabilité du banquier en droit privé français: Jack Vezian, 1977, Librairies Techniques, 26 rue Soufflot, 75005 Paris.
'Commentaire de jurisprudence': Christian Gavalda, *La sémaine juridique,* no. 18651, 1977, Editions Techniques, 110 Boulevard Saint Germain, 75006 Paris.
'Banque—Secret professional—droit de communication des douanes': *Banque,* April 1977.

'Commentaire de jurisprudence': Michel Vasseur, 1977 (pages 66–67), Receuil Dalloz-Sirey, Editions Dalloz, 11 rue Soufflot, 75005 Paris.

'Rapport sur les atteintes portées par le droit français au secret bancaire'; Henri Meyre, May 1979. A seminar paper for the Union internationale et la Fédération suisse des avocats, Basle, Switzerland.

West Germany

Bankgeheimnis und Bankauskunft: S. Sichtermann, 1976, Fritz Knapp Verlag, Frankfurt-am-Main 1.

Bankgeheimnis in Deutschland: S. Sichtermann.

Rechtsgrundlagen des Bankgeschafts: Wilhelm Vallenthin, Fritz Knapp Verlag.

Handbuch des Kredit Geschafts: A. Jahrung and H. Schuck.

'Bankgeheimnis gegenüber den Strafverfolgungsbehörden': Dieter Ungnade, *WM*, no **47, November** 1976.

'Bankgeheimnis und neues Strafprozessrecht': Gerhard Prost, *NJW*, **6**, 1976.

Das Bankwesen in Deutschland, The German Banking System: Schneider, Hellwig and Kingsman (bilingual edition), 1978, Fritz Knapp Verlag, Frankfurt-am-Main 1.

'German law and practice': Jurgen Killius, *THE* 1978.

'Bankgeheimnis in Deutschland': Obermuller, **May** 1979. Paper at a seminar of the Union internationale des avocats, Basle, Switzerland.

Italy

Le Secret Bancaire en Droit Italien, Guido Ruta.

Le Secret Bancaire dans la CEE et en Suisse, 1973, Presses Universitaires de France, 108 Boulevard Saint Germain, 75006 Paris.

This book, which is apparently the only one published in French on the subject, can unfortunately now only be used from a historical point of view as a result of the numerous changes which have taken place since its publication.

The five papers below were given at a conference on banking secrecy organized by the Turin savings bank and the Centre for International Legal Studies (CIDIS), Turin, May 1978.

'Richiesta di informazioni nel processo civile e banche', Gian Franco Fermo.

'Profili penali sostanziali in tema di segreto bancario', Juigi Alibrandi.

'Ragguagli sul segreto bancario, sulle perquisizioni e sui sequestri presso banche nel nuovo codice di procedura penale', Romano Riciotti.

'Il segreto bancario nella prospettiva penale', Pietro Nuvolone.

'L'integrazione dei contratti bancari mediante la clausola di segretezza', Fabio Ziccardi.

Japan

Money and Banking in Japan (The Bank of Japan Research Department): The Macmillan Press Ltd., London, UK.

'Le secret bancaire', Hiroshi Kawai, Yuasa and Hara, May 1979. Section 206, New Ohtemachi Building, 2-1 Ohtemachi 2 Chome, Chiyoda-Ku, Tokyo 100.

'L'endos des chèques à sceaux': Hiroshi Kawai, **May** 1979.

'Dépôts anonymes': Hiroshi Kawai, **May** 1979.

Sweden

'Bank-Sekretessen': Professor Hakan-Nial, 1978. Svenska Bankforeningen, Stockholm.

'Principle of banking secrecy in Sweden': P. G. Persson, **April** 1979. Svenska Handelobank, Stockholm.
'Bank secrecy in Sweden': Lennart Moller, **May** 1979. Advokatbyra, Sturegaten 24, 114 36 Stockholm.

Belgium

'L'habitant du royaume': E. Schreuder. *Annales du notariat et de l'enregistrement.*
Common Market Law (The Reform of Tax Law in Belgium): Me Xavier Bauchau. Stevens and Sons Ltd., 11 New Fetter Lane, London EC4, UK.
'L'impôt sur les revenus en Belgique': Ministère des Affaires Publiques, 15-17 rue Belliard, 1040 Brussels.
'Le secret professional du banquier en droit belge': Me Tahon-Chantraine, 1977. Ferdinand Larcier SA, Brussels.
'Secret bancaire—le Loch Ness financier': Demetriades Psallidas, *Trends-Tendances,* **March** 1977.
'Banking secrecy and taxation in Belgium': *ETR*, June 1977.
'Tax treaties signed by Belgium for the avoidance of double taxation': Philippe-François Lebrun. *European Taxation, Volume 18*, 1978.

Andorra

La Condition Juridique des Vallées d'Andorre: Betrand Belenguier, 1970, Editions A. Pedone, 13 rue Soufflot, 75005 Paris.
'Andorra—a banking center for Spain': P. G. MacDonald Allen. *THSR*, **11**, 1977.
Note d'information, El Banc Agricol i commercial d'Andorra SA, 1978, Andorra la Vella.

Bahrein

Arab Business Yearbook 1976. Graham and Trotman Ltd., 14 Clifford Street, London W1, UK.
'Bahrein exempt companies': *TPI*, March 1978, **5** (3).
'Bahrein': *THW*, 1979.
'Bahrein' (Taxes and investment in the Middle East): 1979, Bureau of Fiscal Documentation, Muiderpoort, 124 Sarphatistraat, Amsterdam C, Netherlands.

Hong Kong

'Hong Kong': J. B. Osbourne, *THE*, 1978.
'Hong Kong': *THW*, 1979.
'Hong Kong: Taxation of financial institutions': Per Borum, *TPI*, January 1979.

British Virgin Islands

The British Virgin Islands—a low tax base with treaty benefits: Marshall J. Langer and Gustav Danielson, 1978, Prentice Hall Inc., Englewood Cliffs, New Jersey, USA.
The British Virgin Islands—United States of America Income Tax Treaty: Marshall J. Langer, 1978, Manx Corp., 9725 South Dixie Highway, Miami, Florida 33156, USA.
'British Virgin Islands': Noel Barton, *THE*, 1978.
'British Virgin Islands': *THW*, 1979.
'BVI bank secrecy': N. Westwood, 1979, Tortola, PO Box 53.

Jersey and Guernsey

'Jersey': Michael M. G. Voisin, Spitz: *Tax Havens Encyclopedia*, Butterworths and Co., London.
'Guernsey': John Nicholas Van Leuven, Spitz: *Tax Havens Encyclopedia*, 1978.
'Channel Islands': Walter H. Diamond: *Tax Havens of the World*, 1978, Matthew Bender, New York.
'Enforcement of a foreign revenue debt in Jersey': Michael M. G. Voisin, *ETR*, 15 May 1978.

See sources on Great Britain for additional material.

Luxembourg

Les Sociétes 'Holding' au Grand-duché de Luxembourg: Delvaux, Reiffers and Elter, 1969, Editions Sirey, 22 rue Soufflot, 75005 Paris, France.
'Le secret bancaire': Albert Dondelinger, 1972, Banque Internationale à Luxembourg SA.
'Le secret bancaire en droit luxembourgeois': *Le secret Bancaire dans la CEE et en Suisse*, 1973 (cited above).
'Exchange controls: Belgium and Luxembourg': parts 1 and 2, *ETR*, **21 January** and **14 February** 1977.
'Investir au Luxembourg': Chambre de Commerce du Luxembourg, 1978, 7 rue Adelaide de-Gaspari, 81503, Luxembourg Kirchberg.
'Luxembourg bank secrecy': Guy H. Urbin, *ETR*, **20 March** 1978.
'Luxembourg bank's reporting requirements': Guy H. Urbin, *ETR*, **3 April** 1978.
'Tax and currency profits of Luxembourg banks': Guy H. Urbin, *ETR*, **24 April** 1978.
'Der Finanzplatz Luxembourg': Albert Dondelinger, *Journal de l'Ordre des experts-comptables luxembourgeois*, **December** 1978.

Singapore and Malaysia

A Source Book on Banking Law in Singapore and Malaysia: Myint Soe, 1977, The Institute of Banking and Finance, Suite 812–813, 8th Floor, International Plaza, Anson Road, Singapore 2.
The Law of Banking and Negotiable Instruments in Singapore and Malaysia: Myint Soe, 1977, Quins Pte Ltd, 404–406 Chinese Chamber of Commerce, Hill Street, Singpore 6.
'Singapore': *THW*, 1979.
'Bank secrecy in Singapore': M. Karthigesu, *June* 1979. Karthigesu and Arul, 2500 Clifford Centre, Raffles Place, Singapore 1.

Isle of Man

'The Isle of Man Banking Act 1975': *THR*, **May** 1976, 3 (5).
'Banking in the Isle of Man': C. A. Cain *TPI*, **May** 1978.
Anatomy of a Tax Haven: The Isle of Man: Mark Solly, 1978. Shearwater Press, Douglas.
'Isle of Man': *THW*, 1979.
'Isle of Man', *THE*, 1979.
'The Isle of Man: survey of a low tax area', H. W. T. Pepper. *European Taxation*, 1979.
'The Isle of Man as a captive centre', *THSR*, **June** 1979.

'Banking secrecy in the Isle of Man', T. W. Cain and Sons, **June** 1979.

USSR

Principes du Droit Soviétique USSR Scientific Academy, Institute of the law and the state, P. Romachkine (Translation: Leon Piatigorski).
'Les banques instruments du développement économique: l'expérience soviétique et des démocraties populaires': *Bulletin du CIEC*, **April** 1975.
'USSR', Instructions concerning the new system of taxation of foreigners, *European Taxation*, **19**, 1979.
'Taxation of work in Russia', *ETR*, **June** 1979.

Bahamas

'The Bahamas—the continuing case against income tax'; *TPI*, **April** 1977.
'The Bahamas': Lennox M. Patton, *THE*, 1978.
'Bank secrecy: Castle Bank and Trust': Oliver P. Gibson, *THSR*, **January** 1978.
'The Bahamas: a complete centre of international finance': Franklyn R. Wilson and Julian Maynard, **November** 1978, Research Committee of the Progressive Liberal Party, Nassau.
'The Bahamas': *THW*, 1979.
Bank Secrecy in the Bahamas: Anthony Thompson, 1979, Higgs and Johnson, 83 Shirley Street, Nassau.

Cayman Islands

The Cayman Islands: An Important Base for Foreign Companies, Marshall J. Langer and W. S. Walter, 1976, US Taxation of Internatonal Operations, Prentice-Hall Inc., Englewood Cliffs, New Jersey, USA.
'Cayman strengthen their secrecy laws': *ITR*, **March** 1977.
'The Cayman Islands as a base for offshore banking and trust company operations': Ian Paget-Brown, 1977.
This booklet, the work of a Cayman lawyer, is amongst the clearest and best-presented works on the subject.

The Cayman Islands: Douglas Calder and Timothy Ridley, 1978.
'Cayman Islands': *THW*, 1979.

Liechtenstein

Liechtensteinisches Landesgesetzblatt (The official gazette of Liechtenstein)
1961 **27 January** 1961, no 3 (law of 21 December 1960)
1965 **14 January** 1965, no 3 (law of 18 November 1964)
1966 **9 November** 1966, no 23 (regulation of 18 October 1966)
1975 **18 August** 1975, no 41 (law of 10 July 1975)
1977 **12 May** 1977, no 28 (order of 19 April 1977)
1978 **5 October** 1978, no 29 (order of 22 August 1978)
'Liechtenstein': Herbert Batliner, *THE*, 1978.
'Liechtenstein': *THW*, 1979.
'Das Bankgeheimnis nach Liechtensteinischem Recht': a lawyer at Vaduz, Liechtenstein, April, 1979.

Vanuatu

'The Anglo-French condominium of the New Hebrides': 1976. Investors Trust Ltd., GPO Box 211, Vila.
'Company Information': 1976, Investors Trust Ltd.
'Bank secrecy in the New Hebrides': S. R. Tatham, 1977, Investors Trust Ltd.
'New Hebrides': *THE*, 1978.
'New Hebrides': *THW*, 1979.

Panama

'Bank secrecy in Panama': Winston Robles, **December** 1973 (opinion).
'Traditional Panama': Colin Hale, *THR*, **July** 1974.
'Reinsurance in Panama': Colin Hale, *THR*, **September** 1974.
'Regimen Legal del Sistema Bancario y de la Comision Bancaria National': National Banking Commission, PO Box 1686, Panama I.
'Panama': Fernando Cardoze and G. A. Galindo, *THE*, 1978.
'Liberal laws create a haven for offshore banking': Panama 1979 — special report: *International Herald Tribune*.
'Panama': *THW*, 1979.
'Bank secrecy in Panama': A. R. de Valdes, **May** 1979. International Service Company Inc. Panama.

Switzerland

The Gnomes of Zurich: T. R. Fehrenbach, 1973, Leslie Frewin Publishers Ltd. 5 Goodwins Court, St Martin's Lane, London WC2, UK.
This very interesting work provides a non-technical overview of the history of Swiss banking.
'Le secret professional du banquier et ses limites' (a study of Swiss law), Jean-Marc Rivier, *La sémaine juridique*, 1974, Editions Techniques, 18 rue Seguier, 75006, Paris, France.
Those Swiss Money Men, Ray Vicker, 1975, Robert Hale and Co., Clerkenwell House, Clerkenwell Green, London EC1, UK.
A non-technical summary which is also very well written.

The Banking System of Switzerland: Hans J. Bar, 1975, Schulthess Polygraphischer Verlag AG, Zurich.
'Le secret bancaire, la Suisse et les autres Etats': Maurice Aubert, **August** 1975, Imprimerie du Journal de Genève.
Complete Guide to Swiss Banks: Harry Browne, 1976, McGraw-Hill Book Co, New York, USA.
This is certainly the most complete practical guide suitable for the non-lawyer, although it is written from the point of view of the US citizen.

L'Extradition et l'Asile Politique en Suisse: Dominique Poncet and Philippe Neyroud, 1976, Barblan et Saladin, Fribourg.
Le Secret Bancaire Suisse: Maurice Aubert, Jean-Philippe Kernen, Herbert Schoenle, 1976, Editions Staempfli et Cie SA, Berne.
Every sphere has its own bible: this is the one for Swiss banking secrecy; it bears the signature of one of the greatest specialists: Maurice Aubert. This remarkable collaboration has resulted in a book which should be on the shelves of any lawyer who specializes in international business. Its only fault — which is also the price of its quality — is that it is certainly very difficult reading for anyone who does not have professional training.

Code des Obligations of 30 March 1911 as at 1 July 1976, Chancellerie federale, Office central des imprimes, 3000 Berne.

Ein Konto in der Schweiz: H. Brestel, P. Kratz, W. Winter, 1976, Fortune Verlag W. Heidelberger, CH-8172 Niederglatt — ZH.

'Swiss banking secrecy' (Its legal basis and limits under domestic and international laws): Maurice Aubert, *TPI*, **January** 1977, **4** (1).

'How to open and operate a Swiss bank account': Charles G. Lubar, *ETR*, **28 February** 1977.

'A guide to Swiss bank accounts': Charles Lubar, *ITR*, **4** April 1977.

'Swiss bank accounts: are their days numbered?': *ETR* **25 April** 1977.

'The future of Swiss bank secrecy': Uri E. Rumati, *TPI* **June** 1977, **4** (1).

Scandale du Crédit Suisse: Max Mabillard and Roger de Weck, **August** 1977, Editions et Publications, Tribune de Genève SA.

This 93-page book was written by two journalists on the subject of the 'Chiasso affair'. It explains what happened very well, but presupposes a certain level of knowledge on the part of the reader.

'Les banques dans notre économie de marché': Hugo Sieber, **30 September** 1977. Paper given at the 64 Bankers' Day at Lucerne.

L'Argent Secret et les Banques Suisses: Jean-Marie Laya, 1977, Editions Belfond, 3 *bis* passage de la Petite-Boucherie, 75006 Paris, France.

This excellent book, written by the editor-in-chief of the Tribune de Genève, provides a very good introduction and is well-written.

'Transfer of bank account upon death': Uri E. Rumati, *TPI*, **January** 1978.

'La convention entre la BNS et l'Association suisse des banquiers rélative à l'obligation de diligence et au secret bancaire': Seminar (Hotel des Bergues), **1 March**, 1978, Geneva business law association.

'La convention relative à l'obligation de diligence lors de l'acceptation de fonds et le secret bancaire': Maurice Aubert, *L'expert-comptable suisse*, **March** 1978, Limmatquai 120, 8001 Zurich.

'Convention entre la Banque nationale suisse et l'Association suisse des banquiers complétant les dispositions sur le secret bancaire': Me Jean-Jacques Magnin, **June** 1978, Office: 2 rue Charles Bonnet, 1206 Geneva.

'Allocution du président de l'association suisse des banquiers': Alfred E. Sarasin, Bankers' Day, 22 September 1978, Berne.

'Swiss bank secrecy again', *ETR*, **27 November** 1978.

'The Swiss banking system': Hans J. Mast, 1978, Credit Suisse.

'Bank initiative threatens bank secrecy': *TMI*, **February** 1979.

'Swiss investments freed of controls', *ETR*, **26 February** 1979.

'Le secret bancaire en droit suisse': Maurice Aubert, **May** 1979, paper to a seminar organized by the Union Internationale et la Federation Suisse des Avocats, Basle.

Appendix III:
Convention on the Need for Caution when accepting deposits and on the use of Banking Secrecy*

(Convention relative a l'obligation de diligence lors de l'acceptation de fonds et l'usage du secret bancaire)

Preamble

Art. 1 The undersigned banks and the Swiss Bankers Association have concluded the following agreement with the Swiss National Bank:
– *in order to prevent through careful identification of clients the anonymous depositing of money or securities in the Swiss banking system;*
– *in order to preserve Switzerland's reputation as a financial centre and to fight against economic crime;*
– *and with a view to confirm, elaborate and fix by means of rules the best practice used in the management of Swiss banks.*

1. The banks to which the convention applies are all those which signed it, together with their Swiss branches but excluding their overseas branches, representative offices and subsidiaries (but see paragraph 13).

2. The convention does not in anyway modify the obligation to observe banking secrecy. It neither can nor will:
   – establish foreign legislation on tax, economic or exchange matters as part of Swiss law or state that it should be observed by the Swiss banks (other than to the extent that international treaties currently in force and Swiss legislation provide for this);
   – depart from existing jurisprudence in the field of international law;
   – modify existing contractual relationships between a bank and its clients.

   Swiss legislation and jurisprudence together with international treaties signed by Switzerland remain the determining factors for banks in Switzerland.

3. The Convention has the effect of codifying, with formal constraints, the current best practice in banking management in accordance with professional ethics; it should not constitute an impediment to normal banking operations.

UNACCEPTABLE ACTIONS

Art 2 The following actions are contrary to the convention:
(a) opening and managing accounts and deposits whose beneficial owners are not known (Articles 3–7);
(b) renting safe-deposit boxes without observing necessary prudence (Article 7);

---

*A document published jointly by the Swiss National Bank and the Swiss Bankers Association on 1st July 1982 which replaces the original agreement signed in 1977. (The text of the convention is given in heavy type.)

(c) assistance in arranging for the escape of capital or tax evasion or similar acts. (Articles 8 and 9).

4. The Convention wishes to ensure the careful identification of every client and allow the authorities to carry out effectively the obligations of informing themselves and providing proof which are imposed on the banks by federal or cantonal law.

5. Any act contrary to the convention constitutes a breach of it and will make the offender liable to the penalties provided by Article 13.

6. The list of actions which in terms of the following articles would be considered as contrary to the convention is exhaustive. The definition of the different acts which constitute a breach is given exclusively in the articles cited in parenthesis in sections (a) to (c). Article 2 does not have any legal force in its own right.

A REQUIREMENT TO EXERCISE CAUTION WHEN ACCEPTING DEPOSITS

Art 3   Identification of the beneficial owner

(1) The banks undertake not to open accounts or accept deposits of securities, nor to make financial placements until they have verified, with the care appropriate to the circumstances, the identity of the true beneficial owner of the funds, and securities.

(2) When an account is opened, securities deposited or when a financial transaction is completed, the identity of both the contracting party and the beneficial owner must be established according to the regulations (paragraphs 10–27).

(3) The identity of the contracting party should also be checked when cash transactions are undertaken involving material sums.

I   Field of application

7. A check on the identity of clients is obligatory (subject to paragraph 18) when opening current accounts, savings accounts and deposits of any kind, whether they are held in the client's name or under a number.

8. Bearer savings books cannot be issued without checking the identity of the depositor. But if the savings book is not left in the custody of the bank, then the bank is not in a position to follow changes of bearer nor to know the beneficial owner.

9. A check on identity is not required for cash transactions taking place over the counter (foreign exchange, purchase and sale of precious metals, payment in cash for certificates of deposit or bonds, cashing cheques etc.). However, if the sum involved is more than Fr. 500 000, the identity of the contracting party must be checked.

II   Identification of the contracting party

A. *Private individuals*

(a) domiciled in Switzerland

10. When the client comes to the bank in person, the bank should check the identity of someone resident in Switzerland by examining some official documents (passport,

identity card, driving licence or similar). Swiss residents known personally to the bank are not required to provide identification.

11. If the relationship with the client is established through correspondence, the bank should check the identity of someone resident in Switzerland through exchange of letters or similar means in order to confirm the address given.

(b) not domiciled in Switzerland

12. When a client with no permanent residence or with a foreign residence comes to the bank in person, the bank should check his identity by examining some official documentation. The client's identity may also be established on presentation of a written introduction from:
    - a foreign branch of the bank, a foreign correspondent bank or a foreign subsidiary of the bank;
    - a client known personally to the bank and considered worthy of trust;
    - a bank appearing in a recognized directory (Bankers Almanac and Year Book, The Bankers World Directory, Polk's World Bank Directory).

13. A bank may only accept recommendations from its branches, correspondents and foreign subsidiaries if it has given them instructions that the identity of clients who are recommended are to be checked in accordance with the Convention.

14. When the relationship with the client is established through correspondence, the bank must require certification of the client's signature by a bank authorized under para. 12 or by a client known personally to the bank and in whom the bank has confidence. It is also necessary to obtain, by exchange of letters or a similar means, a confirmation of the address provided.

B. Legal entities and corporations

(a) based in Switzerland

15. The bank must check that the company's name has appeared in the official Swiss commercial gazette, (FOSC) or appears in the yearbook of the Swiss Commercial Register; if this is not the case the identity of the company should be established through an extract from the commercial register.

16. The identity of legal entities not entered in the commercial register (associations, foundations) should be checked by an exchange of letters or similar means in order to confirm the address given.

(b) based outside Switzerland

17. The identity of the contracting party should be checked by asking for an extract from the commercial register or some similar document (e.g. a certificate of incorporation).

C. Exceptions for clients based in Switzerland

18. There is no requirement for an identity check on a contracting party whose company is based in Switzerland or for an individual when resident in Switzerland when the client wishes to open:
    (a) a salary account;

(b) a savings book, or account, or deposit account or term account, provided that the book or account is a named account and the initial deposit is less than Fr. 50 000.
(c) an account with a cantonal deposit office against the issue of shares when a company is being formed or share capital increased.

The exception allowed under sub-paragraph (a) is also applicable to foreign-based employees whose employer is resident or has its head office in Switzerland, provided that it is the employer who presents the request for an account on behalf of his employees.

III Identification of the beneficial owner

19. When an account is opened or a security deposit made, it is necessary to establish the identity of the person who has effective economic control of the assets.

20. The identity of the beneficial owner should be checked with a care appropriate to the circumstances. The bank may presume that the contracting party is also the beneficial owner. But this assumption is destroyed if any unusual statements are made (see paragraphs 23 and 28-32).

A. Private individuals

21. If the person making the contract states that he is doing so on behalf of a third party the bank should take surname and first name as well as the place and country of residence of the third party.

B. Legal entities and corporations

22. When the person making the contract is acting for a legal entity or corporation, the bank should take its registered name and the place and country of domicile of the legal entity or corporation.

IV Doubtful cases

23. In all doubtful cases the procedure given in article 4 should be followed. This should also be the case where there is any doubt about the identification given or when circumstances cast doubt upon the contracting party being also the beneficial owner (see paragraphs 28-32).

24. This is qualified by the dispositions which relate to those subject to professional secrecy and domicile companies (Articles 5 and 6, paragraphs 33-39 and 40-47).

V Control of procedures

25. The bank should make arrangements to ensure that internal controls and the auditors required by the law can check that the required identifications have been made.

26. The bank should keep a record of the surname, first name and place and country of residence of the contracting party as well as details of the means used to check the identity. Documents provided by corporations and other legal entities should be kept.

27. The information required under paragraphs 23 and 24 concerning the identity of the beneficial owner and that of a physical person who controls a domicile company should also be available.

Art. 4 Procedure in cases where there is doubt

(1) Where the bank has any doubts when an account or deposit is being opened it should require a written declaration from the client in which he confirms that he is acting on his own account or for a third party, and in the latter case should name the person for whom he is acting.

(2) Banks should use a Form A which constitutes an integral part of this convention.

28. If there is any doubt that the contracting party is also the beneficial owner he should be asked to sign the Form A 'Declaration for opening an account or depositing securities'.

29. As a general rule there might be considered to be some doubt when, for example, any of the following situations obtains:
    (a) An account or deposit is requested by someone resident in Switzerland. At the same time a power of attorney is issued to someone (for example a foreigner) who would clearly not have close enough links with the account holder to justify this or other unusual arrangements are made.
    (b) The account or deposit is opened by someone resident in Switzerland whose financial position is known to the bank. The assets provided are out of proportion with the person's financial situation.
    (c) The account or deposit is opened by someone resident abroad and introduced to the bank (see paragraphs 12 and 13). At the same time a power of attorney is issued in favour of someone who clearly did not have sufficiently close ties to the account holder.
    (d) The account or deposit is opened by someone resident abroad who is introduced to the bank (see paragraphs 12 and 13) and whose financial situation is known to the bank. The assets provided are disproportionate to the person's financial position.
    (e) The account or deposit is opened by someone resident abroad who is not introduced to the bank. The bank's discussions at the time of opening the account or deposit reveal some unusual circumstances.
    (f) The account or deposit is opened by letter with someone resident abroad who presents a certified signature (see paragraph 14) but whom the bank does not know personally.

30. If serious doubts remain as to the correctness of the declaration made by the client and cannot be resolved by other explanations, the bank should refuse to open the account or the deposit.

31. The uniform declaration Form A which should be used under the terms of Article 4(2) can be obtained from the secretariat of the Swiss Bankers' Association at Basle. It exists in French, German, Italian and English.

32. Banks have the right to reproduce their own forms which meet their particular needs. These forms must contain the complete text of the uniform declaration. The sections dealing with the extent of banking secrecy and the obligation on banks to provide information as well as those on the system of numbered accounts and

deposits and coded accounts may not be printed in characters which are either larger or smaller than the rest of the text.

Art. 5   Procedures for domiciled companies

(1) The banks must obtain from both Swiss and foreign companies of domicile:

(a) an extract from the commercial register or similar document;
(b) a written declaration on Form A in which the competent authorities indicate who controls the company.

In the terms of this convention companies of domicile are considered to be those entities, companies, foundations, fiduciary organizations etc. which have no commercial or industrial activity in Switzerland nor use any labour in a commercial sense.

(2) When the bank already knows that a company of domicile belongs to a particular group of companies or is aware of the ownership of the share capital and knows the individuals who exert a dominating influence, it may waive the requirement for completion of Form A.

I   Domiciled companies

33. Domiciled companies are considered, without regard to their aims, functions and head office, to be those Swiss or foreign entities which:
    (a) do not have their own offices (registered office with a lawyer, fiduciary organization, bank etc.);
    (b) do not have their own staff working exclusively for them, or have staff who are occupied only with administrative tasks (maintaining accounts or dealing with correspondence on instructions from individuals or companies which control the domiciled company).

34. Swiss entities which have their own profit-making activities and whose administrative board also undertakes the direction of the company (for example a company with a sole shareholder) are not held to be domiciled companies.

II   Division of capital

35. A company is controlled by the person or group of people who own directly or indirectly more than half the capital or voting power, or who exercise in some other recognizable manner a controlling influence.

36. When a company is itself controlled by another legal entity the bank must establish the identity if the individuals who finally exercise a dominating interest and must ask the contracting party to complete the Form A. Paragraph 30 applies to this case.

37. When Form A is waived under Article 5(3) the terms of paragraphs 21, 22, 25 and 26 apply by extension.

III   Identification of the controlling interests in a company

38. The identity of individuals who control a domiciled company must be established and the information preserved in conformity with paragraph 21.

39. If any changes are made in the signatories authorized by a domiciled company for

its dealings with the bank, the latter must repeat the procedure set out in Article 5(1). If the bank is unable to establish clearly which physical persons exercise a major influence on the company, Article 11 applies.

Art. 6 Persons operating under the requirements of professional secrecy

(1) When the client acts through the intermediary of someone who, on the one hand is resident or has his head office in Switzerland, and on the other hand is subject to professional secrecy imposed by law or is a member of a group affiliated to the Swiss Chamber of Fiduciary companies and Accountants, the bank should obtain Form B. This is a declaration that the beneficial owner is known to the intermediary and that the operations envisaged are not contrary to the terms of this convention.

(2) The written declaration is not required for the creation of accounts or deposits for Swiss banks or foreign banks.

I Privileged professions

40. Lawyers and notaries in particular are subject to professional secrecy protected by law in Switzerland (Article 321. Ch. 1, CPS).

41. Fiduciary agents and those responsible for managing capital and are members of a group affiliated to the Swiss Chamber of Fiduciary Companies and Accountants.

42. The Swiss Bankers Association circulates amongst the banks lists of such members from time to time. Bankers should check that the fiduciary agent or fund manager appears on this list.

43. Lawyers, notaries, fiduciary agents and managers who are resident abroad or whose head office is situated abroad must sign Form A in order to indicate the identity of the beneficial owner.

II Signature of the declaration

44. Form B, whose use is set out in Article 6(1) forms an integral part of the convention and may be obtained from the Secretariat of the Swiss Bankers Association in Basle. It is available in French, German, Italian and English. The forms which banks may produce for their own particular needs should contain the complete text of the model form. The confirmation by the person subject to professional secrecy should not be printed in letters any smaller or lighter than the rest of the text.

45. If the professional organization is a company or other legal entity, Form B should be signed in the name of the entity.

46. Anyone subject to professional secrecy in the terms of Article 6(1) may use the special regulations without regard to the fact that he might be acting as an agent or officer of a legal entity or company.

    If the person subject to professional secrecy is an employee of, or a member of, a body directing a bank he may not make use of the special regulations in Article 6(1) on behalf of the bank. He must indicate on Form A for whom he is acting; when he is acting on behalf of a domiciled company he should also give details of the physical persons who exercise a dominant influence.

III Exceptions for banks

47. No declaration is required for accounts or deposits belonging to other banks. Organizations are considered to be banks in Switzerland if they are subject to the provisions of the federal law on banks and savings institutions. Establishments based in other countries are considered to be banks if they comply with the criteria fixed by the State in which they are based.

IV Identification

48. The identity of those representing themselves to be entitled to professional secrecy must be verified in conformity with the procedures set out in paragraphs 10–18; paragraphs 25 and 26 also apply by extension.

B REQUIREMENT TO EXERCISE CAUTION WHEN PROVIDING SAFE-DEPOSIT FACILITIES

Art. 7   Identification and diligence

(1) When providing safe deposit facilities it is necessary to check the identity of the person renting them, following the procedure set out in paragraphs 10–18.

(2) Banks undertake to provide safe deposit facilities only to people in whom there is no doubt, taking into account the standard of vigilance expected from banks, that they are worthy of confidence.

49. Article 7 applies to both individuals and companies, Swiss or foreign.

50. The person taking a safe deposit could be considered worthy of confidence when, for example:
    (a) he already has a business relationship with the bank;
    (b) he is personally known to an employee of or member of the governing body of a bank;
    (c) he is introduced by a client or another bank;
    (d) there is no concrete indication that the safe deposit will be used in connection with any illegal aims.

C PROHIBITION OF ASSISTANCE IN ARRANGING THE ESCAPE OF CAPITAL, TAX EVASION, AND SIMILAR ACTS

Art. 8   Escape of capital

(1) The banks undertake not to provide any active assistance in the transfer of capital from a country whose statutes restrict the placement of funds outside that country.

(2) Active assistance would be considered to be:
(a) organizing meetings with clients outside Switzerland and away from the normal offices of a bank with a view to accepting funds;
(b) participation in organizing operations designed to allow payments to be made abroad when the bank knows, or should know from the circumstances, that the payments are intended in effect to provide an escape for capital;
(c) active collaboration with persons or companies who arrange for the escape of capital or helping this end:
   – by giving them orders;

- *by promising them commissions;*
- *by holding their accounts when these people or companies are resident in Switzerland and the bank knows that they use their accounts for business purposes in order to facilitate the escape of capital:*

(d) giving a client any information about the persons or companies described in sub-paragraph (c).

51. Escape of capital is an unauthorized transfer of assets, made in the form of currency, financial securities or banknotes, from a country which prohibits or limits such transfers abroad by its residents.

52. Article 8 does not apply to transfers of capital from Switzerland to another country.

53. Visits to clients abroad are authorized to the extent that the bank's official does not accept any funds whose transfer is illegal, nor gives any advice on illegal transfers, nor participates in any compensation arrangements.

54. The funds of overseas clients may otherwise be accepted in Switzerland.

Art. 9 Tax evasion and similar acts

The banks must not provide assistance to their clients in manoeuvres designed to deceive either Swiss or foreign authorities, and in particular the tax authorities, by means of incomplete certificates or other statements which might cause errors in other ways.

55. Banks are forbidden to provide their client himself or furnish directly to the Swiss or foreign authorities any incomplete statements or such statements likely to cause errors in other ways. The expression Swiss or foreign authorities includes in particular tax authorities, customs and those responsible for monetary or banking controls.

56. This prohibition applies above all to particular statements requested by the client with the intention of giving them to the authorities. The normal documentation which is maintained on a regular basis, such as statements of account, credit and debit advices, deductions for foreign exchange stock dealing charges and similar expenses, may not be amended by the bank with the intention of carrying out a deception.

57. Statements are considered as incomplete when significant facts are omitted with the intention of deceiving the authorities, for example when the bank, at the client's request, suppresses details of one or more positions in a particular certificate or statement of account. It is not however necessary to mention in statements of account or of security deposits information which relates to other accounts or deposits held in the client's name.

58. Statements are of a nature which might cause errors when the facts are presented in a manner which is contrary to the truth with the intention of deceiving the authorities, for example:
    (a) by indicating dates, amounts or rates which do not correspond with the reality or by creating debit and credit advices which give false information as to the holder of the account;
    (b) by certifying false debits or credits (irrespective of whether or not the certificate corresponds to the bank's books).

D OTHER REQUIREMENTS

Art. 10   Numbered accounts and security deposits

The requirements of this convention apply without any qualification to numbered accounts and security deposits as well as those designated by a code.

59. Numbered accounts and deposits of securities, as well as coded ones and fiduciary accounts and deposits, should be included in any certificates given in respect of a bank's relations with a client.

Art. 11   Breaking off business relations

The banks undertake to break off their relations with a client when the nature of the transactions carried out leads them to suspect that the information as to the economic beneficial owner of funds placed with them, or the renter of safe-deposit facilities, is not correct.

60. Existing relations should be broken off as quickly as it is possible to do without breaking any contract with the client when the bank realises that the client knowingly gave false information about the beneficial owner at the time the account was opened.

61. If the bank is not in a position to make contact with the client, having received instructions by letter, it may delay breaking off relations with the client under terms of paragraph 60 until the next visit from the client or the next correspondence.

Art. 12   Control by auditing bodies

(1) In complying with this convention banks should instruct the auditors required by the banking law, and give them authorization, to make sample tests during the course of the annual audit to ensure that the requirements of the convention have been met. The auditors required by the banking law will communicate any breaches which they discover or which they suspect to the arbitration commission created under Article 14 and to the Federal Banking Commission.

(2) The National Bank will give the text of this convention to the authorized audit bodies together with a list of signatories, thereby giving them the necessary mandate.

Art. 13   Arbitration Commission and penalties

(1) An Arbitration Commission, based in Berne, is charged with examining and taking disciplinary measures against breaches of the terms of this convention. The National Bank and the Swiss Bankers' Association each nominate two members of the Commission which is chaired by a federal judge chosen unanimously by the members. The Commission elects a Secretary.

(2) The National Bank and the Swiss Bankers' Association agree on the appointment of an individual to carry out an investigation. The investigator may then either require that proceedings are opened and a fine imposed, or the suspension of the enquiry. When the investigator requests information from a bank he informs the bank in what way it is involved in proceedings.

(3) The Arbitration Commission may impose a fine of up to Fr. 10m on any bank which has been proven to have broken the terms of the convention. In fixing the amount of the fine the Commission will take into account the seriousness of the breach of the convention, the degree of the bank's guilt and the bank's financial position. The Arbitration Commission will assign the sum received to some public cause.

(4) The Arbitration Commission will rule on procedure; Articles 36–65 of the Federal Law of 4th December 1947 on Federal proceedings in civil courts and articles 22–26 of the Federal Law of 16th December 1943 on legal organization are applicable by extension.

(5) The members of the Arbitration Commission, the Secretary and the person appointed to carry out an investigation are strictly required to preserve professional secrecy concerning the facts which come to their attention during proceedings, being officers of the bank in the sense of Article 47(1) of the banking law. In signing the convention the banks renounce the right to impose banking secrecy concerning the affairs of their clients as regards the Arbitration Commission and the investigator.

(6) The Arbitration Commission will communicate its decisions to the Federal Banking Commission so that the latter may consider whether the people involved in administering and managing the bank still provide 'a guarantee of irreproachable activities' in the terms of Article 3, paragraph 2, section c of the banking law.

62. The National Bank's representatives on the Arbitration Commission must be members of the board of directors, or their deputies, and those of the Swiss Bankers' Association must be members of the administrative Council or the directorate.

63. The Arbitration Commission will periodically advise banks of its decisions to establish jurisprudence, while maintaining both business and banking secrecy.

Art. 14 Entry into force

(1) The convention comes into force on 1st October 1982 and will have effect for a fixed period of five years.

(2) It is renewable tacitly on a year to year basis, provided that the Swiss Bankers' Association or the National Bank do not determine it by giving three months' notice.

(3) Every bank which has signed the agreement has the right to withdraw from it, subject to three months' notice, before the end of each full year of its operation, but the earliest withdrawal would be to take effect at 30th September 1987.

(4) The banks authorize the Council of the Swiss Bankers' Association to modify the agreement, with the agreement of the National Bank, in the light of experience.

64. The power given in Article 14(4) does not confer on the Swiss Bankers' Association the power to amend the essential aspects of the convention to the detriment of the signing banks.

65. Neither the Swiss Bankers' Association nor the National Bank may individually give an authentic interpretation of the convention. Any such interpretation may only be provided on a joint basis.

Index

Abrahams case, 107
Actio injurarium, 4
Administration, 45
Africa, 107
Agen Court of Appeal, 121
Agreement completing contract for opening ordinary account and deposit, 51
Agreement for opening account and depositing securities, 41–46, 49
Agreement for opening current account and deposit, 46
Algeria, 75, 81, 94, 95
Alsted, Peter, 129
Alternative trusts, 63, 64
Andorra, 30, 148–152
   back-to-back loans, 151
   banking secrecy, 149–150
   banks and banking system, 149
   currency, 148
   exchange control, 149, 150
   financial market, 151
   geographical, historical, and economic situation, 148
   instruments of banking secrecy, 150
   international agreements likely to undermine banking secrecy, 150–151
   legal basis and penalties, 149
   non-residents' market, blind and official, 151
   personal comments, 151–152
   population, stability, communications, and legal system, 148
   practice of banking secrecy and foreign economic powers, 150
Anglin, Judge, 105
Anglo-Saxon law, 61–64, 66, 77, 79, 93, 103, 104, 107, 110, 114
Anonymous companies, 231
Anonymous entity, 79
Anonymous structures, 66–67
Apparatchiks, 186
April game, 99
Argentarii, 4
Aubert, Maurice, 8, 15

Australia, 110–111
Austria, 254–55

Back-to-back loans, 6, 23, 36, 151, 157, 162, 166, 173, 180, 184, 190, 200, 208, 214, 219, 224, 232, 238, 249, 261
Bahamas, 16, 23, 58, 68, 101, 167, 192–201, 208, 229
   back-to-back loans, 200
   banking secrecy, 196–198
   banks and banking system, 195–196
   blind market and official market for non-residents, 200
   currency, 193
   exchange control, 194, 199
   financial market, 200
   geographical, historical, and economic situation, 193
   instruments of banking secrecy, 198
   international agreements likely to undermine banking secrecy, 200
   legal basis and penalties, 197
   personal comments, 201
   population, stability, communications, and legal system, 193
   practice of banking secrecy and foreign economic powers, 198
   taxation, 200
Bahamian Chamber of Commerce, 196
Bahrein, 153–157
   back-to-back loans, 157
   banking secrecy, 155
   banks and banking system, 154–155
   currency, 154
   exchange controls, 154
   financial market, 156
   geographical, historical, and economic situation, 153
   instruments of banking secrecy, 155–157
   international agreements likely to undermine banking secrecy, 156
   personal comments, 157

Bahrein *continued*
  population, stabilty, communications, and legal system, 153
  practice of banking secrecy and foreign economic powers, 156
Bahrein Monetary Agency, 154
Bank books, 111
Bank deposit certificates, 11–26
Bank of England, 60
Bank of France, 72
Bank of France Ltd., 72
Bank of Nova Scotia, 68
Bank of Portugal, 135, 136
Bank of Sark, 72
Bank of Tokyo, 106
Bank Secrecy Act of 1970, 99, 100
Banker, role of, 3
Banking documents, xi
Banking havens, x, 92, 146, 192, 253
Banking infernos, x, xi, 92, 114
Banking loopholes, 260–267
Banking secrecy
  absence of, 95
  absolute, x, 12
  at time of death, 76–80
  birth of, 5
  British protection in, 95
  cases in which banker is relieved of, 94
  conditions for lifting, 255
  desire for, 9–26
  direct instruments of, 39–57, 76–78
  forms of, x
  general history, 3–8
  hostility towards, 138
  indirect instruments of, 57–67, 76, 78–80
  instruments of, 150, 155, 160, 165, 171, 178, 183, 189, 198, 206, 212, 217, 223, 231, 237, 246
  international, 5
  international agreements likely to undermine, 150, 156, 161, 165–166, 172, 179, 183, 190, 200, 207, 212, 218, 224, 232, 237, 248
  market for, 20–21
  principle of, 4, 141
  reasons for seeking, 10
  recent history, 27–32
  Rolls-Royces of, 68–75
  true, 10
  true limits of, 269
  value of, 137
  violations of, 48
  withholding of, 9

Bankruptcy, 13–16, 126
  French, 15–16
  Swiss, 15–16
Barclays Bank, 97
Bare trustee, 62
Bearer certificates, 260–261
Belgian-Luxemburg Institute (BLEU), 175
Belgium, 140, 180
Beneficially owned trust, 63
Beneficiary who is non-resident, 60
Bermuda, 95
Bills of exchange, 43
Bookmakers, 97
Bretton Woods agreement, 21, 23, 24, 156, 166, 172, 179, 200, 207, 212, 232, 237
British Virgin Islands, 106, 163–167
  back-to-back loans, 166
  banking secrecy, 164
  banks and banking system, 164
  blind market for non-residents, 166
  currency, 163
  exchange controls, 163, 165
  financial market, 166
  geographical, historical, and economic situation, 163
  instruments of banking secrecy, 165
  international agreements likely to undermine banking secrecy, 165
  legal basis and penalties, 164–165
  official non-resident market, 166
  personal comments, 167
  population, stability, communications, and legal system, 163
  practice of banking secrecy and foreign economic powers, 165
  specific agreements, 166
Butterfield and Son Ltd., N. T., 95

Calvin, 4
Campione d'Italia, 256, 257
Canada, 95, 103–106, 109, 167
Canadian Bank of Commerce, 104–106
Canadian Bankers' Association, 103
Captive bank, *see* Offshore captive bank
Castle Bank, 102, 199
Catalan law, 149
Cayman Islands, 14, 92, 96, 101, 102, 167, 192, 199, 202–208, 229
  back-to-back loans, 208
  banking secrecy, 204
  banks and banking system, 203
  blind maket and official market for non-residents, 208

Cayman Islands *continued*
　currency, 202
　exchange control, 202, 206–207
　financial market, 208
　geographical, historical, and economic situation, 202
　instruments of banking secrecy, 206
　international agreements likely to undermine banking secrecy, 207
　legal basis and penalties, 204
　personal comments, 208
　population, stability, communications, and legal system, 202
　practice of banking secrecy and foreign economic powers, 206
　specific agreements, 207
　taxation, 207
Central Bank of the Bahamas, 199
Chambost, Edouard, 11
Channel Islands, 168–174
Cheques, 43
Chiasso affair, 33
Clients' complaints, 43
Clinch case, 95–96
Commercial society, 30–32
Common law, 61, 104, 105, 114, 153, 204
Communications, 42
Compensation, 43
Condominium of the New Hebrides, 220
Costa Rica, 256
Criminals and criminal organizations, 24–25
Currency smuggling, 19
Current account, 4, 43, 47
Custodial dues, 44
Customs officer, 120
Customs service, 120

Death, banking secrecy at time of, 76–80
Defective execution of an instruction, 42
de Lima, Pieres, 136
de Molay, Jacques, 4
Denmark, 129–131
Deposit regulations, 44
Deutsche Bundesbank, 115
Diplomatic bag, 20
Diplomatic service, 19
'Dirty money', 11, 12, 25
Discretionary trust, 62
Disguised trust, 62
Domiciliary company, 36
Donaldson, Baswell, 195
Doneghue case, 93–94

Drug trafficking, 20
Duplicate keys, 111

East Germany, 23
Equity, 61
European Legal Cooperation Agreement, 179
Exchange controls, 5, 16–24, 30, 31, 70, 78, 99, 149, 150, 154, 161, 163, 165, 169, 171, 174, 176, 178, 182, 186, 189, 194, 199, 202, 206–207, 210, 216, 218, 221, 227, 234, 240–241, 247–248

False invoicing, 12
False names, 54, 198, 217
Federal Bank, 115
Federal Banking Commission, 35
Federal Republic of Germany, *see* West Germany
Fehrenbach, T. R., 7
Fiduciary agreement, 46
Fiduciary contracts, 6
Field affair, 96
Field case, 102
Financial authorities, 116
Financial captives game, 72
Financial police, 127, 128
Finland, 141
First World War, 5
Fiscal bankruptcy, 13–16
Fiscal Code, 116
Fiscal law, 100
'Fishing expeditions', 122, 138
Fleming, Donald M., 196, 197
FLN (Algerian National Liberation Front), 26, 81–90, 264
Florence, 4
Florida, 102
France, 12, 13, 15, 16, 18, 66, 79, 115, 118–125
Free captives, 69–70
Free justice, 119–120

Geheime Stadt Polizei, 5
General conditions, 42–44, 52
Geneva, 4, 5, 90
Geneva Business Law Association, 34
Germany, 5–7
Gestapo, 5–6
Golden rule, 105
Great Britain, 13, 16, 17, 92–97, 169
　jurisprudence is not necessarily justice, 93

Great Britain *continued*
  unusual transactions, 95–96
Greeks, 3
Guardia di finanzia, 127
Guernsey, 14, 16, 17, 72, 92, 168–174, 199
  back-to-back loans, 173
  banking secrecy, 170
  banks and banking systems, 169–170
  blind market for non-residents, 173
  currency, 168
  exchange control, 169, 171, 174
  financial market, 173
  instruments of banking secrecy, 171
  international agreements likely to undermine banking secrecy, 172
  legal basis and penalties, 170–171
  official non-resident market, 173
  personal comments, 173
  population, stability, communications, and legal system, 168
  practice of banking secrecy and foreign economic power, 171–172
Guide des Paradis Fiscaux, xi
Gulags, 38
Gulf States, 10

Hammourabi Code, 3
Heavy reserves, 71
Hong Kong, 158–162, 228, 235
  back-to-back loans, 162
  banking secrecy, 160
  banks and banking system, 159
  blind and official market for non-residents, 161
  currency, 158–159
  exchange control, 161
  financial market, 161
  geographical, historical, and economic situation, 158
  instruments of banking secrecy, 160
  international agreements likely to undermine banking secrecy, 161
  legal basis and penalties, 160
  personal comments, 162
  population, stability, communications, and legal system, 158
  practice of banking secrecy and foreign economic powers, 160–161
  taxation, 161
Hungary, 209–214, 262
  back-to-back loans, 214
  banking secrecy, 210
  banks and banking system, 210
  blind market for non-residents, 213

Hungary *continued*
  currency, 210
  exchange control, 210
  financial market, 213
  instruments of banking secrecy, 212
  international agreements likely to undermine banking secrecy, 212
  legal basis and penalties, 211
  official market for non-residents, 213
  personal comments, 214
  practice of banking secrecy and foreign economic powers, 212
  specific agreements, 212
  taxation, 213

Income and Corporation Taxes Act, 95
Informers, 118
Inheritors' reserve system, 77
Inland Revenue, 14
Insurance, 46
Insurance in transit, 44
Interbank market, 70, 73
Interest
  at wholesale prices, 70
  ban on charging, 4
International agreements, 150, 161, 165–166, 172, 179, 183, 190, 200, 207, 212, 218, 224, 232, 237, 248
International finance, 153–157
International Monetary Fund, 22, 156, 179, 200
IRS, 50, 51
Isle of Man, 181–184
  back-to-back loans, 184
  banking secrecy, 182
  banks and banking system, 182
  blind market for non-residents, 183
  currency, 181
  exchange control, 182
  financial market, 183
  geographical, historical, and economic situation, 181
  instruments of banking secrecy, 183
  international agreements likely to undermine banking secrecy, 183
  legal position and penalties, 182
  official non-resident market, 184
  personal comments, 184
  population, stability, communications, and legal system, 181
  practice of banking secrecy and foreign economic powers, 183
Italian Exchange Control Office, 128
Italy, 12, 63, 110, 115, 126–128

Jamaica, 207, 208
Japan, 23, 132–133, 262, 264–267
Jersey, 13, 14, 16, 17, 59, 60, 66, 92, 168–174, 199
 back-to-back loans, 173
 banking secrecy, 170
 banks and banking system, 169–170
 blind market for non-residents, 173
 currency, 168
 exchange control, 169, 171, 174
 financial market, 173
 instruments of banking secrecy, 171
 international agreements likely to undermine banking secrecy, 172
 legal basis and penalties, 170–171
 official non-resident market, 173
 personal comments, 173
 population, stability, communications, and legal system, 168
 practice of banking secrecy and foreign economic power, 171–172
John Doe summons, 100, 101
Joint deposits, 44
Julius Ceasar, 4
Jungholz, 255, 257–258
Juno the Counsellor, 4

Kamikaze, 263
Kawai, Hiroshi, 133, 262
Kawamoto, Mr., 133
Kleinwalsertal, 255–257
Knight, D. B., 108
Knights Templar, 4

Latin countries, 13
'Laundering', 25
Law-breaking, 19
Law of gravity, 105
Lebanon, 155, 253
Legal counterfeiting, 18
Legal entity, 76, 78, 79
Legal evasion, 124
Legal incapacity, 42
Lettered accounts, 39
Lex visigothorum, 4
Liechtenstein, 60, 61, 66, 67, 215–219
 back-to-back loans, 219
 banking secrecy, 216
 banks and banking system, 216
 blind market for non-residents, 219
 currency, 216
 exchange control, 216, 218
 financial market, 219

Liechtenstein *continued*
 geographical, historical, and economic situation, 215
 instruments of banking secrecy, 217
 international agreements likely to undermine banking secrecy, 218
 legal basis and penalties, 217
 official market for non-residents, 219
 personal comments, 219
 population, stability, communications, and legal system, 215
 practice of banking secrecy and foreign economic powers, 218
 specific agreements, 219
 taxation, 218
Lien, 43
Life tenant, 61
Local exchange control, 59–60, 73
London Accepting House Committee, 182
London Clearing House, 182
Loopholes, *see* Banking loopholes
Luxemburg, 175–180, 229
 back-to-back loans, 180
 banking secrecy, 176–177
 banks and banking system, 176
 blind market for non-residents, 179
 currency, 175
 exchange control, 176, 178
 financial market, 179–180
 geographical, historical, and economic situation, 175
 instruments of banking secrecy, 178
 international agreements likely to undermine banking secrecy, 179
 legal basis and penalties, 177
 official non-resident market, 180
 personal comments, 180
 population, stability, communications, and legal system, 175
 practice of banking secrecy and foreign economic powers, 178
 specific agreements, 179
 taxation, 178

Malaysia, 253
Manos, Judge, 199
Mather, L. C., 108
Mazaham, D., 108
Mexico, 142
Moller, Me Lennart, 137
Monaco, 30, 61, 79, 80
Moneta, 4
Monetary Authority of Singapore (MAS), 234–237, 253

Monies received, 45
Morgan, Judge, 204
Morocco, 149
Motives, 10
Mu-kimei, 262-267

National Federation of Bankers' Associations, 132
Natsu-in, 262-264
Nauru, 192, 224, 254
Nazi Germany, 138
Negus treasure, 81
Net losses, 260-261
Netherlands, 143
New Hebrides, 220
Nial, Pr Hakan, 137
Nixon case, 102
Norway, 142
Numbered accounts, 39, 46-48, 51, 54, 185, 187, 188, 198, 217, 229, 231

OECD, 11
Offshore banking units (OBUs), 153-157
Offshore captive, 68
Offshore captive bank, 68-75
Offshore financial platforms, 70
Open deposits, 45
Overseas bank accounts, 16
Overseas deposits, 45

Panama, 60, 65-67, 135, 211, 226-232
    back-to-back loans, 232
    banking secrecy, 229-231
    banks and banking system, 228
    blind market for non-residents, 232
    currency, 227
    exchange controls, 227
    financial market, 232
    geographical, historical, and economic situation, 226
    instruments of banking secrecy, 231
    international agreements likely to undermine banking secrecy, 232
    legal basis and sanctions, 229
    official market for non-residents, 232
    personal comments, 232
    population, stability, communications, and legal system, 226
    practice of banking secrecy and foreign economic powers, 231
Paper banks, 71-72, 164, 192
Parallel guarantee financing, *see* Back-to-back loans
Parasites on society, 9-11

Penal Code, 118
Peterson v. Idaho First National Bank, 99
Political secrets, 25-26
Political society, 30-32
Politics, 81-90
Portugal, 114, 134-136
Postmortem instrument, 55-56, 78
Power of attorney, 55
Precedents, 14
Private agreements, 59-66, 78, 79
Protected trust, 64
Protection, 130
Protector for virtuous trusts, 64-66
Pseudonym accounts, 39

Recreation of bearer instruments, 263-264
Responsibility, 46
Roman law, 63, 64, 79, 114
Romans, 3, 4
Roving depositor, 264, 265
Royal Bank of Canada, 106

Safe deposit, 55-56, 111, 121, 124
Safekeeping, 44, 45
St Thomas Aquinas, 4
St Vincent, 258
Sarasin, Alfred E., 33, 196, 247
Scheduled Territories, 169, 171, 182, 194
Sealed account, 133
Sealed deposits, 45
Seals, 262-264
Second World War, 6
Secrecy, 44
Securities, 52
Security measures, 10, 48
Shah of Iran, 81
Share dealings, 95
Shell companies, 74
Shinyo-shokai, 132
Signature by means of number or assumed name, 53
Signatures, right of disposal and control of, 42
Singapore, 58, 228, 233-238
    back-to-back loans, 238
    banking secrecy, 235
    banks and banking system, 235
    blind market for non-residents, 238
    currency, 233
    exchange control, 234
    financial market, 238
    geographical, historical, and economic situation, 233

321

Singapore *continued*
  instruments of banking secrecy, 237
  international agreements likely to undermine banking secrecy, 237
  official market for non-residents, 238
  personal comments, 238
  population, stability, communications, and legal system, 233
  practice of banking secrecy and foreign economic powers, 237–238
  specific agreements, 237
Sociedad anonyma, 66
Societé anonyme, 66
South Africa, 107–109
Spain, 136, 141
Statements, 44
Summonsing practice, 100–109
Sutherland case, 97
Sweden, 137–139
Swiss-American Treaty, 28
Swiss Bankers Association, 7, 34
Swiss National Bank, 34, 35, 241
Swiss Penal Code, 6
Switzerland, xi, 6–10, 13, 15, 21, 25, 27, 33–39, 59, 66, 77, 78, 80, 89, 101, 132, 149, 192, 196, 208, 215, 239–250, 264
  back-to-back loans, 249
  banking secrecy, 242–246
  banks and banking system, 241–242
  blind market for non-residents, 249
  Civil Code, 242
  currency, 239–240
  exchange controls, 240–241, 247–248
  financial market, 249
  instruments of banking secrecy, 246
  international agreements likely to undermine banking secrecy, 248
  legal basis and penalties, 242–246
  official market for non-residents, 249
  personal comments, 250
  practice of banking secrecy and foreign powers, 246–248
  specific agreements, 248
  taxation, 248

Task assessment, 116
Tax amnesty, 31
Tax authorities, 13, 96, 99, 100, 101, 104, 106, 108–110, 120, 125, 127, 138, 143, 161, 178
Tax avoidance, 10–11, 96
Tax collectors, 3
Tax debts, 13

Tax evasion, 11–13, 25, 101, 104, 116, 117, 124, 261
Tax frauds, 116
Tax havens, 11, 14, 261
Tax inspection, 12, 138
Tax revision, 138
Tax treaties, 130
Taxation, 71, 73, 94, 161, 172, 178, 189, 200, 207, 213, 218, 248
Taxpayers, 9–11
Taylor case, 13–14, 170, 172
Termination of business relations, 43
Third-party accounts, 89, 264
Thomson, Anthony, 197
Toku-betsu, 262
Tournier case, 93, 99, 103, 107, 110, 182, 196, 198, 204, 222, 223, 236
Trade unions, 17
Transmission errors or losses, 42
Trapezites, 3–4
Trust deed, 61
Trust-instrument, 61
Trust property, 61
Trust with right of decision, 62
Trusts, 61
Turks and Caicos Islands, 259

Union Bank of Switzerland, 104, 105
United Kingdom, *see* Great Britain
United States, 6–8, 14, 15, 25, 27, 51, 92, 96, 98–102, 106, 167, 196, 199, 206, 208, 231
USSR, 185–190
  back-to-back loans, 190
  banking secrecy, 186
  banks and banking system, 186
  blind market for non-residents, 190
  currency, 185–186
  exchange controls, 186, 189
  financial market, 190
  instruments of bank secrecy, 189
  international agreements likely to undermine banking secrecy, 190
  legal basis and penalties, 187–188
  official non-resident market, 190
  personal comments, 190
  practice of banking secrecy and foreign economic powers, 189
  reason for banking secrecy, 185
  taxation, 189

Vanuatu, 220–225
  back-to-back loans, 224

Vanuatu *continued*
  banking secrecy, 221
  banks and banking system, 221
  blind and official markets for non-residents, 224
  currency, 220
  exchange control, 221
  financial market, 224
  geographical, historical, and economic situations, 220
  instruments of banking secrecy, 223
  international agreements likely to undermine banking secrecy, 224
  legal basis and penalties, 222
  personal comments, 224–225
  population, stability, communications, and legal system, 220
  practice of banking secrecy and foreign economic powers, 223–224
Vasseur, Michel, 123, 124
Virtuous trusts, protector for, 64–66
Vnechtorgbank, 188

Wensleydale, Lord, 105
West Germany, 23, 115–117, 256
Westwood, N., 164, 167
White-collar crimes, 101
Wholesale prices, 70
Wills, 78
Withdrawals, 44, 46